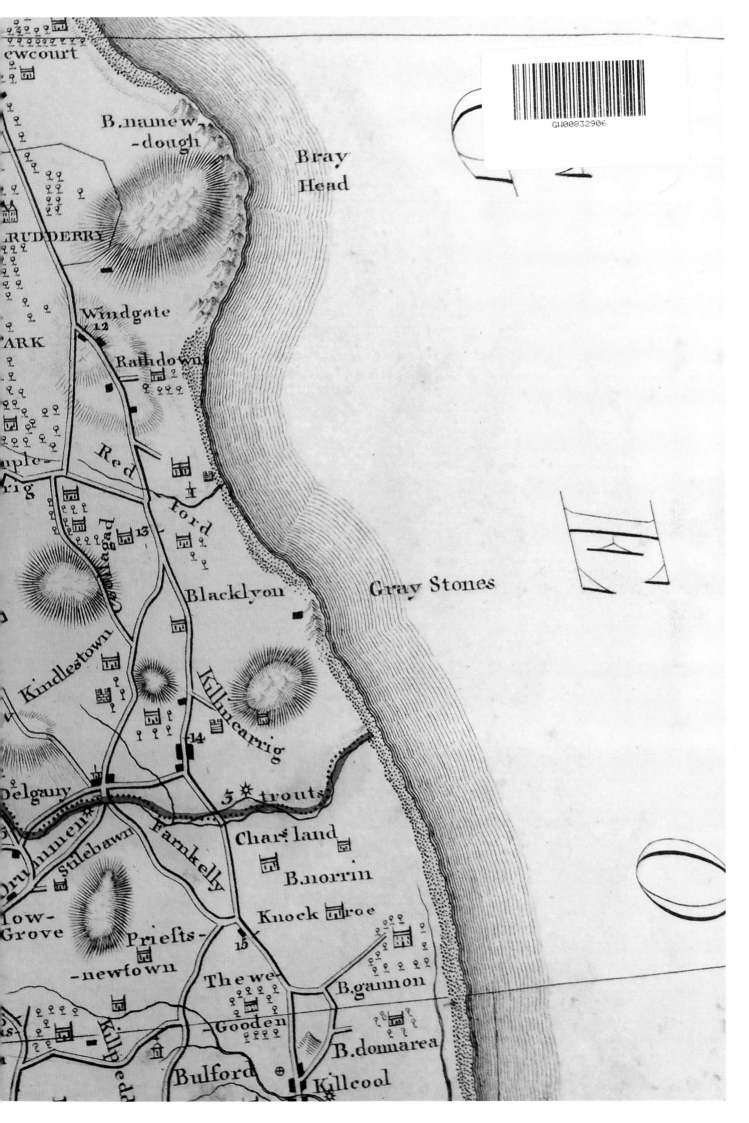

ewcourt

B. namew
-dough

Bray
Head

CRUDDERRY

Windgate
12

PARK

Rathdown

Red

uple-
rig

Ford

Gray Stones

Blacklyon

Cloonagad 13

Kindlestown

Kilmcarrig

14

Delgany

5 trouts

Drummen

Stilebawn

Farnkelly

Chars.land

B.norrin

Knock roe

low-
Grove

Priests-

15

Thewe

B.gannon

-newtown

Kilpead

Gooden

Bulford

B.donnarea

Killcool

A Pictorial History of

GREYSTONES

&

ITS COASTAL ENVIRONS

1760 to 2018

A collection of old photographs, letters,
documents and historical records.

Compiled by

Derek Paine

&

Gary Paine

First published in 2018 by Martello Press Ltd.,
Blackrock, Co. Dublin, Republic of Ireland

Martello Press
quality printers

A CIP catalogue record for this book is available from the British Library

ISBN 978 1 9998357 8 1

To Greystones people at home and abroad

FRONT DUST COVER PHOTO: Photograph taken in the 1890s of Rochfort Doyle sailing across the mouth of Greystones harbour in his open clinker sailing boat with its small gaff mainsail. The two storey house, *Yarra Yarra*, which stands to this day, can be seen on the extreme left with a wooden hut on the beach in front of it. To the right of it and slightly set back are the cottages in The Bawn (originally known as Strand Cottages). Fronting directly onto the beach (no sea wall had yet been built) is the line of cottages, including the appropriately named *Wave Cottage* and *Spray Cottage,* that were eventually washed away between 1929 and 1931. Subsidence of the end section of the north wall, built in 1888/1889, with its granite bollard, is visible on the left. The photograph is one of a pair of photographs taken on the same day, the second of which is featured on page 149.

BACK DUST COVER PHOTO: 1890s scene at Greystones railway station with at least six carriages waiting outside the station. A horse and cart, laden with goods including a box of Sunlight soap, is proceeding up Church Road, most likely to supply shops including Edwards' Greystones Supply Stores and George Enright Doyle's shop, Stanley Stores. Sunlight soap was manufactured by Lever Brothers at Port Sunlight on The Wirral in Merseyside, from where it was shipped all over the world. The box of soap in the photo had most likely just been unloaded at Dublin port and despatched to Greystones by rail.

FRONT COVER INSIDE: Section of Jacob Nevill's map of County Wicklow published in 1760. The road south from Bray Head continued through Blacklyon, passing *Blacklyon House* and on to Killincarrig, without any detour to the sea. The area beside the rock outcrop was known as "Gray Stones". St. Crispin's Cell and the ruin of Rathdown Castle are marked at Ennis' Lane, just north of the stream at Red Ford. To the south of Killincarrig, the Three Trouts Stream is marked, with Charlesland to the south of it. Further south is *Ballygannon House*, the home of the Scott family. *Ballydonarea House* is also shown.

BACK COVER INSIDE: Section of the plan drawn in 1876 which formed part of the "Book of Reference" that was presented to the House of Commons Select Committee at Westminster in July 1877 for Parliament to approve the construction of the Greystones Water Supply. Importantly, it shows the various houses and their occupiers at the time and reveals the still relatively undeveloped seaward side of both Church Road and Trafalgar Road.

CONTENTS

Acknowledgements

This book, like the previous seven, would not have been possible without the help of many people who have provided photographs and documents for copying as well as information. I would like to thank the following, as well as those mentioned in the previous books.

Gary Acheson	Jack Clarke	John Ferns	Noel Kennedy	Linda Paine
Harry Acheson	Naomi Combe	Niall Ferns	Suzy Kenny	Tanya Paine
Derek Archer	Andrew Crawford	Trevor Fisher	Elizabeth Kirwan	Rosemary Raughter
Eric Archer	Mary-Anne Creedy	John Flynn	Zenon Kopik	John Richardson
Robin Archer	Marcia Cuthbert	Pat Flynn	Betty Lowe	Peter Robbie
Barbara Barker	Joseph Davy	Ken Ging	Richard Lowe	Noeleen Scott
Eric Barker	Maurice Dodd	Kim Ging	Carmel Lynch	Denis Slattery
Sarah Barnes	Brendan Doyle	Robert Gunning	Dick Martin	David Spurling
Martin Barrett	Brian Doyle	Caroline Harberd	Tom McGlynn	Eric Spurling
Peter Bateman	Ciaran Doyle	Billy Hayden	John McGowan	Ozzy Spurling
Gavin Beattie	James Doyle	Jimmy "Jago" Hayden	Tom McKeown	Carmel Stokes
Joe Behan	Paddy Dunne	Gudmundur Helgason	Gráinne McLoughlin	Joe Sweeney
Kevin Brady	Keith Egan	Ali Higgins	Gwen McNiff	Noreen Talbot
Bernard Byrne	Andrew Evans	Amy Higgins	Peter Murtagh	Joe Taylor
John Byrne	Clifford Evans	Richard Haines	Richard Nichols	Bryan Thompson
Paul Byrne	Norman Evans	Herbie Hill	David Nixon	Anne Walker
Daragh Cafferky	Patrick Evans	Leo Ireton	Tommy Norgrove	John Whiston
Áine Carson	Telford Evans	Alan Jones	Dave O'Connor	Hayley Whiting
Reg Chambers-Jones	Val Evans	Brod Kearon	Hazel Paine	Len Williams

With special thanks also to

National Archives, Dublin	Parliamentary Archives, Westminster	National Archives, Kew
Gwynedd Archives, Caernarfon	Library & Archives Canada, Ottawa	Military Archives, Dublin
Australian Military Archives, Canberra	Commonwealth War Graves Commission	British Newspaper Archive, Boston Spa
British Library, London	Guildhall Library, London	National Library of Ireland, Dublin
Dublin City Library & Archive	National Photographic Archive of Ireland	The Irish Architectural Archive
National Slate Museum, Llanberis	World Rugby Museum, Twickenham Stadium	National Maritime Museum, Dún Laoghaire
Association of Yachting Historians	Royal National Lifeboat Institution Archives, Poole	Lloyd's Register Foundation, London
UK Ship Register, Cardiff	Cumbria Archives & Local Studies Centre, Whitehaven	The Irish Air Corps
Shipwrecks UK	Troon & Ayrshire Family Historical Society	www.uboat.net
Greystones Cricket Club	Greystones Archaeological & Historical Society	Greystones Golf Club
Greystones Rugby Club	Éire Óg Greystones GAA Club	Greystones Rowing Club
Greystones Sailing Club	Greystones Ridge Angling Club	Greystones Tennis Club
Wicklow RNLI Lifeboat	Getty Images for their permission to reproduce the photograph at the top of page 266 under licence.	

The previous 7 books, all of which are now out of print, are as follows:

A Pictorial History of Greystones 1855-1955
(black dust cover, 160 pages), compiled by Derek Paine and published by Martello Press Ltd in 1993.

Another Pictorial History of Greystones 1870-1990
(green dust cover, 208 pages), compiled by Derek Paine and published by Martello Press Ltd in 1994.

A Pictorial History of Kilcoole, Newcastle, Newtownmountkennedy, Glen o' the Downs, Delgany & Greystones 1860-1985
(terracotta dust cover, 240 pages), compiled by Derek Paine and published by Martello Press Ltd in 1996.

A Pictorial & Written History of Greystones 1846-1986
(blue dust cover, 240 pages), compiled by Derek Paine and published by Martello Press Ltd in 1998.

A Pictorial History of Greystones, Bray & Enniskerry 1835-1980
(black dust cover, 232 pages), compiled by Derek Paine and published by Martello Press Ltd in 2001.

A Pictorial History of Greystones 1884-2005
(silver dust cover, 240 pages), compiled by Derek Paine and published by Martello Press Ltd in 2005.

A Pictorial History of Greystones & its Environs 1754-2007
(gold dust cover, 256 pages), compiled by Derek Paine & Gary Paine and published by Martello Press Ltd in 2007.

Foreword

My memories of visits to Greystones during the summer holidays in the 1950s and 1960s never fade away. Staying in *Wavecrest* at the harbour, from where my great-grandfather established his coal import business in the 1870s, I absorbed some of the sights, sounds, smells, etc. of Greystones at that time. The pony rides in the paddock field beside *Glencoe*, the spluttering of a Seagull outboard engine starting up to take anglers out for the day's catch, the music and noise from the penny slot machines at the Anchor Cafe, the smell of the fishermen's nets drying on the wall across the road from our house, the sound of conversation at the top of the old boat slip, where "our elders" gathered as sunset approached, the swimming and diving competitions held in the harbour which were great entertainment, with much camaraderie among our age group, and the Ormonde Cinema, another popular venue, with its ever changing films to see. All of these are vividly etched in the mind.

Moments in time pass quickly into memory, those that are captured in a photograph remain locked in time forever. We are very fortunate to have had Derek Paine assemble his rich archive of old photographs and records, particularly during a time when preservation of such things was not viewed as important as it is today. Photographs are a visible record of how times were, the haystacks that can be seen on the grassy areas in the old images before the advent of the motor car, a reminder of the presence of the horse and cart. On those summer visits, I can recall my grandfather, Arthur Patrick Evans and one of his sons, Leonard Evans, who was a teenager when the last of the sailing schooners called to Greystones reminiscing about those bygone times. Information imparted by them and meticulously written down by Leonard's cousin, Dr. Leslie Doyle, has helped tell the story of that particular part of the history of Greystones in this and the previous books.

The history of Greystones is of course much so more than the harbour and its activities. In this book, the first in the series to include colour and with 296 pages, the largest to date, we gain a unique insight into some of the connections between Greystones and important events. These include World War One, the Easter Rising and the suffragette movement. We also learn more about the shops, hotels and businesses in Greystones down the years, the town's electrification, its lifeboat, the coast guards, as well as the pure unusual, a proposed Greystones to Glendalough railway in 1874.

The pace of changes in Greystones has accelerated in recent years as we embrace the future and remember the past. Through Derek Paine's lifelong compilation of his archive of material on its history, as well the dedication of his son, Gary, in completing this 8th book, his legacy to us is further enhanced. Greystones people can justifiably feel proud that their town has one of the best documented pictorial local histories of any in Ireland. I hope this latest book brings enjoyment to each and every reader.

Andrew Evans,
Rochdale,
United Kingdom
Summer 2018

INTRODUCTION

In August 1973, when my father held his first exhibition of old photographs of Greystones in the former St. Patrick's National School on La Touche Place, he did not envisage the depth of interest it would generate locally. In that pre-internet era, when the town was much smaller than today, over 1,400 people attended, highlighting the historical interest and visual attraction that old photographs engender. Importantly, it led to local families generously making additional old photos and documents available for copying, enhancing the archive of material he had begun to assemble in the 1950s. Subsequent exhibitions held in the 1980s and early 1990s in the annexe of The Burnaby drew similar levels of interest, such that consideration was given to the idea of publishing a book. In 1993, Derek published the first of his seven Pictorial History of Greystones books. Since the publication of the last book in 2007, as more old photographs were unearthed and previously unpublished material from my father's archive identified, we had been steadily compiling the draft of an 8th book. My only regret is that it wasn't published before my father passed away, but I am delighted to have now brought it to publication. On his regular visits to my house in London, we spent many hours together at the National Archives in Kew, the House of Lords Records Office in Westminster and the British Library. There is a curiosity in uncovering the past, never quite knowing what a dusty box file of old documents will reveal. Attending postcard fairs, our searches, though often fruitless, would occasionally reward us with a previously unseen, rare, locally published old Greystones postcard. The one featured on page 289 is an excellent example. Accompanying my father on his walks around Greystones, we would bump into locals who would say "*I've discovered an old photo of such and such, would it be of interest?*", inevitably adding to the archive of material. For example, the very old photograph on page 207 of harvest time at Temple Carrig was provided by the Richardson family of Blacklion, following a chance meeting by the Gap Bridge on the North Beach, shortly after publication of the last book. On a par with the best photos featured in the previous books, its detail provides a unique glimpse into a bygone era of our locality.

I acknowledge all the people who appear in photographs, those who are no longer with us, as well as all those mentioned in this and the previous books, for providing photographs and information. Whilst I am reluctant to highlight any particular contributors over others, two in particular, sadly no longer with us, deserve special mention again. Firstly, the late Dr. Leslie Doyle, great-grandson of John Doyle (1793-1855). John Doyle played a significant role in the development of Greystones. In addition to being the owner of the Greystones built coal schooner, *Belle Vue*, he also built the coast guard cottages at Kenmare Terrace on the lower part of Trafalgar Road, as well as other houses close by. One of the founding members of Greystones Rugby Club in 1937, Leslie had a vast knowledge of the history of Greystones, handed down from his father and grandfather. He was instrumental in the completion of the first four books in this series. My father always eagerly looked forward to Leslie's visits home and the inevitable discussion that centred on the latest nugget of the town's history that Leslie had uncovered. Secondly, the French family, in particular Samuel A. French and his sister Henrietta, to whom the people of Greystones owe a huge debt of gratitude. I am pleased to say that this current book includes some previously unpublished information from both the Doyle and French family archives and we are indebted to them for preserving these records.

ABOVE: Samuel A. French with his sister, Henrietta, at Greystones railway station c.1907.

Samuel A. French and Henrietta French were assiduous collectors and keepers of documents and records relating to the development of Greystones and its social history, from the late 19th century through and beyond the first half of the 20th century. Their contribution, in terms of retention of historical material relating to the town, is of a similar historical importance as the classic old photos of Greystones and other towns the length and breadth of Ireland taken by their grandfather, Robert French. Robert French was Chief Photographer for the Lawrence Collection of photographs, now held by the National Photographic Archive (NPA) in Dublin. He was a regular visitor to Greystones, where he stayed at *Trippleton Cottage* on Bellevue Road, the family home of his son, Samuel H. French. A number of Robert French's old glass negatives of various views in Greystones were bequeathed to my father. These photographs, some of which are different to the Robert French Greystones photos held by the NPA in Dublin, have featured in the previous books. The photograph on the back of the dust jacket is one of these. Originally included in Book No.5, this photograph was erroneously developed back to front and was small and dark. Having now been digitally scanned from the original glass negative using the very latest technology, it is published now in its full glory. Arrangements are currently being made with the NPA for the donation of this and other glass negatives to be added to their existing collection of old photographs of Greystones.

INTRODUCTION

Particular thanks are due to Elizabeth Kirwan, Curator of the National Photographic Archive in Dublin and the team for kind permission to reproduce a number of photographs. The NPA has recently digitally scanned many of the Greystones glass negatives in high resolution. Details not apparent to the naked eye in the originally developed photographs are now visible. A number of these are included throughout the book. Also of historical significance are photos from a family photo album, held by the NPA, which belonged to Thomas MacDonagh and his wife Muriel (nee Gifford). The series of photos, taken during a family holiday in Greystones in September 1915, with their son and baby daughter at the harbour and the South Beach, bely the events which would shatter the family just seven months later during Easter 1916 and again the following year. They are a reminder of what a rich seam of photographic history can be revealed from an old family photograph album. They reminded me of the Flavelle family photographs taken during their holidays in Greystones between 1899 and 1903 which featured in Book Nos.3, 4 & 5. A previously unpublished photo of the family on the cliff walk is included in this book.

In the text, references are made to the previous books in this series, the list of which is shown in order of date published on page iv. The identities of people in the photographs (where known) read from left to right. Certain individuals' names have been defined with initials and dates in order to distinguish them from others with the same name. Some words, which have more than one spelling in use, such as coast guards (the Irish spelling) have been spelt so, rather than the single word spelling used in the UK. Every effort has been made to ensure the accuracy of these and any errors or omissions will be corrected in future editions of the book. In general, house names, ships, etc., along with newspaper reports appear in italics throughout the book. The series of books has evolved over the years. Colour photographs of the town and the harbour area from the mid-1950s onwards are included for the first time in this latest book. Although the earlier books in the series covered Greystones and its immediate environs, the remit in this book has been expanded east across the Irish Sea. This book includes information about harbours and ports in England, Scotland and Wales that had important maritime links with Greystones. These harbours assisted in the development of Greystones and contributed to the thriving town it is today. The sailing routes taken by the wooden schooners which operated between Greystones and harbours and ports in England, Scotland and Wales, primarily for the import of coal (with occasional cargoes of slate, bricks and cement) are discussed. Among these, the Greystones built and owned schooner, *Belle Vue* (mid 19th century) and the Greystones owned schooner, *Velinheli* (late 19th / early 20th century) were the respective workhorses for local coal importers, John Doyle and Arthur Evans.

The book opens with the section of Jacob Nevill's 1760 map of County Wicklow reproduced on the inside of the front cover. This reveals the rock outcrop, unconnected to the road south from Bray Head, known simply at that time as "Gray Stones". A photograph of the page from the Coast Guard Establishment Book listing the names of the men who initially served at the first coast guard station at Blacklion, following the appointment of its first Chief Officer, Thomas Lamb Wood on 1st February 1821, has been reproduced by kind permission of the National Archives in Kew, London. Linking in with this and published for the first time, are the plans from the indenture signed between John Doyle and the Board of Trade in 1842 for the construction of the coast guard cottages at Kenmare Terrace on what is now Trafalgar Road, but which at that time was a private road leading to the field owned by George Evans. Of note also in this book is information relating to Greystones during both World Wars. The restrictions on the use of lights in houses during 1918 when the German U-boat threat to shipping became acute is briefly touched on, along with a chapter devoted to the Coast Watching Service stationed at Look Out Post No.8 on Bray Head during World War Two. This chapter covers the events surrounding the night of 30th / 31st May 1941, when the men on watch reported the waves of German Luftwaffe aircraft heading north along the Wicklow coast. That night Dublin's North Strand was bombed, with the loss of 28 lives.

I wish to thank Joe Behan of Martello Press for his assistance over the last 25 years, not just in publishing this latest book, but also all of the others in the series. Particular thanks for writing the foreword is also due to Andrew Evans, great-great-grandson and great-grandson respectively of Greystones' two foremost schooner owners, John Doyle and Arthur Evans. The quality of some of the photographs and images included throughout the book reflect their age and condition. Whilst modern technology enables some enhancements, this is not always the case. However, I feel that it is better to include them as they are, rather than exclude them. Examples of these include the photograph on page 101, which, though grainy, is the only known image of a schooner in Greystones harbour with all her sails up. Furthermore, although some of the photos have featured in the earlier books, they have been included again in this book, either because the quality of the image is superior to that previously published, or because they warrant inclusion again to add depth to the subject being covered. I am also grateful to Jimmy "Jago" Hayden for his input, particularly in providing details and endeavouring to date many of the images from the NPA collection. He, like my father, spent his youth in and around Greystones harbour in the 1940s. In 2015, following in-depth research on the subject, Jimmy presented a paper to the Greystones Archaeological & Historical Society in which he pieced together the likely sequencing of a number of the Robert French photographs of Greystones. This paper can be accessed online.

This year marks 25 years since the publication of Book No.1. Reprints of both Book No.1 and other books in the series may be considered for publication in the future.

Gary Paine
Greystones
September 2018
garytpaine@gmail.com

The obituary below appeared in *The Irish Times* on Saturday 23rd April 2016.

A renowned builder of boats and collector of Wicklow photos

Derek Paine

- -

Born: October 12th, 1931
Died: April 10th, 2016

- -

Derek Paine, who has died aged 84, led a life intimately and devotedly connected to the sea and to the community in which he lived. He was a renowned builder of boats and a collector of photographs and like ephemera, which he compiled into seven volumes, a unique legacy chronicling the social history of his beloved Greystones.

Paine's rear garden in the north Wicklow seaside town at times resembled a small boatyard. From his clutter-filled workshop there emerged a succession of repaired and newly built wooden boats.

At the same time, his house accumulated an ever-growing number of photographs as his interest in local history became more widely known and people handed over their collections for posterity.

Paine's deepest maritime affection was for the *Water Wag*, a 13ft-long clinker built sailing boat and the oldest "one design" dinghy in existence. *Water Wag* enthusiasts have been racing the timber boats since 1887 and the class was re-invigorated in the 1980s, largely due to the craftsmanship of Paine, as the Wag Club, based in Dún Laoghaire, acknowledged by declaring him an honorary life member.

Derek Paine was born in the upper bedroom of Glencoe, one of the few homes, then fronting on to Greystones North Beach, to survive the sea storms of 1929-1931. Through the small front bedroom window on the gable, among the first sounds he would have heard were gulls and waves breaking on the pebbles.

Model boats

His parents were Ernest Paine and Emily (nee Thompson). Ernest was a traveller for Berger Paints but also made model boats for Helys department store. Paine's uncle, George Thompson, was a lieutenant commander in the Naval Service and captained the *LE Macha* when, in 1948, it repatriated to Ireland the remains of the poet W.B. Yeats from France.

Above: Derek Paine with a model he built of a *Water Wag*.
Photograph: JACK CLARKE

A grandfather, Robert Thompson, spent 22 years in the Naval Service. Colour blindness prevented Derek following their lead, although he attended the Hibernian Marine School in Clontarf with that in mind. Instead, his working life was in insurance and finance, but retirement in 1986 allowed him to indulge his boat building passion to the full. He built four new *Water Wags* and restored to sailing some 15 others, as well as keeping afloat innumerable other small craft.

Greystones postcards

Paine's other consuming interest germinated from an idle interest in Greystones postcards and other documents relating to the town, that he began collecting in the 1950s. By the 1970s, he had sufficient to mount photographic exhibitions.

Gradually Paine assembled a priceless archive of images from the mid-19th century to the early years of the 21st century, covering Greystones, Delgany, Bray, Enniskerry, Kilcoole and Newtownmountkennedy. The archive formed the basis of his Pictorial History of Greystones series of books, the first of which he published in 1993. In seven volumes (with material for an eighth, which son Gary is contemplating), they chronicle the emergence of Greystones from the Victorian and Edwardian era through the 20th century – a comprehensive social history of a small town.

Paine was active in the Greystones Civic Association, under whose auspices he was instrumental in acquiring the base of the Kish Lighthouse in 1966 to extend and protect the now demolished original Victorian harbour, as well as the two ships' anchors which survive to this day. He was a founding member of Greystones Sailing Club and had a boat moored in the harbour for many years. He was a devoted family man. A favourite pastime in retirement, when he was not tinkering in his workshop, was walking the coast at Kilcoole or around Bray Head with his dog, Tyson.

Derek Paine is survived by his wife Hazel and their three children, Linda, David and Gary, six grandchildren and a brother, Stanley.

ABOVE: Photograph of the lifeboat house, *Glencoe*, *Alberta* and *Yarra Yarra*, three of the houses on the North Beach to survive the 1929-1931 storms which destroyed the line of cottages and houses, the ruins of which are visible further up the North Beach. The view contrasts with that of the photograph on the front cover taken several decades earlier which shows the line of cottages intact.

ABOVE: Family photo taken in 1939 on the North Beach Road in front of the Thompson family home, *Glencoe*. Note the wooden fishermen's hut at the top of the boat slip. Back row: Ernest Paine, Stanley Paine, Doreen Bertram (nee Thompson), Mr. Fitzgerald, Emily Paine (nee Thompson) and Derek Paine. Front row: Flo Thompson, Dorrie Thompson (nee Archer), Mary Thompson, Robert Thompson and Alec Thompson, who served in the South Irish Horse in World War One.

BELOW RIGHT: Family reunion in the front garden of *Glencoe* in the 1940s for Robert and Mary Thompson and their five children, Alec, George (in Irish Naval uniform),William, Maisie Underwood (nee Thompson) and Emily Paine (nee Thompson). Robert Thompson was born in 1856 and orphaned at the age of two. He was raised by the Massey family at *Fuchsia Cottage*, the derelict ruin of which was located until earlier this year just north of the entrance to the SEK International Spanish school at *Belevedere Hall* in Windgates. In 1872, he walked from there to Dún Laoghaire, where he enlisted in the Royal Navy aboard *HMS Vanguard*, the ill-fated guard ship of the Eastern Irish District. Three years later he served aboard *HMS Penelope*. This was one of the seven Royal Navy ships of the First Reserve Squadron ordered to undertake a summer cruise around Ireland in 1875. It was at the end of this cruise that another ship in the squadron, *HMS Iron Duke*, in fog, accidentally rammed and sank *HMS Vanguard*, 11 miles east north east of Bray Head. Robert Thompson served in the Royal Navy for 22 years until 1894, before eventually returning to Greystones in 1926, where he lived at *Glencoe* until his death aged 90 in 1946. He is buried in Redford cemetery at The Grove.

ABOVE: Robert Thompson (right), the owner of *Glencoe* and his son, George (centre) together with Mr Trent (left), in February 1930 inspecting damage to *Jubilee Castle* / *Rosetta Fort*. It was located just north of where the ruin is on the extreme right in the photo at the top of the page.

ABOVE: 1941 photo of Ernest Paine with his two sons, Derek (rear) and Stanley (front) on a donkey in front of *Glencoe*. The field adjacent to the lifeboat house (where *Harbour View* apartments now stand) was let out for pony and donkey rides for many years during the summer months. The donkey in the photo was owned by the Martin family of *Killeen Cottage*, Rathdown Road.

ABOVE: Photograph taken in 1938 of Derek Paine on North Beach Road in front of *Glencoe* with *Yarra Yarra* and its porch gable entrance visible in the background. Note the shingle spilling over the wall and onto the road. This was a regular occurrence from the storm action of the sea.

ABOVE: Photograph of Ernest and Emily Paine, with their three children, Joan Fisher (nee Paine), Derek and Stanley (holding the family dog) taken around 1942 in the front garden of *Glencoe*. The family lived at the house during World War Two.

BELOW: 1937 photo of Derek Paine learning to sail off the North Beach with Greystones harbour in the background.

ABOVE: 1950s photograph of Derek Paine preparing to sail from Greystones harbour in his clinker built dinghy, *Joan*. The boat was one of two built jointly by his father, Ernest, together with Willie Redmond in 1948/1949. The boat was later lost in a storm at Greystones harbour, with only the metal ring from the end of its mooring rope and its rudder recovered.

ABOVE: Photograph of the 1948-49 Greystones Football Club under-18 team taken in Arch Field. Back row: Kevin Glynn, Billy Manweiler, J. Coffey, Donie Doyle, Derek Paine and Seamus Whiston. Front row: John Dougan, Billy Hayden, Godfrey Holloway, E. O'Brien and Willie Mitchell. Greystones Football Club was established in 1924.

RIGHT: Derek Paine and his son, David, preparing his *Matilda* yacht to sail from Greystones harbour in 1977. The flagstaff can be seen in the background, protruding above the harbour buildings. A rowing boat is about to be wheeled down the slip and a number of trailers from boats that have been launched are visible on the beach. The concrete lip of the Kish base is visible. The chain suspended from it connected to the heavy mooring chain from which the boats' moorings in the harbour were set. A similar heavy chain can be seen running across the beach. Each autumn, this chain was lifted in order to prevent it from being buried during the winter storms.

ABOVE: Derek Paine and Don Mclean photographed beside the flagstaff at Greystones harbour in 1970. At the time, both men served on Greystones & District Civic Association as Hon. Secretary and Chairman respectively and both had yachts moored in the harbour for a number of years.

ABOVE: The organising committee comprising Derek Paine, Dr. Leslie Doyle, Victor Lowe and Ozzy Spurling, photographed in August 1973 at the opening of the inaugural exhibition of old photographs of Greystones. This was held in the old St. Patrick's National School on La Touche Place.

ABOVE: Derek Paine, Dr. Leslie Doyle and Victor Lowe at the opening of the exhibition of old photographs of Greystones in 1985, held in aid of the RNLI in the annexe of The Burnaby.

DEREK PAINE

Greystones had a fine tradition of boatbuilding down the years, beginning with the Arthur Connor built schooner, *Belle Vue,* in 1839. This was carried on by Henry Evans (1808-1898) who built many boats to the rear of *Emily House* beside the turnpike. In the 20th century, the craft of boatbuilding was maintained most notably by boatbuilders such as John Spurling and Willie Redmond (refer to Book No. 7).

RIGHT: Derek Paine building his first *Water Wag,* named *Skee,* in his workshop in 1984. In the late 19th century, *Water Wags* were regular visitors to Greystones, competing in their own designated race at the Greystones Regattas of 1889, 1890 and 1891. During those years, *Water Wags* from the The Royal Irish Yacht Club, The Royal St. George Yacht Club and the Dublin Bay Sailing Club in Dún Laoghaire sailed down the coast Greystones to enter the races.

6th RACE—1.40 p.m.
*Sailing Race—Water-Wags and Class C of D.B.S.C., under
D.B.S.C. Rules.—About 5 Miles.*
·First Prize, £3 ; Second Prize, £1 10s. ; Third Prize £1.
Ida. J. R. Boyd, R. I. Y. C. *Red and White Vertical.*
Rose. Louis Meldon, D. B. S. C. *Red.*
Intacta. J. Keily, R. St. G. Y. C. *Blue.*
Eva. J. B. Middleton, R. I. Y. C. *Pink.*
Yum-Yum. R. Lee, D. B. S. C. *Light Blue.*

ABOVE: Extract from the official programme for the 1889 Greystones Regatta held on Thursday 22nd August 1889. The race was won by *Rose* in a time of 2 hours and 51 minutes, beating *Ida* by 1½ minutes.

Listed above, Eva, was built in 1887. Owned by the Middleton family of the Shankill Corinthian Sailing Club, she was the very first *Water Wag* ever built. For the centenary of the class, the *Water Wag* Club commissioned Derek Paine to build a new *Water Wag,* named *Eva,* in honour of the first ever *Water Wag*. Launched in Dún Laoghaire in 1987, she is still sailing to this day.

LEFT: Derek Paine checking the spars on his 4th *Water Wag, Little Tern* (Sail No.36), which he built in 1996. The name was chosen in reference to the colony of little terns that return each summer from Sub-Saharan Africa to nest among the stones on Kilcoole Beach. The little terns are featured in Book No. 5. The *Water Wags* are a familiar sight for walkers on Dún Laoghaire pier every Wednesday evening during the summer, where they have raced within the harbour for over a century. This *Water Wag* followed *Skee* (Sail No.32, built in 1984), *Eva* (Sail No.33, built in 1987) and *Chloe* (Sail No.34, built in 1990).

RIGHT: Classmates in the infants' class of St. Patrick's National School, Greystones in 1935, Frank Doyle and Derek Paine photographed on 18th August 2013 attending a ceremony to unveil a plaque at Greystones harbour. The plaque was in memory of John Doyle, Coxswain of the Greystones Lifeboat. In October 1892, John Doyle, his brother William and Herbert, William's son, drowned in the harbour whilst attempting to assist the schooner, *Mersey*. Frank was the grandson of William Doyle and the nephew of Herbert Doyle.

THE BRANDY HOLE

On Wednesday 25th August 1847, a turning of the sod ceremony took place to commence the works to bring the railway line around Bray Head to Greystones. The chosen spot was at the Brandy Hole.

Reporting on the occasion, *The Freeman's Journal* noted that "*at 2.00pm the Chairman of the Waterford, Wexford, Wicklow & Dublin Railway, the Earl of Courtown, dug up some earth with a spade which was presented to him and at that moment explosions were heard, from where blasts were set off by way of beginning the work*". The correspondent reporting on the proceedings also noted that "*if there was difficulty in descending, the labour in the ascent from the Brandy Hole proved the lungs and limbs of those engaged in it. The important and gratifying ceremony which all had witnessed, as well as the glorious weather, cheered all onward and the hillside was surmounted most successfully*".

ABOVE: View of the beach at Bray Head adjacent to the small promontory which housed the smugglers' cavern that was known as the Brandy Hole. The ruin of a building constructed later is visible on the plateau.

Those first sounds of dynamite blasting through the rock to commence the works ultimately dealt a mortal blow to the smuggling activities that gave the Brandy Hole its name. Soon the rock blasted by the railway company had filled up the smugglers' cavern and its ability to serve as a smuggling hideaway was rendered defunct.

With its rocky sea cliffs and hidden landing spots, Bray Head's rugged coastline lent itself to smuggling. The establishment of the Preventive Guard Station at Blacklion (forerunner of the coast guards) in 1821 provided a visible deterrent along the nearby coastline. The station was equipped with two boats, a large open boat called a galley, with oars, mast and sails and a smaller open clinker built boat called a gig. The station's 15 strong compliment of men, drawn mainly from outside the locality, were principally engaged in the detection and prevention of contraband activities. Each evening, in calm conditions, the boatmen of the station rowed out to patrol the coast. The relocation of the coast guards from Blacklion to a purpose built station comprising of interlinked cottages at Kenmare Terrace in 1843 on the lower part of Trafalgar Road further bolstered their presence. Importantly, the new station also included a watch house (refer to the plan on page 118), manned by the boatmen. The cottages' sight lines extended northeast to the area known as the Red Rocks and beyond to the Cable Rock, Bray Head's most easterly point.

Long before the arrival of the preventive guard, Bray Head had acquired a reputation for smuggling. The activities centred on the natural cavern known as the Brandy Hole. It was sufficiently well established to be noted as a feature on the Ordnance Survey map of the area in 1838.

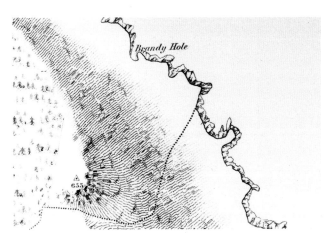

Whilst smuggling by its nature is prone to being embellished in local folklore, there are a number of written accounts dating from the latter part of the 19th century and early part of the 20th century that shed some light on the history of the Brandy Hole. The most detailed of these information sources comes from a book of Irish Tales by Dr. Campion, published in 1869. The publication entitled *The Last Struggles of the Irish Sea Smugglers: A Historical Romance of the Wicklow Coast,* was largely centred on a fictional smuggler, "Wild Willy", who was active in his profession along the Wicklow coast, including the Brandy Hole. The book contains factual information relating to the Brandy Hole. The introduction, written by Campion, draws on his research with people in the locality familiar with the subject. The book's preface notes that "*it is from some of such exciting fragments of past exciting lore that the author has selected passages and incidents of his present story*".

ABOVE: The Brandy Hole on Bray Head marked on the 1838 Ordnance Survey map surveyed by Capt. Tucker and Lieutenant James of the Royal Engineers.

In his introduction, Campion further notes that whilst Wicklow has had innumerable tourists' guides, "*very few, if any condescended to dip into the pineal of the old Head, to people its cliffs with anything but sheep and wild goats, or to peep into its vast gorges and sounding sea-caverns that lie and slumber and dream and murmur at its spacious and foam-muffling base. Very few, if any, have sat down with the goatherd or the white headed peasant, as they lay musing on those wild defiles and taken the trouble of learning from their lips those little dottings of the past*".

To set the scene within his fictional tale, Campion draws on the factual accounts given to him by locals remembering back to a time 50 years or more before. The following excerpt provides us with possibly the most accurate written account of what the Brandy Hole was and how it came about to be a geographic feature marked by that name on the Ordnance Survey map of 1838.

"*On the eastern side of the Head is one remarkable spot - indeed, the most remarkable spot of that vast promontory; its site is at present indicated by the middle or second tunnel of the Wicklow Railway. Here there was an immense spacious cavern, with its great mouth widely open to the sea and its various chambers piercing far into the bowels of the earth, shooting both laterally, directly and extensively, until they all formed one enormous emporium, not only for the inroads of the raging ocean and its weeds and shells and disjected members of wrecks, its gulls and puffins, herons and cormorants, its sea-calves, porpoises and dogfish; but also for the large contraband trade, that needed all its ample accommodation for its perpetual contributions.*

Into this great gulphing throat of crags and earth, whole ship-boats, fully laden with smuggled goods, were easily able to make way, even at the flow of the tide, for there was quite room enough to steer to the right or left at all times, out of its influence and to discharge their cargoes high and dry into the many departments prepared for them. Here there was perfect security for all secret purpose; for proceedings were carried on so well, silently and effectively, by the sea marauders, that either the coast guard knew nothing of the use the famous cavern was put to, or they were afraid to venture their persons into those secret recesses, where it was a natural deduction from common calculation that they would remain henceforth, until the last trumpet called them forth to eternal judgement.

Immediately over this cavern and on a line with the circuitous pathway, or goat-track, that encircled the whole hill, was another cavern, but of a very different description indeed; for it was dug down into the heart of the mountain in rather a slanting direction, some fifty or sixty feet deep, but leaving no trace about how it had been effected; for the earth exhumed had been carefully flung into the sea and the mouth of the cave thickly set with ferns, mosses, briars and brambles.

The appearance of this excavation was not by any means enticing to adventurers, comers or goers, to peep into its sombre recesses, much less to investigate the depths of its deep. There was, however, a facile way to penetrate this black gulph, for rude hewn steps for that purpose were well known to the enlightened, although muffled up from common view by the natural vegetable growth which had been so ingeniously coaxed into the service of the industrious sappers and miners of its formation.

There were also secret steps and pathways from the cavern below, equally well covered and concealed and by which a person above, by means of a rope, might either assist parties to climb expeditiously upwards, or else drag up large bales of goods of every kind for stowage in the earth-cave just described and from which they might be readily distributed to purchasers in all directions.

Both the earth and sea caves are now only spoken of as the Brandy Hole, the site of both being utterly obliterated by the enterprising man of science, who burst and bored through earth and rock and crag and cavern, until both caves disappeared before his magic power and now constitute part and portion of the Wexford line. But immediately before this scientific transformation, the Brandy Hole ended its notoriety and existence in a very inglorious manner indeed and in one also very unworthy of the famous owners and fabricators of those wonderful dungeons.

It appears that a few fishermen wandering about this place on the Head, stumbled upon the earth cave and through bravado or foolhardiness determined to see the bottom of it, even if it went down into the sea. Accordingly, they descended very cautiously at first, but by and by, feeling the secret steps under their feet, finished their descent without any further difficulty. Arrived at the end of their journey, they popped upon some hard round body, which, after striking a light, they discovered to be nothing more or less than a keg of first rate French brandy. It was a solitary occupant and very probably was the last sample of the kind that ever adorned the same uninviting premises.

Without any delay, the prize was broached and the precious liquor set squirting into the throats of the thirsty souls, who never before met such an extraordinary chance. But their feast was conducted with so little moderation and their love of the potent liquor increasing as they quaffed, the hapless result was, that some lay smothered by the vile excess and others reeled homewards, but only to lie down on their sick beds and spend week upon week before their ultimate recovery. Such was the last traditional use made of the now betunneled Brandy Hole, the theatre of so many remarkable exploits".

In addition to Dr. Campion's book published in 1869, there are a number of other references to the existence of smuggling activities at Bray Head. The following report appeared in *Saunders's Newsletter* dated Monday 22nd June 1789. "*A revenue cutter pursued and captured a smuggling wherry on Saturday morning off Bray Head. The wherry was laden with geneva, tobacco and raw silks. Some boats from the shore seeing the situation of the wherry put to sea and received all the silk, which they landed before the cutter could come up . The prize was brought to the Custom House.*" The geneva referred to in this report was a spirit similar to gin, distilled from grain and flavoured with juniper berries, commonly produced in the Netherlands.

In *The Tourist's Illustrated Handbook for Ireland with Maps & Illustrations*, published in 1853 the author wrote the following. "*At the foot of Bray Head may be seen the railway now being constructed to the town of Wicklow; while beneath lies a natural basin known as the Brandy Hole, so called from the facilities it gave to smugglers; and many a hand to hand encounter has it been the scene of between the daring defrauder of the revenue and the coast guard*".

An article published almost a century ago also provides an insight into the Brandy Hole on Bray Head. In response to a story concerning smuggling along the coast to the north of Dublin, *The Evening Herald* dated 26th November 1920 published the following: "*A reader, following up the account the other day of the smuggling that was carried on down to a century ago by the people of Fairview and Clontarf, says that some of the inhabitants of the wild and lonely coast of Wicklow were even more notorious contrabandists about that time. A series of caverns under Bray Head especially lent themselves readily to the concealment of smuggled goods, pushed in from vessels under cover of night or in misty weather. One of these, still remembered locally as the Brandy Hole was an immense awning in the cliff, with its entrance opening to the sea and having several chambers extending far under the hill. Into this, the smugglers were easily able to steer their fully laden little boats and discharge their contents in the natural storehouses within. The Brandy Hole was furnished with a second entrance which was an artificial one. It gave access to the treasure cave from the land and was carefully concealed from the uninitiated by a thick growth of bracken and brambles. Every trace of this interesting relic of a romantic traffic was wiped away during the construction of the Dublin and South Eastern Railway".*

The Weekly Freeman, which was the weekend edition of *The Freeman's Journal* included the following in its edition of Saturday 4th December 1920. "*It is difficult for one to realise that at certain periods around our coasts there existed and flourished to a large degree, communities of outlaws particularly along the thin, bleak and barren shores of the counties of Dublin and Wicklow, who carried on a promiscuous mode of living in the capacities of smuggling, privateering and even piracy. Extravagant and far-fetched as this assertion must seem to many, there are numerous records to be found in files of old newspapers and journals that go to prove conclusively that how numbers of sea robbers carried on a thriving trade and there are romantic stories preserved in which their doings and adventures are recorded. Taking Ringsend as a starting point, that was at one time an important port, heavily armed privateers during the period of the war with France about the years 1778 & 1780, set out under French and American colours and were frequently rewarded with prizes by the French for the capture of trading vessels, which they brought around the Land's End to Brest. These cruisers were quickly built for great speed and two of them lay off Bray Head and in fact at various points on the east and south coasts, such as Waterford, Cork & Cape Clear. Their owners and commanders made a great deal of money by such means, in so much that their example was soon followed by lesser fry, including smuggling crafts who joined in such warfare and they too were enabled to obtain letters of marque from the French and joined in the war against England, to return to their places of plunder with a goodly supply of prize money. These freebooters frequented in numbers the Irish Sea*".

In *The Weekly Freeman's Journal* dated 14th April 1923, in an article headed "*Smuggling in Ireland*", H.T. Hunt Grubb, commented in detail about smuggling in olden times in Dublin. In addition, he wrote that "*the system of smuggling at Bray was even more extensive than at the north side of the city. Bray was at that period only a fishing village and Bray Head had several hiding places for contraband goods, principally a large cavern called the Brandy Hole. This strangely enough consisted of two natural caves, one situated above the other and connected by a shaft. The upper portion communicated with the heights above and there was an opening to what was known as the goat track and was covered with bramble bushes. The upper cave afforded the smugglers a safe retreat as well as sleeping accommodation, likewise a repository for merchandise. The lower cave opened upon the sea and it extended for a long distance under the hill where there was sufficient water to allow boats laden with goods from the ships outside to be taken far within and unloaded. From this rendezvous, smuggling vessels would set out in the thick darkness or in mist and then sail openly to Dublin or some other port where they would discharge their legitimate cargoes.*

The caves now only remain a memory and a tradition. One can quite imagine the fierce and terrible encounters that took place between the excise men and the smugglers on that dangerous part of the coast and the shoreline of Co. Wicklow was even more bleak and desolate than that of the County of Dublin before described. The Brandy Hole has been completely obliterated. At the time of the construction of the railway round the Head it was filled in, yet people travelling by train pass over the very spot which is about half way round the Head*".

In 1963, *The Evening Herald* published another article entitled "*When the smugglers set sail for Bray Head.*" In it the reporter, Hugh Clifton, wrote the following: "*The wild and desolate coast of early 18th century Wicklow afforded so many facilities for smuggling that Government efforts seldom interrupted the well-laid schemes of the contrabandists. The latter's customary plan was to send their goods ashore in small craft under cover of mist or darkness to pre-arranged hiding places, then to sail innocently on to Dublin or elsewhere, with their legal cargo.*

The natural uniformity of Bray Head's shoreline lent itself to the adaptation of the places for landing or concealing contraband. The most suitable spot was known as the Brandy Hole. It was half a mile along the coast from where the present road crosses the railway line at the Head. Here was a large cavern, with its entrance opening seawards and with many offshoots extending underneath the Head. So the smugglers under dim lantern light, crept ashore to this natural storehouse and discharged their loads into various "holds" prepared for them. Directly over this cavern and convenient to a goat track encircling Bray Head, a slant-wise shaft had been constructed by the smugglers' allies ashore. This linked up with another chamber near the surface, its entrance being concealed by thick undergrowth, thus providing, for those in the know, a means of entry to the cavern from the slopes of the Head.*

Steps and platforms were also provided so that a person on land, by means of a rope, could help fellow smugglers to climb out, or, if necessary, drag up bales of goods from the cavern to the upper chamber, or from the latter to the useful goat track. The secret of these Ali Baba subterranean activities must have been kept for a long time, because in a pretty little cottage at the southern end of Bray strand (there was no promenade then), lived an elderly woman and her daughter. Ostensibly, the pair made a living from collecting and selling pebbles peculiar to the district. However, tradition has it that the older lady was, with others, an active agent for the contrabandists. Her agency must have been a profitable one because she is reputed to have died wealthy. It is said that she was a woman of great courage and went about armed. That on one occasion, no doubt under cover of darkness, she was involved in an affray with the Preventive Men. For it seems that when authority got wise to the trade plied at the Brandy Hole, Bray Head was the scene of some fierce melees between law men and lawbreakers. The caves concerned were demolished during the construction of the railway and the inlet in the cliffs, still known as the Brandy Hole is the sole memorial of the smugglers' Open Sesame! on Bray Head*".

In the early 1800s, smuggling activity in the Irish Sea centred principally in the waters around the Isle of Man. This area was a particular haven for contraband, given the island's tax free status. On 16th August 1844, *The Dublin Monitor* newspaper noted that there were 16 revenue cutters based at Kingstown (Dún Laoghaire). Under the headline "*Capture of a Smuggler*", it also reported that "*Her Majesty's revenue cutter, Prince Albert, Lieutenant Croker, R.N., captured at seven o'clock a.m. yesterday, after a chase of two hours, off the Calf of Man, the cutter, Ceres, of 52 tons belonging to Flushing, with a crew of ten men. She had on board 51 bales of tobacco of 310lbs each. Her boat being absent, the captors suspected what she was about and returned in search of her, whom they found with 62 bales, which the smugglers evidently wished to put on board a suspicious looking schooner that was dodging about for the purpose. The pilot of the Ceres is the noted Jos. Wells, who was pilot of the Eliza, formerly captured*".

There are two other places associated with smuggling along the east coast which have the word "Brandy" in their names. There is another Brandy Hole at Dalkey, near Bullock, that was used to smuggle goods. Further north in County Down, there is a smugglers' path named The Brandy Pad. This led inland from the coast through the Mourne mountains in which smuggled goods, landed on the beach under cover of darkness, were spirited away through the mountains on the backs of small ponies.

ABOVE: Painting of a Royal Navy cutter. The cutters used by the revenue service and also by smugglers were similar, utilising the design's attributes of speed and manoeuvrability.

ABOVE: This is one of the oldest photographs taken on Bray Head. The image is from a *Carte de Visite* published in 1872. It shows a gentleman in a hat and long coat standing above the Brandy Hole tunnel. He is pointing towards the whitewashed timber bridge which traversed the cleft in the cliffs known as The Ram's Scalp, over which the original railway line ran through the Brabazon tunnel. On 9th August 1867 this spot was scene of a serious accident when the 6.20am Dublin bound train from Enniscorthy (the then terminus) crashed through the left side handrail, resulting in two fatalities. In 1876, a second tunnel, known as the Ram's Scalp tunnel, was blasted through the rock to the left of the Brabazon tunnel. It remains in use today. In the photograph, the shoreline at the northern end of the shingle beach at the Brandy Hole is just visible. On 25th August 1847, the cutting of the sod took place to commence the construction of the railway line around Bray Head to Greystones near this spot. *The Dublin Mercantile Advertiser* dated Friday 19th October 1855 reported that "*the first experimental trip on this line from Bray to Wicklow was made on Saturday*".

LEFT: 2005 photograph showing a DART, having just exited the Brandy Hole tunnel, heading north past the Brandy Hole beach (heavily armoured with boulders), about to proceed through the Ram's Scalp tunnel. The disused Brabazon tunnel, which is visible from the flagstaff at Greystones harbour, can be seen to its right.

ABOVE: 155 years after the railway company blasted out the rock to construct the Brandy Hole tunnel, filling up the smugglers' cave that was the Brandy Hole, they returned. In the photograph, taken in July 2002, the Brandy Hole beach disappeared under a bed of boulders to protect the railway. Though nature has returned a small area of shingle beach at its southern end, it will require much stronger forces of nature to open up the smugglers' cavern that was the Brandy Hole, to enable a return to the illicit activities of the past.

ABOVE & BELOW: Two old postcards showing the road known as The Carriage Road, which was built by the Earl of Meath across the top of Bray Head. The upper photograph is looking north towards where the cross was later erected on 23rd September 1950 to commemorate Holy Year. The lower photograph is looking south towards the obelisk monument that was erected by W.G. Morris of Windgates to commemorate Queen Victoria's Golden Jubilee in 1887. This can be seen protruding on the horizon at the highest point on Bray Head (241m, 791ft). The Carriage Road was accessed through the gate opposite the old main entrance to the Kilruddery Estate on the Bray side of the Southern Cross roundabout. The road wound its way close to where the cross is today before turning south and zigzagging across the top to near where the Ordnance Survey marker is now located. *The Wicklow Newsletter* dated 26th August 1916 noted that *"the carriage road up Bray Head is open daily and the walk round the Head to Greystones affords unsurpassed views of sea and mountain scenery"*.

LEFT: Members of the Flavelle family who holidayed in Greystones between 1899 and 1903, photographed sitting on the Victoria obelisk on the summit of Bray Head. The obelisk was erected in 1887 and blown up by an unknown group of men on 11th November 1933. It was subsequently replaced by the present day Ordnance Survey marker shown in the colour photo below.

ABOVE RIGHT: The catalogue for the auction held in Dublin on 3rd February 1920 for the sale of the "*Morris Estate*" by the vendor, Major George William Sterne Morris, born in 1879 in *Windgate House*, the son of William George Morris. The estate comprised approximately 360 acres, 135 acres of which were let to tenants and 225 acres of which were "*in the occupation of the vendor.*" The 10 lots included "*almost the entire village of Windgate, situated on the south side of Bray Head*", right across to the railway line. It included 12 houses and cottages, *Rathdown Cottage,* among them. With regard to Lots 8, 9 & 10 which covered a combined area of just under 50 acres, the auction noted the existence of an 1868 granting of certain rights which permitted the Rev. Peter Marsh and his heirs liberty to exploit any mineral deposits, plus "*all liberty of hawking, fishing, fowling or pursuing game on the lands.*" The area where the original railway line ran south from Bray Head before traversing the bridge at Ennis' Lane was known as Morris' Bank and included a crossing point known as Morris' Crossing. This is featured in Book No.7.

BELOW: August 2010 view looking south from the Ordnance Survey marker on the summit of Bray Head overlooking Greystones and the coastline at Ballygannon and on to Wicklow Head in the distance.

BRAY HEAD WORLD WAR TWO LOOK OUT POST

Friday 30th May 1941 began like any other day for the two-man watch on duty at Look Out Post No.8 of the Coast Watching Service situated on the southern slopes of Bray Head. Weather conditions were moderate and during the course of the day, no events of note were recorded. It appeared just another routine day, with the watch phoning McCormick's coal distributors in Bray late morning to order more coal. As midnight approached, the men prepared for the changeover of the watch, with Messrs. Wheeler and Doyle handing over to Messrs. Davies and Salmon. No sooner had the new watch taken over than the sound of aircraft travelling north was heard. Over the course of a frantic 20 minute period between 00.02hrs and 00.22hrs, the watch followed the set procedure, phoning Air Defence Command in Dublin on no fewer than five occasions to pass on the information. By the time dawn broke on Saturday 31st May 1941, death and destruction had been brought to Dublin's North Strand - the toll of fatalities would eventually rise to 28.

BELOW: The timeline of events below describes the bombing of Dublin's North Strand on 30th / 31st May 1941 and the role played by Look Out Post No.8 on Bray Head in observing events and relaying information up the line of command to Air Defence Command in Dublin. Acknowledgements are due to both the Military Archives, Cathal Brugha Barracks, Dublin, for affording access to the log books and also to Michael Kennedy for his book, *Guarding Neutral Ireland,* as valuable sources of the information below. The observations made by the watch manning the Bray Head Look Out Post No.8 are highlighted in green in the table below. Timings and other relevant information relating to the events surrounding the bombing are overlaid within the timeline table.

Friday 30th May 1941

Time	Events / Messages / Incidents / Action Taken
23.40hrs	Look Out Post No.14 at Carnsore Point observed the first wave of aircraft heading north along the Wexford coast. A further wave of incoming aircraft heading north were observed at 23.48hrs.
23.48hrs	The air raid alarm was sounded in Dublin and a code "Yellow" preliminary air raid warning was issued. Dublin's air defences comprising the city's anti-aircraft guns, searchlights and men went on standby.
23.56hrs	Look Out Post No.9 on Wicklow Head *"Sound of aircraft 7 miles southeast of post, going north, visibility moderate. Emergency on, heard continuous sound of aircraft going north from 00.00hrs to 01.45hrs."*
23.58hrs	Air raid warning code "Red" was issued to the gun crews manning the city's anti-aircraft artillery. *"The reports from Air Defence Control carried information that seemed to indicate a developing threat to the city."*

Saturday 31st May 1941

Time	Events / Messages / Incidents / Action Taken
00.02hrs	Look Out Post No.8 on Bray Head: *"Heard sound of aircraft 8 miles southeast of post, travelling north, visibility moderate, phoned Air Defence Command."*
00.03hrs	Look Out Post No.8 on Bray Head: *"Heard sound of aircraft 3 miles southwest of post, travelling north, flying high, visibility moderate, phoned Air Defence Command."*
00.10hrs	Look Out Post No.8 on Bray Head: *"Heard sound of aircraft southeast and southwest of post, travelling north, at 00.15hrs heard sound of aircraft southeast of post travelling northeast, visibility moderate, phoned Air Defence Command."*
00.20hrs	Look Out Post No.8 on Bray Head: *"Heard sound of heavy explosions northeast of post, visibility moderate, phoned Air Defence Command."*
00.22hrs	Look Out Post No.8 on Bray Head: *"Heard sound of number of aircraft southeast of post, travelling north, visibility moderate, phoned Air Defence Command."*
00.30hrs	Look Out Post No.8 on Bray Head: *"Heard sound of aircraft 2 miles southwest of post, travelling north over post, also heard more aircraft 4 miles southeast of post, travelling north, visibility moderate, phoned Air Defence Command."*
00.34hrs	Look Out Post No.14 at Carnsore Point observed the last of the 3 waves of Luftwaffe bombers passing north along the Wexford coast.
00.35hrs	Clontarf Battery was the first of the Dublin anti-aircraft defences to open fire, discharging 4 rounds at an aircraft caught in a searchlight beam heading north to the east at around 7,000 feet.
00.46hrs	Look Out Post No.8 on Bray Head: *"Heard sound of aircraft 3 miles south of post, travelling northwest. 00.50hrs heard sound of aircraft 3 miles northeast of post, travelling southwest, visibility moderate, phoned Air Defence Command."*
01.07hrs	Look Out Post No.8 on Bray Head: *"Heard sound of aircraft 3 miles southeast of post travelling north, also more southeast of post going north, also heard sound of a number of explosions east of post, phoned Air Defence Command."*
01.13hrs	Look Out Post No.8 on Bray Head: *"Heard sound of aircraft 6 miles south and southwest of post going north, phoned Air Defence Command."*
01.25hrs	Look Out Post No.8 on Bray Head *"Heard sound of aircraft 3 miles south of post travelling north, also a number of explosions east of post, visibility moderate, phoned Air Defence Command."*
01.27hrs	Look Out Post No.8 on Bray Head: *"Heard sound of 2 very large explosions east of post."*
01.28hrs	Clontarf and Ringsend Batteries opened fire almost simultaneously on 2 planes coming from the north.
01.30hrs	The first of the 4 bombs dropped on Dublin, estimated at 250lbs fell on the North Circular Road near the junction with North Richmond Street. A shop was demolished and a house set on fire, but there were no casualties. The second 250lbs bomb fell almost at the same time, a couple of hundred yards from the first at the junction of Richmond Cottages and Summerhill Parade, injuring one woman who died 2 weeks later in hospital.
01.30hrs	Collinstown Bofors Gun Battery opened fire, discharging 2 rounds, the second at 01.45hrs.
01.30hrs	Stillorgan Battery and Ballyfermot Battery (01.31hrs) opened fire on the same 2 planes.
01.30hrs	Look Out Post No.8 on Bray Head: *"Sighted very bright flashes north of post, visibility moderate, phoned Air Defence Command."*
01.32hrs	The third of the four bombs, again estimated at 250lbs fell on the Phoenix Park, shattering windows in Áras an Uachtaráin.
01.36hrs	Look Out Post No.8 on Bray Head: *"Heard sound of aircraft 3 miles south of post going north, visibility moderate."*
01.40hrs	Look Out Post No.8 on Bray Head: *"Heard sound of aircraft 3 miles southwest of post going north, phoned Air Defence Command."*
02.03hrs	Look Out Post No.8 on Bray Head: *"Heard sound of aircraft 3 miles northeast travelling south, visibility moderate, phoned Air Defence Command."*

Time	Events / Messages / Incidents / Action Taken
02.05hrs	The fourth and largest of the bombs, estimated at 500lbs landed on the tram tracks on the North Strand opposite the junction with North William Street, with the explosion heard across the city. 25 houses were demolished and a further 45 had to be demolished. By 22.00hrs on 31st May, the bodies of 17 victims had been recovered. The final death toll would reach 28.
02.10hrs	Wicklow Head Look Out Post No.9 *"heard aircraft 6 miles northeast of post heading southeast."*
02.14hrs	Look Out Post No.8 on Bray Head: *"Heard sound of aircraft 4 miles west of post travelling south, also heard a lot of explosions east of post, visibility moderate, phoned Air Defence Command."*
02.15hrs	The aircraft believed to be the one which dropped the large bomb on the North Strand passed Wicklow Head.
02.30hrs	The emergency was called off.
03.15hrs	Call from Bray Guards.
03.50hrs	Look Out Post No.8 Bray Head: *"Heard sound of aircraft northeast of post, then sighted it passing post, type Junker."* This aircraft is believed to have been a straggler from the main waves of bombers. Dalkey Look Out Post No.7 is recorded as having shot at this aircraft with machine gun fire as it passed by. Dalkey Look Out Post was incorporated into a larger military establishment which had a searchlight and sound detectors.

BELOW: The log book entries for Look Out Post No.8 on Bray Head for 30th and 31st May 1941. Examination reveals that at 00.03hrs on Saturday 31st May 1941 Luftwaffe bombers flew over Greystones.

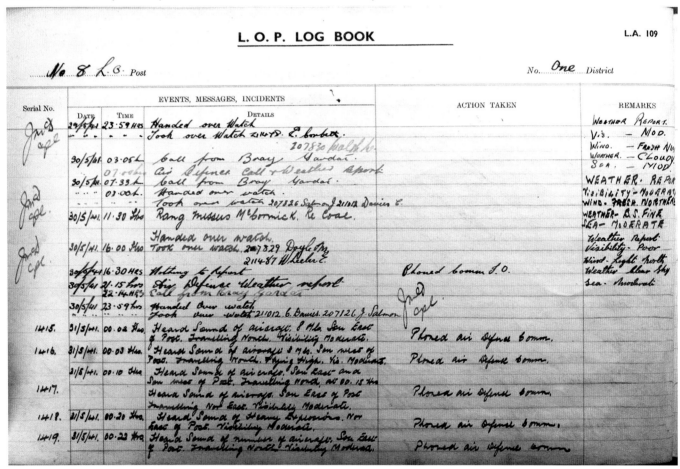

BELOW: The log book entry made at 03.50hrs on 31st May 1941 clearly identifying a Junkers flying south past Bray Head.

BELOW: A World War Two German Luftwaffe Junkers bomber.

RIGHT: Bofors 40 mm light anti-aircraft guns which were deployed at Collinstown.

RIGHT: Vickers 3.7 inch heavy anti-aircraft guns which were deployed at Ringsend and Clontarf.

BRAY HEAD WORLD WAR TWO LOOK OUT POST

Whilst the truth of why Dublin was bombed by the Luftwaffe on 31st May 1941 may never be known, the consensus view is that it was the result of a tragic mistake made by two of the large number of German bombers that flew up along the Irish coast that night. The log book for May 1941 for the Bray Head Look Out Post No.8 reveals that the activity level in the skies above Bray Head reached a peak during that month. There was scarcely a night that the din of aircraft flying along the Wicklow coast was not heard. It was well known that the Luftwaffe used the geographic reference point of Bray Head and the lights of Dublin on their bombing raids over Liverpool. Planes regularly flew up the Irish coast at a distance of five miles, just outside the three mile territorial limit, before banking to the east and heading for Liverpool.

In April and early May 1941, Belfast was blitzed on a number of nights, with the death toll reaching more than 900. It was quite common for German aircraft to become lost in their search for the docks of Cardiff, Liverpool and Belfast. It was paramount that the crew and aircraft return safely to Germany. This necessitated the jettisoning of the aircraft's bombs to lighten the plane and preserve fuel to ensure a successful return to Germany. It is telling that, in the five minutes prior to the dropping of the first bomb on Dublin at 01.30hrs on that fateful night, the men in the Bray Head Look Out Post recorded hearing loud explosions on two separate occasions out to sea as the majority of German aircraft jettisoned their bombs. Sadly for the people of the North Strand it appears that two of the German aircraft inadvertently jettisoned theirs over the city and not the sea as intended, with tragic consequences. Three nights before the North Strand bombing, on 28th May 1941, over 50 German bombers flew up along the Wicklow coast, observed by the men on watch on Bray Head. They almost bombed Dublin in error, but passed to the east of the city. They were possibly looking for Cardiff or Liverpool, but seeing that the land differed to their bomb-aimer's map, they dropped their bombs off the coast instead. The Bray Head look out post recorded hearing continual loud explosions and seeing bright flashes out to sea between midnight and 02.00hrs.

ABOVE: Members of the Coast Watching Service stationed at Look Out Post No.8 on Bray Head during World War Two. Back row, left to right: R.J. Nolan, Joseph Naylor, Cecil Davies, Michael Doyle. Front row, left to right: C. O'Toole, J. Cleary, L. Wheeler.

BELOW: The roll of personnel who manned Look Out Post No.8 on Bray Head at the commencement of its operations in 1940.

ABOVE RIGHT: Photograph of the Look Out Post at Ardmore in Co. Waterford, built to the same modular design, which shows how the Bray Head Look Out Post looked prior to its demolition.

At total of 82 look out posts were built or reconditioned between 1939 and 1942, constructed to a uniform identical design using 137 pre-cast concrete blocks. The Bray Head Look Out Post was one of nine located between Howth Head and Carnsore Point. These were considered among the most important of the posts around the coast in regard to reporting any incursions into Irish air space. It was from these nine look out posts that news of a potential air attack on Dublin from the south would be first relayed. After the end of the war, the look out posts were shut down, with many falling into disrepair. Today, around 50 of them are still standing and a number still have their "EIRE" markings in neatly laid out stones adjacent to them. The Bray Head marking was revealed, still largely intact in July 2018, when a large fire on Bray Head scorched the grass back to the earth. Donegal retains the highest number of surviving "EIRE" markings, where eight of them can still be seen on headlands.

ABOVE & BELOW: The ruins of Look Out Post No.8 on the southern slope of Bray Head, adjacent to the cliff walk in April 2016. Its location gave sweeping views north to Dalkey Island, across to Howth and south to Ballygannon and Wicklow Head.

LEFT: Aerial photograph taken by the Irish Air Corps following the fire on Bray Head in July 2018. Through the subsequent efforts of a number of local volunteers including Denis Slattery, John Byrne, Fiachra White and Brian Hassel in cutting back the scorched vegetation and tidying the area, the "EIRE" marking and a faint trace of the digit "8" above it denoting Look Out Post No.8 on Bray Head was once again clearly revealed.

ABOVE: Photograph taken in the summer of 1995, the previous time a large fire on Bray Head extended to the seaward side of the cliff walk to reveal the "EIRE" marking made from whitewashed stones. Located between the Look Out Post and the cliff edge, the first line of stones form part of the box surround. Beyond it, the "E", "I" and "R" can be seen.

RIGHT: "EIRE" marking for Look Out Post No.9 on Wicklow Head was placed on the eastward side of the original 1781 built octagonal lighthouse tower (the most westerly of Wicklow Head's three lighthouses). The "EIRE" markings were added during 1942-43 to each of the 82 look out posts that stretched around the Irish coast from Ballagan Point in Co. Louth to Inishowen Head in Co. Donegal. A list of the 82 LOPs, their locations and numbers, was given to all allied pilots.

BRAY HEAD WORLD WAR TWO LOOK OUT POST

Each look out post was manned 24 hours, seven days a week by a rotating watch of two men on duty in either 8 or 12 hour shifts. One man operated the telephone inside the post, the other patrolled outside, observing the sea, air and coast. Details of events, messages, incidents and action taken were recorded, each with a serial number, date and time. Examination of the nine log books that cover Look Out Post No.8 on Bray Head between 1940 and 1945 reveals that very detailed observations were made by the coast watchers of objects and events in the air, on the land and in the sea. It is clear that the men were strongly encouraged to report and record everything, no matter how innocuous. An object seen floating out at sea towards Greystones turned out to be nothing more than a wicker basket. On another occasion, the threat was more real when a trawler, southeast of the Kish Light Vessel, reported that it had to cut its nets free after snagging a floating mine. Whilst these events are interesting, the Bray Head Look Out Post No.8's most important observations were undoubtedly the recording of the waves of Luftwaffe bombers flying up the Wicklow coast on the night of 30th / 31st May 1941, one of the most significant World War Two events that impacted Ireland, the bombing of Dublin's North Strand.

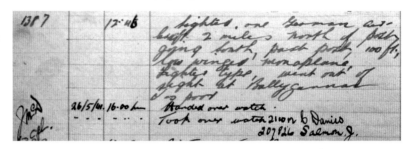

ABOVE: The Wicklow Head Look Out Post No.9's ominous entry on 31st May 1941, the night the Luftwaffe bombed Dublin's North Strand *"Heard continuous sound of aircraft going north 00.00hrs to 01.45hrs."*

ABOVE: Photograph of *Rose Cottage,* on the Bray to Greystones road at Windgates with its distinctive thatched roof. This was the home of Michael Doyle. He served with the Coast Watching Service during World War Two and was stationed at Look Out Post No.8 on Bray Head. On 30th May 1941, he finished his eight hour watch from 16.00hrs to 00.00hrs. At 00.03hrs on 31st May 1941, the first wave of Luftwaffe bombers was observed heading north by the watch that took over.

ABOVE: Log book entry dated 26th May 1941 for Look Out Post No.8 on Bray Head recording that at 12.46hrs the watch *"sighted one German aircraft, 2 miles north of post going south past post, 100 feet, low winged monoplane, fighter type, went out of sight at Ballygannon".*

Selected entries from the Look Out Post log books are reproduced below. They give a sense of the events and sounds that were seen and heard on Bray Head by the men of the Coast Watching Service during World War Two.

Date	Time	Events / Messages / Incidents / Action Taken
8th May 1940	11.20hrs	*"Sighted convoy 12 miles S.E. of L.O.P. travelling N.E., 6 merchant ships, 1 submarine, 2 escort ships & 1 destroyer. Nationality unknown. Visibility good."*
2nd June 1940	00.55hrs	*"Phoned Greystones Gardai enquiring if there were any boats out belonging to Greystones as there was a light observed about two miles off shore and sound of outboard engine. They said they would investigate."*
5th July 1940	07.30hrs	*"Call from Greystones Gardai re floating object seen by men fishing. 14.08hrs, Call from Greystones Gardai stating that object which they reported to us was a wickerwork basket 4ft x 3ft."*
7th July 1940	17.21hrs	*"2 submarines sighted from the Wicklow Look out Post, to keep sharp look out for them."*
8th July 1940	00.30hrs	*"Received call from Dalkey Look Out Post informing us that they had received information from a local, that there was something like gun flashes off Wicklow. 00.33hrs, Rang Gardai to see if they had seen anything like gun flashes. They reported that there was nothing to report."*
14th Sept 1940	13.35hrs	*"Sighted 1 battleship and 2 cruisers 10 miles east of post. Battleship seemed stationary, 2 cruisers going south, also a small black object which appeared to be a submarine, all travelling south, nationality unknown, visibility good. 13.45hrs, further to report above, sighted 2 cruisers and 1 battleship southeast of post, close to the others travelling south, nationality unknown."*
17th October 1940	01.55hrs	*"Heard sound of 7 heavy explosions east of post in the distance, visibility moderate."*
1st March 1941	11.09hrs	*"Sighted one bomber 9 miles east of post travelling south, nationality unknown, visibility good, phoned Air Defence Command."*
5th March 1941	22.00hrs	*"Observed the reflection of search lights in the sky, 18 miles northeast, phoned Air Defence command."*

BRAY HEAD WORLD WAR TWO LOOK OUT POST

Date	Time	Events / Messages / Incidents / Action Taken
16th March 1941	12.50hrs	*"Call from Captain O'Sullivan, Military Barracks, Bray re machine gun fire south of Greystones, to know if we heard it (we didn't hear it)."*
7th May 1941	09.20hrs	*"Aircraft reported in serial number 1314 has been circling round two colliers and Kish Lightship, she then turned and went south, visibility good."*
9th May 1941	01.20hrs	*"Heard sound of 10 heavy explosions northeast & east of post, visibility good, observed 2 flashes."*
14th May 1941	22.35hrs	*"Rang Greystones military re morse signalling in the vicinity of Wicklow. 22.40hrs, rang Wicklow L.O.P. re above. 22.45hrs Greystones rang telling us that they would communicate with Bray to see if they were out signalling. Wicklow L.O.P. rang informing us that they were signalling to Bray."*
16th May 1941	08.26hrs	*"Sighted 7 trawlers in convoy formation 9 miles southeast of post, travelling north, these trawlers appear to be mine sweepers, visibility good."*
29th May 1941 Events of the night of 30th / 31st May 1941 are covered on pages 20 and 21.	00.22hrs	*"Heard sound of aircraft 8 miles south of post, travelling north, height 10,000 feet, visibility poor. 00.26hrs, heard sound of two heavy explosions northeast of post and 1 bright flash sighted in same direction. 00.28hrs, heard sound of 1 heavy explosion northeast of post, visibility poor. 00.30hrs, heard sound of aircraft 8 miles southwest of post travelling north, height 10,000 feet, nationality unknown, visibility poor. 00.35hrs, heard sound of aircraft 7 miles south of post travelling north over post, height 200 feet, nationality unknown, visibility poor. 00.36hrs, heard sound of 2 explosions, heavy, northeast of post. 00.58hrs, heard sound of aircraft 8 miles south of post, travelling north, height 10,000 feet, visibility good. 01.04hrs, heard sound of 2 heavy explosions, southeast of post. 01.07hrs, heard sound of 2 heavy explosions northeast of post and numerous others, some seem very distant. 01.15hrs, heard sound of 4 very heavy explosions northeast of post, seemed very near."* Under the "Action Taken Column" in the log book was the following entry: *"Reported at 01.20hrs, Air Defence engaged and too busy, only took time and direction of travel in each case marked x."* 01.30hrs, *"heard sound of a number of aircraft 7 miles southeast of post going north over post and continuous explosions north and northeast of post. 01.53hrs, heard sound of aircraft southeast of post going north."* 08.45hrs, sighted one high winged monoplane, twin engine, double tail bomber, 5 miles southwest of post travelling southwest, nationality unknown."*
31st May 1941	23.55hrs	*"Heard sound of aircraft 7 miles southeast of post going north, visibility moderate."*
1st June 1941	00.09hrs	*"Heard sound of aircraft 7 miles southeast of post going north, visibility moderate. 00.13hrs, heard sound of aircraft 6 miles southeast of post going north. 00.10hrs, heard sound of 1 heavy explosion north of post. 00.26hrs, heard sound of aircraft 6 miles southeast of post going north. 00.32hrs, heard sound of aircraft going north over post. 00.38hrs, heard sound of aircraft 2 miles west of post going north. 00.42hrs, heard sound of aircraft over post, going north, visibility moderate. 00.35hrs, call from Air Defence ending emergency.* Under the "Action Taken Column" in the log book was the following entry: *"aircraft also heard at 00.50hrs, 00.55hrs, 00.58hrs and at 01.45hrs, but found it impossible to get through to Air Defence. 19.50hrs Distr. Offr. visited post."*
2nd August 1941	18.40hrs	*"Sighted a buoy drifting south, 3 miles northeast of post, visibility moderate. 19.30hrs, call from Greystones Gardai asking us to inform them if buoy changed its course they would investigate. 20.15hrs, rang Greystones Gardai informing them that there was a boat out at object. 20.25hrs, observed boat towing object towards Greystones at 20.25hrs. 21.25hrs, Greystones Gardai rang informing us that object picked up was a buoy."*
12th March 1942	10.25hrs	*"Call from Bray Gardai with following message: Information has been received here that a mine was observed on the sea about 12 miles east of the Kish Lightship by the officers and crew of the Mail Boat, Hibernia on their inward & outward journeys on 11th & 12th, precaution to be taken."*
11th June 1942	21.30hrs	*"Rang Greystones Gardai re large object floating in water 1 mile east of post, informing them sailing boat had inspected same and was proceeding into Greystones. Asked them to question them and find out what it was and to ring me back. 22.05hrs, Greystones Gardai rang informing us that they had asked people in boat about object referred to was two bales of straw."*
8th July 1942	08.12hrs	*"Call from Bray Gardai informing us that they had received a message from Howth saying that there was one mine sighted east southeast of the Kish Lightship by fishermen. 08.33hrs, call from Bray Gardai saying they had received another message from Howth Gardai at 03.00hrs, a fisherman's nets got caught in a mine and had to cut them away, 8 miles east southeast."*
6th Feb 1943	10.30hrs	*"Call from Greystones Gardai re sheep on rocks. 10.40hrs, phoned Greystones Gardai, informed them sheep were still there."*
3rd Sept. 1944	15.55hrs	*"Phoned Greystones Gardai ref. object washed ashore 1 mile south of post. Description 2 feet long, rounded at both ends, at one end an eye, the other a point. 16.02hrs, phoned Eastern Sector with above report. 18.46hrs, call from Greystones Gardai ref to object on beach was small mine. 21.00hrs, Capt. Murphy phoned Greystones Gardai re object on beach."*
4th Sept. 1944	08.30hrs	*"Rang Greystones Gardai re object on beach - found to be a container."*

LEFT: August 2010 photo of a train about to enter the mile long tunnel under Bray Head. In the top right corner, the gable ends of St. Crispin's Cell, believed to date from the 16th or early 17th century, are visible in the field adjacent to the houses in Redford Park. In the foreground is the cliff walk which now carries on in a straight line, bisecting the field, having previously veered to the left at the indentation in the cliffs known locally as Morris' Bank. The change in the route of the cliff walk at this point followed regular diversions inland from its original course along the edge of the marl cliffs on the North Beach, which were prone to constant erosion.

LEFT: 1980s photograph of the lime kiln that stood approximately 40 metres inland from the 2nd Gap Bridge, prior to its removal by Wicklow County Council. A larger lime kiln also existed 400 metres to the south of this, on whose site *Jubilee Castle / Rosetta Fort* was later built.

BELOW: Photo taken in 1945 looking towards an ivy clad St. Crispin's Cell, with only a single house and Coolagad visible in the background.

RIGHT: Photo taken in 2005 showing the ruins of Captain Charles Tarrant's house, adjacent to the level crossing at Ennis' Lane, with Bray Head in the background. In 1771, Captain Tarrant acquired 20 acres of land including the farmhouse. A significant figure in the history of Irish engineering and transportation, he was a surveyor, architect, painter and cartographer.

He served as surveyor on the Grand Canal project as well as taking a role as advisor to the Wide Streets Commission, which laid out the Georgian streets and squares of Dublin. For the latter he was engaged to oversee the construction of the buildings on the south side of Dame Street. In addition, he also played an important role in establishing the Barrow Navigation scheme. He died at Ashbury, Berkshire at the age of 89 on 18th March 1818. Close to St. Crispin's Cell once stood Rathdown Castle, whose "*ruinous masonry, now all grass grown*" was commented upon by G.N. Wright in *A Guide to the County of Wicklow* published in 1827. He further commented that "*the base of one large square tower may still be seen, the walls of which are four feet in thickness*".

RIGHT: Another previously unpublished photograph of the Flavelle family near the cliff walk at Morris' Bank. The family spent summer holidays in Greystones from 1899 and 1903, staying at *Magheralin*, the single storey house that stood until recently at the corner of Church Road and Rathdown Road. Book Nos. 3, 4 and 5 include several other photos from the Flavelle family album taken during their holidays in Greystones.

BELOW: Wicklow County Council sign confirming that the cliff walk was closed until further notice "*due to slippage*". The constant need to move the path several feet inland from the cliff edge due to regular erosion eventually led to its present diversion.

LEFT: Demolition of the 2nd Gap Bridge on 8th October 2008. The bridge was built as part of the 1888/1890 "Rathdown Deviation" which resulted in the railway line being moved inland from the 1st (Ennis') Gap Bridge, which carried the railway from its commencement in 1855. The 2nd Gap Bridge became redundant following the opening of the mile long tunnel which the Board of Trade sanctioned for passenger traffic in February 1918.

ABOVE: 1995 photo of the access road to the sewage works at the Gap Bridge being moved inland due to erosion. On the left is Darcy's field, which for a couple of years in the mid 1970s was a pitch and putt course, prior to being converted into sports pitches used by both Greystones Football Club and St. David's School, with shipping containers serving as changing rooms.

SOUTHERN SLOPES OF BRAY HEAD TO GREYSTONES

February 2018 marked the centenary of the opening of the mile long tunnel for passenger traffic. On 17th October 1917 the first train passed through on a trial basis and the last of its more than four million lining bricks was put in place on 20th November 1917. For many years the line had been affected by erosion from the sea and the run off of water from the slopes of Bray Head. Book No.7 includes a number of complaints from the travelling public to the railway company about the dangerous condition of the original railway line (often in very descriptive terms).

LEFT: Pre 1917 photograph showing the original railway line as it exited the Cable Rock tunnel and ran along Morris' Bank towards the Gap Bridge above the North Beach. Note the thatched railway storage building on the seaward side of the railway line and the ruined walls and gable ends of the old farm building on the crest of Bray Head above the Cable Rock tunnel. The Cable Rock, Bray Head's most easterly point, can be seen in the distance on the extreme right of the photo.

An edition of *Irish Society* dated 27th June 1891 featured the cliff walk, noting that the path at that time gave the walker "*the choice of proceeding along the railway bank or by the pebbly beach.*"

ABOVE RIGHT: Photograph taken in March 2017 showing the last remaining visible intact section of the series of sea walls which were built to protect the railway as it ran along the banks on its approach to Greystones after exiting the Cable Rock tunnel. This point lies at the extreme end of the North Beach, close to the area known as the Red Rocks.

ABOVE: A Dublin, Wicklow & Wexford Railway steam train heading along Morris' Bank in 1898 along the original track towards Greystones.

RIGHT: Fighting a losing battle, as a team of workmen carry out repairs to the wooden piling on the North Beach in this pre 1917 photograph. The series of wooden groynes driven into the beach to help prevent erosion can be seen as a steam train heads south towards Greystones.

ABOVE: This photograph uniquely shows all three approaches of the railway from Bray Head to Greystones. On the right, at the edge of the cliff, is the original Ennis' (Gap) Bridge, over which the railway ran from 1855 until 1890. This original bridge survived until the 1940s, when the army blew it up due to its dangerous condition. The arch of the second Ennis' (Gap) Bridge is visible to its left, in line with the roof of the railway cottage, adjacent to the present railway line. This bridge was built when the line was moved inland as part of the "Rathdown Deviation" and was completed between 1888 and 1890. It carried the railway until the present route through the mile long tunnel was opened in 1918 and was demolished in October 2008. Further inland, the lime kiln (demolished in the 1980s) on Ennis' Lane is visible, with vegetation protruding from its top. The linesman's cottage owned by the Dublin, Wicklow & Wexford Railway is visible on the seaward side of the present railway line.

ABOVE: Photograph taken in the 1890s showing the original Ennis' (Gap) Bridge just left of centre, with its protective sections of sea wall flanking both sides. When this photograph was taken, the railway line had been moved inland to pass over the 2nd Ennis' (Gap) Bridge. Telegraph poles running adjacent to the railway line are visible. Along the shoreline the sea wall and protective buttresses can be seen. Book No.7 includes information relating to this stretch of sea wall which was originally built to protect (unsuccessfully) the original railway line. A Dublin bound steam train can be seen travelling along Morris' Bank towards the Cable Rock tunnel.

RIGHT: The ruins of the linesman's cottage photographed in the early 1970s. It had a water tank adjacent to it, with a spout that could swivel out to provide water to the passing steam engines. A second linesman's cottage, originally known as *Jubilee Cottage*, which was on the opposite side of the railway line, slightly to the north and extended over time, now forms one of the houses on New Road (just visible in the top photograph on page 37).

LEFT: Photograph taken in 1939 of David and Lorna Fox sitting on the ruins of the 1st Gap Bridge on the North Beach, by then imperilled by erosion.

BELOW: June 2007 view from the 2nd Gap Bridge over which the railway passed until 1918. It then formed part of the cliff walk for more than 80 years prior to its diversion inland. A number of the outer granite coping stones had already succumbed to erosion when this photo was taken.

ABOVE: Photograph showing extensive sections of the sea wall at the base of the cliffs as a steam train heads south towards Greystones.

BELOW: View of the 2nd Gap Bridge photographed in May 2008, five months prior to its demolition.

ABOVE: 1890s photograph of the Jubilee Siding creosoting plant belonging to the Dublin Wicklow & Wexford Railway. It was located just to the north of *Jubilee Castle / Rosetta Fort,* whose turreted roof is visible beyond the shed on the right-hand side of the photo. The siding was used by the railway company to creosote the railway sleepers and telegraph posts that were used on the line. It also included a large dipping tank on site. Note the two masted coal schooner in the harbour in the distance.

ABOVE: Washing drying on a line on the North Beach beside the wooden huts adjacent to the stream that provided a supply of fresh water. The depression in the land just to the right of the roof of the last house in The Bawn is the sand pit which was located where New Road is now. In the distance, standing out from the trees, is *Belvedere Hall*.

ABOVE: A number of washerwomen, wearing hats and long dresses, some holding parasols, can be seen chatting in front of the wooden huts. During the summer months, many of the fishermen's wives from the cottages on the North Beach earned supplementary income for their families washing and drying clothes on the beach, both for residents and the annual influx of visitors who rented houses in Greystones for the summer months. A large cart can be seen on the roadway opposite the two storey house.

RIGHT: Photograph taken in the mid 1970s showing the gully where the stream ran its natural course out over the shingle.

RIGHT: Map drawn in 1876 as part of the "Book of Reference" which was presented to the House of Commons Select Committee in July 1877 for Parliament to approve the construction of the Greystones water supply. As can be seen, *Glencoe*, *Alberta* and *Yarra Yarra* had not yet been built. The only houses shown on the North Beach were eight of the cottages which were subsequently washed away. The ten cottages in The Bawn are also shown. The small coalyard to the rear of *Wavecrest* and the larger one to the rear of what is now The Beach House, owned by Arthur Evans, are also marked. The large lime kiln upon which *Jubilee Castle / Rosetta Fort* was subsequently built is marked on the extreme right of the map.

This lime kiln was one of at least five that are known to have existed along the coast near Greystones, all of which were in close proximity to streams. The one featured on page 26 was the most northerly of these. The lime kiln shown on the opposite page was the largest of the five. Though not appearing on the 1838 Ordnance Survey map, it is possible that this lime kiln was used when the original 1847 jetty was being built. A lime kiln was known to have existed at the end of Trafalgar Road on the site where Spendlove's coffee house is now located. The 1838 map shows another just south of The Breaches between Kilcoole and Newcastle, possibly removed when the railway to Wicklow was built in the 1850s. Nowadays, the only surviving lime kiln along the stretch of coast near Greystones is visible from the railway line. It is preserved as a feature on Charlesland Golf Course (the 2nd hole is named *Lime Kiln*), just south of where the Three Trouts Stream enters the sea at the northern end of the course.

Lime became an important product in the 18th and 19th centuries for its use in agriculture and construction. It was used as a component of mortar as well as a wash to protect the outside of buildings from the elements. Lime kilns, similar in design to those at Greystones, existed along the coast of Cardigan Bay in Wales. The absence of limestone in County Wicklow necessitated its import by coasting vessels. Skerries in north County Dublin was a major source of limestone, which abounded on the shoreline. It was quarried and brought to the Wicklow coast in coasting vessels. Here it was jettisoned close to the shoreline in front of the kilns and collected at low tide.

The May 1836 minutes of the House of Commons Committee on the proposal to build the Dublin to Drogheda railway line noted the following evidence provided by Mr O'Dwyer, Harbour Master at Skerries. "*All the limestone that is carried from Skerries is sent to Wicklow and they get it as fast as they can.*" When questioned further, he noted that it was carried there "*by the Wicklow boats*" who paid "*2 shillings a ton for it in Skerries.*" Three years earlier, on 26th February 1833, *The Southern Reporter & Cork Commercial Courier* reported on a storm which lashed the east coast of Ireland, mentioning that "*six boats, with limestone, from Skerries to Wicklow, were, for the most part, lost and damaged.*" Notwithstanding the opening of the railway line to Wicklow in October 1855, limestone continued to be shipped by sea from Skerries. *The Evening Freeman* dated 7th February 1861, in its notice of windbound ships, noted the *William & Betsey* sailing from Skerries to Wicklow with a cargo of limestone. The other material which lime kilns required for the production of lime was a type of anthracite coal dust (prevalent in South Wales) known as culm.

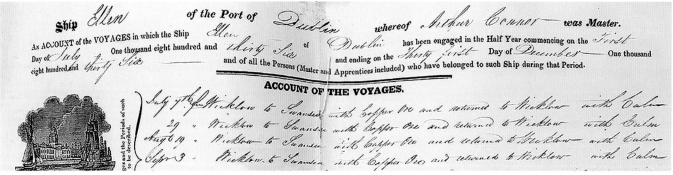

ABOVE: Log Book for the schooner, *Ellen* between 1st July 1836 and 31st December 1836 when she regularly sailed from Wicklow to Swansea. Exporting copper ore from the Avoca mines, she carried culm on the return voyage. It was likely that the culm was then disbursed into smaller boats to supply fuel to fire the lime kilns that were built along the coast near Greystones.

ABOVE: Charlesland Golf Course under construction in 1991 with the lime kiln preserved within the landscaping of the course.

RIGHT: In order to make lime, the limestone had to be heated to 800 to 900 degrees centigrade to remove the carbon dioxide to produce calcium oxide or quicklime. An arched opening at the base of the lime kiln enabled air to ventilate through a small aperture or draw hole, above which the fire was lit. The furnace which tapered to the draw hole was lined with fire bricks to prolong its life. Alternate layers of limestone and culm were then introduced through the opening at the top using a mixture of between three and five parts limestone to one part culm. The burning process generally lasted between three and five days. It is reported that they burned with a transparent blue flame, emitting a thick acrid yellow smoke. The resultant product, known as quicklime, was then left to cool for a further four to five days before being raked out of the kiln. Given its corrosive nature, it was then left in heaps to absorb rainwater in a process called slaking. Farmers then spread it on the land in a ratio of 4 tons of lime to 1 acre.

LEFT: Golfers heading towards the 3rd tee in April 2018.

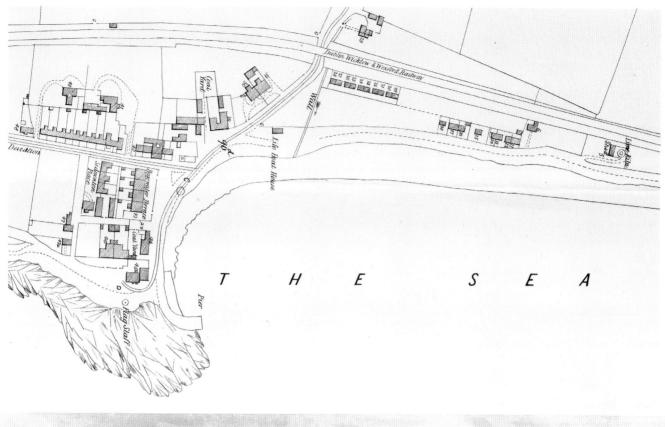

ABOVE & BELOW: Photograph taken from the flagstaff in the 1880s showing the first cottages on the North Beach. On the extreme right is the large lime kiln, with its arch shaped vent on its southern wall. Neither this lime kiln nor the smaller one further north were marked on the 1838 Ordnance Survey map. However the kiln shown above was marked on the 1876 map published as part of plans to construct the Greystones piped water supply from Temple Carrig. The two storey house to the right of the lifeboat house is *Alberta*, without the porch and balcony added later.

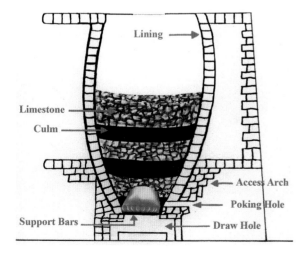

At night when in full operation with its blue flame, the lime kiln would have formed an impressive sight, casting a glow on the sea when viewed from the rocks at the flagstaff.

ABOVE: Foundations of the new houses being built on the former sites of Greystones Sailing Club and Greystones Ridge Angling Club in August 2016.

ABOVE: Photograph taken during the 1890s with the whitewashed three storey *Jubilee Castle / Rosetta Fort* standing out at the end of the road.

ABOVE: Close-up view of *Jubilee Castle / Rosetta Fort* with its balcony visible on the seaward side of the building.

ABOVE: Photograph taken in the 1890s showing a fine view of the cottages on the North Beach. Behind them, the line of telegraph poles can be seen along the original route of the railway, prior to its re-routing in 1917.

ABOVE: View in the 1880s with only *Alberta* on this part of the North Beach Road. A horse and cart can be seen passing under the railway arch.

ABOVE: The above photograph was taken around 1917. It shows the railway line running along the banks over the 2nd Gap Bridge and also the new embankment under construction, veering off to the left to link up with the mile long tunnel. The freshly whitewashed *Jubilee Castle / Rosetta Fort* again forms a striking image at the end of the road. The high section of wall on the beach in front of it was built to protect it from the ravages of a northeasterly (partial remains of the wall can be seen in the bottom photo on page 37). It remained a prominent feature on the beach until it too succumbed to the ravages of the sea in the 1980s. To the left of *Jubilee Castle*, two large vertical wooden poles can be seen, lashed together at the top. They were on the site of what was known as the Jubilee Siding, where the Dublin & South Eastern Railway had its creosoting plant. These poles were used to hoist telegraph poles and railway sleepers into a dipping tank containing creosote. A horse can be seen standing in the shade under a tree in the paddock field.

ABOVE: Photograph taken in the late 1890s again showing lines of washing hung out to dry on the beach next to the wooden huts. The newly built Grand Hotel with its flag flying from its top can be seen in the distance.

ABOVE: The view in 1970 following the completion of works organised by Greystones & District Civic Association, which saw the levelling of the ruins of the North Beach houses that were washed away, to create an unsurfaced car park.

ABOVE: Another view post 1917 showing the modern day railway approach south from the mile long tunnel. The linesman's cottage can be seen adjacent to the track beyond the bend in the line. Opposite with its white gable end, on the landward side of the railway line and some distance from the track, is the second linesman's cottage (now a house on New Road). Both cottages were built by The Dublin & South Eastern Railway.

ABOVE: View in the 1880s prior to the extension of the pier and before *Jubilee Castle / Rosetta Fort* was built. A coal schooner is alongside the 1847 jetty. The Grand Hotel had not yet been built and the building on the corner of Trafalgar Road and Victoria Road, where Spendlove's is now located, is single storey.

ABOVE: Another photo showing the levelling undertaken in 1970 to build the car park. In the photograph, the rough road seen veering to the left was the entrance to the former council dump and the ruins of the wall built to protect *Jubilee Castle / Rosetta Fort* are visible on the beach.

Between 1929 and 1931, storms washed away almost all of the houses along the road fronting onto the North Beach. Whilst the precise impact of the removal of thousands of tons of stones from the beach over preceding decades cannot be fully quantified, there is no doubt it was a contributory factor in their demise. Prior to the construction of the original jetty at Greystones harbour in 1847, the local fishermen were aware that the area around the rocks filled up with shingle during a northeasterly, only for it to return to the beach following a southeasterly. This formed part of the evidence gathered by the local Fisheries Inspector, John Madden, in his report dated January 1828, which was submitted to the Commissioners of Fisheries as part of a proposal to construct a pier at Greystones (as featured in Book No.7).

Following the construction of the original jetty and particularly after its extension between 1886 and 1888, the harbour was increasingly prone to becoming choked with sand and shingle following northeasterly gales. The schooners which regularly sailed to Greystones loaded gravel ballast from the North Beach prior to departing on their return voyages to ports such as Whitehaven, Troon and Garston. Aside from its stabilisation attributes, the gravel was of high quality, readily saleable and contributed towards the financial returns of the schooner owners if sold. Indeed it was felt that this practice was beneficial in helping to alleviate the silting of the harbour. The gravel was sold by the La Touche Estate to schooner owners including Arthur Evans, J.G. McEntagart and William H. Dann. In addition, gravel was sold to local builders who used it for driveways and paths, as well as to dress the tops of walls. Some of the latter still survive today around the harbour area at Bayswater Terrace and the lower part of Trafalgar Road.

ABOVE: Gravel ticket dated 24th May 1916 permitting William H. Dann to take 9 tons of gravel ballast from the North Beach for his coal schooner, *Joseph Fisher*.

ABOVE: Thomas Foley collecting a cartload of gravel from the North Beach. George Archer, on behalf of the landowner, the La Touche Estate, charged sixpence a load.

ABOVE: Removal of gravel from the North Beach in the early 1900s for use as ship's ballast or as construction materials. A horse and cart can is heading up the beach to add to several large piles of stones already outside the lifeboat house (refer also to page 102).

Over the years, gravel was also removed without permission. Book No.4 includes an account of a court case heard in July 1896, when a high court action was taken by the La Touche Estate against a number of local residents, who it alleged had removed gravel from the beach without permission. The court found in favour of the plaintiff, Francis La Touche, and an injunction was granted to restrain the defendants from digging or carrying away sand, shingle, gravel or stones.

By 1899 the steam ship, *SS Dunsyre,* was calling to Greystones, to take on board significant quantities of gravel which it brought to Dublin. In May 1902, Thomas Hewson, residing at *Jubilee Castle / Rosetta Fort* took a court case against his landlord, Peter La Touche, alleging that the property was being undermined by the removal of sand and gravel from the beach. *The Irish Times* reported that "*prior to 1900 Mr La Touche allowed a certain amount of gravel to be removed to build houses on the estate. In 1900 (counsel said) he began to sell sand, stones and gravel from the beach, which were taken away in carts, boats and steamers, to the amount of 18,000 loads, in consequence of which the sea now invaded the plaintiff's premises*".

The Wicklow Newsletter & County Advertiser dated 29th April 1916 reported that "*Mr E. Archer, Greystones, writing on behalf of 17 residents living on The Beach, Greystones, asked the Council to replace the drinking fountain protection wall, which the great storm of last November practically swept away. A few years ago, the Council originally constructed the wall, but so seriously did itself and the adjoining walls become damaged that the fountain was thrown down, pipes burst and even yet it was down in the gravel below the level of the ground rendering it difficult to access. He impressed on the Council the necessity for building the wall and putting a strong base under the fountain, or the next autumn storms would certainly demolish the roadway and fountain*".

This was a prelude to the catastrophic events that would unfold just over a decade later which resulted in a beach community having to abandon their homes due to the forces of nature.

Jubilee Castle / Rosetta Fort was built for Dublin barrister, Thomas Hewson, on the former site of the lime kiln in 1897, the year of Queen Victoria's diamond jubilee, from which it derived its name. In the May 1902 legal case mentioned on the previous page, Thomas Hewson was unsuccessful in seeking an injunction to restrain the La Touche Estate from removing stones from the beach. *The Irish Times* reported that "*owing to the taking away of sand from the beach, the sea broke up actually against the walls of the castle.*" Thomas Hewson subsequently moved to *Burlington House* on Victoria Road and the house was lived in by his brother, the Rev. Henry Hewson. According to *Thom's Directory* the change in name to *Rosetta Fort* occurred around 1913, but longtime Greystones residents still refer to it as *Jubilee Castle.*

BELOW: This advertisement was placed in *The Freeman's Journal* on Saturday 6th March 1920 in respect of the three storey *Rosetta Fort*. The five bedroom property was available on a lease of about 200 years. Just under ten years later, the building succumbed to the sea.

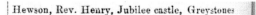
Hewson, Rev. Henry, Jubilee castle, Greystones

Young, Wm. John, Rosetta villa 15*l*.

Walker, A., Seafort Cottage £1 10s.
Wave cottage—Vacant £2 10s.
Young, Wm. John, Rosetta-fort £15

ABOVE: Extracts from *Thom's Directory* showing the change in the building's name over time. The 1912 extract listed Rev. Henry Hewson as living at *Jubilee Castle*. The 1914 extract shows it had changed ownership and name, with John William Young listed as living at *Rosetta Villa* (it retained this name until 1918 when it was renamed *Rosetta Fort*). The final extract is from 1929, the year before *Rosetta Fort* collapsed. It shows a neighbouring property, the appropriately named *Wave Cottage,* already vacant!

POSSESSION TO PURCHASER
ROSETTA FORT, HARBOUR ROAD GREYSTONES.

Nice comfortable residence, situated in one of the best parts of this favourite seaside resort. Contains—sittingroom, diningroom, 5 good bedrooms, kitchen. House stands on about half an acre. Head Rent. £5. Lease about 200 years. Vacant Possession will be handed to purchaser. Card to view premises from Auctioneers.
F. G. SHARPE, Esq., LL.D., Solicitor, 16 College Green.

RIGHT: A woman (possibly the owner, Mrs Young) standing beside the ruins of *Jubilee Castle / Rosetta Fort* in February 1930 with its distinctive turret topped roof.

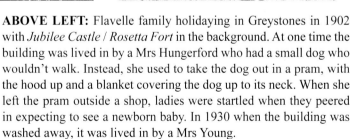

ABOVE LEFT: Flavelle family holidaying in Greystones in 1902 with *Jubilee Castle / Rosetta Fort* in the background. At one time the building was lived in by a Mrs Hungerford who had a small dog who wouldn't walk. Instead, she used to take the dog out in a pram, with the hood up and a blanket covering the dog up to its neck. When she left the pram outside a shop, ladies were startled when they peered in expecting to see a newborn baby. In 1930 when the building was washed away, it was lived in by a Mrs Young.

The Wicklow People dated 21st January 1977 reported "*heavy seas last week washed shingle away to reveal the old steps and boundary walls of Jubilee Castle.*"

ABOVE: In December 1989 a storm removed the bank of shingle on the North Beach to reveal the remains of the sea wall built in vain to protect the houses that were washed away between 1929 and 1931.

RIGHT: View from the DART in July 2017 looking towards the area where *Jubilee Castle / Rosetta Fort* once stood.

ABOVE: Photograph taken in June 2017 of the newly built row of houses to the right of *Yarra Yarra* (the blue house on the left).

ABOVE: View in the early 1930s of the ruins of the North Beach houses washed away between 1929 and 1931. *Yarra Yarra* is on the extreme left and to its right are the ruins of the houses including *Pierview*. The whole front section of the collapsed *Jubilee Castle / Rosetta Fort* lies on the beach, with the remainder of the structure standing precariously.

ABOVE: 1930 photo showing *Yarra Yarra* with its bay windows on the extreme left. Most of the houses that were standing in the photographs on the opposite page had now been washed away, with just ruins remaining. The photograph shows the ruins of the houses including *Pierview*, the home of Willie Archer. In conversation with Gary Paine in May 2017, Willie's nephew, Eric Archer, then aged 97, recalled being in *Pierview* as a ten year old boy with his father, Ted and his uncle, Willie. With a storm surge due at the next high tide, Eric watched his father and uncle move a piano from the lounge of *Pierview* into the safety of a neighbouring house in The Bawn where the Lawless family lived. The piano ultimately survived, *Pierview* didn't.

ABOVE & BELOW: Photographs taken in February 1930 showing the storm damage to the sea wall and road along the North Beach. In the top photograph, an exposed water pipe can be seen following the washing away of the road. Further along, the sea wall has been destroyed and a number of residents are surveying the damage. At this time, the houses and cottages were still intact. The lifeboat house is visible in the distance as well as the gable roof of *Glencoe* and the bay window of *Yarra Yarra*. In the photo below looking from the triangle, the destruction of the sea wall is visible to the onlookers who have driven down to observe the damage.

Strand-cottages.	
1 Lynch, P.	£1 15s.
2 Whiston, M.	£1 15s.
3 Daly, John	£1 15s.
4 Keddy, Michael	£1 15s.
5 Green, Michael	£1 15s.
6 Ryan, Joseph	£1 15s.
7 Byrne, P.	£1 15s.
8 Doyle, Mrs.	£1 15s.
9 Smith, Miss	£1 15s.
10 Doyle, Miss	£2 5s.
Spray Cottages.	
1 and 2—vacant	

Sea Beach-road. North.	
Archer, Wm., Pierview cottage	£3
Curling, A., Kiln cottage	£2 10s.
Evans, James, Yarra Yarra	£21
Evans, Samuel, Novara	£12
Hill, R. H., The Bungalow	£10
Hinds, Mrs. Christina, Le Cote	£12
Lawless, Hugh, Woodbine cott.	£10
Leggett, J., Seaforth	£5
Murphy, J., Somerton-cottage	£9
Spray cottage—vacant	£5 5s.
Thompson, Robert, Glencoe	£25
Tucker, H., jun., Alberta	£9 13s
Walker, A., Seafort Cottage	£1 10s.
Wave cottage—Vacant	£2 10s.
Young, Wm. John, Rosetta-fort	£15

LEFT: Extracts from the 1928 edition of *Thom's Directory* listing the names of residents of Strand Cottages (today known as The Bawn) and the 15 houses fronting onto the North Beach along what was known as Sea Beach Road North. The list of residents' names should not be viewed as definitive, as a number of other family names of residents whose houses were subsequently washed away are included in the various press reports that follow. These include families such as Kinsella, Darcy, Hennessy, Mahon, Crumpling, Hobson and McCullagh.

BELOW: The following press reports reveal the gradual destruction of the houses along Greystones North Beach between 1929 and 1931.

The Irish Independent - 26th December 1927.

Under the headline, "*Mountainous Seas Lash Coast*", the paper reported "*Heavy seas broke over the harbour at Greystones and the piers, which are already in a dilapidated condition were still further damaged. The residents of about 30 cottages spent a very anxious time and were in great danger of being flooded by the waves swept down upon the North Beach. As a precaution, they were obliged to barricade their doors to prevent the water entering their homes.*"

The Belfast Newsletter - 19th February 1929.

Under a story headed, "*Fury of the Waves, Sea Wall Washed Away at Greystones*", the paper reported "*Great waves pounded the coast of County Wicklow last night and swept away the protecting wall that was built along the North Beach Road, Greystones, at a cost of £3,000 some years ago. The roadway was undermined by the waves and at midnight only a narrow strip remained. The residents in the houses near the road, nearly all large detached or semi detached villas were greatly alarmed and some of them went to hotels for the night. It is believed that the foundations of the houses may be damaged unless some form of protection against the sea can be provided without delay.*"

ABOVE: The southern end of the seawall breached by the waves, with a large section of the road carried away by the waves. Residents can be seen carrying furniture from the houses in order to store it in a safer location.

The Belfast Newsletter - 21st February 1929.

Under the headline, "*Greystones Wall - Protection Collapses Under Tidal Pressure*", the paper reported "*further extensive damage was caused yesterday to the new protection wall along the North Beach, Greystones (Co. Wicklow), which began to collapse on Monday night. At about 3.20 yesterday morning at high tide, about 50 feet of the wall collapsed and undermined the roadway in front of the houses. A further portion is tilted over. The people living in the houses are in a very nervous state and afraid to sleep. One woman said that when the wall was falling she thought there was an earthquake. A number of silver coins - about a dozen - have been dug up on the beach in front of the collapsed wall - one four shilling piece was dated 1609.*"

Unidentified newspaper clipping - 25th February 1929.

Under the headline "*Terrific Tide brings new Menace to Greystones - Railway Line Only Way to Get to Houses - Removal of Furniture*", the paper reported "*a terrific tide and heavy sea visited Greystones at 12.30 this morning and covered the roadway in front of the cottages, which have been threatened during the past few days. The people living on the North Beach have now no pathway left. The sea is 12 feet only from two of the houses. The people have no means of getting to their houses except by the railway line. Over 150 feet of the water main which ran along the roadway has been carried away, leaving the people with no water supply. The electric light coils are now only a few feet from the sea. The four feet wall in front of one of the houses was carried away before my eyes. The people have removed their furniture to back houses. They show great reluctance to leave their homes, which in most cases were built by the occupants themselves. There has been no storm, but a heavy ground swell was this morning washing 30 feet high over the remaining portion of the wall, which is now about totally demolished.*"

Unidentified newspaper clipping - 26th February 1929.

Under a story headed "*Families in Flight from Menace of the Sea - The Greystones Peril Continues - Raging Tide Today*", the paper reported "*the heavy sea raging along the eastern coast continues to play havoc with the roadway on the North Beach at Greystones. The scene this morning was one of great destruction on the North Beach. One would think there had been an earthquake in the vicinity this morning and to add to the discomfort of the residents of the locality, there was a heavy fall of snow during the morning and men of the working class, living in this area, were obliged to climb over several walls in order to get to their work. At one o'clock today, there was a tremendous high tide, with the result that a raging sea lashed over the crippled wall, mountains high. A large number of workmen were engaged during the day dismantling four cottages which are threatened with destruction. Seven families have now left their homes in the flooded area.*"

The Irish Examiner - 28th February 1929.

Under the headline "*Sea Wall Disappearing - Further Encroachments at Greystones*", the paper reported "*Further encroachment of the sea at the north shore in the vicinity of the breach in the sea wall resulted from yesterday evening's tide, which swept through the southern opening and tore away some fifty feet of the shingle backing from the wall. The breach in the wall is being enlarged and a further section of the wall is in danger and five additional houses may soon be exposed to the mercy of the sea .*

The boundary walls and gateways of four houses collapsed yesterday evening and it is feared that the morning tide will undermine the houses themselves. The owners of the cottages are endeavouring to save as much of the materials as can be carried away before the houses fall into the sea.

On each side of the 100 feet gap, there is a slight banking of the shingle at the front of the wall, which it is hoped will resist the draw of the receding waves and hold out sufficiently long to enable the raising of a new rampart behind the doomed cottages, with side-long reaches to the still standing portions of the wall north and south of the gap.

All day long yesterday, curious spectators came down to the North Beach and stood by the hour watching the waves roaring through the gap in the wall. The occupiers of the threatened cottages stood with gloomy faces watching the waves pounding the unprotected earth bank, carrying away the ground below.

If the sea continues its inroad until the higher ground on which the cottages stand is washed away, the low land behind will be flooded and the railway line beyond will eventually be involved. Happily, this contingency is at present remote. Fortunately, the northern end of the defence wall remains intact and there are no signs of any damage up to the present, although it experienced a very severe buffeting yesterday.

The committee of St. Kilian's Hall has kindly arranged for some of the inhabitants to take temporary shelter there, whilst others are moving their belongings to other quarters. The dismantling of the houses continued and they now present a forlorn spectacle.

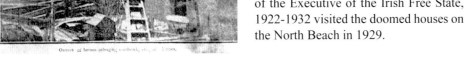

Owners of houses salvaging woodwork, etc., at Homes.

ABOVE: Owners of houses on the North Beach salvaging timber and other fittings.

RIGHT: William T. Cosgrave, President of the Executive of the Irish Free State, 1922-1932 visited the doomed houses on the North Beach in 1929.

Yesterday, the Board of Health Architect (Mr R.M. Butler), again visited the place for the purpose of submitting a report.

A Press Association message says:- Last night, a heavy sea beating along the coast wrought further havoc, with the roadway by the beach, where a scene of great destruction was revealed this morning. An exceptionally high tide flowed with great force, washing to a great height over the tottering walls.

Workmen were today occupied dismantling the threatened cottages and already seven families have abandoned their homes. Doubtless all the houses on the front are doomed to destruction. Doors were wrenched from their hinges by the male members of the disturbed families, who also removed window frames and other fixtures that may be of other use elsewhere. The railway line too is in danger, as it will be at the mercy of the sea when the barrier of the houses is removed. President Cosgrave, accompanied by another Minister, visited the scene at Greystones today and saw for himself the damage that was caused by the sea."

Unidentified newspaper clipping - 16th November 1929.

Newspaper reported that "*A heavy southeast wind and high tide swept over Greystones last night. Beginning at about 10.30, it lasted until after midnight. Residents in the vicinity of the North Beach, where the storm of February last wrought so much havoc were petrified and in a pitiable state. Several families had to leave their homes. The boundary wall for about 20 yards and gate in front of the cottages were washed away and the sea dashed through the front doors. Some damage was done also to the water main and the electric light system in the area. A high tide raged this morning at 10.30, but it died down quickly and the wind changed to the northeast".*

The Irish Independent - 19th November 1929.

Under the headline *"Coast Erosion in Storm"*, the newspaper reported that *"further gaps have appeared in the sea wall at Greystones following Saturday's storm and there is now a breach of about 150 yards. The front walls of six houses were entirely washed away. Several electric light standards were undermined and fell, causing the current to be cut off, while the water main was also injured and the supply fountain endangered".*

Unidentified newspaper clipping - 5th December 1929.

Under a story headed *"Houses Swamped By Sea - Storm Causes Considerable Damage at Greystones"*, the newspaper reported that *"Greystones was swept by a storm of unusual violence last night. Waves from the sea washed against the houses at the North Beach and the inhabitants were terror stricken. At about 11 o'clock the sea washed through the houses and into the backyards and considerable damage was caused. The children, who were unable to go to sleep last night presented a pitiful sight this morning. The houses were again flooded by the tide this afternoon. Waves 50 feet high were washing over the houses".*

The Irish Independent - 13th December 1929.

Under the headline *"Coast Erosion, Menace to Greystones"*, the paper reported that *"the erosion of the coast at the North Beach, Greystones, still continues and the sea is slowly but relentlessly eating away the land upon which fourteen cottages stand. When The Irish Independent representative visited the scene it was quite apparent that the fate of these dwellings is sealed and that it is merely a matter of time and weather until they are completely destroyed by the waves.*

The breach which was made last February in the newly constructed protection wall has been widened to the extent of about 100 yards by the gales of the last few weeks. It was extremely fortunate for the residents, the representative of The Irish Independent was informed, that the storms blew from the west. Had the wind swept up from the southeast with the same force, it would have been impossible to estimate the damage, but certainly many more of the cottages would have been wiped out.

As it is, the beach road leading to the houses has disappeared and the yawning chasm of about 200 yards is partly filled with shingle. In the opinion of those familiar with the scene, further protection works would not be of the slightest avail. The little front gardens of several of the dwellings have, with their walls, been swallowed up by the sea and the occupants must now exercise great care in gaining an entrance to their homes. The debris thrown up by the recent storms, even though the wind was not bearing directly upon the place, has been deposited further landwards, beyond the fronts of several of the houses, a sinister indication of the unrelaxing advance of the sea upon this portion of the coast.

The fronts of four cottages have been protected by wood and the occupants have taken up residence in small habitations at the back. This has been done as a precaution against the front of the dwellings collapsing into the sea. Amongst those whose houses are now threatened are: Mr M. Whiston, Mrs Byrne, Mr W. Kinsella, Mr J. Leggett, Mr J. Whiston, Mr J. Walker, Mrs Hennessy, Ms A. Darcy, Mr B. Mahon, Mrs McCullagh, Mr Hobson, Mrs Crumpling, Mrs Curling, Mr John F. Evans and Mrs Young".

Unidentified newspaper clipping - 17th January 1930.

Under the story *"Families Flee from Ruined Homes - Cottagers' Plight in Greystones - Ravages of the Sea"*, the paper reported *"Greystones was again visited by terrific seas and a spring tide last night when great damage was done along the North Beach. Practically the entire row of cottages along the shore have been literally wiped out and the beach is strewn with the wreckage of these buildings.*

ABOVE: Residents of the North Beach houses standing amid the scene of utter desolation, with the sea wall thrown down by the waves and the roadway and front gardens of the houses washed away.

Six or eight families have fled from their ruined homes and at present only four houses remain intact towards the Greystones end of the beach and these are in imminent danger. One of the water mains has been carried away by the storm and some 60 yards of the remaining portion of the sea wall have disappeared."

<u>*The Irish Examiner - 18th January 1930.*</u>

Under the headline "*Families Homeless*" the paper reported "*Seven dwelling houses on the North Beach, Greystones, Co. Wicklow, were engulfed by a heavy sea in the early hours of this morning and collapsed. The occupants, realising the danger which was yesterday, had left the houses. Over twenty people have been affected. The houses which collapsed this morning included the four which were affected by the storms last year and had been abandoned by their owners. The three others destroyed were occupied by Mrs Kinsella and family, James Legett and family, Wm. Whiston and family and the Misses Darcy. Two other houses are now in imminent danger and workmen are at present engaged in salvaging the doors, windows and other equipment. The sea wall which had been specially constructed to protect these houses, was also damaged by the sea today and has now practically disappeared. Yesterday, there was a heavy sea rolling in from the southeast and the waves began to pound at the bank in front of the houses. Knowing that there was an exceptionally high tide at one o'clock this morning, the residents began to move their furniture and household utensils to their neighbours' houses. This morning waves 40 feet high thundered against the front walls of the houses. At least three families are rendered homeless and dependent upon the charity of their friends for shelter.*"

<u>**Unidentified newspaper clipping - 31st January 1930.**</u>

Under a story headed "*Heavy Seas Again Wash Greystones - Damaged Houses Swept into the Water*", the paper reported "*Greystones was again visited by a terrific tide and raging sea, accompanied by heavy rain and a gale from the southeast at 12 noon today. Six or seven houses already dismantled by previous storms have been washed into the sea. The sea wall in front of Mrs Young's house, Rosetta, locally known as Jubilee Castle has been demolished by the waves. The building is in danger of being undermined and will hardly stand against tonight's tide. Mrs Young has removed part of her furniture, but fears the loss of the remainder. Mr James Evans of Yarra Yarra has also cleared out some of his furniture. Up to late afternoon, the gale was still raging & a heavy tide is expected tonight.*"

<u>*The Irish Independent - 1st February 1930.*</u>

Under the headline "*Waves Wash Away Houses at Greystones*", the paper reported "*The sea lashed into a rage and waves broke with fury along the seashore from Greystones to Blackrock, playing havoc with the remnants of the houses on the North Beach, Greystones and those which had been abandoned. Six of the remaining houses on the North Beach were swept away by a tremendous sea this morning. One after another they collapsed and fell into the surf, the broken walls being taken up and thrown back again. The remaining portion of the sea wall at the north end was smashed and torn away and further breaches were made in the shore.*

As a result, Rosetta Fort, formerly known as Jubilee Castle, is now endangered and to obviate any danger, the residents commenced the removal of their furniture from it today. Several motorists travelled down to Greystones to watch the ravages of the storm. One gentleman had an exciting experience when a big wave broke over his saloon car, smashing the windscreen and he was obliged to drive it to a place of greater safety."

============= **The Aftermath** =============

In 1929, the Greystones Utility Society was established to assist and look after householders on the North Beach who had or were likely to lose their houses due to the inroads of the sea. The Society comprised the householders who met to discuss where and

how they could build a new home. The minute book for the Society notes that several potential sites were identified and eventually fields owned by Mr Maguire at the railway arch and Mr Carr at Blacklion and Jink's Hill were selected. Another site at Church Avenue, owned by D. Evans was not pursued as he did not wish to sell. The sites were purchased with the aid of government grants. It would appear that the grants were awarded on a sliding scale and possibly linked to the value of the original house on the North Beach in addition to how dangerous its position was.

The following people received sites or plots of land at Blacklion on the east side of the road from approximately opposite St. Bridget's Park to near Church Lane:- Mr Hobson, Mr Lawless, Mr Johnston, Mrs Young, Mr Keddy, Mr Curling, Mr John Evans, Mr Sam Evans, Mr James Evans and Mrs McCullagh. The Great Southern Railway Company had an option on a plot of land at Jink's Hill on Rathdown Road, to be used in the event that it became necessary to move the railway line further inland. Owned by Mr Carr and known locally as the "Railway Plot", the company agreed to release this site and plots were given to the following:- W. Archer. E. Archer, W. Spurling and R. Thompson.

A third field, owned by Mr Maguire, was obtained by the Council. This field was near the railway arch and dwellings were built for other residents from the North Beach. Grants awarded to the owners of the North Beach houses ranged from £60 to R. Thompson to £90 for Mrs Grace Young, with £75 to W. Spurling, £75 to James Evans, £85 to Sam Evans, £82 to H. Lawless, £82 to W. Archer, £80 to Mrs McCullagh, £82 to J. Hobson, £82 to A. Curling and £82 to John Evans.

The cost of the average dwellings, all of which were bungalows, was £520 without the provision of hot water. With the goals of the Greystones Utility Society having been duly met, it was wound up by its secretary, Edward Archer on 11th November 1933.

RIGHT: Some of the North Beach residents who lost their homes. Included are Winnie Kinsella, James Whiston, Lena Salmon, Mrs Peter Byrne and Bert Curling.

ABOVE: View from the flagstaff in August 2007, with the dock almost completely silted up. Only five of the concrete steps leading from it onto the pier are exposed.

ABOVE: View from the flagstaff in August 2017.

ABOVE: June 2007 view of the storm wall at the back of the old pier. At the time of the pier extension in 1887 and 1888, the original storm wall of the 1847 jetty was removed and replaced by the storm wall shown above. In addition to the pier being lengthened, the dock was blasted out and the boat slip and north wall were also constructed. The storm wall was popular with both anglers and the more daring swimmers, who used to dive from its lofty height.

ABOVE: Punching through the 1888 storm wall in May 2008 to create an access platform to enable lifting cranes to position the concrete blocks of the new pier in place.

ABOVE: A second access gap is punched through the storm wall in June 2008. The dock, having been dredged of sand, disappears under tons of soil as a roller compacts the top layer of stones.

ABOVE: A diver descending a ladder at the back of the old pier in July 2008 in order to check the correct alignment of the initial concrete blocks laid for the new pier on the sea bed.

ABOVE: Photograph taken in July 2008 with only the end section of the 1888 storm wall remaining intact. The surface of the old pier was used as a platform for the crane to lift the large pre-cast concrete blocks into place to form the new pier.

ABOVE: A crane lifts one of the initial pre-cast concrete blocks into place to form the new pier in July 2008.

ABOVE: The new storm wall taking shape in April 2010.

ABOVE: Construction of the inner pier at the marina entrance in December 2009.

ABOVE: View in August 2009 showing the work in progress of the new piers, with a large pile of boulders awaiting transfer. The erosion of the old cliff walk running along the top of the cliffs adjacent to the field is evident.

ABOVE: A crane lifting one of the steel piling sections into place as work progresses on the northern pier in April 2009.

ABOVE: View from Windgates in December 2009, with five large crawler cranes engaged in the construction of the project. A substantial number of the large pre-cast concrete blocks, produced by the temporary cement batching plant, can be seen in the foreground, with an equal amount stacked in front of *Rockport* (pale blue house) and *Wavecrest* (yellow house).

ABOVE: Pumping cement into the end of the southern pier in December 2009.

ABOVE: Showing the changing coastline in August 2010.

RIGHT: February 2011 aerial photograph showing the infilling of top soil and the extent of land reclamation as the marina development takes shape.

ABOVE: View in April 2009 with the temporary causeway built on top of the old north wall towards the right of the photo.

ABOVE: Northern and southern piers nearing completion in August 2009.

ABOVE: Entrance to the marina section taking shape in April 2010.

ABOVE: View of the marina basin now enclosed and steel piling in place in May 2010.

ABOVE: The old and the new, with the upper bay window of *Yarra Yarra*, which survived the storms of 1929-1931 and the first of the new houses of the marina development under construction in February 2016.

ABOVE: View of the first of the new houses being built in February 2016 with Coolagad and the two Sugarloaf mountains.

ABOVE: The line of new houses progressing in March 2016.

ABOVE: The boardwalk under construction in September 2018.

ABOVE: Photograph taken in the 1880s prior to the construction of the boat slip (1888). The entrance arch to the coalyard owned by John Doyle (1793-1855) and later by his son, John Doyle II (1836-1883) can be seen. The arch had been removed by the time that the photograph at the bottom of the page was taken several decades later. A man can be seen in a white shirt standing with his back against the crab wall. The wall derived its name from the time when the sea reached the rocks around its base at high tide and crabs would hide in the holes and crevices. Prior to the extension of the pier in the 1880s, the southeasterly gales would scoop up the shingle from this area and deposit it on the North Beach, only for the next northeasterly gale to return the shingle to the harbour.

Greystones.   Co. Wicklow.

maternal grandfather, Robert Watson was born Enright Doyle's & reared in greystones. He recalled, as a boy, in 1860s being able to fish from "the Crab wall"

ABOVE: Extract from a letter written in May 1981 by Dr. Leslie Doyle recalling a time during the 1860s when it was possible to fish from the crab wall.

LEFT: Postcard sent in 1904 showing the top of the crab wall at a time when there was a wide expanse of shingle on the beach.

ABOVE: Summer day at the bottom of the boat slip with several people swimming off the Cúl of the Rock adjacent to it.

ABOVE: Floodlit view of the old boat slip, with *Rockport, Wavecrest,* Bayswater Terrace and Bethel Terrace.

ABOVE: Room with a view. A lady gazes out from the upstairs of Bayswater Terrace on a still day in 1959, the year the fishermen's huts and viewing area on their roof was constructed. A truck with Evans Motors livery on its side can be seen beside a VW camper van. Three people are in conversation at the crab wall, whilst two others are about to dive in off the north wall.

ABOVE: 1880s photograph of the first post office and savings bank in Greystones located in *Rockport*. This was run by George Watson who lived with his family above the grocery shop next door. On the 1901 census, George Watson was listed as a grocer. By 1906 the shop was a pharmacy, run by James R. Guest and his wife, Johanna, who also rented out rooms in *Rockport* to visitors. These regularly included Bill and May Beckett (parents of playwright, Samuel Beckett) who always timed their visits to coincide with the annual swimming gala. Note the sign above the window "*Money Order Office / Post Office / Savings Bank*" and the two letter posting slits in the wall below the window sill. To the right of the "*Post Office / Postal Telegraph Office*" sign above the door is ducting, encasing the telegraph wire that connected to telegraph wires which ran along the railway line. At this time, this was main means of communication between Greystones and the outside world. Book No.7 includes information about the laying of the underwater telegraph cable in 1886 from Nevin in North Wales that came ashore at the Winding House, 200 metres south of Newcastle station. It was the method by which the Greystones Lifeboat was alerted when it was called out on its launches. The grocery shop is well stocked, with signs in the window advertising Irish butter and bacon. When the above photograph was taken, neither the boat slip nor inner dock had been constructed, in contrast with the photograph below.

ABOVE: Late 1890s photograph with the flag flying above the Grand Hotel, which opened in 1894. Note that the door to the former Post Office in *Rockport* has been bricked up, with a window in its place. Watson's shop next door, with a horse and cart outside and Arthur Evans, Coal Merchant, to the right of it at *Wavecrest,* are bathed in the late afternoon sun.

ABOVE: 1969 view from the top of the boat slip looking towards Great and Little Sugarloaf. A number of barrel shaped lobster pots with their orange nylon mesh can be seen in the foreground. There are more than 30 clinker built fishing boats pulled up above the high water mark and onto the grassy area. The large orange fishing boat pulled up in front of the car belonged to the Dublin City Sea Angling Club. Throughout the 1960s and into the 1970s, the club kept four or five of these boats at Greystones, similarly painted. Two of them, painted pale blue on the inside and orange on the outside, can be seen in the photograph on the top of the opposite page. Three rows of neatly laid out fishing nets lie drying in the sun on the concrete hard standing in front of the fishermen's huts. The bus shelter (removed in 1997) can be seen directly opposite The Beach House. Also visible is the original railway arch built in 1855 and replaced in 1971 by the current bridge, following the introduction of double-decker buses.

The 1871 built lifeboat house was still its original size and missing its round granite finial on the southern end of its roof. At this time, it was known as the Anchor Cafe, with candy floss a speciality. The stream that today enters the harbour through a culvert, ran open between *Glencoe* and the wall of the paddock field where pony rides were offered in the summer. It ran out onto the beach, forming a depression in the shingle before entering the sea on the Bray side of the north wall. *Alberta* and *Yarra Yarra* to the right of *Glencoe* are two more survivors of the 1929-1931 storms, the latter only just. The overgrown ruins of the houses washed away can be seen further up the beach.

In 1970, Greystones & District Civic Association acquired the area encompassing the ruins and levelled it to create an unpaved car park. A line of large boulders was put in place to protect the access road and car park from any encroachment by the sea during storms. Agreement had been made between the Civic Association and the newly formed Greystones Sailing Club for the latter to be provided with a leasehold site upon which to build a clubhouse and pen and these were constructed in 1971. In 1977, Greystones Ridge Angling Club followed suit and built its club premises further up the roadway. In the distance, the red roofed, double gable front of the house, originally named *Barbaville,* can be seen (refer also to photo on page 293).

BOTTOM RIGHT: Summer scene in the mid 1950s, with prams left at the edge of the sand and families enjoying a flat calm day at the edge of the water. The photograph shows clearly the collapsed end of the pier, which suffered significant damage during a storm in February 1912, when a section fell into the sea creating a gap in the storm wall. Swimmers can be seen perched where the dislodged granite blocks at the end of the 1847 jetty once were. These had been dislodged by the bowsprit of one of the coal schooners during a storm in October 1910. This damage had remained unrepaired since that time and the blocks were eventually reset when major repairs were made to the surface of the pier during the summer of 1958.

ABOVE: Photograph taken from the roof of the old bus shelter at low tide in the early 1960s. Around half a dozen fishing boats are moored close to the pier, with a clinker built *Mermaid* sailing boat moored on the extreme left. The collapsed end section of the pier is visible in the sea and the protective steel railing at the end of the pier is just visible. An expanse of rock extends up the beach. In March 1974, additional top soil was spread over the rocks between the fishermen's huts and the top of the boat slip to create a more extensive grass slope. No mast is visible at the flagstaff beyond *Rockport House*. Its reintroduction by the Civic Association did not happen until 1971. A couple of people are leaning against the yellow railings on the roof of the fishermen's huts built in 1959, where coin operated binoculars enabled the public to look out to sea or swivel around to view the mountains.

OLD TIMES AT THE HARBOUR

In the early 1960s, a marine engineer advised that the badly broken end section of Greystones pier was in need of protection. In 1963, a newly constructed base for the Kish Lighthouse in Dublin Bay had been damaged by a storm. A new base was subsequently built for the lighthouse and the damaged one was stored in Dún Laoghaire. Greystones & District Civic Association arranged for this base to be towed to the harbour.

ABOVE: Photo taken from the flagstaff at 6pm on Thursday 4th August 1966 as a crowd of people gathered on the pier to await the arrival of Kish base, which can be seen being towed towards Greystones in the distance. It took two tugs a total of seven hours to complete the task. While the Kish base made the harbour more prone to silting up, which necessitated periodic dredging, within the stringent financial constraints of the time, it nevertheless helped prolong the life of the original harbour over the following decades.

ABOVE & BELOW: Series of photographs taken of the Kish base arriving on 4th August 1966. At that time, there was still a grass slope down onto the beach on the seaward side of the 2nd Gap Bridge. The remains of the protective wall of *Jubilee Castle / Rosetta Fort* can be seen just to the left of the tug's mast.

OLD TIMES AT THE HARBOUR

RIGHT: The 102 foot diameter structure weighing 3,500 tons being held in position. Standing on the Kish base are Ken Williams (diver), Ned Sparks (contract manager), Geoff Jackson (engineer) and Derek Paine (Greystones & District Civic Association).

BELOW & BELOW RIGHT: Photographs taken in October 1967 showing storm damage to the Kish base, with its deck collapsed. As a result of this, it underwent substantial armouring with large boulders and cement.

BELOW & RIGHT: Construction of the causeway at the end of the pier.

ABOVE: Early 1970s view showing the Kish base protected by large boulders. The large white boat with the mahogany upper deck belonged to Jimmy Kearon. The *Mermaid* with the white canvas tarpaulin moored near the Kish belonged to Derek Paine.

ABOVE & BELOW: Rough sea with waves breaking over the storm wall onto Greystones pier in November 1962. The specification of the building works for Greystones pier dated 25th August 1886 stipulated that there were to be six granite mooring posts, including the two existing ones from the 1847 jetty. They were required to measure 22 inches in diameter at the top, tapering to 20 inches in diameter at their base. They were set in 24 inch square blocks, embedded 3 and half feet down below the surface of the pier, in a concrete mass 6 feet square.

ABOVE: Wave breaking over the pier in November 1962.

ABOVE: Wave crashing over the back of the pier in the early 1960s prior to the arrival of the Kish base.

ABOVE: Storm at Greystones harbour on 25th April 1981. The "blow hole" on the pier, through which the braver kids of the time used to achieve "lift off" by standing on a piece of plywood, can be seen in full swing on the extreme right, spouting water. Following a storm in February 1979, a large hole appeared in the back of the pier and a pipe was inserted, running through to the harbour side with an air vent to relieve pressure on the pier's surface.

ABOVE & BELOW: Photographs taken on 26th August 1986 showing the aftermath of Hurricane Charley which battered the Irish coast. The hurricane, which originated in the Gulf of Mexico a fortnight before, was tracked as it crossed the Atlantic, passing just south of Ireland on 25th August. Winds of 65mph (105km/h) were recorded and several 24 hour rainfall records were set during the storm. The River Dargle in Bray burst its banks, flooding some areas to a depth of 5 feet (1.5 metres), forcing around 1,000 residents to evacuate their homes. Greystones harbour was strewn with flotsam and jetsam, the roots of a tree can be seen washed up just to the right of the mast of the *Mermaid,* which had been pulled up to the relative safety of the top of the boat slip.

ABOVE: Tree trunks line the shore of the harbour at low tide following the aftermath of Hurricane Charley. Yachts in the harbour including a *Westerly 22*, *Matilda* and a *Stardrift 28*, can be seen swinging from their moorings and a fishing trawler is pointing towards the pier.

BELOW: Wreckage from boats smashed to pieces piled up against the wall of the dock.

ABOVE & BELOW: A large crowd on Greystones pier in the early 1900s watching two men duelling in a pole fight. In the lower photo, an even larger crowd watch a swimming gala. Note the end of the pier was still intact.

ABOVE: Hats galore as spectators watch a diver competing in the diving competition in 1910. A tent erected near the storm wall in the background served as a temporary changing area.

BELOW: Spectators gathered opposite *Rockport* and *Wavecrest* in 1910 to observe the aquatic competitions, as children in the boat in the foreground get a close-up view of the action.

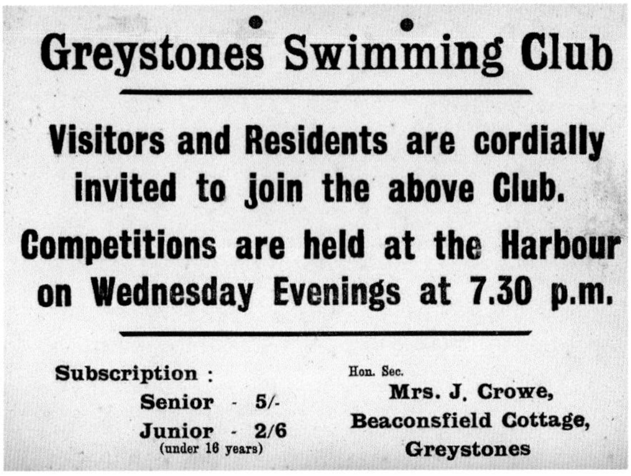

Greystones Swimming Club

Visitors and Residents are cordially invited to join the above Club.

Competitions are held at the Harbour on Wednesday Evenings at 7.30 p.m.

Subscription :
Senior - 5/-
Junior - 2/6
(under 18 years)

Hon. Sec.
Mrs. J. Crowe,
Beaconsfield Cottage,
Greystones

ABOVE: A pre 1954 advertisement for Greystones Swimming Club.

ABOVE: Greystones Swimming Club embroidered badge from the mid 1950s. Costing 1s & 6d, club members were required to have these sewn onto their togs when competing at swimming galas.

ABOVE: A swimming gala in the 1930s.

BELOW: A large crowd watching a water polo match in the harbour. These were regularly held as part of the annual swimming gala.

ABOVE RIGHT: Ticket for the Grand Aquatic Gala held at Greystones harbour in August 1917. The events included the Graceful Diving Championship of Leinster and a water polo match, Greystones versus County Dublin.

LEFT: Swimming gala at the harbour in the 1920s. Note the army band with their white music sheets on the pier beside the storm wall. Some of the braver spectators have climbed on top of the exposed end of the pier. The close-up photograph shows the timber diving board erected at the end of the 1847 jetty. It also shows an excellent view of the double steps at the end of the pier, with the upper ones leading nowhere following the storm in February 1912 which knocked a gaping hole in the storm wall.

Like rowing and sailing, swimming has a long established tradition in Greystones. While the early regattas comprised rowing and sailing races only, the 1884 Greystones Regatta programme of events included a swimming race. *The Freeman's Journal* dated 30th August 1884 reported that the 250 yard swimming race was won by F. McPhail. The following year's regatta featured the "*Greystones Residents' Swimming Race*" over a distance of 200 yards. The result was: 1st place, Allan Price, prize £1, 2nd place, J.D. Wynne, prize 10 shillings and 3rd place, Arthur Price. Dublin Swimming Club was established in 1881 and by 1885 it was organising its own swimming race for club members at Greystones harbour as part of the Greystones Regatta. In the late 1800s, Greystones Swimming Club was established. It was run for many years by local residents, with Louis Meldon, Arthur Hughes and Thomas Hewson (who built *Jubilee Castle*) among its stalwarts. All three were also active members of the management committee for the Gentlemen's Bathing Place on Marine Road. The programme for the Greystones Regatta held on 10th August 1891 included, as event No.16, starting at 5pm, an 8-a-side water polo match lasting 20 minutes. This was played between members of Blackrock Aquatic Polo Club, Dublin Bay Swimming Club and Sandycove Swimming Club. By the late 1890s, at the Bray end of Bray Head, Bart Naylor, a Bray fisherman and boatbuilder took a lease on what is now called Naylor's Cove. He erected bathing boxes and a small pier at the Cove to encourage swimming and diving there.

With the increasing popularity of Greystones as a summer resort in the early 1900s, the Greystones Life Saving Society was formed. As well as promoting swimming, the society also fulfilled an important role in ensuring water safety for the town's residents and summer visitors. Along with Greystones Swimming Club it was active in the organisation of the aquatic galas held at Greystones harbour from the early 1900s onwards. At the 1906 gala, the graceful diving competition was won by G. Meldon, whilst a water polo match saw J. Beckett's VII defeat J.C. Meldon's VII by 2 goals to 1. Pembroke Swimming Club's Jim Beckett, uncle of Nobel Laureate Samuel Beckett, was one of the leading Irish swimmers of his generation. Of the 80 Irish Championships swum between 1893 and 1914, only the prolific George Dockrell with 20 Championship wins eclipsed Beckett's 9 Championships. The Becketts were a keen swimming family. Bill Beckett, father of Samuel, served as Hon. Treasurer of Dublin Swimming Club in 1894 and 1895 and as Captain in 1896. He was a regular visitor to Greystones, staying with his young family at *Rockport,* run as a boarding house by J. Guest overlooking the harbour. With the dock offering a sheltered spot to learn to swim and Arthur Evans' schooner, *Velinheli,* regularly unloading coal on the pier, there was plenty to occupy the young Samuel Beckett.

In 1913 Greystones hosted the 220 yards Championship of Ireland, which was won by J.S. Brady of Clontarf. In the 1920s swimming galas were held annually at the harbour and in 1926 the Irish Amateur Swimming Association selected Greystones as the venue to host the All-Ireland Swimming Championships. On 14th August a huge number of spectators thronged the pier and every vantage point from the flagstaff to the top of the boat slip and across to Bayswater Terrace. It proved highly successful for competitors from the north of Ireland, with Miss Absolom of Bangor retaining her title as Irish ladies' diving champion. In the men's 220 yards swimming championship J. Jenkins of the Clonard Swimming Club in Belfast became Irish champion in a time of 2 minutes 53.5 seconds. The galas continued throughout the 1930s and by the middle of that decade the facilities (now sadly dilapidated) at Naylor's Cove on Bray Head were also significantly enhanced through the construction of the tidal swimming pools and concrete changing facilities. Bray Cove Swimming Club also hosted annual galas at this venue during its hey day.

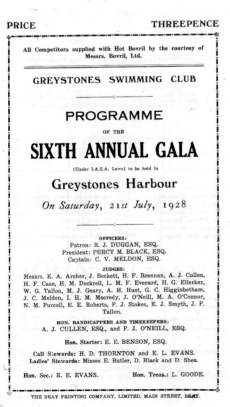

LEFT: The programme for the 1928 swimming gala hosted by Greystones Swimming Club with Bovril supplied to all competitors. The names of the various officials on the front cover include a number of well-known Greystones families (such as Meldon and Stokes) who had long associations with swimming locally. Jim Beckett was one of the judges. Another was Dublin born Noel M. Purcell. He was a regular participant at Greystones swimming galas. At the 1916 gala in the harbour, he scored both goals for Blackrock in their 2-0 win against Greystones in the water polo match. Four years later he won a gold medal as part of the Great Britain water polo team at the 1920 Olympic Games in Antwerp. At the Paris Olympics in 1924, he captained the Irish water polo team, which also included Jim Beckett. Purcell scored both of Ireland's goals in the 4-2 Olympic quarter final defeat to Czechoslovakia. He also won 4 caps for Ireland at rugby in 1921.

RIGHT: Diving at Greystones in the 1920s.

By the 1950s, Greystones Swimming Club had a growing membership composed of residents and summer visitors. Regular dances were held at both the Clyda Hotel and the Grand Hotel as fundraisers and social events. A highlight of the Greystones Swimming Club calendar was the annual swimming race from the harbour to the gentlemen's bathing place. This event was open to club members only and was generally held in the mid-point of the season, often attracting a large number of spectators. At the annual Wicklow Regatta, by this time a long established aquatic festival which included swimming in its programme, the 1955 event attracted over 400 competitors from clubs. Greystones Swimming Club took 1st place in both the men's and ladies squad races. In the under 16 age category, Deirdre McCartan and P. Evans took 1st & 2nd place respectively in the girl's diving. Deirdre McCartan later went on to marry Ronnie Drew of The Dubliners.

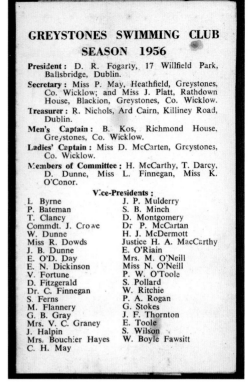

GREYSTONES SWIMMING CLUB
SEASON 1956

President : D. R. Fogarty, 17 Willfield Park, Ballsbridge, Dublin.
Secretary : Miss P. May, Heathfield, Greystones, Co. Wicklow; and Miss J. Platt, Rathdown House, Blackion, Greystones, Co. Wicklow.
Treasurer : R. Nichols, Ard Cairn, Killiney Road, Dublin.
Men's Captain : B. Kos, Richmond House, Greystones, Co. Wicklow.
Ladies' Captain : Miss D. McCarten, Greystones, Co. Wicklow.
Members of Committee : H. McCarthy, T. Darcy, D. Dunne, Miss L. Finnegan, Miss K. O'Conor.

Vice-Presidents :

L. Byrne	J. P. Mulderry
P. Bateman	S. B. Minch
T. Clancy	D. Montgomery
Commdt. J. Crowe	Dr P. McCartan
W. Dunne	H. J. McDermott
Miss R. Dowds	Justice H. A. MacCarthy
J. B. Dunne	E. O'Riain
E. O'D. Day	Mrs. M. O'Neill
E. N. Dickinson	Miss N. O'Neill
V. Fortune	P. W. O'Toole
D. Fitzgerald	S. Pollard
Dr. C. Finnegan	W. Ritchie
S. Ferns	P. A. Rogan
M. Flannery	G. Stokes
G. B. Gray	J. F. Thornton
Mrs. V. C. Graney	E. Toole
J. Halpin	S. Wilson
Mrs. Bouchier Hayes	W. Boyle Fawsitt
C. H. May	

★ GREYSTONES SWIMMING CLUB ★

ANNUAL GALA

Saturday, 11th July, 1959

At 3 p.m.

BETWEEN GREYSTONES, MULLINGAR AND TULLAMORE SWIMMING CLUBS

Open 400 Yards Handicap Ladies' and Gents
ENTRANCE FEE 2/6

ADMISSION TO PIER 1/-

AFTER THE GALA COME TO

GALA DANCE

LA TOUCHE HOTEL,
GREYSTONES

Music by Tom Gerrity and his Band

DANCING 9-1 ★ ADMISSION (inc. tax) 5/-
(ADMISSION BY TICKET ONLY.)

Tickets May be obtained from any Member of the Committee or the La Touche Hotel

ABOVE: 1959 photo of the swimming raft which was moored to the pier.

BELOW: Dances were regularly held during the 1950s at the Grand Hotel and the Clyda Hotel.

GREYSTONES SWIMMING CLUB

N° 180

Supper Dance

GRAND HOTEL, GREYSTONES

FRIDAY, 20th JULY 1956

Music by Chris Ryan and his Band

Dancing 9-3 — Evening Dress

TICKETS 12/6
(From members of the Committee)

G.S.C. N° 180 SUPPER First Sitting 12 o'clock

LEFT: Members of Greystones Swimming Club photographed on the pier in the 1950s. Included are Michael Nichols, Trishy May, Dodo Platt, Carmel Stokes, Kathleen O'Connor, Greg Cunniam, Miklos Kos, Baylor Kos, Bobby Meldon and Collette Bateman.

GREYSTONES SWIMMING CLUB

Easter Monday Dance

will be held in

CLYDA HOTEL, GREYSTONES

Harry Hogg and his Orchestra

Dancing 9-1

ADMISSION - - 5/-
(By Ticket 3/6)

RIGHT: Gráinne McLoughlin participating in a raft race at Greystones Harbour in August 2002. The race was held as part of Greystones Arts Festival and raised funds for Wicklow RNLI Greystones won the junior race and Wicklow town won the senior race.

ABOVE: View of Swan's Rock exposed on the South Beach in the 1890s. When coal schooners first sailed to Greystones before the original jetty was built at the harbour in 1847, the coal was unloaded just off the South Beach into smaller flat-bottomed boats or barges from where it was landed by porters at Swan's Rock. In recent years this rock feature has been buried under shingle. It is named after a Mr Swan who at one time worked at the nearby coalyard. *Pigot's Directory of Ireland* published in 1824 noted that, at that time, both Bray and Wicklow Town had established coal merchants, with George Seymour operating as a coal and slate merchant in Bray and George D. Ronan operating as a coal merchant in Wicklow Town.

BELOW: The coalyard marked at the bottom of the 1838 Ordnance Survey map was operated by the Seymour family at one time and was known as Seymour's coalyard. It was located where the car park and playground are today. At the time Greystones was just a few scattered dwellings. On the 1841 census it was too small to be separately returned and was included within Delgany Parish, comprising of 351 houses, split into 3 segments: (i) *"Rural Portion"* with 1,888 persons (covering an area of 3,946 acres and what is now Greystones) (ii) *"Delgany Town"* with 201 persons and (iii) *"Killincarrig Town"* with 179 persons. Of the 2,268 total population, just over one quarter were listed as visitors.

With no harbour affording shelter in a storm, the schooners were often at the mercy of the weather. *The Cumberland Pacquet & Ware's Whitehaven Advertiser* dated 8th October 1839 reported that the Whitehaven based schooner, *Myrtle*, *"was driven on shore, wind at N.E. off Greystones on the week of Tuesday last and has since become a complete wreck. Her crew, who remained upon the wreck from night-fall on Tuesday until daybreak on Wednesday, when they succeeded in getting on shore, by the aid of a rope fastened to a buoy, have lost all their clothing etc by the unfortunate occurrence. The Myrtle was coal-laden, but we believe was tolerably well covered."*

The following two pages show the links between various local schooner owning families which included the Doyle, Cuthbert, Evans and McGill families. It was the Doyle family who became the first Greystones schooner owners in 1839, following the lead shown by the Cuthbert family, who operated schooners out of Bray. In the mid 1830s, William Cuthbert was importing coal from Whitehaven to Bray in his schooner, *William & Margaret*. By the end of the decade, his brother-in-law, John Doyle had commissioned the construction of his own schooner, *Belle Vue*. The era of Greystones owned schooners importing coal had begun. Over the following eight decades, schooner owners and coal importers including Arthur Evans, John George McEntagart and William H. Dann followed the trail blazed by John Doyle of importing coal under sail to Greystones.

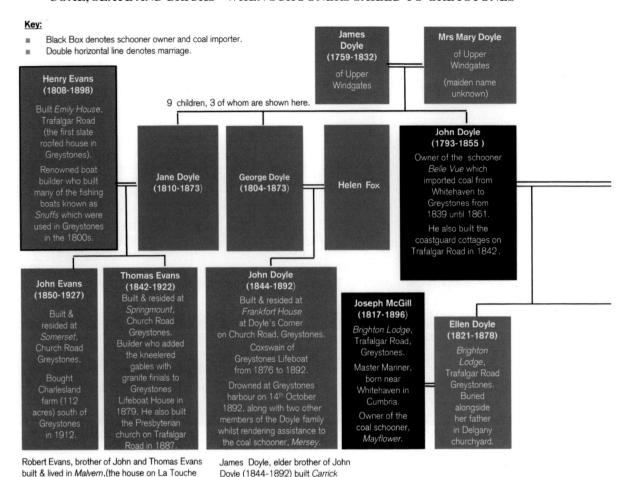

Key:
- Black Box denotes schooner owner and coal importer.
- Double horizontal line denotes marriage.

James Doyle (1759-1832) of Upper Windgates

Mrs Mary Doyle of Upper Windgates (maiden name unknown)

9 children, 3 of whom are shown here.

Henry Evans (1808-1898)
Built *Emily House*, Trafalgar Road (the first slate roofed house in Greystones).
Renowned boat builder who built many of the fishing boats known as *Snuffs* which were used in Greystones in the 1800s.

Jane Doyle (1810-1873)

George Doyle (1804-1873)

Helen Fox

John Doyle (1793-1855)
Owner of the schooner *Belle Vue* which imported coal from Whitehaven to Greystones from 1839 until 1861.
He also built the coastguard cottages on Trafalgar Road in 1842.

John Evans (1850-1927)
Built & resided at *Somerset*, Church Road Greystones.
Bought Charlesland farm (112 acres) south of Greystones in 1912.

Thomas Evans (1842-1922)
Built & resided at *Springmount*, Church Road Greystones.
Builder who added the kneelered gables with granite finials to Greystones Lifeboat House in 1879. He also built the Presbyterian church on Trafalgar Road in 1887.

John Doyle (1844-1892)
Built & resided at *Frankfort House* at Doyle's Corner on Church Road, Greystones.
Coxswain of Greystones Lifeboat from 1876 to 1892.
Drowned at Greystones harbour on 14th October 1892, along with two other members of the Doyle family whilst rendering assistance to the coal schooner, *Mersey*.

Joseph McGill (1817-1896)
Brighton Lodge, Trafalgar Road, Greystones.
Master Mariner, born near Whitehaven in Cumbria.
Owner of the coal schooner, *Mayflower*.

Ellen Doyle (1821-1878)
Brighton Lodge, Trafalgar Road Greystones.
Buried alongside her father in Delgany churchyard.

Robert Evans, brother of John and Thomas Evans built & lived in *Malvern*, (the house on La Touche Place where the shop Paraphernalia is today)

James Doyle, elder brother of John Doyle (1844-1892) built *Carrick Cottage* at Doyle's Corner.

ABOVE: Built by Henry Evans, *Emily House* beside the entrance to the turnpike on Trafalgar Road, the first slate roofed house in Greystones.

Greystones Parish.

Rector—Rev. EDWARD S. DAUNT, A.M., Rectory.
Lay Reader—R. CATHCART DOBBS, Knockdolian.

This issue of our Parish Magazine registers the death of Henry Evans, of Emily House, and the baptism of his youngest great grandchild.

The kindly old man was well-known in Greystones, where he was born early in the century, and his numerous descendants are among the most respected and enterprising members of our community. It is worthy of note that he built the first slated house in this sea-side village, which has since continued to increase and prosper.

He was for long a consistent Christian, his simple faith in his Saviour never failed, and as the infirmities of old age increased his longing desire was to depart and be with Christ. The attendance at his funeral was unusually large, and his remains were interred in the Delgany Cemetery after service in the adjoining church, when the Rev. E. S. Daunt gave an earnest and impressive address.

ABOVE: Henry Evans (1808-1898).

ABOVE RIGHT: Extract from the February 1898 *Calary, Delgany, Derrylossory, Greystones, Killiskey & Newtownmountkennedy Parish Magazine* about the passing of Henry Evans. In a letter written by Dr. Leslie Doyle to Derek Paine in January 1984, he commented on the magazine extract as follows: *"The item about the death of Henry Evans of Emily House in his 90th year is of some importance in the records of Greystones in the 19th century. I know who he was, as my father often talked about him to me. I may have told you before, he was a shipwright of some renown and he built the fishing ships and boats in the sheds behind Emily House along by the turnpike. No doubt, he built the three yawls in his name (Kite, Hawk and Eagle) in 1849 and 1850 contained in the Greystones Fishing Register."*

The Doyle family were originally from Newcastle. James Doyle, the son of John Doyle (1730-1803), a miller and farmer was born at the Corn Mill in 1759. Around the early 1790s, James Doyle and his wife Mary moved to Windgates where he had a holding and a bakehouse. The family subsequently moved to Greystones (harbour area), then consisting of only a few fishermen's cottages. James Doyle died on 24th May 1832, aged 73 and is buried in Newcastle cemetery. By this time, his son John Doyle, had served for a number of years as a tidewaiter within the preventive waterguard (a forerunner to the coast guards). This enabled him to see at first hand how profitable it was to own and operate schooners, in particular importing coal at a time when the railway had not yet come to Greystones.

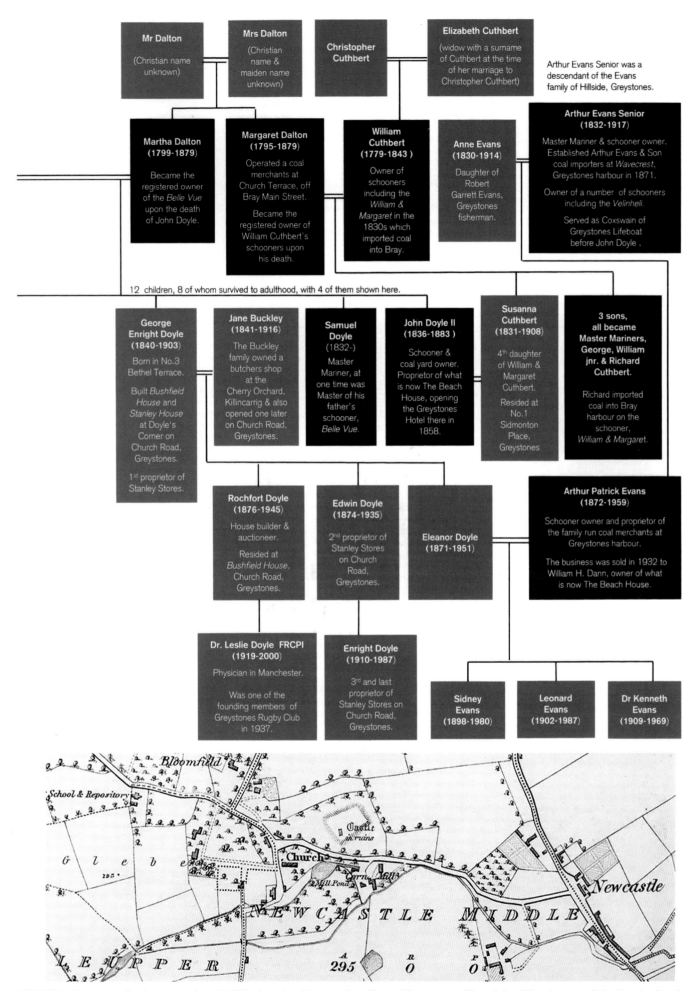

Mr Dalton
(Christian name unknown)

Mrs Dalton
(Christian name & maiden name unknown)

Christopher Cuthbert

Elizabeth Cuthbert
(widow with a surname of Cuthbert at the time of her marriage to Christopher Cuthbert)

Arthur Evans Senior was a descendant of the Evans family of Hillside, Greystones.

Martha Dalton (1799-1879)
Became the registered owner of the *Belle Vue* upon the death of John Doyle.

Margaret Dalton (1795-1879)
Operated a coal merchants at Church Terrace, off Bray Main Street.
Became the registered owner of William Cuthbert's schooners upon his death.

William Cuthbert (1779-1843)
Owner of schooners including the *William & Margaret* in the 1830s which imported coal into Bray.

Anne Evans (1830-1914)
Daughter of Robert Garrett Evans, Greystones fisherman.

Arthur Evans Senior (1832-1917)
Master Mariner & schooner owner. Established Arthur Evans & Son coal importers at *Wavecrest*, Greystones harbour in 1871.
Owner of a number of schooners including the *Velinheli*.
Served as Coxswain of Greystones Lifeboat before John Doyle .

12 children, 8 of whom survived to adulthood, with 4 of them shown here.

George Enright Doyle (1840-1903)
Born in No.3 Bethel Terrace.
Built *Bushfield House* and *Stanley House* at Doyle's Corner on Church Road, Greystones.
1st proprietor of Stanley Stores.

Jane Buckley (1841-1916)
The Buckley family owned a butchers shop at the Cherry Orchard, Killincarrig & also opened one later on Church Road, Greystones.

Samuel Doyle (1832-)
Master Mariner, at one time was Master of his father's schooner, *Belle Vue*.

John Doyle II (1836-1883)
Schooner & coal yard owner. Proprietor of what is now The Beach House, opening the Greystones Hotel there in 1858.

Susanna Cuthbert (1831-1908)
4th daughter of William & Margaret Cuthbert.
Resided at No.1 Sidmonton Place, Greystones

3 sons, all became Master Mariners, George, William jnr. & Richard Cuthbert.
Richard imported coal into Bray harbour on the schooner, *William & Margaret*.

Rochfort Doyle (1876-1945)
House builder & auctioneer.
Resided at *Bushfield House*, Church Road, Greystones.

Edwin Doyle (1874-1935)
2nd proprietor of Stanley Stores on Church Road, Greystones.

Eleanor Doyle (1871-1951)

Arthur Patrick Evans (1872-1959)
Schooner owner and proprietor of the family run coal merchants at Greystones harbour.
The business was sold in 1932 to William H. Dann, owner of what is now The Beach House.

Dr. Leslie Doyle FRCPI (1919-2000)
Physician in Manchester.
Was one of the founding members of Greystones Rugby Club in 1937.

Enright Doyle (1910-1987)
3rd and last proprietor of Stanley Stores on Church Road, Greystones.

Sidney Evans (1898-1980)

Leonard Evans (1902-1987)

Dr Kenneth Evans (1909-1969)

ABOVE: Ordnance Survey map dated 1838 showing Newcastle village. The corn mill and dwelling house of the Doyle family were next to the mill pond and church. Newcastle parish records and minutes for the late 18th century refer to "*John Doyle of the mill holding.*"

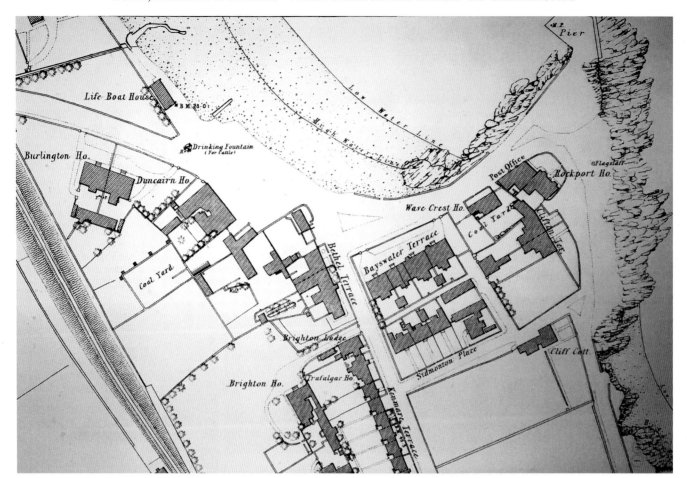

ABOVE: Ordnance Survey sheet of the harbour area dated 1883. It shows the buildings built by John Doyle (1793-1855) which included Kenmare Terrace, *Trafalgar House, Brighton House, Brighton Lodge* and Nos, 1, 2 and 3 Bethel Terrace. His son, John Doyle II, subsequently developed what is now The Beach House and also built Bayswater Terrace. John Doyle's elder brother, William lived at *Cliff Cottage* and owned all the land between it and where the Garda Station is today. Arthur Evans' two coalyards can be seen (behind his house, *Wavecrest* and behind what is now The Beach House).

ABOVE: Martha Doyle, nee Dalton (1800-1879).　　**ABOVE:** John Doyle (1793-1855).

ABOVE: John Doyle's headstone in Delgany churchyard. Its obelisk, almost Ordnance Survey marker shape is appropriate for a man who played a very significant part in helping put Greystones on the map.

Originally from Bray, Martha Dalton married John Doyle on 1st September 1817 in St. Paul's Church, Bray. The above oil painting portraits (which measure 32 inches by 28 inches) were commissioned by John Doyle during the 1840s when he lived at Bethel Terrace on Trafalgar Road. He is holding his telescope, a reminder of his association with the sea, from his time as a 16 year old supernumerary tidewaiter at Wicklow in 1809, through to becoming a Greystones ship owner in 1839. The paintings hung at the family home in Bethel Terrace for many years after both he and Martha had died. In the early 1900s, an auction was held there and realising they were going under the hammer, his grandson Edwin Doyle, purchased them to keep them in the family. Dr. Leslie Doyle recalled that the paintings hung in his uncle Edwin Doyle's dining room at *Stanley House* all through his childhood in the 1920s. Leslie's cousin, Eric Doyle had the paintings professionally restored and they hung in his home, *Whitfield House,* on the corner of Church Road and Bellevue Road (until recently, the doctors' surgery), for a number of years. Following his death, ownership passed to a nephew and they remain within the Doyle family. Today they hang in the Portland, Oregon, USA home of John Doyle's great-great-grandson, Brian Doyle.

ABOVE: 2018 view of the buildings built by the Doyle family and enhanced over the years. It was whilst living at Bethel Terrace, to the left of the anchor in the above photo, that John Doyle commissioned the building of the schooner, *Belle Vue* which began importing coal from Whitehaven to Greystones in March 1839. His coalyard was located directly behind where Spendlove's is today. The anchor positioned on the triangle was the first of the two acquired by Greystones & District Civic Association in the late 1960s, the second larger anchor, acquired in 1972, is located at the flagstaff.

In 1809, at the age of 16, John Doyle became a supernumerary (trainee) tidewaiter at Wicklow harbour. One or more tidewaiters were put aboard vessels as they entered port (on the tide) and their duty was to remain on board until the discharge of the cargo was complete. In essence they were to ensure that no goods were imported without the proper duty being paid. They were part of the preventive or water guard service and were sometimes called preventive officers. Between 1809 and 1818, John Doyle was promoted to the position of tidewaiter. The Establishment Books for H.M. Customs & Port Duties in Ireland reveal that in 1818 and 1820 he was working as a tidewaiter at Wicklow. By December 1826 he was still working as a tidewaiter, but in London and in a letter written that year he mentioned that he was "*praying to be removed from London to Wicklow*". John and Martha had 12 children, the eldest was born in 1818. His sixth child, William, born in 1829 was the first to be baptised in Delgany. He also saw service in Kenmare in County Kerry and Westport in County Mayo. It was from his time posted at the former that Kenmare Terrace on Trafalgar Road is so named.

His experience gained from working as a tidewaiter was to prove formative, as he realised the financial reward to be gained by owning trading ships. In addition, his brother-in-law, William Cuthbert, who was 14 years his senior was, by the mid 1830s a schooner owner, importing coal into Bray aboard his 36 ton schooner, *William & Margaret*. The Cuthbert family of Bray were themselves related through marriages with other ship owners, including the Beggs and Carey families who operated along the east coast. The latter imported coal to harbours in north County Dublin. The seeds of John Doyle's entrepreneurship had been sewn. and he was about to join the ranks of Wicklow's ship owners and coal importers. Throughout his life he was acknowledged locally as being an expert tap-dancer and he went on to be, albeit briefly, Greystones' first post master.

RIGHT: The entry dated 1st May 1809 in the Minute Book of the Irish Revenue Board & Irish Board of Customs, recording the appointment of John Doyle as a supernumerary tidewaiter at Wicklow.

LEFT: Dates of birth of John and Martha Doyle's twelve children. The list, written in pencil, was found in a bible with John Doyle's name in the fly-leaf. Four of their children died in childhood, with the surviving eight all being mentioned in John Doyle's last will and testament dated 1855. A number of the names are of particular note. Samuel Doyle, born May 31st 1834, became a master mariner and was, from August 1852 master of his father's schooner, *Belle Vue,* before he later settled in Castletown, on the Isle of Man. John Doyle II (his elder sibling, John Doyle I, had died in childhood and it was customary for the next boy born to be given the same name as a deceased sibling) was born May 29th 1836. John Doyle II went on to own The Beach House prior to it being owned by J.G. McEntagart. The penultimate name on the list is that of G. E. Doyle, born October 27th 1840. George Enright Doyle went on to build *Bushfield House* and *Stanley House* (where Fenton Fires is today) where he opened his shop, Stanley Stores. John and Martha Doyle had 55 grandchildren.

73

COAL, SLATE AND BRICKS - WHEN SCHOONERS SAILED TO GREYSTONES

In around 1830, John Doyle's parents, James and Mary had moved from Windgates to Greystones, residing in *The Long Cottage*, situated where *Wavecrest* is today. In May 1832, James Doyle died aged 73 and his widow, Mary, lived on at the cottage which, in addition to being located very close to the rocks and the sea, also had a yard behind it. In the late 1830s, John Doyle commissioned an Arklow shipwright, Arthur Connor, to build him a schooner in this yard. On 10th February 1839, Connor signed the certificate of construction for the schooner and she was registered at the port of Dublin on 27th February 1839. In recognition of where she was built, she was called *Belle Vue*, the name of the country home and estate of the La Touche family, owners of the land upon which her keel had been laid. Dr. Leslie Doyle wrote in June 1985 that the "*schooner was launched using tree trunks as rollers, down rather smooth rocks where the boat slip now stands (silted up). The launching was the occasion for a celebration. An ox was roasted and spirits flowed where Coolnagreina is now (the Y.W.C.A. guest house). The ox was roasted on the lawn in front of the house. The schooner took pit props from around the Delgany / Greystones area to Whitehaven and coal back to the Greystones jetty (harbour was not built until the late 1880s)*".

ABOVE: Roasting the ox was a traditional way to celebrate a major event.

ABOVE: This photograph was taken in the 1880s prior to the construction of the boat slip and dock. It shows *Wavecrest* (to the right of Watson's shop) behind which the schooner *Belle Vue* was built in 1838/1839. Launched over the rocks using wooden rollers, the 52 ton *Belle Vue* is believed to be the largest vessel ever built in Greystones.

LEFT: Official transcript obtained from the UK Shipping Register in Cardiff in the 1960s by Dr. Leslie Doyle. It provides a detailed summary of the *Belle Vue*, which was first registered as No.11 in 1839 with Dublin as its port of registry. This registration was later cancelled, with the ship registered anew at Dublin as No.1 on 15th January 1853. Her registration was then transferred to Ardrossan in Ayrshire in February 1863 following her subsequent sale to Scottish owners.

In addition to William Cuthbert, another established Bray schooner owner and coal importer in the mid 1830s was George Seymour. He was the owner of the schooner, *Better Luck Still,* which like the Cuthbert's *William & Margaret*, imported coal from Whitehaven. Records for the *Better Luck Still* reveal that during the first half of 1837 she imported Whitehaven coal into Bray on no fewer than ten occasions - she was constantly back and forth. John Doyle would undoubtedly have sought advice from George Seymour, prior to engaging Arthur Connor to build the *Belle Vue*. Both the *Better Luck Still* and the *Belle Vue* were similar in terms of length, breadth and tonnage. The *Belle Vue* was however one foot shorter and one foot wider, which likely helped her survive a number of major storms.

74

ABOVE: The Certificate of Registry for the *Belle Vue* dated 15th January 1853 upon her re-registration at the Port of Dublin. Whilst her tonnage was subsequently altered from 52 tons to just under 46 tons on 24th March 1857, this is believed to be more likely due to a change in measurement basis rather than a revision of the schooner's actual structure.

Writing in 1985, Dr. Leslie Doyle recalled a discussion he had with Stephen Doyle, son of Robert Doyle (1843-1913), the youngest child of John and Martha about which he noted the following. "*John Doyle (1793-1855) was said to have been involved in two sea rescues, one, a German ship which was wrecked on the North Beach, half to one mile north of what is now the harbour. Stephen Doyle stated that the ship was called the Prince of Prussia (I have never been able to substantiate the vessel's name). The crew was boarded with John Doyle for two to three weeks. In recognition of his efforts and rescue, the Emperor of Prussia gave John Doyle a Certificate of Commendation. The Certificate went to John's eldest surviving son, William, it is not now extant. The second rescue was that of a fishing vessel in difficulties at sea. He called for volunteers on the space which now lies in front of The Beach House. The rescue gave rise to the doggerel, often recited by Stephen Doyle.*

Oh where is brave John Doyle of Greystones?
or, er a stout hero from Wicklow to Bray,
is he at home, or is he at sea,
sure it's twelve months off our native shore,
he saved us all from a watery grave.

Another epic, recited many times related to a severe, prolonged snowfall (unusual in Greystones). The very small community at Greystones ran out of flour for bread making. John Doyle went to his uncle's mill and farm at Newcastle and brought the much needed flour, laden onto packhorses back to Greystones."

COAL, SLATE AND BRICKS - WHEN SCHOONERS SAILED TO GREYSTONES

During the era when schooners sailed to Greystones, while slate, brick and cement were imported, coal was by far the largest import by tonnage. Census records for Greystones show only a gradual increase in population during the latter half of the 19th century. By 1881 the population still numbered just 405, gradually rising from 516 in 1891 to 856 in 1901, before increasing to 1,226 in 1911. A proposal was made in 1907 to bring town gas to Greystones and notice was given that an application was intended to be made during the 1908 session of Parliament in Westminster. A bill proposed the construction of gasometers on a site between Victoria Road and the railway line but the plan never materialised. Instead coal remained the main source of energy for Greystones and ensured a steady demand for English, Welsh and Scottish coal imported into Greystones harbour. The slate ports of Porthmadog and Port Dinorwic (now known as Y Felinheli) were known to have periodically exported slate to harbours along the east coast of Ireland. The gradual rise in population and resultant housebuilding, along with the need to replace thatched roofs on some of the older cottages with slate, resulted in slate from the slate quarries in North Wales being imported into Greystones harbour on occasions. It was perhaps no coincidence that the first slate roofed house in Greystones, *Emily House*, belonged to a boatbuilder, whose larger boats (luggers) were well capable of sailing to Wales.

ABOVE: Whitehaven harbour on the coast of Cumbria, from where John Doyle's schooner, *Belle Vue* departed on her maiden return voyage back to Greystones on 28th March 1839. For more than 22 years, until her last recorded arrival in 1861, the *Belle Vue* regularly imported Whitehaven coal to Greystones.

RIGHT: The Miners Memorial which was unveiled beside Whitehaven harbour in June 2005 in memory of those who worked in the town's mining industry. It features a pillar of coal surrounded by four figures, a deputy overman representing mine management, a mines rescue man representing safety and rescue work, a coalface worker depicting manpower and a screenlass to illustrate hardship and poverty. Whitehaven's mines suffered from firedamp (methane) and many lives were lost in underground explosions. In the same year as the *Belle Vue's* maiden voyage, 23 men and boys were killed in an explosion at its William Pit, when a boy's open light caused the methane to combust.

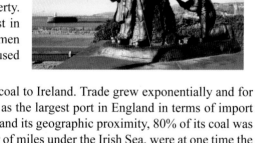

Whitehaven harbour was originally developed in 1632 for the export of coal to Ireland. Trade grew exponentially and for two decades, during the late 18th century, Whitehaven ranked 2nd only to London as the largest port in England in terms of import and export tonnage. Given Ireland's comparative lack of indigenous coal reserves and its geographic proximity, 80% of its coal was imported from Whitehaven in 1700. The coal mines, which extended out a number of miles under the Irish Sea, were at one time the deepest in the world. By 1835 Whitehaven, with 443 ships registered there, was still the 5th largest port in England due to its export of coal. In addition to Greystones, schooners regularly carried coal from Whitehaven to harbours all along the east coast including Wicklow, Bray, Bullock, Kingstown, Malahide, Skerries, Balbriggan, Drogheda and Dundalk. *The Cumberland Pacquet & Ware's Whitehaven Advertiser* dated 23rd November 1852 reported that "*the demand for Whitehaven coals in Dublin has been very firm*".

In the photograph above, the large chimney air vent known locally as "The Candlestick" can be seen. This was built in the mid-1840s when the Wellington Pit, the greatest of all Whitehaven's coal mines was sunk. The building in the foreground is reputed to be the house in which the Dublin born author of *Gulliver's Travels*, Jonathan Swift, lived in for three years during his childhood, part of which was spent in Whitehaven. The photo shows the west pier on the left, completed in 1832 and the north pier on the right, completed in 1841 (refer also to the map shown on page 100).

So numerous were the ships calling to Whitehaven, they posed a problem for the harbour authorities. Conscious not to have their harbour choked with discharged ballast, the instructions issued by the trustees of the Port Harbour and Town of Whitehaven in May 1846 stipulated that "*all vessels arriving with ballast must discharge the same into hoppers (which are provided by the trustees of the harbour to prevent any return thereof), for which they are chargeable with 6d for every ton of ballast so discharged.*" Masters of vessels that flouted the regulations were fined. There was thus an incentive for the *Belle Vue* to carry pit props from the La Touche Estate as ballast, avoiding the 6d charge per ton as well as boosting profits by selling the props to the mine owners.

The map on the following page shows the principal routes of the schooners that sailed to Greystones over the 77 year period, from the launch of John Doyle's *Belle Vue* in 1839 through to William H. Dann's *Joseph Fisher* in 1916. With the continuing dilapidation of Greystones harbour, combined with improvements made at Wicklow harbour and quayside, the *Joseph Fisher* switched to importing coal into Wicklow from September 1916 onwards.

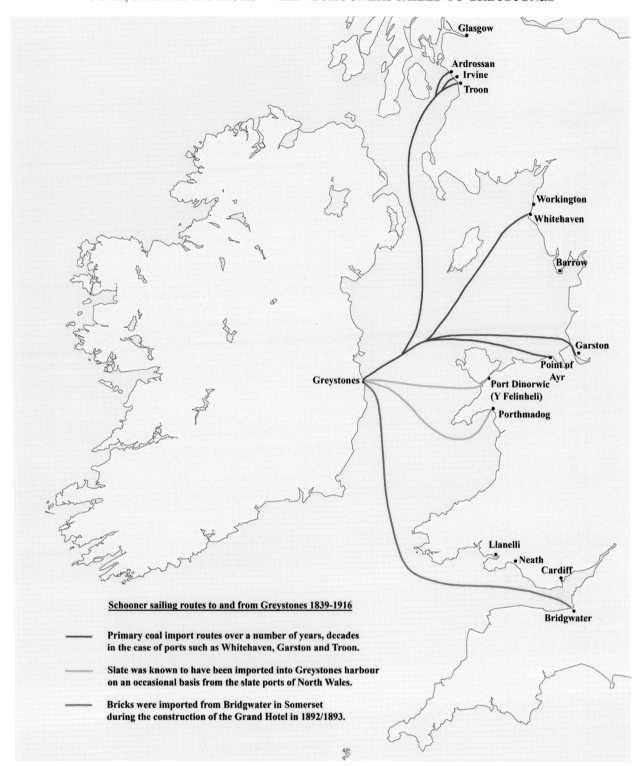

Schooner sailing routes to and from Greystones 1839-1916

—— Primary coal import routes over a number of years, decades
in the case of ports such as Whitehaven, Garston and Troon.

—— Slate was known to have been imported into Greystones harbour
on an occasional basis from the slate ports of North Wales.

—— Bricks were imported from Bridgwater in Somerset
during the construction of the Grand Hotel in 1892/1893.

ABOVE: The map also shows ports and harbours where occasional visits were made to and from Greystones. These included ports in South Wales which it is known the *Belle Vue* visited, as well as Barrow where it is known pit wood was exported to on the *Henry*.

BELOW: The details from the "*Shipping Intelligence*" section of *The Cumberland Pacquet* newspaper which recorded ships that sailed from Whitehaven harbour for the week commencing Monday 25th March 1839. Newspaper reports of arrivals and sailings routinely misspelled details of the ships and their masters. The master's name was listed as Casson on the *Belle Vue's* maiden return voyage to Greystones on Thursday 28th March 1839. It is believed it should have read Carson, as the *Belle Vue's* first master, according to her statutory returns under the Shipping Act, was Robert Carson. Also accompanying the *Belle Vue* as she sailed that

Susanna, Cuthbert, Cardiff. Lady Gordon, Bridson; Derby-haven. Lively, Cowell; Patrick, Cowley, Peel. Better Luck Still. Park, Bray. John & Mary, Herbert, Balbriggan. Dart, M'William, Whithorn. Myrtle, Dixon ; Swallow, Moore, Newry. Poplewell, Jones, Chester. Joannes, Finnigan, Dundalk. George Grant, Walsh. Garliestown. Adelaide, Beggs, Malahide. * Brunswick, M'Culloch, Dundrum. Caledonia, Tear ; Hunter, Cottiman, Ramsey. Industry, Holmes, Duddon. Bellevue, Casson, Greystones.—29. Orcadian, M'Gill, Liverpool. Ann, Beaver, Annan.—April 1. Mary Ann and Eliza, Jones, Barrow. Active, Anderson, Dumfries. Utility, Gill; Tampico, Winder ; Camilla, Reid ; Brothers, Hannah, Dublin. Catherine and Ellen, Craine ; Victoria, Christian ;

day was the *Better Luck Still* owned by the Bray coal importer, George Seymour. It appeared from those early newspaper reports detailing shipping arrivals and sailings that it was quite common for Greystones and Bray bound schooners to, whenever possible, accompany each other on the journey across the Irish Sea. Also noted in the newspaper clipping is the Bray schooner, *Susanna*, owned by the Cuthbert family, which was sailing from Whitehaven to Cardiff with coal. When the *Belle Vue* arrived in Whitehaven on her second voyage from Greystones on Tuesday 16th April 1839, she was accompanied by the *Better Luck Still* from Bray.

COAL, SLATE AND BRICKS - WHEN SCHOONERS SAILED TO GREYSTONES

The table below lists details of ships sailing to and from Greystones between 1839 and 1916 sourced from local newspapers, historical records and ships' log book books (those that have survived) that recorded details of their voyages including cargo. An asterisk in the cargo column indicates the likely cargo given the ship's port of departure.

Date	Ship	From	To	Cargo	Source / Comments
15th Mar 1839	*Belle Vue*	Greystones	Whitehaven	-	*The Cumberland Pacquet & Ware's Whitehaven Advertiser.* Master's name was Carson. Maiden voyage of the *Belle Vue* from Greystones to Whitehaven.
28th Mar 1839	*Belle Vue*	Whitehaven	Greystones	Coal *	*The Cumberland Pacquet & Ware's Whitehaven Advertiser.* Master's name was Carson. Maiden voyage of the *Belle Vue* from Whitehaven to Greystones and she was accompanied by the *Better Luck Still*, which departed from Whitehaven for Bray on the same day.
16th Apr 1839	*Belle Vue*	Greystones	Whitehaven	-	*The Cumberland Pacquet & Ware's Whitehaven Advertiser.* Master's name was Carson. Second voyage of the *Belle Vue* from Greystones to Whitehaven. She was accompanied by the *Better Luck Still,* which arrived in Whitehaven from Bray on the same day.
24th Apr 1839	*Belle Vue*	Whitehaven	Greystones	Coal *	*The Cumberland Pacquet & Ware's Whitehaven Advertiser.* Master's name was Carson. Second voyage of the Belle Vue from Whitehaven to Greystones and she was accompanied by the *Seymour*, which departed from Whitehaven for Bray on the same day.
11th Sept 1839	*Belle Vue*	Whitehaven	Greystones	Coal *	*The Cumberland Pacquet & Ware's Whitehaven Advertiser.* Master's name was Kearon. The *William & Margaret* and the *Better Luck Still* also departed Whitehaven for Bray on the same day.
27th Dec 1839	*Belle Vue*	Whitehaven	Greystones	Coal *	*The Cumberland Pacquet & Ware's Whitehaven Advertiser.* Master's name was Cairns. The *Susannah*, with its master, Cuthbert, departed the same day for Bray, as did the *Utility* for Dublin, whose master was Captain Joseph McGill. The future son-in-law of John Doyle, the owner of the *Belle Vue,* he later resided on Trafalgar Road, Greystones and he is buried beside John Doyle in Delgany.
4th Feb 1840	*Isabella*	Whitehaven	Greystones	Coal *	*The Cumberland Pacquet & Ware's Whitehaven Advertiser.* The *Isabella* was a smack, built in Perth, Scotland. She was owned by William Middleton.
14th Mar 1840	*Lowther Castle*	Whitehaven	Greystones	Coal *	*The Cumberland Pacquet & Ware's Whitehaven Advertiser.* The schooner, *Lowther Castle* was built in Whitehaven and was owned by its master, William Middleton. The vessel was named after the ancestral family home of the Lowther family, who were instrumental in the establishment of coal mining in the Whitehaven area.
2nd July 1840	*Belle Vue*	Whitehaven	Greystones	Coal *	*The Cumberland Paquet & Ware's Whitehaven Advertiser.* Master's name was Thompson. The *William & Margaret,* with its master, Cuthbert and the *Robert Seymour*, with its master, Burton, both departed Whitehaven for Bray on the same day as the *Belle Vue.*
9th Nov 1840	*Belle Vue*	Whitehaven	Greystones	Coal *	*The Cumberland Paquet & Ware's Whitehaven Advertiser.* Master's name was Thompson.
31st Mar 1846	*Belle Vue*	Greystones	Neath (Giant's Grave) Wales.	-	*Shipping & Mercantile Gazette.* Master's name was Kearon.
15th Oct 1846	*Belle Vue*	Strangford	Greystones	Coal *	*Shipping & Mercantile Gazette.* The *Belle Vue* had put in to Strangford Lough which was used as a sanctuary during storms, having departed Whitehaven. Another vessel, *Resolution*, bound for Greystones having departed Ayr also put into Strangford Lough.
15th May 1848	*Belle Vue*	Greystones	Whitehaven	-	*Shipping & Mercantile Gazette.*
17th July 1849	*Belle Vue*	Greystones	Whitehaven	-	*The Cumberland Paquet & Ware's Whitehaven Advertiser.* Master was Cairns.
25th Feb 1850	*Belle Vue*	Greystones	Whitehaven	-	*Shipping & Mercantile Gazette.* Master's name was Cairns. Six vessels were reported departing Whitehaven on 24th February bound for Dublin, Baldoyle, Malahide, Rush, Balbriggan and Dundalk.
4th June 1853	*Belle Vue*	Whitehaven	Greystones	Coal *	*The Carlisle Patriot.* Master's name was Samuel Doyle.
12th Feb 1854	*Belle Vue*	Whitehaven	Greystones	Coal *	*The Carlisle Journal.* Master's name was Samuel Doyle.
4th May 1854	*Belle Vue*	Whitehaven	Greystones	Coal *	*The Cumberland Paquet & Ware's Whitehaven Advertiser.* Master's name was Samuel Doyle. On the same date, 4 vessels departed Whitehaven for Kingstown, Dublin, Rush, Balbriggan and Dundalk. The *Belle Vue's* log for this period recorded that her crew of 3 included Whitehaven born, John Thaile, aged 38.
1st May 1855	*Belle Vue*	Whitehaven	Greystones	Coal *	*The Cumberland Paquet & Ware's Whitehaven Advertiser.* Master's name was Samuel Doyle.
12th Jun 1855	*Patrick*	Dublin	Greystones	Bricks	*The Freeman's Journal.* The *Patrick* was a 36 ton vessel whose master was Denis Kavanagh of Arklow. This voyage was four months before the railway opened.
3rd Nov 1855	*Belle Vue*	Whitehaven	Greystones	Coal *	*The Carlisle Patriot.* Master's name was Samuel Doyle.
24th Oct 1856	*Mermaid*	Whitehaven	Greystones	Coal *	*The Carlisle Journal.* Master's name was Morgan.
19th Apr 1857	*Belle Vue*	Llanelli	Greystones	Coal *	Ship's Log Book. Her subsequent voyage was to Neath in South Wales and back.
7th May 1857	*Industry*	Greystones	Whitehaven	-	*The Cumberland Paquet & Ware's Whitehaven Advertiser.* Master's name Campbell. 53 ton schooner owned by James Tyrrell of Arklow.

COAL, SLATE AND BRICKS - WHEN SCHOONERS SAILED TO GREYSTONES

Date	Ship	From	To	Cargo	Source / Comments
8th Oct 1859	*Belle Vue*	Whitehaven	Greystones	Coal *	*The Carlisle Journal.* Master's name was Fields. The Fields name had a long maritime association with Greystones, being one of the original fishing family names in the locality.
27th Apr 1860	*Belle Vue*	Neath	Greystones	Coal *	*The Carlisle Journal.* Master's name was Fields.
11th May 1860	*Greyhound*	Whitehaven	Greystones	Coal *	*The Carlisle Journal.* Master's name was Carnes. The *Greyhound* was acquired by Martha Doyle, widow of John Doyle (1793-1855) in December 1858.
28th Oct 1860	*Belle Vue*	Whitehaven	Greystones	Coal *	*The Cumberland Pacquet & Ware's Whitehaven Advertiser.* Master's name was Fields.
19th June 1861	*Belle Vue*	Whitehaven	Greystones	Coal	*The Evening Freeman.*
4th Sept 1861	*Mersey*	Greystones	Whitehaven	Ballast	*The Freeman's Journal.* The first newspaper record listing ballast (stones from the North Beach) as cargo on a wind bound vessel, sailing out of Greystones.
14th Sept 1861	*Tees Packet*	Whitehaven	Greystones	Coal	*The Freeman's Journal.* The vessel was a 60 ton vessel registered in Dublin.
12th Nov 1861	*Mary Tatham*	Glasgow	Greystones	Coal	*The Freeman's Journal.* The *Mary Tatham* was a 56 ton vessel registered in Dublin.
12th Nov 1861	*Belle Vue*	Ardrossan	Greystones	Coal	*The Freeman's Journal.* Last known recorded date for the *Belle Vue* importing coal into Greystones harbour, more than 22 years after her first voyage.
6th Aug 1862	*Eliza & Mary*	Liverpool	Greystones	Coal	*The Freeman's Journal.*
22nd Sept 1862	*Clans*	Greystones	Whitehaven	Ballast	*The Freeman's Journal.* The *Clans* was a 63 ton vessel registered at Greenock.
6th Jan 1863	*Richard*	Whitehaven	Greystones	Coal	*The Evening Freeman.* Master's name was Finnigan. 34 ton vessel.
22nd May 1863	*Mary Tortain*	Whitehaven	Greystones	Coal	*The Evening Freeman.* On the same day, vessels were also reported as bringing coal from Whitehaven to Bray and Balbriggan and from Troon to Wicklow.
23rd July 1863	*Joshua*	Liverpool	Greystones	Coal	*The Irish Times.*
10th Feb 1864	*Alert*	Liverpool	Greystones	Coal	*The Evening Freeman.*
2nd Oct 1865	*Richard*	Garston	Greystones	Coal	*The Freeman's Journal.* 35 ton vessel owned by R. Flanagan of Wicklow.
4th April 1866	*Morning Light*	Whitehaven	Greystones	Coal	*Saunders's Newsletter.* The *Morning Light*, 78 tons was registered at Dublin.
23rd May 1866	*Maid*	Whitehaven	Greystones	Coal	*Saunders's Newsletter.*
30th July 1866	*Henry*	Greystones	Barrow	Pit wood	*The Freeman's Journal.* The *Henry*, a 64 ton vessel, first registered in Dublin in 1856 was owned by Henry Fox of Wicklow.
14th Aug 1866	*Morning Light*	Whitehaven	Greystones	Coal	*The Freeman's Journal.*
15th Aug 1868	*Morning Light*	Workington	Greystones	Coal	*Saunders's Newsletter.*
1st Mar 1867	*Morning Light*	Whitehaven	Greystones	Coal	*Saunders's Newsletter.* On the same day, *Thomas Ferguson* departed Whitehaven for Bray.
24th Oct 1868	*Prince Waterloo*	Whitehaven	Greystones	Coal	*Saunders's Newletter.* Built in Wicklow in 1816, the *Prince Waterloo* was a 64 feet, 63 ton schooner which was later lost at Hoylake on 9th March 1875.
24th Oct 1868	*William & Henry*	Greystones	Whitehaven	Ballast	*The Freeman's Journal.*
8th Sept 1876	*Morning Light*	Ardrossan	Greystones	Coal *	Ship's Log Book. Owned by John Doyle II (1836-1883) of Greystones.
27th July 1877	*Thomas*	Glasgow	Greystones	Coal *	*Shipping & Mercantile Gazette.* Master's name was Jones.
25th Mar 1878	*Morning Light*	Troon	Greystones	Coal *	*Shipping & Mercantile Gazette.* Master's name was Kinsella.
7th Jun 1879	*Sarah Jane*	Whitehaven	Greystones	Coal *	Ship's Log Book. Arklow built (1851) & owned. The *Sarah Jane* was a 46 ton schooner. In 1883 she was acquired by Arthur Evans of Greystones.
19th Oct 1880	*Sarah Jane*	Greystones	Liverpool	-	*Manchester Courier & Lancashire General Advertiser.*
21st July 1882	*Sarah Jane*	Troon	Greystones	Coal *	Ship's Log Book. Troon developed under the 4th Duke of Portland who enlarged the harbour and created the first proper railway in Scotland (Kilmarnock & Troon Railway) to transport coal from the mines (of the Ayrshire Coalfield) near Kilmarnock.
16th July 1883	*Sarah Jane*	Greystones	Troon	Ballast	Ship's Log Book.
16th Sept 1883	*Sarah Jane*	Greystones	Irvine	Ballast	Ship's Log Book.
19th Aug 1884	*Sarah Jane*	Troon	Greystones	Coal *	*The Glasgow Herald.*
26th May 1885	*Sarah Jane*	Greystones	Troon	-	*The Glasgow Herald.*
1st Jun 1885	*Sarah Jane*	Troon	Greystones	Coal *	*The Glasgow Herald.*
10th July 1886	*Sarah Jane*	Garston	Greystones	Coal	Ship's Log Book, with the entry "*95 tons of coal*".
20th Aug 1886	*Sarah Jane*	Greystones	Troon	Ballast	Ship's Log Book.
24th Aug 1886	*Sarah Jane*	Troon	Greystones	Coal	Ship's Log Book, with the entry "*90 tons of coal*".
2nd Oct 1886	*Sarah Jane*	Greystones	Troon	-	*The Glasgow Herald.* On 24th Oct 1886 the *Sarah Jane*, laden with coal from Troon was driven ashore at Greystones and wrecked (*The Freeman's Journal*).
25th Jun 1887	*Mersey*	Whitehaven	Greystones	Coal *	Ship's Log Book. Earliest record of the *Mersey* importing coal to Greystones.
6th May 1889	*Mersey*	Ardrossan	Greystones	Coal *	Ship's Log Book. The *Mersey* was the schooner, owned by J.G. McEntagart, proprietor of what is now The Beach House.
5th July 1889	*Mersey*	Garston	Greystones	Coal *	Ship's Log Book.
7th Aug 1889	*Mersey*	Runcorn	Greystones	Coal *	Ship's Log Book.

COAL, SLATE AND BRICKS - WHEN SCHOONERS SAILED TO GREYSTONES

Date	Ship	From	To	Cargo	Source / Comments
8th Feb 1891	*Mersey*	Irvine	Greystones	Coal *	Ship's Log Book.
26th Aug 1891	*Mersey*	Greystones	Troon	Ballast	Ship's Log Book.
23rd Sept 1892	*Mersey*	Garston	Greystones	Coal *	Whilst still at Greystones harbour on 14th October 1892, three members of the Doyle family were drowned trying to render assistance to the *Mersey*.
23rd Apr 1893	*Velinheli*	Greystones	Bridgwater	-	*Lloyd's List.* To obtain bricks for the construction of the Grand Hotel.
21st Jun 1893	*Velinheli*	Bridgwater	Greystones	Bricks *	Ship's Log Book. Bricks for the construction of the Grand Hotel.
16th Oct 1893	*Mersey*	Greystones	Troon	Ballast	*The Glasgow Herald.*
3rd Apr 1894	*Mersey*	Troon	Greystones	Coal	*The Glasgow Herald.*
5th May 1894	*Eva*	Troon	Greystones	Coal	*The Glasgow Herald.* The *Eva* later imported coal from Garston to Wicklow harbour. She was later lost with all her crew in July 1915.
29th May 1894	*Velinheli*	Garston	Greystones	Coal *	Ship's Log Book.
4th Oct 1894	*Mersey*	Greystones	Troon	Ballast	Ship's Log Book.
13th Sept 1895	*Velinheli*	Troon	Greystones	Coal	*The Glasgow Herald.*
13th Feb 1896	*Velinheli*	Irvine	Greystones	Coal	*Glasgow Herald.* Irvine is on the Ayrshire coast between Ardrossan and Troon.
1st Apr 1896	*Mersey*	Troon	Greystones	Coal *	Ship's Log Book.
10th Oct 1896	*Mersey*	Point of Ayr	Greystones	Coal	*The Morning Post.*
22nd Jun 1897	*Mersey*	Point of Ayr	Greystones	Coal	Ship's Log Book.
4th Nov 1897	*Velinheli*	Point of Ayr	Greystones	Coal *	Ship's Log Book.
14th Nov 1898	*Welsh Prince*	Greystones	Dublin	-	*The Freeman's Journal.*
15th Apr 1899	*SS Dunsyre*	Greystones	Dublin	Gravel	*Irish Independent.* Steam ship that took gravel from the North Beach, Greystones. Glasgow built, the 176 ton, 100 feet long *SS Dunsyre* was launched on 28th January 1899. She sank in a storm on 1st April 1900 en route from Neath to Cork, fully laden with coal.
16th Jun 1899	*William & Henry*	Liverpool	Greystones	Coal *	Ship's Log Book.
18th Mar 1898	*Mersey*	Garston	Greystones	Coal *	Ship's Log Book.
10th Aug 1898	*Velinheli*	Garston	Greystones	Coal *	Ship's Log Book.
3rd Jun 1899	*Mersey*	Garston	Greystones	Coal *	Ship's Log Book.
19th Jun 1899	*SS Portaferry*	Greystones	Dublin	Gravel	*The Irish Independent.* Steam ship which took gravel from the North Beach.
18th Oct 1899	*Mersey*	Point of Ayr	Greystones	Coal	Ship's Log Book.
5th Apr 1900	*Mersey*	Point of Ayr	Greystones	Coal *	Ship's Log Book.
22nd Apr 1900	*Velinheli*	Point of Ayr	Greystones	Coal *	Ship's Log Book.
23rd May 1901	*Velinheli*	Liverpool	Greystones	Coal *	*Lloyd's List.*
24th May 1901	*Mersey*	Garston	Greystones	Coal *	Ship's Log Book.
23rd July 1901	*Eva*	Liverpool	Greystones	Coal *	*Lloyd's List.*
24th Jun 1902	*Mersey*	Garston	Greystones	Coal *	Ship's Log Book.
25th Jun 1902	*Velinheli*	Point of Ayr	Greystones	Coal *	Ship's Log Book.
18th Nov 1902	*Mersey*	Point of Ayr	Greystones	Coal *	Ship's Log Book.
8th May 1903	*Mersey*	Garston	Greystones	Coal *	Ship's Log Book.
14th Sept 1903	*Velinheli*	Garston	Greystones	Coal *	Ship's Log Book.
7th Feb 1904	*Mersey*	Garston	Greystones	Coal *	Ship's Log Book.
25th Mar 1904	*Federation*	Runcorn	Greystones	Coal *	*Lloyd's List.*
19th Jun 1904	*Emma Alice*	Garston	Greystones	Coal *	Ship's Log Book. The *Emma Alice* was owned by Patrick Reilly of Bray.
12th Oct 1904	*Velinheli*	Point of Ayr	Greystones	Coal *	Ship's Log Book.
6th Nov 1904	*Mersey*	Point of Ayr	Greystones	Coal *	Ship's Log Book.
20th Jun 1906	*Velinheli*	Garston	Greystones	Coal *	Ship's Log Book.
9th July 1906	*Confido*	Liverpool	Greystones	Coal *	*Lloyd's List.* In May 1905, J.G. McEntagart purchased the 49 ton, 80 feet long ketch, *Confido* to replace the *Mersey* (wrecked off Anglesey in January 1905).
29th Jun 1907	*Velinheli*	Point of Ayr	Greystones	Coal *	Ship's Log Book.
2nd July 1907	*Federation*	Greystones	Runcorn	-	*Lloyd's List.*
8th Apr 1907	*Confido*	Liverpool	Greystones	Coal *	*Lloyd's List.* William H. Dann purchased the *Confido* on 8th January 1907 from J.G. McEntagart for £600. The master's name was Booth.
16th July 1907	*Confido*	Garston	Greystones	Coal *	*Lloyd's List.*
27th May 1908	*Velinheli*	Garston	Greystones	Coal *	Ship's Log Book.
7th May 1909	*Velinheli*	Point of Ayr	Greystones	Coal *	Ship's Log Book.
28th May 1909	*Velinheli*	Garston	Greystones	Coal *	Ship's Log Book.
27th July 1909	*Velinheli*	Garston	Greystones	Coal *	Ship's Log Book.

Date	Ship	From	To	Cargo	. Source / Comments
7th Sept 1909	*William & Margaret*	Liverpool	Greystones	Coal *	Lloyd's List. The *William & Margaret* was owned by Edward Tyrell of Arklow in 1909. She was built in 1846 and was owned by the Cuthbert family of Bray (mainly Richard Cuthbert) from new until 1900. She replaced an earlier *William & Margaret* (built in 1829 and broken up in 1846) which was owned by William Cuthbert, brother-in-law of John Doyle 1793-1855.
18th Oct 1909	*Velinheli*	Widnes	Greystones	Coal *	Ship's Log Book.
12th Sept 1910	*Velinheli*	Garston	Greystones	Coal *	Ship's Log Book.
6th May 1912	*Velinheli*	Runcorn	Greystones	Coal *	Ship's Log Book.
29th Jun 1912	*Velinheli*	Greystones	Garston	Ballast	Ship's Log Book.
12th July 1912	*Joseph Fisher*	Garston	Greystones	Coal *	Ship's Log Book
7th Jun 1913	*Velinheli*	Widnes	Greystones	Coal *	Ship's Log Book
28th Jun 1913	*Joseph Fisher*	Garston	Greystones	Coal *	Ship's Log Book.
30th Apr 1914	*Joseph Fisher*	Garston	Greystones	Coal *	Ship's Log Book.
28th Jul 1914	*Joseph Fisher*	Greystones	Garston	-	Ship's Log Book. The *Joseph Fisher* departed Greystones harbour the day World War One broke out. She would later become a casualty of the war.
20th Nov 1914	*Joseph Fisher*	Garston	Greystones	Coal *	Ship's Log Book,
24th Sept 1916	*Joseph Fisher*	Garston	Greystones	Coal	Ship's Log Book.

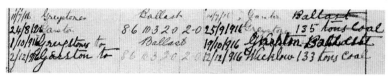

ABOVE: Section of the log book of the *Joseph Fisher* detailing her voyages between 1st July 1916 and 31st December 1916. On 25th September 1916 she arrived in Greystones from Garston with a cargo of 135 tons of coal. This is believed to be among the last recorded arrivals, if not the final one, into Greystones harbour of a locally owned sailing schooner. For the remainder of 1916 she imported coal into Wicklow harbour only. Her log book for the period 1st January 1917 to 30th June 1917 reveals that she imported coal from Garston to Wicklow harbour exclusively. Though her log book record of voyages for the second half of 1917 has not survived, the entries for the first half of 1918 again record her regularly importing coal from Garston to Wicklow harbour only, returning with timber on the return voyage. Examination of local newspaper reports of the time do not show any reports of Greystones owned schooners entering the harbour after 25th September 1916.

=== ⚓ ===

The *Belle Vue's* first master, following her launch in 1839, was Robert Carson. He was replaced briefly by Robert Kearon in January 1840. John Thompson became master in May 1840 and he held the position until the mid 1840s, when George Kearon took on the role. In February 1848 Edward Kearons was master. Arthur Patrick Evans confirmed to Dr. Leslie Doyle in the mid 1950s that, shortly before his marriage to Eleanor Anne Doyle (daughter of George Enright Doyle and granddaughter of John Doyle 1793-1855), he and Eleanor Anne had visited Arklow in 1896. Whilst there they met Edward Kearons, almost half a century on from when he had served as master of the *Belle Vue* and he likely reminisced about the days importing coal from Whitehaven to Greystones.

ABOVE: The statutory form, signed by George Kearon, master of the *Belle Vue*, which was filed with the Custom House in Whitehaven on 5th August 1845. It details the ship's voyages from 1st January 1845 to 30th June 1845. She was *"employed in the coasting trade from Whitehaven to Greystones."* Two of the crew, John Fields and Michael Fields, were Greystones born. The Fields family were one of the oldest fishing families in Greystones and are featured in detail in the fishing section of Book No.7. The above voyages pre-dated the construction of the original jetty at Greystones harbour, which was not built until 1847. In fair weather, the coal would have been discharged at the rocks upon which the boat slip was later built and taken from there by cart to John Doyle's coalyard, which was situated near where the Boat Yard Gallery is today.

COAL, SLATE AND BRICKS - WHEN SCHOONERS SAILED TO GREYSTONES

From the few log records for the *Belle Vue* which have survived, it is noteworthy that during the winter months she was laid up at Dublin to avoid the risk of her loss during the worst of the winter storms. Her log record for the first half of 1857 records her as *"laying up at Dublin"* between 1st January and 17th March. She then sailed to Whitehaven before arriving in Greystones on 22nd March. She next made six voyages to Whitehaven and two to South Wales (Llanelli and Neath) before arriving back to Greystones on 30th June. From the information passed down through the Doyle family the *Belle Vue* was always regarded as being a very well built vessel. This is further confirmed by her successfully surviving a number of major storms during her existence.

LEFT: The report published in *The Illustrated London News* dated 23rd March 1844 notes that *"one of the most violent storms ever known upon the Irish coast blew from the eastward on Friday morning and Saturday. The injuries sustained by vessels and the damage done to property in Kingstown has been very considerable"*. Towards the bottom of the report, it described *"the schooner, Belle Vue, of Greystones, perfect wreck"*. The description of her status as a *"perfect wreck"* was noteworthy. Importantly, she was not described as *"sunk"*, a *"total wreck"* or *"in pieces"* as was often the description used when a vessel was lost. The term *"perfect wreck"* is a descriptive rather than a definitive technical term. While the *Belle Vue* gave every appearance of being in a terminal state, she survived to sail another day. Her crew's sense of relief would have been tinged with sadness as *"the schooner, Seymour of Bray, coal laden from Whitehaven, was overwhelmed by a sea when crossing the Burford Bank and all hands perished"*. The *Seymour* was built in Whitehaven in 1836 and owned by the Bray coal merchant, George Seymour. She was a 63 ton, 57 feet long, almost 15 feet wide, two masted schooner. The Burford Bank runs north south along the seabed at the entrance to Dublin Bay and the sea above it can be rough in stormy weather. The *Seymour* didn't benefit from the broader build that the *Belle Vue* had. The latter was over a foot wider and eight feet shorter than the *Seymour*. When the *Belle Vue* made her second voyage from Whitehaven to Greystones on 24th April 1839, the *Seymour* also departed the same day bound for Bray.

A familiar sight to walkers along Dún Laoghaire's East Pier is an imposing granite memorial to Captain John McNeil Boyd of *HMS Ajax* and five of his men, who lost their lives trying to rescue the crews of the schooners *Neptune* and *Industry*. The vessels were smashed against the rocks at the back of the pier and seven of the nine crew members drowned during the severe storm that lashed the east coast on 8th and 9th of February 1861. Between Howth Head and Wicklow Head, over the course of two days, 29 ships and many of their crew were lost. The *Belle Vue* was one of a number of coal schooners that departed Whitehaven as the storm was gathering. Bound for Greystones with her cargo of coal, against the odds, she managed to make it to the relative sanctuary of Dún Laoghaire harbour, but only just.

Eleven vessels were wrecked inside Dún Laoghaire harbour and a trail of destruction was witnessed all along the coast. Two vessels foundered at the Muglins with all hands lost and a similar fate befell two vessels off Greystones. At Wicklow harbour, ten crew members belonging to three schooners from Whitehaven, Maryport and Ardrossan were drowned during the storm. At Bray the brig, *Endeavour* from Drogheda, was wrecked but her crew rescued. Lloyd's of London recorded 135 ships lost around the coasts of Britain and Ireland, their highest number ever recorded for a single day.

The Wicklow Newsletter dated 11th February 1861 noted that a contributory factor towards the scale of the destruction was the following. *"The vessels laden with coal had been detained during the earlier part of the week by a westerly gale. The change which had taken place in the direction of the wind gave reason to believe that these ships would attempt to cross the channel. The Whitehaven coal brigs generally wait for a northeasterly wind"*.

The Dublin Weekly Nation dated 16th February 1861 reported that four of the crew of the brig, *Mary* of Warrenpoint, were drowned when she broke up on the shore at Greystones. It also noted the following. *"A most remarkable fact is that this brig was towed out of Whitehaven by the Belle Vue of Greystones, but the latter was more fortunate than her consort, for she was able to make the harbour at Kingstown, although in a disabled condition, her masts having gone over the side"*.

ABOVE: The Captain Boyd Memorial on Dún Laoghaire's East Pier.

Samuel Doyle became the master of the *Belle Vue* in August 1852 and her owner the following year. On 8th June 1859 the *Belle Vue* was sold to his mother, Martha, widow of John Doyle. The vessel's last recorded voyage to Greystones was in November 1861 when she sailed from Ardrossan. Her ownership by the Doyle family eventually ceased in March 1862, when she was mortgaged for £160 to John Barr, proprietor of Ardrossan Colliery. For the remainder of 1862 she brought coal from both Ardrossan and Troon to Dublin. In January 1863, William McJannett, a ship broker also based in Ardrossan acquired 100% ownership of the *Belle Vue*.

LEFT: Between January and September 1863, the *Belle Vue* regularly imported coal from Ardrossan to Bowmore harbour, home to one of Scotland's foremost whiskey distilleries. Bowmore is on Islay, the southernmost of the Inner Hebrides and its distillery's whiskey maturation warehouses are the oldest in Scotland.

During 1864, the *Belle Vue* regularly sailed from Ardrossan to Belfast and Derry with coal. In early August, she sailed up the River Clyde to Bowling, just up river from Dumbarton. There she was loaded with coal from the Lanarkshire coalfields destined for yet another voyage from Britain to Ireland. She cast adrift, headed down river and out into the Firth of Clyde bound for Belfast. Early on the morning of Saturday 6th August, when off Holy Isle on the east coast of the Isle of Arran, she sprang a leak. Fortunately there was time for her crew of three to get into her boat and make landfall at Lamlash. A quarter of a century after her launch, the little ship that had, more than any other, kept the home fires of Greystones burning between 1839 and 1861 slipped below the waves.

The Glasgow Herald.

No. 7671.—PUBLISHED DAILY. TUESDAY, AUGUST 9, 1864. PRICE

Lamlash, August 6.—The schooner *Bellevue*, Robertson, from Bowling to Belfast, with coals, sprung a leak and foundered off Holy Isle, Arran, early this morning. The crew, three in number, were saved in their boats and landed here.

ABOVE: The report on the loss of the *Belle Vue* in *The Glasgow Herald* dated Tuesday 9th August 1864.

BELOW: Extract from the copy register for transmission to The Chief Registrar of Shipping which provided detailed information on the *Belle Vue*. The final entry relating to a ship was always written in red ink. Usually these read "*vessel broken up*", "*vessel wrecked*" or "*sold foreign*". In the case of the *Belle Vue*, her final entry reads "*vessel lost*" 6/8/'64", formally recording her ultimate fate.

BELOW RIGHT: 1880s photograph showing the livery stables wall behind which John Doyle had his coalyard, which was operated after his death by his son, John Doyle II. Note again the house on the corner of Trafalgar Road and Victoria Road is single storey (where Spendloves is today).

WANTED, an honest, sober, steady, unmarried man, as GENERAL WORKMAN; he must understand the care of a horse, and to stand in a coal yard: must be well recommended by last employer. Wages, 10s. per week and an apartment to live in. Apply to Mr. John Doyle, Greystones.

ABOVE: Advert published in *The Wicklow Newsletter & County Advertiser* dated 3rd June 1865 seeking a general workman for John Doyle II's coalyard on wages of 10 shillings per week.

John Doyle II, like his father, had an entrepreneurial spirit. In addition to running a coal merchants, he also developed the premises which is now The Beach House, opening the Greystones Hotel there in 1858. He also built Bayswater Terrace. He had married into the Cuhbert family, schooner owners and coal importers in Bray. During the mid 1860s, his brother-in-law Richard Cuthbert, owned the 78 ton vessel, *Morning Light*, which regularly imported coal to Greystones from harbours including Whitehaven and Ardrossan. By the mid 1870s, John Doyle II had acquired the *Morning Light* from Richard Cuthbert and she continued to import coal from the Ayrshire coalfields from Troon and Ardrossan to Greystones.

Telegraphic Address:—"IRON, DUBLIN." Telephones:—Nos. 311 and 2632

ROSS & WALPOLE, LTD.,

Engineers, Millwrights,

:: :: *Boiler Makers,* :: ::

Iron and Brass Founders,

NORTH WALL IRON WORKS,

ON ADMIRALTY LIST. DUBLIN.

SHIPS DOCKED AND ALL REPAIRS EXECUTED WITH DESPATCH

ABOVE: The original cast-iron mushroom shaped bollard photographed at the top of the old boat slip in June 2007, prior to its removal and storage for safe keeping the following year by the contractors engaged in constructing the new harbour. With the distinctive patina on its lettering, from over 120 years of wear, its 1888 date commemorated the year the boat slip was constructed. It was placed with the intention of aiding the launch of the second Greystones Lifeboat, *Richard Browne,* in the event of her being called out to assist with a rescue. The boat slip was built as part of the second of the four major construction phases relating to the development of Greystones harbour when, in addition to the slipway, the dock was blasted out, the pier extended and the north wall constructed. The bollard was specially cast by the company, Ross & Walpole Limited, who were one of the firms engaged in the harbour improvement works.

Ross and Walpole were an important part of the Dublin shipbuilding industry through the latter part of the 19th century which was centred around the Graving Dock at the North Wall. Whilst the larger steel ships of between 100 and 3,000 tonnes were the preserve of firms such as the Dublin Dockyard Company and Vickers, Ross & Walpole Limited built a number of smaller vessels and are most famous for building the majority of the second fleet of Guinness barges, taking over the contract from Harland & Wolfe. The barges made by them brought the Guinness barrels from the brewery's own jetty at its St James' Gate site down the Liffey to Dublin Port. Ross & Walpole also made a number of iron bridges for the Dublin, Wicklow & Wexford Railway Company as well as some of the iron bridges on the Grand Canal.

ABOVE: Fine view looking towards the top of the old boat slip with Arthur Evans & Son Coal Merchants sign over the entrance to the small coalyard to the rear of *Wavecrest*. The cast-iron Ross & Walpole bollard can be seen at the top of the boat slip.

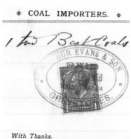

Mr. Arthur Evans, a well-known resident of Greystones, is the owner of a jackdaw which seems possessed of somewhat rare accomplishments for one of its kind. The bird in question has long been in the habit of turning on the cock of a filter, so as to allow the water to triple gently, and permit of his enjoying the cooling draught. He much relishes a bath, and when sufficient water has been poured into the bowl, he calls out lustily, "Stop! Stop!" He will hold a penny on his head while the words, "Ready! present! fire!" are repeated, and will then discharge the coin. He delights in hiding articles, and when disporting himself on the top of the house will wag his tail, slowly or quickly, in accordance with the word of command.

ABOVE: *The Wicklow People* dated 3rd December 1892 included the above interesting snippet.

ABOVE: Arthur Evans, born on 26th February 1832, was the son of Robert Grattan Evans, a fisherman and farmer. He married Anne Evans, the daughter of Robert Garrett Evans, also a fisherman and farmer at Christ Church, Delgany on 23rd July 1856. The marriage register recorded his profession as "*Mariner*". Arthur Evans was, like John Doyle (1793-1855), a man of the sea and an entrepreneur of his day. During the 1860s, he was part owner of two Greystones fishing luggers (*Lily* and *May Flower*) and one yawl (*Flower*). In 1872, he diversified into coal and shipping, owning and part owning various schooners, as well as chartering them when demand dictated. His coal importation and distribution business operated from *Wavecrest*. In addition to the coalyard there, his larger main coalyard was to the rear of where The Beach House is today. Following his death in 1917, the coal business was carried on by his son, Arthur Patrick Evans, until he sold it upon his retirement, aged 60, to William H. Dann in 1932. Arthur Evans owned a number of houses in Greystones, including *Kinvara* and *Orahova* on Church Road. He also built seven houses at the top of Killincarrig Road.

RIGHT & BELOW: The counterfoil entry from the fishing register (right) for the lugger, *May Flower*, owned by Arthur Evans. She fished out of Greystones from 1863 and was subsequently converted into the service vessel for the Codling Bank Light Ship off the Wicklow Coast. Arthur Evans held the contract to service this navigation marker for many years. The Account of Voyages for the *May Flower* covering the 2nd half of 1890 below shows that she sailed from Dún Laoghaire on set dates three times a month, weather permitting. The *May Flower* was subsequently replaced by a small trawler, the *Electric*, which Arthur Evans commissioned John Tyrrell & Sons of Arklow to build specially for fulfilling the contract to service the Codling Bank Light Ship. The contract ended in 1920 and the *Electric* was sold to a Wexford buyer by his son, Arthur Patrick Evans in 1922.

No. 341

FISHERIES—IRELAND.
Act 5 & 6 Vic. Chap. 106.

District _Kingstown_ Letter _A_
APPLICATION TO REGISTER.
The "_May Flower_"
Port or Place to which belonging, ... } _Greystones_
Owner _Arthur & John Evans_
Description of Vessel or Boat, how rigged, what Sails used, &c. } _Lugger. 5 Sails_
Mode of Fishing _Herring_
Tonnage _12 tons_
Length of Keel _40 feet_
No. of Men _7_ } Usually employed.
No. of Boys _0_ }
Signature of Applicant _Arthur Evans John Evans_
Residence _Greystones_

Above particulars Certified to be correct.
Signature _W. H. Harris_
Rank _Lieutenant_
Station _Greystones_ in _Kingstown_ District.
Dated this _20th_ day of _May_ 1863.

No. allotted _26_ of _1st_ Class.
No of Certificate _26_
Date of Registry _23rd May /63_

LIST D.
ACCOUNT OF VOYAGES AND CREW OF HOME TRADE SHIP, TO BE DELIVERED HALF-YEARLY TO THE SUPERINTENDENT OF A MERCANTILE MARINE OFFICE.

Name of Ship	Official Number	Port of Registry	Registered Tonnage	REGISTERED MANAGING OWNER		MASTER			Date of Commencement of Half-year	Date of Termination of Half-year
				Name	Address	Name	No. of Certificate (if any)	Address		
May Flower	95-314	Dublin	17.95	Arthur Evans	Wavecrest Greystones	Matthew Doyle		13 Cumberland St. Kingstown	July 1st 1890	Dec 31st 1890

ACCOUNT OF VOYAGES (*)

Attending Codling Bank Light Ship from Kingstown on 1st 10th and 20th of each month or as soon after as weather permits each trip occupying about twelve hours

COAL, SLATE AND BRICKS - WHEN SCHOONERS SAILED TO GREYSTONES

Book No.7 includes a detailed timeline history of the development of Greystones harbour. Whilst there was always a strong desire locally to construct a pier, coupled with a financial commitment towards its cost given by the La Touche family, ultimately a lack of finance precluded its development until 1847. The original jetty built that year enabled schooners to tie up alongside it, but gave very limited shelter to any craft in rough seas. The arrival of the lifeboat in 1872, which had to be launched over the shingle beach on its carriage, immediately highlighted the need for a boat slip to be built, a point which the lifeboat inspector made at the time. By April 1875, the records of the Greystones Lifeboat reveal that the Board of Works were *"now about to construct a slipway 10 feet wide for the use of the coast guard."* The lifeboat committee confirmed that the Institution would be prepared to bear the additional cost involved in making the slipway 16 feet wide to accommodate the *Sarah Tancred* on her carriage.

In 1878, the annual report for the Commissioners of Public Works in Ireland noted that an application *"to construct a quay and landing slip with approaches at Greystones was not recommended."* In a letter dated 7th August 1883 to the Editor of *The Dublin Daily Express*, engineer James Price wrote *"from an intimate knowledge of most of the coast and fisheries of Ireland, I do not think there are 25 places unprovided with harbours possessing so many advantages as Greystones, both for facility of construction and certainty of its at once being used largely for fishing, in fact the population are first class seamen and well accustomed to fishing. Perhaps it is not generally known that the prize for best essay on the preservation of nets, offered by Baroness Burdett-Coutts to the whole Kingdom was won by Mr Arthur Evans of Greystones, the speaker for the fishermen at the meeting on Saturday. Trevor, who spoke is skipper of a schooner of Mr Evans, who trades in coal at Greystones and he states that except in one point he knows of no anchorage equal to the tough marly bottom outside the pier at Greystones. If one twenty fifth part of the £250,000 be allocated to Greystones, it will truly be a sound and useful application of the money, forming a near refuge, even for the boats of strangers."*

Baroness Burdett-Coutts was the granddaughter of Thomas Coutts, who founded the bank, Coutts & Co. She was a noted philanthropist who supported many causes, one of which was the promotion of the fishing industry in Ireland. A copy of the winning essay written by Arthur Evans in 1874 which was entered in the competition organised by Baroness Burdett-Coutts is included in Book No.4. The essay, titled "Essay on the best means to prevent nets from rotting", was published in London and formed a valuable guide for fishermen to follow around the coasts of Britain and Ireland.

After much agitation, a Government grant of £20,678 was eventually approved to build a harbour at Greystones comprising of (i) a concrete pier 200 feet long, measured on the wharf's coping and 35 feet wide exclusive of the parapet, with two flights of steps and six mooring posts (ii) a concrete boat slip 156 feet long or thereabouts and 20 feet wide (iii) an inner dock for small boats, with an approach road around the side to the pier and (iv) a concrete groyne 345 feet long or thereabouts.

Following the construction of the original jetty at the harbour in 1847, schooners sailed to Greystones harbour. Their numbers increased following the pier extension in 1887 and 1888. Many of the old photos of the harbour show up to three schooners tied up alongside the pier at any one time. Nevertheless, schooners sailing to and from Greystones harbour did so within its constraints. These included its largely unprotected aspect which laid it open to the brunt of storms. This was starkly illustrated in 1892 and 1910 with tragic consequences (for the Doyle families in the case of the former). The situation wasn't helped by an unwillingness by either Wicklow Grand Jury or the government to assume responsibility for the harbour following the enhancements made in the late 1880s and undertake the necessary repairs to the dilapidating structure. Likewise, the issue of the harbour silting up which greatly impacted the ability of schooners to operate, except during high tide, was never properly addressed. Despite all this, through the determined efforts of men like Arthur Evans, Greystones harbour did manage to enjoy a period when a significant tonnage of coal was imported. On 29th May 1891 Arthur Evans acquired the former slate-carrying schooner, *Velinheli,* for £850. Her previous owner was John Deane, of Blackburn, Lancashire, a slate merchant, who used the ship to export slate from the Dinorwic quarry in Gwynedd, out through Port Dinorwic (now Y Felinheli) on the Menai Strait to various ports around Britain and Ireland.

ABOVE: Photograph taken from the railway bridge in the late 1880s with a schooner in the harbour and the lifeboat house with its round granite finials on its gable ends. Note the fishing snuffs pulled up onto the grass and the flagstaff dressed with flags.

ABOVE: Photograph taken in the early 1970s prior to the spreading of topsoil over the rocks to form a grassy bank. As part of the works to extend the pier, the boat slip was also constructed in 1888. It was a favourite spot for people to gather in the evening sun.

ABOVE: Details of Kingstown shipping for Monday 30th July 1866 published in *The Freeman's Journal*. Among the "windbound" vessels was the *Henry*, a 64 ton vessel owned by Henry Fox of Wicklow, which departed Greystones for Barrow carrying a cargo of pit wood. It is known that the *Belle Vue* regularly exported timber from Greystones (sourced from the La Touche family estate at *Bellevue*) for use as pit props in the coal mines at Whitehaven. It is thus not surprising that timber was also exported from Greystones to nearby Barrow to be used in its ore mines. Pit wood, principally sourced from estates in Windermere and Argyleshire, enabled Barrow's steel works (using its locally mined ore) to become the largest in the world during the latter half of the 19th century. During the mid to late 1860s many Wexford vessels exported pit wood. *The Wexford Independent* dated 1st September 1866 listed five vessels departing Wexford with pit wood (three of which were bound for Barrow). Half a century later, when J.G. McEntagart's schooner, *Mersey*, was wrecked on Anglesey in January 1905, she was carrying a cargo of pit props from Bray to Garston. The information about the two vessels listed as "off the harbour" in the above clipping is also interesting, with the *Neptune* arriving from Norway carrying a cargo of ice. This was at the height of the summer, in an era before electric refrigeration.

ABOVE: Press clipping from *The Manchester Courier & Lancashire General Advertiser* newspaper dated Thursday 21st October 1880. Greystones takes its place alongside the likes of New York, Rangoon, Montevideo and Valparaiso in the "*Liverpool Shipping News*" section listing vessels "*Arrived*" and "*Sailed*", with the arrival into Liverpool of the schooner, *Sarah Jane,* on Tuesday 19th October 1880. The *Sarah Jane* was a 46 ton schooner registered at Dublin. Acquired by Arthur Evans in 1883, she was driven ashore and wrecked at Greystones in October 1886 carrying a cargo of coal from Troon.

FOLLOWING PAGE: Series of photographs discovered a number of years ago in an old album given to the National Maritime Museum in Dún Laoghaire, to whom we are grateful for their kind permission to reproduce here. Taken in 1891, they provide the best known photographic record of a collier under sail approaching Greystones harbour and discharging her coal. In the lower photograph, the ripple on the water on her port bow can be seen as she lowers her anchor in advance of entering the harbour.

Collier entering Greystones Harbour Co Wicklow 1891

Collier coming to an anchor - Greystones

same

Discharging coal – Greystones

ABOVE & RIGHT: 1880s photograph of a top-sail schooner tied up to the 1847 jetty discharging coal. The close-up section on the right shows a full lift of coal sacks being hoisted from the hold, with men on the pier operating the lifting crane using a pulley block system. Two crew men, partially obscured by the rigging, can be seen on the deck of the schooner supervising the unloading. A simple ladder, placed between the schooner's gunwale and the jetty, served as a gang plank.

THE HARBOUR, GREYSTONES

ABOVE: Colourtone postcard from the early 1900s featuring Arthur Evans' coal schooner, *Velinheli,* moored alongside the extended pier. Smoke from a Dublin bound steam train running along Morrris' banks can be seen.

ABOVE: Photograph taken in the 1880s of a schooner alongside the 1847 built jetty prior to its subsequent extension between 1886 and 1888. *The Dublin Daily Express* dated 9th October 1888, reported that "*the jetty was formerly approached by a steep road along the edge of the rocks*". The newspaper further reported that following the construction of the dock, the new approach onto the pier "*had an incline of only 1 in 25, to the manifest benefit of horses employed in drawing loads from the vessels*". The photograph also reveals a fine view of the natural rock formation prior to the blasting out of the dock and construction of the boat slip.

ABOVE: Discharging coal in 1911. The crack in the upper storm wall which collapsed the following year creating a gap is visible.

ABOVE: Early 1900s photograph of the *Velinheli* alongside the pier, with the *Mersey* and the *Reciprocity* abreast. Kneeling on the left, repairing whelk pots, is George Archer, eldest son of Edward Archer (the last Coxswain of the Greystones Lifeboat). The "sallies" used for weaving the pots were made of hazel or willow, soaked several days before use to make them pliable.

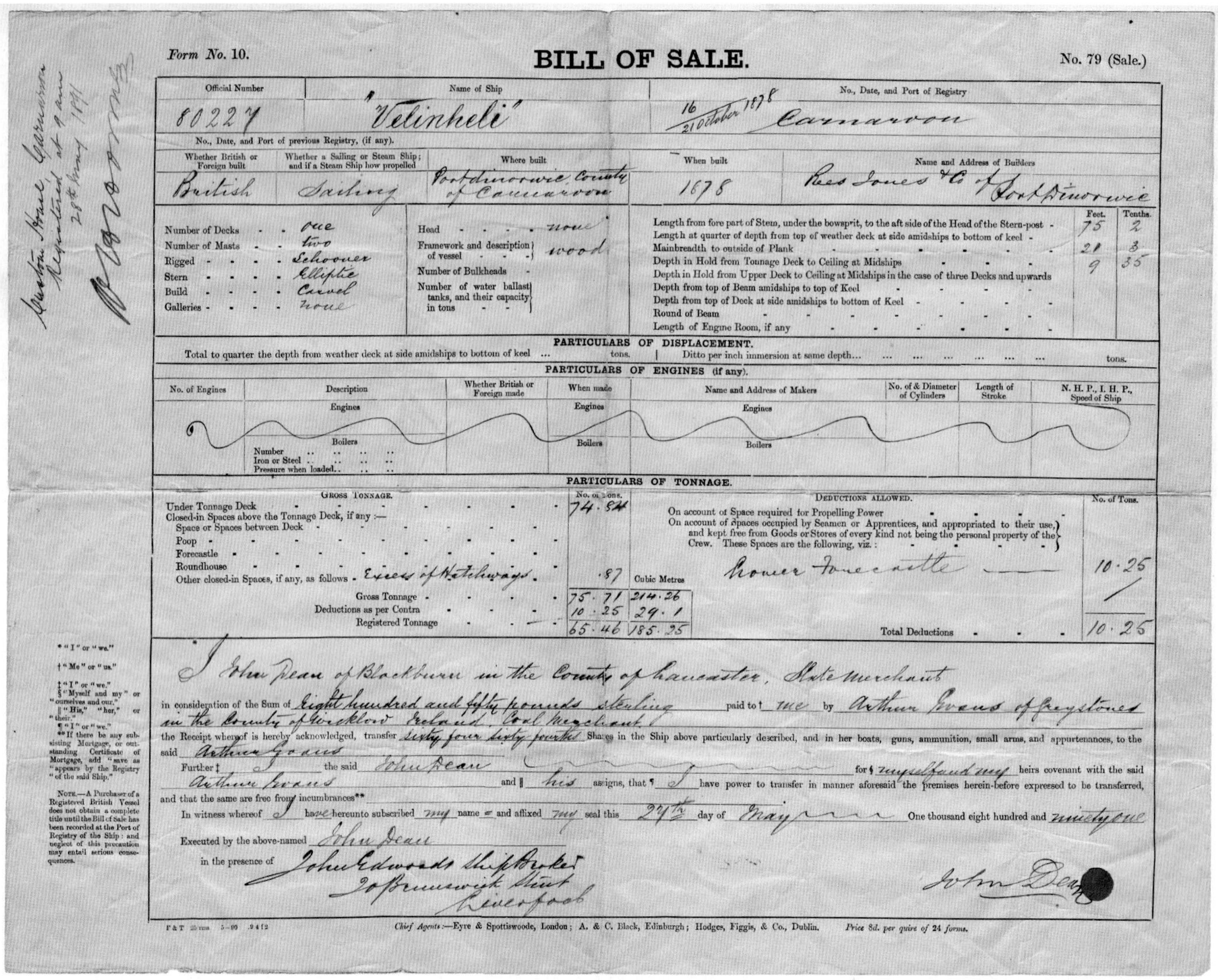

Form No. 10.

BILL OF SALE.

No. 79 (Sale.)

The image shows an original handwritten Bill of Sale document for the ship "Velinheli", Official Number 80227, registered at Carnarvon, built 1878 by Rees Jones & Co. of Portdinorwic. Built British, Sailing, at Portdinorwic County of Carnarvon. One deck, two masts, Schooner rigged, Elliptic stern, Carvel build. Gross tonnage figures and registered tonnage 65.46. The sale is from John Deane of Blackburn in the County of Lancaster, Slate merchant, in consideration of eight hundred and fifty pounds Sterling paid by Arthur Evans of Greystones in the County of Wicklow, Ireland, Coal Merchant, dated 27th day of May one thousand eight hundred and ninety one.

ABOVE: The original bill of sale dated 27th May 1891 for the £850 purchase of the 1878 built *Velinheli* by Arthur Evans of Greystones from its previous owner, John Deane, a slate merchant. It was in this year that the two largest slate quarries, Penrhyn and Dinorwic, began to invest in steam ships, which were more cost-effective to operate in the slate trade. Wooden schooners like the *Velinheli* which had exported slate were sold to ship owners to operate as coastal trading vessels, in the shipment of coal in particular.

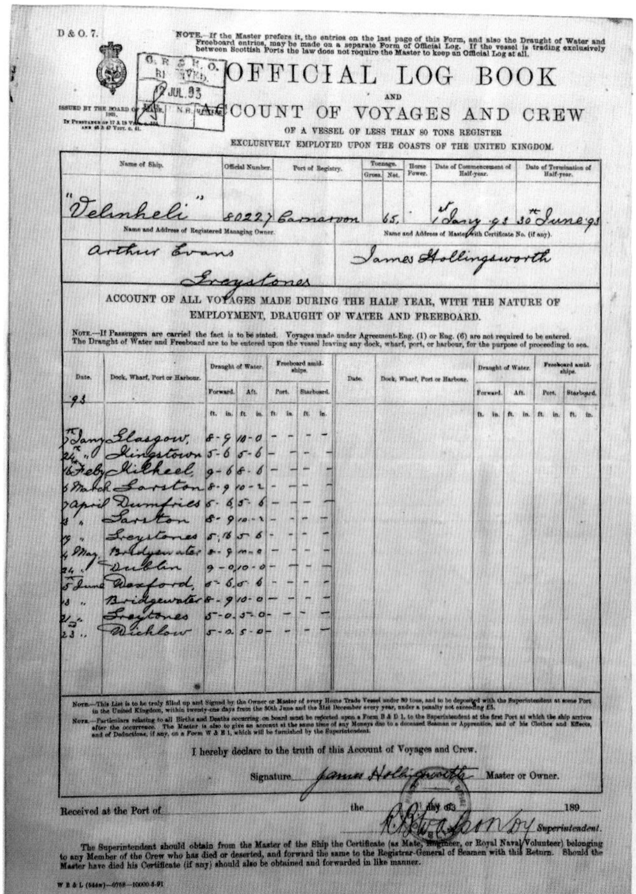

The image shows an Official Log Book page for the "Velinheli", Official Number 80227, Port of Registry Carnarvon, Tonnage 65, covering the half year 1 January 1893 to 30 June 1893. Registered Managing Owner Arthur Evans, Greystones. Master James Hollingsworth. It contains an account of all voyages made during the half year, listing ports including Glasgow, Kingstown, Kilkeel, Garston, Dumfries, Garston, Greystones, Bridgwater, Dublin, Wexford, Bridgwater, Greystones, Wicklow.

LEFT: Log book of the *Velinheli* covering the six month period from January to June 1893. Arthur Evans & Son imported 130 tons of bricks in 1892-1893 and the log entry for June 1893 records the *Velinheli* sailing from Bridgwater in Somerset to Greystones. Bridgwater was famous for red brick production and this shipment coincided with the construction of the Grand Hotel on Trafalgar Road, which opened in June 1894.

ABOVE: Pre 1910 photograph of the *Velinheli,* either coal-laden or in-ballast alongside Greystones pier.

ABOVE: Broadside view of the *Velinheli* in 1911 coming alongside Greystones pier.

LEFT: The only known photograph of the crew of the *Velinheli*. The man on the left was the ship's cook. It was common for ships to have a cat on board and when the *Velinheli* was rammed and sunk in January 1915, all four crew members plus the cat survived. In a letter to Derek Paine in December 1986 about the era when schooners sailed to Greystones, Dr. Leslie Doyle wrote that "*the Velinheli particularly was part of the Greystones folklore in the two decades before 1910, the final 20 years of the golden age of the harbour area*". With her top-sail rig, the *Velinheli* was undoubtedly the most majestic of all the Greystones schooners during the near eight decades when sailing ships called to the harbour. The name *Velinheli* is the anglicised version of Y Felinheli (the modern name of Port Dinorwic on the Menai Strait where she was built). Felinheli means salt water mill in Welsh.

ABOVE: Fine view of the *Velinheli* alongside the pier in Bray harbour in March 1906. This was after she had run aground on the beach just south of the harbour, before being re-floated.

COAL, SLATE AND BRICKS - WHEN SCHOONERS SAILED TO GREYSTONES

John George McEntagart was born in Kolcatta (Calcutta), India in July 1847, the son of an army sergeant. In 1884 he acquired what is now The Beach House, after the death of John Doyle II (1836-1883). This also included the coal import business and coal store which continued to be supplied by various schooners sailing to Greystones. In 1889, with the completion of the pier extension at Greystones, J.G. McEntagart acquired the *Mersey*, a 49 ton schooner built in Runcorn in 1842. She had been under the ownership of John Nolan of Wicklow since the 1860s, predominantly employed importing coal to Wicklow harbour. Despite her age, over the following decade and a half she was the main vessel supplying McEntagart's coal merchants at the harbour. In October 1892, she was involved in the tragedy in which three members of the Doyle family (including the Coxswain of the Greystones Lifeboat, John Doyle) drowned, with J.G. McEntagart entering the sea from the beach in a vain attempt to try to save them.

Fifteen months later in January 1894, the *Mersey* was again caught in a storm at Greystones harbour. Two of her crew stranded aboard her were rescued by the coast guards using the breeches buoy and rocket apparatus. The *Mersey* herself was beached and successfully re-floated at high tide three days later, sustaining only minor damage to her stern post. In October 1896, she was bound for Greystones, laden with coal from Point of Ayr when she got into difficulties in rough seas off the north coast of Anglesey. Her crew of three had to be rescued by the Cemaes Bay RNLI Lifeboat but the *Mersey* survived to sail another day.

By 1901, J.G. McEntagart sought to devote more time to his other main business, the Empire restaurant at 29 Nassau Street, Dublin. He placed an auction notice seeking to dispose of his entire Greystones business, comprising of his licensed premises, then known as The Beach, as well as his coal schooner, *Mersey*. The sale did not proceed however and he continued to run the business, eventually selling it to the manager of The Beach, William H. Dann in January 1907. By this time, the *Mersey* had fallen victim to a huge storm that engulfed the whole of Britain and Ireland on 15th January 1905. The sea at Southend froze over to a distance of 200 yards from the shore and three feet of snow fell across the north of Ireland as gales battered the coastline. The 63 year old *Mersey*, bound for Garston with a cargo of pit props from Bray, was driven ashore and wrecked near Black Point, the easterly most point on Anglesey. Fortunately her crew were safely evacuated, but her loss prompted J.G. McEntagart to seek a newer replacement.

In May 1905 he bought the *Confido*, a 69 ton two masted ketch, 80 feet in length. Built in Galmpton, Devon in 1885, she had mainly operated on the east coast of England. Sadly, the *Confido* was not to enjoy the narrow escapes that the *Mersey* had once enjoyed. Exactly a year to the day after William H. Dann had signed a £600 mortgage provided by J.G. McEntagart to finance his purchase of the *Confido*, she was wrecked at Arklow in a storm on 8th January 1908.

ARKLOW WRECK.

The wreck of the Greystones ketch Confidio off Arklow. The vessel was bound for Kynochs with 130 tons of coal, and it was with great difficulty the crew were saved.

The Wicklow Newsletter dated 11th January 1908 reported that *"efforts were made to save the vessel, but nothing could be done for her as she swung with a suddenness and a velocity round the pier head which defied any services put forth to prevent her being cast ashore. She was tossed like a cork on the waves until she ran into an angle formed by the pier and the plateau of sands on the north side of the harbour, where she foundered after a terrible struggle. The men aboard were in great danger and when the ship was gone, attention was turned to their rescue. At first it was considered advisable to bring out the lifeboat, but as the Confido was quite close to the pier, the crew climbed out along the jib boom and got on terra firma after a very thrilling experience, the captain and the mate being the last to come ashore. They were drenched through and through and were taken in charge by the local people, members of whom gave all the assistance in their power. All night the vessel was watched, but this morning it was discovered she was a total wreck and at 10 o'clock she was breaking in pieces, the sea washing through her"*.

Her certificate of registry noted her status in March 1899 as a *"recovered wreck"* in Faversham, Kent. Sadly, she was now beyond repair and in an attempt to recoup some of his losses, William Dann instructed an Arklow auctioneer, Daniel Condren, to sell her as a wreck (masts, rigging, windlass, etc.) the following month. The final entry in her official register, written in red ink as was customary, stated *"registry closed 27th April 1908, vessel about to be broken up, advice received from owners"*.

Arthur Evans & Son had suffered the loss of the 46 ton schooner, *Sarah Jane*, laden with coal from Troon and driven ashore and wrecked at Greystones in October 1886. Since her purchase in 1891, the *Velinheli* had encountered her share of near misses, such as her deliberate scuttling in Greystones harbour four years later. *The Wicklow People* dated 26th October 1895, under the story, *"A Greystones Vessel In Distress"* reported the following. *"On Tuesday the schooner, Velinheli, laden with 140 tons of coal, bound from Garston to Greystones was in distress at the last named place and in consequence of the heavy sea that was running, it was deemed advisable to sink her. Her bottom was auger-bored shortly afterwards and she sank just inside the harbour. If this had not been done, the probabilities are that she would have been wrecked on the beach. The vessel, which is owned by Mr Arthur Evans, Greystones, was successfully floated on Thursday evening"*.

Just over a decade later, she survived another scare. On 20th March 1906, with a cargo of coal from Garston for coal merchant, John Plunkett of Quinnsboro Road, Bray, the crew was anxious to enter Bray harbour ahead of high tide and an impending storm. Mistiming her entrance, she grounded her bow on the sand and was blown onto the beach just south of the harbour, her crew securing her before evacuating. *The Irish News* dated 22nd March 1906 highlighted her precarious status, reporting that *"the ship is in a very dangerous position and may become a wreck"*. The report also noted that the Clyde Steamship Company's tug, *Flying Sprite,* based at Dublin port had been unsuccessful in attempting to pull her off the beach. She was eventually re-floated, albeit with some damage to her keel, resulting in her hold leaking, causing her cargo to be water damaged.

ABOVE: *Velinheli* aground on Bray Beach in March 1906.

COAL, SLATE AND BRICKS - WHEN SCHOONERS SAILED TO GREYSTONES

In October 1910, a storm at Greystones harbour badly damaged three vessels, the *Velinheli, Reciprocity* and the *Federation*. The repercussions were far reaching. Marine insurance for trading vessels entering Greystones harbour was no longer available following this event. With the harbour decaying and constantly prone to silting up, the loss of insurance cover significantly impacted the tonnage of coal imported from this point onwards. The photographs taken in October 1910 on this and the following two pages have been digitally reproduced from the original glass negatives, using the latest high resolution scanning technology. For the first time they reveal in clearer detail the substantial damage caused to the vessels.

ABOVE: The *Velinheli* and *Reciprocity* lie next to the 1847 jetty with a group of men just visible through their rigging inspecting the damage. Two horses and carts can be seen making their way along the beach after unloading cargo from the *Federation,* aground by the boat slip. The flagstaff is just visible on the extreme right. The two children are believed to be Samuel A French and his sister, Henrietta.

ABOVE: Three men can be seen on the bowsprit of the *Velinheli*, securing her sails and rigging. The damage caused to the corner of the 1847 jetty, when the bowsprit of the *Reciprocity* dislodged some of the blocks during the height of the storm, can be clearly seen. Laden with coal and half submerged, the *Reciprocity* was driven under the stern of the *Velinheli*, shearing off her aft, port and starboard bulwarks revealing her ribs. The damage to the bulwarks on the aft of the *Velinheli* is also visible.

ABOVE, BELOW & OPPOSITE PAGE: The *Federation* is aground on the beach, her bow secured by a chain. A heavy swell is still rolling into the harbour as a number of men are on the deck of the stricken *Reciprocity*, with one of her spars in the water tied to her starboard side. Like the *Federation*, she was a ketch, with her fore mast higher than her aft or mizzen mast. Book Nos.1 & 2 include photos taken earlier during the storm showing the *Reciprocity's* mizzen mast and boom still in place. The mast and yardarms of the *Velinheli* are visible on the left of the photo on the opposite page.

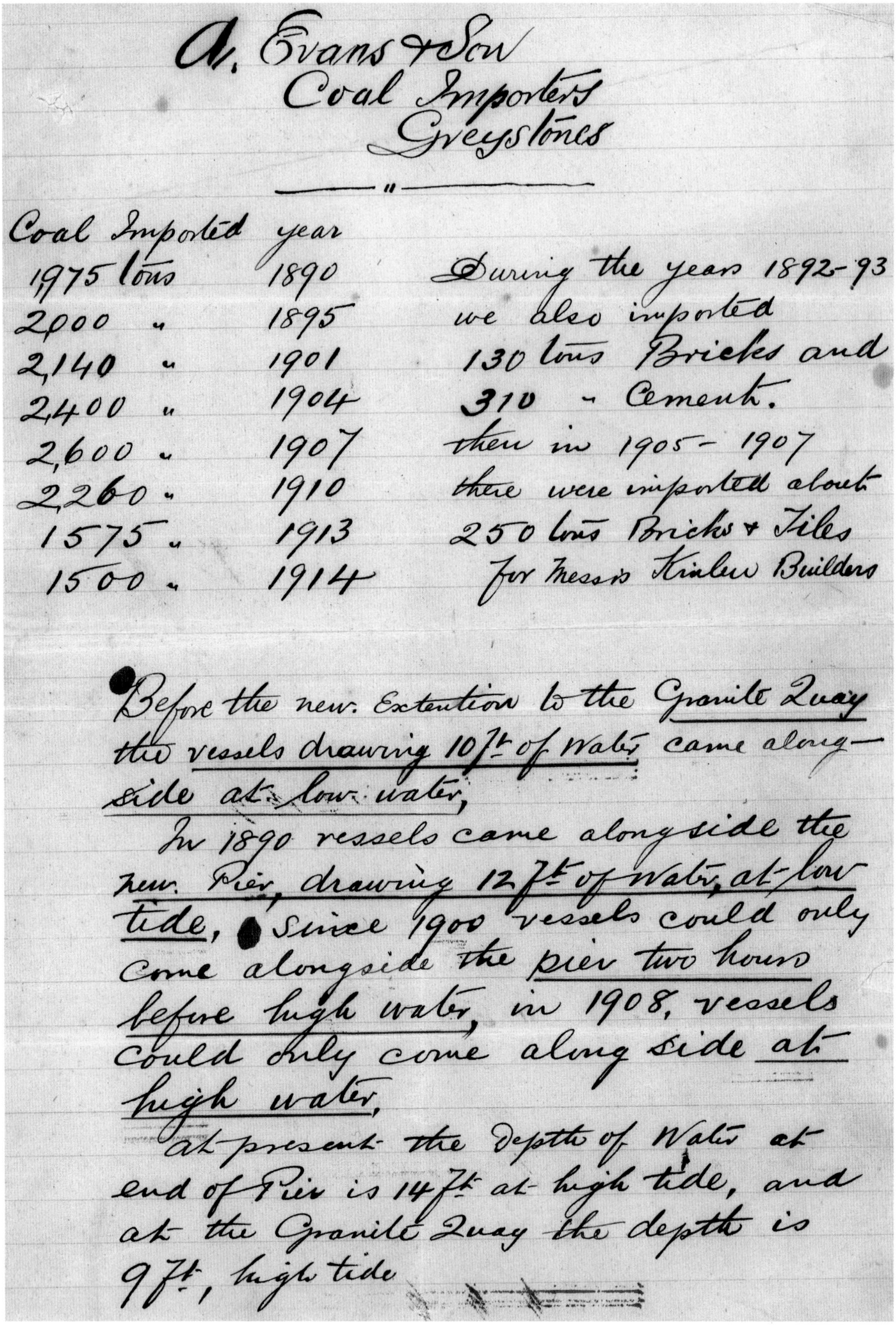

A. Evans + Son
Coal Importers
Greystones

———"———

Coal Imported	year
1975 tons	1890
2000 "	1895
2,140 "	1901
2,400 "	1904
2,600 "	1907
2260 "	1910
1575 "	1913
1500 "	1914

During the years 1892-93 we also imported 130 tons Bricks and 310 " Cement. then in 1905 - 1907 there were imported about 250 tons Bricks + Tiles for Messrs Kinlen Builders

Before the new. Extention to the Granite Quay the vessels drawing 10ft of Water came alongside at low water,

In 1890 vessels came alongside the new. Pier, drawing 12ft of Water, at low tide, Since 1900 vessels could only come alongside the pier two hours before high water, in 1908, vessels could only come along side at high water,

At present the depth of Water at end of Pier is 14ft at high tide, and at the Granite Quay the depth is 9ft, high tide

ABOVE: One of the most important historical documents relating to the era when schooners sailed into Greystones. It was written around 1915 by Arthur Patrick Evans, son of Arthur Evans senior, who established the family run coal import and distribution business in 1872. The business was run from *Wavecrest*. It is believed that the document was prepared as part of a submission to seek assistance regarding the silting up of the harbour. In addition to recording the depth of water in the harbour, it details the tonnage of coal imported from 1890 through to 1914. Note the substantial decrease in volumes post 1910, when marine insurance cover for vessels entering Greystones harbour was no longer obtainable. It also recorded that 130 tons of bricks and 310 tons of cement were imported during the years 1892-93. This coincided with the building of the Grand Hotel (La Touche Hotel), which officially opened in June 1894. It also recorded the tonnage of bricks and tiles which were imported for Messrs. Kinlen Builders between the years 1905-1907. P.J. Kinlen of *Montrose*, Church Road, was a builder and contractor who built the Holy Rosary Church as well as a number of houses in The Burnaby, where Kinlen Road is named after him. By way of comparison, Bray harbour imported 7,672 tons of coal and 21,000 bricks through sailing vessels in 1900.

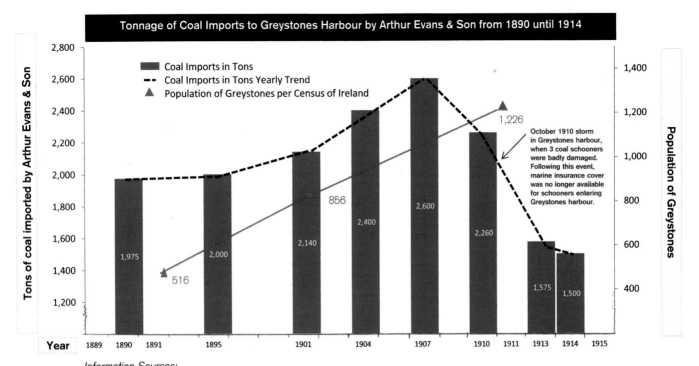

Tonnage of Coal Imports to Greystones Harbour by Arthur Evans & Son from 1890 until 1914

Legend:
- Coal Imports in Tons
- Coal Imports in Tons Yearly Trend
- Population of Greystones per Census of Ireland

Data labels: 1,975; 2,000; 2,140; 2,400; 2,600; 2,260; 1,575; 1,500

Population markers: 516; 856; 1,226

October 1910 storm in Greystones harbour, when 3 coal schooners were badly damaged. Following this event, marine insurance cover was no longer available for schooners entering Greystones harbour.

Information Sources:
Arthur Evans & Son, Coal Importers, "Wavecrest", Greystones Harbour.
Census of Ireland Population Statistics for Greystones for 1891, 1901 & 1911, as disclosed in Thom's Directory.

BELOW: Mounted photograph entitled "*Greystones Wreck*" showing the *Velinheli* and the sunken *Reciprocity* in Greystones harbour following the October 1910 storm. It was taken by Jesse St. Aubyn, photographer, of *Annaville*, Church Road (formerly of *Brooklands House*, Trafalgar Road). The handwriting provides additional information about the three damaged vessels "*Schooner, Velinheli, Reg. Dublin, owner, A. Evans & Son, Flat Barge, Reciprocity, Reg. Liverpool, on charter to A. Evans & Son, Flat Barge, Federation was ashore on beach inside the harbour, on charter*". The *Reciprocity* and *Federation* were also known as "*Liverpool Flats*" or "*Welsh Flats*". Their barge-like flat bottoms were ideally suited to tidal harbours along the North Wales coast, as they remained upright at low tide. Accordingly their design also helped them contend with the challenges posed by the silting up of Greystones harbour.

RIGHT: Whilst Anglesey did have some coal reserves (known as levels), these were small, opencast mine deposits, located inland for local consumption. Point of Ayr, lying at the northern most point of the Welsh mainland was the closest geographically of all the coal harbours visited by the schooners importing coal to Greystones. It formed part of the North Wales Coalfield. As with Whitehaven, the pit heads were beside the sea. Schooners had to time their arrival and departure as they could only access the loading quay at high water. Throughout the 1890s and 1900s Arthur Evans, J.G. McEntagart and William H. Dann all regularly imported coal from Point of Ayr. It and Garston had become the main coal exporting points for Greystones schooners by this time. Coal mining at Point of Ayr continued after privatisation and ceased in 1997 when the pits were closed. In September 2015, a memorial featuring the headframe from one of the former Point of Ayr coal shafts was unveiled to mark the history of coal mining along this stretch of the Welsh coast.

POINT OF AYR COLLIERY FFYNNONGROEW

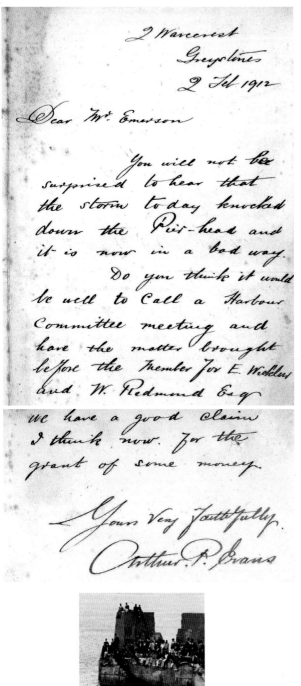

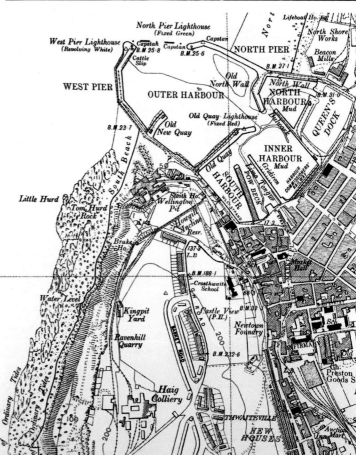

ABOVE: Map of Whitehaven dated 1923 showing the Wellington Pit on the headland overlooking the harbour. Sunk by John Peile between 1838 and 1845, it was likely that much of the coal imported to Greystones came form this pit. Coal mining in Whitehaven ceased in 1986 when the Haig Colliery (marked towards the bottom of the map) closed.

LEFT: Letter written by Arthur Patrick Evans dated 2nd February 1912 to John Emerson who was Honorary Secretary of the Greystones Harbour Committee at the time.

OPPOSITE PAGE RIGHT: William Redmond M.P., referred to in the letter was the younger brother of John Redmond, leader of The Irish Parlimentarty Party. He took an interest in the deteriorating state of Greystones harbour and had visited it with the Chief Secretary for Ireland, Augustine Birrell in October 1910 following the damage caused by a storm (refer also to the section on the suffragettes on page 198). He served in World War One and was killed in action at the Battle of Messines Ridge in Flanders on 7th June 1917. He was posthumously awarded the Légion d'Honneur by the French Government.

ABOVE: Close-up photo showing the gap in the storm wall of the pier caused by the storm in February 1912.

BALLINA PARK,
ASHFORD,
Co. WICKLOW.
Wicklow 4218.

6th February 1978

Dear Mr.Payne,

With reference to your letter about Greystones in the Wicklow People the enclosed photograph may be of slight interest. Taken in 1915 when we as children were taken to Greystones for a Summer holiday it shows the sailing ships that brought in the coal in those days.

The coal was unloaded by means of a bucket and winch hauled up by the horse shown in the picture. No dieselengines or fork lift trucks in those days.

Standing watching is probably my brother, with governess and friend.

Yours sincerely,

(Charles Tighe)

ABOVE: The response from Mr Charles Tighe of Ashford, Co. Wicklow in reply to a letter from Derek Paine to *The Wicklow People* in 1978 seeking old photos and information about the coal schooners that used to import coal into Greystones. As previously mentioned, coal schooners continued to import coal into Greystones after 1910, albeit in fewer numbers, despite the inability to obtain marine insurance. Group Captain Charles Tighe OBE DFC was a member of the Tighe family which, at one time owned estates in Wicklow and Kilkenny, including *Woodstock House* at Inistioge. He joined the Royal Air Force in 1925 as a pilot officer. He rose through the ranks to squadron leader and finally to group captain during World War Two, when he was present at the fall of France. Mentioned in despatches, he won a Distinguished Flying Cross in 1936 for operations in Palestine. He was awarded an OBE in 1946.

ABOVE: John Emerson, Hon. Secretary of the Greystones Harbour Committee in 1912.

ABOVE: Taken from an old album, this is believed to be the only known photograph of a schooner with all her sails up in Greystones harbour. It is dated 1910.

Throughout the era of schooners sailing from Greystones, integral to ensuring a safe voyage was their use of ballast. Gravel removed from the North Beach was the principal form of ballast used. This practice was undoubtedly a contributory factor towards the houses on the North Beach being washed away between 1929 and 1931. Jim Kinsella, who ran his coal merchants business in Blacklion for many years, was interviewed in *East Coast* dated 26th April 1974. He recalled the days when his father, "Blacktop" Kinsella, was employed by Arthur Evans & Son. "*My father worked at the old schooners, clearing the coal boat, Velinheli. She used to be around 140 tons. It used to work out about a quid a week in pay. Start at six o'clock each morning and finish at two o'clock the next day with 38 tons of ballast in her. Ballast would be stones off the beach. I think it was around a tanner a ton or eight pence a ton they paid at the time for ballast.*"

RIGHT: "Blacktop" Kinsella and Cornelius Salmon having their lunch on the bench opposite Dann's.

LEFT: A little part of Greystones that is forever Scotland. The 650 metre long, 10 metre high and up to 28 metres wide Ballast Bank at Troon was made from ballast stones and sand deposited by the coal schooners arriving over many decades to take on coal. A similar man-made ballast bank exists (most of which has largely disappeared due to redevelopment) at Irvine, seven miles north along the Ayrshire coast. It was known locally as "Wee Ireland", in reference to the schooners arriving with ballast from Ireland. A number of Greystones schooners, including the *Velinheli* and the *Sarah Jane,* imported coal from both Troon and Irvine after depositing ballast stones taken from the North Beach upon their arrival in Scotland (see also page 38). The Ballast Bank today provides protection for Troon's marina. The view from its top, looking 14 miles due west across the Firth of Clyde is to Holy Isle, off Arran, the final resting place of John Doyle's Greystones built schooner, *Belle Vue.*

BELOW: The account of voyages for the 46 ton Arklow owned vessel, *Sarah Jane,* for the second half of 1883 shows that she brought ballast from Greystones to both Troon and Irvine.

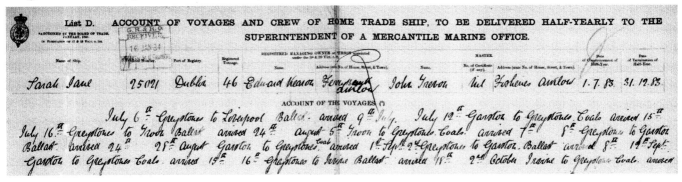

LEFT: Jim Kinsella standing at the entrance to his coalyard in Blacklion (also shown in the May 2018 photograph above). When Arthur Patrick Evans retired and sold his coal business to William H. Dann in 1933, Jim Kinsella set up his own coal business at Blacklion.

COAL, SLATE AND BRICKS - WHEN SCHOONERS SAILED TO GREYSTONES

The outbreak of World War One added another dimension to the challenges facing the schooners that crossed the Irish Sea on their regular coal runs. In addition to having to cope with the usual problems posed by unpredictable weather, it wasn't long into the war that the threat from German U-boat activity became apparent. The German Navy had 36 U-boats in commission when the war started. Though the initial focus was to target warships, the sinking of the British steamship, *Glitra*, captured and scuttled by the German U-boat *U-17* on 20th October 1914 off Norway, signalled that the threat to merchant shipping was real. By February 1915, the German Navy had added a further nine U-boats to its fleet, taking the total to 45. Capable of operating at sea for up to three weeks at a time, the U-boats were well able to attack shipping in the Irish Sea. December 1914 was a quiet month during which the German Navy did not sink a single enemy ship. Before sunrise on 1st January 1915, the U-boat *U 24* crept up on the 15,000 ton pre-dreadnought battleship, *Formidable*, torpedoing her at point-blank range of 100 metres in the English Channel, with the loss of 547 lives. On 21st January the first merchant ship, the 1,301 ton British steamer, *Durward*, to be sunk by a U-boat in almost two months went down off the Belgian coast. The threat to shipping in the Irish Sea was growing and the German U-boat commanders knew that the approaches to Liverpool offered many targets should they wish to attack. On 30th January six British steamers, totalling just under 12,000 tons, were sunk in a single day (three in the English Channel and three off Liverpool sunk by U-boat *U 21*).

For Arthur Evans the increased risk was apparent. The *Velinheli* regularly sailed to Garston to import coal and thus had to negotiate the waters of Liverpool Bay when entering and leaving the Mersey. This was wartime and every precaution had to be taken to minimise the risk. It was on the evening of Monday 25th January 1915, when the *Velinheli* had departed Garston and was in Liverpool Bay that it was sunk in a collision with the *S.S. Laertes*, indirectly as a result of the U-boat threat. Leonard Evans, who was 12 years old at the time, wrote the following to Dr Leslie Doyle in 1978. *"The Velinheli was lost in 1915 near the Bar Lightship during a submarine scare in a collision with the steamship, Laertes (from South Africa), all vessels sailing without lights at this time. The crew were saved as the S.S. Laertes' bow was into the vessel amidships and when the crew were aboard the Laertes, the latter reversed her engines and the Velinheli went down. The Admiralty Court awarded the owners compensation equivalent to the repair cost incurred in the storm at Greystones in October 1910 when three vessels were damaged, approximately one eighth of the value of the vessel."*

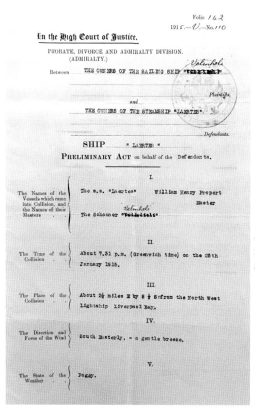

ABOVE: The Admiralty Court proceedings for the case brought by the owners of the *Velinheli* against the owners of the *S.S. Laertes*.

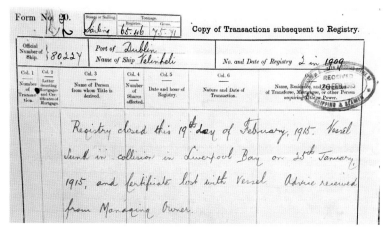

ABOVE: The final entry in the registry for the *Velinheli*. Her port of registry for most of her ownership by Arthur Evans remained Carnarvon (now Caernarfon), only transferring to Dublin on 6th March 1909.

ABOVE: Port Dinorwic (Y Felinheli) c.1890. Just visible in the distance is the old shed and slipway where the *Velinheli* was built and launched in 1878.

Though the report carried in *The Liverpool Echo* mentioned that there was a dog on board the *Velinheli* at the time of her loss, the story passed down through the Evans family is that the animal in question was the ship's cat, which was rescued along with the crew prior to her sinking. The loss of the *Velinheli* was keenly felt in Greystones. For almost a quarter of a century she had been back and forth importing English, Welsh and Scottish coal. Her topsails had been a familiar sight on the horizon as she sailed towards the harbour. Until this point she always had luck on her side, emerging safely from being driven ashore at Bray in 1906, as well as surviving the severe storm at Greystones harbour in October 1910. For Arthur Evans & Son the decision whether to replace her was straightforward. The compensation received in no way reflected her true value. Furthermore, the issues besetting the harbour, in particular its lack of depth especially at low tide, coupled with the crumbling state of the pier and north wall, meant that she was not replaced. Two weeks after the sinking of the *Velinheli* the 2,183 ton *S.S. Laertes* was sailing from Liverpool via Amsterdam bound for Java with a general cargo. She came under torpedo and gunfire attack from U-boat *U2* off the Netherlands. Though Lloyds' records listed her damaged, she lived to sail another day. As with the *Velinehli*, eventually her luck ran out. On 1st August 1917, whilst off Prawle Point in Devon, she was torpedoed and sunk with the loss of 14 lives.

COAL, SLATE AND BRICKS - WHEN SCHOONERS SAILED TO GREYSTONES

The danger faced by schooners in the Irish Sea during World War One was starkly demonstrated by the story reported in *The Wicklow Newsletter* dated 22nd September 1917. Under the headline, "*Arklow schooner sunk - Four of the crew killed by shell fire - Story of sailor who escaped (Passed by Censor)*", the report of the incident was as follows:

"*Last week a brief notice in the daily papers announced the sinking of an Arklow schooner, the Jane Williamson and the killing of four of the crew by shell-fire when they were escaping from their vessel in their small boat. This account we can now substantiate and give with it the particulars of the inhuman treatment meted out to our brave Irish sailors by the U-boat.*

The Jane Williamson was the property of Messrs. Kearon & Tyrell, Arklow, a company which is known throughout the world and which has already suffered severely in shipping losses. The crew comprised Robert Valentine Kearon, aged 40 years and third son of Mr Robert Kearon, Beulah, Arklow, master; John Vullman, mate, an Englishman; John Proctor, Wicklow Terrace, Arklow; Joseph Keegan, Wicklow; J. Cassidy, a Donegal man and John Deacon, Cahore, Co. Wexford. Loaded with coal the vessel left Swansea in company with two schooners and all went well until Monday when it arrived off Cornwall. In the account given by John Proctor, it appears that by mid day on Monday they were off the Cornish coast and at that time the other vessels were so far ahead as to be out of sight, but two other schooners were visible. Suddenly, firing was heard away in front and for almost three hours the repeated explosions were audible. Naturally the crew became extremely anxious and that anxiety became a concrete fact when about 3pm, a submarine rose to the surface near the other schooners, and having shelled them first, sank them in turn.

Finished its vile work, the U-boat at 3.30 approached the Arklow schooner to within 700 yards and as it remained low in the water, which was running with a heavy swell, it was partly submerged for the greater part of the time. A shot was fired, and the shell whizzing overhead, burst against the sea on the other side of the vessel. A few moments, pregnant with anxiety elapsed and then the submarine crept nearer by 200 yards and a second shot was fired. This time the rigging suffered and the cordage fell upon the deck. The crew, fearing for their lives, could not comprehend the tactics, for no order was issued as to what they were to do, though Proctor believes they were a warning for them to leave the vessel to her fate, but this reading of the shots was only evident from the subsequent happenings. Submerging, the U-boat disappeared and then about three minutes later, re-appeared off the schooner's stern and calmly approached to within 20 yards, apparently for the purpose of reading the name and port of the vessel. Though within speaking distance at that moment, the crew of the U-boat gave no instructions, but again submerged. Over 20 minutes elapsed and the crew saw no sign of the enemy and they began to hope that they were being allowed to proceed safely on their course. Indeed, so hopeful were they that some pursued their customary work about the vessel, others partook of dinner, which in the excitement and terror had been justifiably forgotten.

But at 4 o'clock the enemy re-appeared, some 150 yards away, on the vessel's port side, the gun was stripped and three or four shells were fired against the unfortunate vessel in quick succession, damaging the rigging, sails and bulwarks. The crew rushed to the boat, which unhappily was on the same side and in almost direct line with the firing, they prepared to launch her. Just then they saw smoke issuing again from the U-boat's gun and, involuntarily, all stooped beneath the shelter of the boat and bulwark. Keegan, who was next to Proctor, was struck with the shrapnel and fell, instantly killed. The boat was lowered. Proctor, leapt into her, quickly followed by Cassidy, Deacon and the captain. The mate loosened the rope and prepared to push off, leaving the body of Keegan lying on the deck. Just as Proctor started sculling from the boat's stern, Deacon and Cassidy seized the oars to pull and the mate pushed off. Another shot rang out and exploded at the boat. Whether it was a direct hit on the small boat, or was the rebound of the exploding shrapnel from the vessel, the men could not determine, but the boat was very severely damaged and all members of the crew received injuries. Proctor escaped with a slight scratch on the left side of the face, but the other unfortunate men were mangled and torn, particularly the two sailors. Their heads, bodies and limbs were dreadfully wounded and they must all have suffered untold agony, lying so uncomfortably in the boat, unattended, bleeding and mangled.

Keeping wonderful possession of his senses, Proctor seized the mate and pulled him into the boat and then sculled away around the stern, just as another shell exploded and on to the other side of the vessel, seeking shelter from further bombardment. The Germans followed him and signalled to him to come nearer. Fearful of the consequences, he drew near and then saw that in the conning tower of the submarine, there were two officers and about three men. On the deck, there was one big man attending the gun and about three or four others talking and laughing unconcernedly among themselves. Without further molestation, the submarine, expending another shell on the sinking vessel, steamed away. One can imagine poor Proctor's horror when, looking about him, he saw Cassidy dead and the others to all appearances dying and he alone amid his heart-rending surroundings out on the open sea. Cassidy's head and body had been terribly lacerated and he died almost immediately. Deacon's side, the captain's side and leg and Vullman's back and one foot were wounded. He could do practically nothing for them to alleviate their sufferings or to render their positions less comfortable.

When the submarine had finally disappeared, bent on further murders, the captain suggested to Proctor to hoist the sail, but he was afraid that should he seen, the U-boat would suspect him of signalling or decoying and he refused to risk it. All that evening, all through the night, he rowed the boat until his hands were raw with blisters. The vessel had been 15 or 18 miles off shore, but darkness setting in, he could not manage to reach the coast. Three hours after the attack, Deacon died. Next day about noon a patrol trawler saw the derelict boat and took the exhausted and wounded men on board and then headed for Penzance, the wounded were taken to hospital, where the captain, despite every care and attention, died of his wounds and the effects of his protracted exposure about mid-day on Wednesday. Vullman is slowly recovering, while proctor was quickly himself again.

When the heartbreaking news was conveyed to Arklow, the townspeople, shocked and grieved, extended their sincere sympathy to the relatives of the captain and his men. William and Granville Kearon went across to Cornwall and having attended the inquest on the bodies, brought back the body of their brother for interment in the family burial ground. The remains were conveyed from Fishguard to Arklow by Messrs. Kinloch's steamer, River Avoca (Captain Thos. Tyrrell) and landed at the dock jetty in Arklow on Sunday morning. The funeral took place at 3pm from Beulah, his late residence, to St. Saviour's Churchyard, Kilbride. Captain Kearon had been sailing since he was 16 years old and having quickly obtained the position of master, had captained his ships for the last 20 years. The Jane Williamson, his father's property, was a fine ship and he had been master of her for the last seven years. She was bound from Swansea on her ill-fated voyage with coal for Cherbourg. His men were sincerely attached to him, for his manner and abilities endeared all to him. Son of a sea-faring man, he knew and recognised the dangers of the profession, he loved it and was proud of his work and in that knowledge and in that pride, he was able to win the sincere admiration and respect of his crews.

The Rev. Coster officiated at the funeral and read the service over the remains in the church. The congregation, which filled St. Saviour's sang the hymn, Jesus still lead on, as the body was conveyed out of the church to the grave. All this time, shots from the garrison were fired at intervals in token of regret and honour. The entire town turned out to the funeral, thus expressing their sympathy with the relatives in their terrible affliction. The soldiers of the garrison, under the command of Major Beamish attended, while the captains of ships had specially attended from all parts. This was indeed the most impressive part of the ceremonies, for such a spontaneous, universal expression of sympathy was totally unexpected under the circumstances. Arklow and other captains left their ships in Runcorn, Liverpool, Bristol, Swansea, Cardiff, Plymouth, London, Portsmouth, even from ports in Scotland, as well as many ports in Ireland, to attend the funeral and to show their regret and esteem for their old comrade. Rarely has such an impressive funeral been seen before in Arklow.

The chief mourners were: Robert Kearon (father), William, Samuel, Walter (Dublin), C. Henry and Granville Kearon (brothers), Joseph and Wm. Kearon (uncles) and Ernest E. Bulmer (Australian Navy), cousin. Rev. J.W. Harrison, curate of St. Saviour's, Arklow, was also present at the graveside. Numerous beautiful wreaths and floral tributes were sent by relatives and friends and laid on the grave, including one from Messrs. Watkins and Ticquet, shipping agents, London.

An inquest was held at Penzance on the remains of the three men, Robert Kearon (skipper), John Cassidy and John Deacon (seamen). Evidence having been given by the two sole survivors of the crew, that the submarine opened fire on the schooner from 150 yards range, and that the Germans, laughing at the survivors, rendered no aid. The jury returned a verdict of wilful and diabolical murder. Proctor, whose safe return home was hailed with delight by his relatives and friends, looks splendid after his horrible ordeal and gives a most intelligent account of his experiences. He feels very deeply for his unhappy master and colleagues and was sorry he could not do more for them all. He is a most popular young man in the town and his bravery and presence of mind, in the face of such appalling dangers have materially added to the esteem in which he is held."

=======================

Coming nearly two years after the storm which resulted in marine insurance no longer being available for vessels entering Greystones harbour, it was quite a bold move that saw William H. Dann acquire the 70 ton schooner, *Joseph Fisher,* in June 1912. Built in 1866 by Robert McLea in Rothesay on the Isle of Bute, she was one of 40 vessels built at his yard between 1855 and 1872. She was named after the son of James Fisher, founder of the Barrow based shipping and marine services company, James Fisher & Sons Plc., which today is quoted on the London Stock Exchange. The *Joseph Fisher* spent her early years sailing out of Barrow. In 1893 she was acquired by a Scottish owner based at Campbelltown on the Kintyre Peninsula and in May 1902 she was sold to James Stafford of Wexford, who used her for coal importing. He subsequently sold her to William H. Dann. She regularly carried coal from Garston to Greystones until her last recorded arrival into Greystones harbour on 25th September 1916. After this date she sailed to Wicklow instead, carrying timber on her return voyages. By 1916, Thomas Miller & Co. coal merchants and steamship owners of Bray, were expanding their fleet of steam ships used for importing coal into Wicklow harbour. The business had acquired steamships with specially designed long hatches which made them ideally suited to the Wicklow trade, where a new crane had also recently been installed on the quayside. With the higher carrying capacities of the steamships, the economics of the coal importing business was shifting away from the traditional sailing schooners whose days were becoming numbered. For the *Joseph Fisher*, it was a very different threat that subsequently ended her days.

ABOVE: One of the schooners in the above photograph of Greystones harbour is known to be the *Joseph Fisher.*

ABOVE: The German Navy U-boat *UB 64* which, under the command of Sub-Lieutenant Ernst Krieger, sank the Greystones owned coal schooner, *Joseph Fisher,* on 15ᵗʰ September 1918, 16 miles east north east of the Codling Bank. On the same day, *UB 64* also sank two other sailing vessels. These were the 94 ton ketch, *Mary Fanny*, en route from Garston to New Ross with a cargo of coal (sunk 14 miles east south east of the Codling Bank Light Vessel) and the 89 ton ketch, *Energy*, en route from Garston to Youghal with a cargo of coal (sunk 18 miles northeast of the Codling Bank Light Vessel). The three vessels were among ten sunk by *UB 64* during a nine day period between 13ᵗʰ September 1918 and 21ˢᵗ September 1918, with the loss of 70 lives. Of these, the largest was the 4,952 ton steamer, *Barrister*, torpedoed and sunk with the loss of 30 lives on 19ᵗʰ September, nine miles off the Chicken Rock Light House southwest, of the Isle of Man. She was en route from Glasgow (via Liverpool) to the West Indies, carrying a general cargo as well as mail. Richard Roche, in his book, "*Tales of the Wexford Coast*", mentions that when German U-boats were operating off the south coast of Wexford during World War One, on occasions, they sent dinghies ashore for supplies of fresh water, eggs and vegetables. These were usually exchanged for bottles of Schnapps. One resident of Kilmore Quay maintained that it was Germans who stole three of the six drills of cabbage plants he had planted behind the lifeboat house. No one contradicted him.

PARTICULARS OF DISPLACEMENT.		
Total to quarter the depth from weather deck at side amidships to bottom of keel	27½ Tons.	Ditto per inch immersion at same depth
PARTICULARS OF ENGINES (if any).		

Registry closed 27th September 1918 vessel sunk in Irish Sea by enemy submarine on 1918. Certificate lost with vessel. Advice received from Owner per Form 20 received 30.9.18

ABOVE: The entry in the register for the *Joseph Fisher* noting "*vessel sunk in Irish Sea by enemy submarine on 15ᵗʰ September 1918*". Her sinking came less than a month before the Kingstown to Holyhead mail boat, *RMS Leinster,* was torpedoed and sunk on 10ᵗʰ October 1918 just outside Dublin Bay. With more than 500 lives lost, it remains the greatest loss of life ever in the Irish Sea.

Vessel.	Official No.	Sail x Stm. S.	Date of loss	Sold.	Broken up Etc.	War loss	Rets received	Remarks 129
Joseph Fisher	54543	x	15.9.18	-	-	✦	Cert. 27.9.18	S.17.12.17

ABOVE: Extract from the register listing ships lost at sea during world war one. Of the 37 vessels listed alphabetically alongside William H. Dann's *Joseph Fisher* on page 129 of the register, just over half were, like her, marked by a red cross to indicate their official status as a "*War Loss.*"

When the *Joseph Fisher* was owned by William H. Dann, she was skippered by Buckie Booth. The mate was Thomas Corish, the cook was Billy Hayden and the boy seaman was William "Sniper" Vickers. Mr Vickers, interviewed in Wicklow in 1983 in his 87ᵗʰ year, was able to tell the story of this vessel. He said that the gaff on the main mast was used with two snatch blocks to unload and load. He was on board when the ship sailed on her final voyage on Saturday 14ᵗʰ September 1918. She had departed Garston and early next morning the man on watch thought he saw a submarine periscope. The skipper immediately ordered the men to swing out the lifeboat. Shortly afterwards, a shell exploded in the water just ahead of them and the skipper gave the command to take to the lifeboat. The next shell hit the *Joseph Fisher* and she sank very quickly. The crew were in their lifeboat for many hours before they were picked up by a passing schooner, the *Laudsdale,* and landed at Peel on the Isle of Man.

ABOVE: Billy "Sniper" Vickers photographed at the age of 86 attending the exhibition of old photographs of Greystones held in the annexe of The Burnaby in 1983. At the time he was one of the last surviving crew members from the era when sailing schooners imported coal to Greystones harbour.

COAL, SLATE AND BRICKS - WHEN SCHOONERS SAILED TO GREYSTONES

On 5th February 1918, as it was heading past Rathlin Island, the *SS Tuscania*, became the first ship carrying US troops to Europe to be torpedoed and sunk during the war, with the loss of 210 lives. The front page of *The Wicklow Newsletter* dated 9th February 1918 contained a copy of "*The Lights (Ireland) Order of 17th January 1918*" which was issued by Admiral Lewis Bayly, Commander-in-Chief, Competent Naval Authority, Queenstown. The Order, which came into force on 10th February 1918, placed a prohibition on lights in "*all places in Ireland within five miles of the coast*". The Order gave powers to naval, military and police authorities to ensure that it was strictly adhered to.

Lights Visible from Sea.

GREYSTONES HOUSEHOLDERS PROSECUTED

ABOVE & BELOW: Headline from *The Wicklow Newsletter* dated 5th October 1918, which reported on proceedings at Bray Petty Sessions Court, under the sub-heading "*Lights in Houses*".

"*District Inspector Molony prosecuted Frederick Williams, Slievoy House, Greystones for exposing a light which was visible at sea. Sergt. Turnbull said when he saw the light at 11.45pm he rang at the door and got no answer. On making inquiries next day, the lady in the house admitted having a light in the room. The window had no blind. The Chairman stated the defendant had written a letter in which he stated there was a blind on the window. Witness said that might refer to another occasion since then when he again had to warn the defendant, but on the first occasion, there was no blind. District Inspector Molony said he stated in the letter that on inspection of the blinds on the windows, a constable had expressed satisfaction. Witness said he was unaware of that happening. They were getting any amount of trouble in Greystones.*

The D.I. said the order was important having regard to facts they all knew of. The Chairman agreed as to its importance and as it was the first offence they imposed a fine of 10s and costs. Mr Molony said up to the present they had been content with serving cautions, but it was because there was considerable trouble and they disregarded the cautions, that proceedings were instituted. Richard Gorman, Braemar Hotel was summoned for a like offence. Coast guard Buchanan gave evidence of finding the light visible from the sea in the house. There was no attempt made to screen the light. He had personally cautioned the defendant on four occasions as to lights. Defendant said he had warned the people in the house about the lights. Mr Molony said it was the owner's responsibility to ensure that blinds were in the windows. As it was not the first time he had been warned, the Chairman said he would be fined £1 and costs."

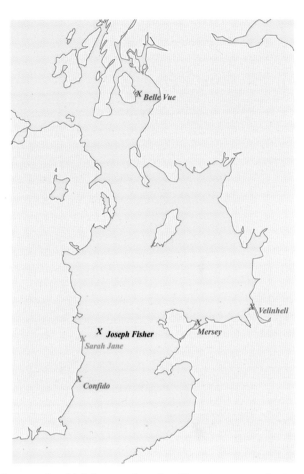

BELOW & ABOVE RIGHT: Table and map showing the where six of the vessels which imported coal to Greystones were lost.

Ship	Year Built	Built	Owner	Date of Loss / Location on map	Comments
Belle Vue	1839	Greystones	William McJannett (at the time of her loss), previously the Doyle family of Greystones)	6th August 1864 X	Ship sprang a leak en route from Bowling (Glasgow) to Belfast carrying a cargo of coal and sank off Holy Isle on the east coast of the Isle of Arran. Crew got off safely and made landfall in the ship's boat at Lamlash on the Isle of Arran.
Sarah Jane	1851	Arklow	Arthur Evans	23rd October 1886 X	Dragged her anchor when attempting to ride out a storm at Greystones. She was driven ashore and broken up in heavy seas at the next high tide, laden with her cargo of coal from Troon.
Mersey	1842	Runcorn	J.G. McEntagart	15th January 1905 X	Driven ashore in a storm and wrecked at Penmon, near Black Point, Anglesey whilst en route from Bray to Garston with a cargo of pit props. Crew got off safely. Three members of the Doyle family were drowned trying to assist the *Mersey* in Greystones harbour in 1892.
Confido	1885	Galmpton (Devon)	William H. Dann	8th January 1908 X	Wrecked in a storm at Arklow on 8th January 1908. Crew got off safely by crawling along her jib boom before scrambling onto land.
Velinheli	1878	Port Dinorwic (Y Felinheli, Menai Strait)	Arthur Evans	27th January 1915 X	Rammed and sunk by the 2,183 ton steamship, *Laertes* of South Africa, off New Brighton, Liverpool Bay at the entrance to the Mersey. Crew of four (including the ship's cat) were taken on board the *Laertes*.
Joseph Fisher	1866	Rothesey (Isle of Bute)	William H. Dann	15th September 1918 X	Torpedoed and sunk by the German U-boat, *UB 64*, 16 miles east north east of the Codling Bank Lightship. Crew got off safely, taking to the ship's boat. They were picked up by a passing schooner and brought to Peel on the Isle of Man.

COAL, SLATE AND BRICKS - WHEN SCHOONERS SAILED TO GREYSTONES

BELOW: Various old bills for Greystones schooner owning coal importers.

BELOW: Various old bills and adverts for Greystones coal merchants.

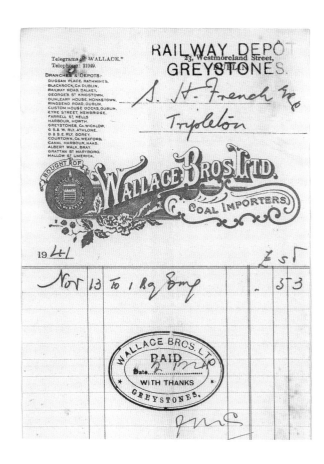

June 30. 1941

Mr French
Tripleton Cott

McKENZIE & KINSELLA,
Coal Merchants

BLACKLION and GREYSTONES, Co. Wicklow

June 21	¼ ton Coal	21/-
24	¼ ton	21/-
		42/-

Feb 25 1941

Mr French
Tripleton Cott

McKENZIE & KINSELLA,
Coal Merchants

BLACKLION and GREYSTONES, Co. Wicklow

Jan 31	½ ton coal	37/-
Feb 26	½ ton coal	41/-
		£3 18 0

June 24 1941

To _Mr French_
Tripleton Cott

Please Receive from

McKenzie & Kinsella,

Coal, Slack and Coke Stores,

Blacklion, Greystones.

½ Emergency
¼ Tons of _____ Coal Value £ : :

Signed _W_

RAILWAY DEPOT
23, Westmoreland Street,
GREYSTONES.

S. H. French Esq
Tripleton

Telegrams "WALLACE."
Telephone : 21049.

BRANCHES & DEPOTS :-
DUGGAN PLACE, RATHMINES.
BLACKROCK, Co. DUBLIN.
RAILWAY ROAD, DALKEY.
GEORGE'S ST, KINGSTOWN.
DUNLEARY HOUSE, MONKSTOWN.
RINGSEND ROAD, DUBLIN.
CUSTOM HOUSE DOCKS, DUBLIN.
EYRE STREET, NEWBRIDGE.
FARRELL ST, KELLS.
HARBOUR, HOWTH.
GREYSTONES, Co. WICKLOW.
G. S. & W. RLY. ATHLONE.
D. & S. E. RLY. GOREY.
COURTOWN, Co. WEXFORD.
CANAL HARBOUR, NAAS.
ALBERT WALK, BRAY.
GRATTAN ST MARYBORO.
MALLOW ST, LIMERICK.

BOUGHT OF
WALLACE BROS LTD.
COAL IMPORTERS

19 41 £ 5

Nov 13	To 1 Bg Smp		-	5 3

WALLACE BROS. LTD.
PAID
Date
WITH THANKS
GREYSTONES.

Est. 1933 _20/3/70_ 19

Mr Evans
KananKilly

THOMAS KINSELLA
FUEL FACTOR
BLACKLION, GREYSTONES

½ ton Coal

in 8 Bags   £6-14-0

Above No.
Greystones 77

2 Wave Crest
Greystones
August 1932.

Arthur Evans & Son, coal merchants, Greystones begs to inform their customers that they have retired from business and disposed of their coal yards to Mr. William H. Dann, *coal merchant*, of The Beach Greystones ~~who intends to amalgamate our former business with his own.~~

~~We find in our books~~

We enclose particulars of some items appearing in our books against you ~~and we shall thank you for as remittance~~ Kindly let us have payment of same to facilitate the winding up of our business

Yours faithfully
Arthur Evans & Son

ARTHUR EVANS & SON,
COAL MERCHANTS,
GREYSTONES.

Beg to inform their numerous friends and Summer Visitors that, from long experience, buying for Cash from Best English Collieries, they can give the Best Value.

ABOVE: Advertisement dated 1907.

ABOVE & BELOW: The end of an era. After 70 years of importing and distributing coal to Greystones, this was the draft of the circular sent to the customers of Arthur Evans & Son in August 1932, informing them that the business had been sold to William H. Dann of The Beach, Greystones. The sale of the business for the amount of £300 included one horse, a cart, various chattels and implements as well as the stock of coal.

1 Horse £25
2. sets Harness £6
2. Coal Drays £15
1. Block Dray £3
2. Scales £8
3. Shovels 10/=
2. (tons) Coal Bags 15/=
Hay 25/=
Oats + Straw 13/6
1 1/4 tons Coke @ 37/6 ton
tons Best Coal @ 40/= ton
tons Wigan @ 36/= ton

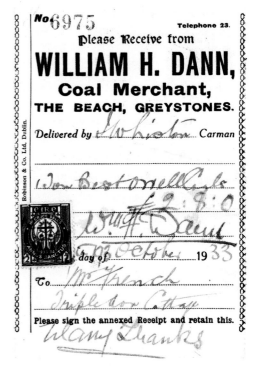

No 6975   Telephone 23.
Please Receive from
WILLIAM H. DANN,
Coal Merchant,
THE BEACH, GREYSTONES.
Delivered by _____ Carman
_____
Wm H Dann
_____ day of October 19 33
To Mr French
Triple ton Cottage
Please sign the annexed Receipt and retain this.
Many Thanks

ABOVE: Delivery note from 1933, by which time the former Arthur Evans & Son coal business had been incorporated into the existing coal business of William H. Dann.

LEFT: Arthur Evans & Son Greystones Coal Store sign still on the wall of the field at the rear of Dann's a number of years after the sale of the yard. John Dann, wearing the overcoat can be seen supervising the ploughing of the field.

ABOVE: Arthur Patrick Evans , photographed in the garden of *Ardmore House* in 1951 with grandsons, Andrew and Richard.

ABOVE: When Arthur Patrick Evans sold his coal business in 1932, he maintained his ownership of *Wavecrest* at the harbour for a number of years. He contracted his cousin, Rochfort Doyle, to build *Ardmore House* on Church Road in 1935. This became his retirement residence until his death in January1959. *Wavecrest* remained in the Evans family who used it as a holiday home up until the 1960s.

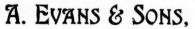

A. EVANS & SONS,

Coal Merchants,

THE HARBOUR, GREYSTONES.

Best Orrell, Wigan,

and Kitchen Coals.

At Lowest Cash Prices.

RIGHT: Arthur Evans (1832-1917) and his son Arthur Patrick Evans (1872-1959) lie beside each other in the cemetery at The Grove. From the information shown in the graph on page 99, Arthur Evans & Son imported in the region of 50,000 tons of coal into Greystones harbour over the quarter of a century preceding World War One.

ABOVE: Photograph taken in 1958 showing the five great-grandsons of Arthur Evans, schooner owner and coal importer, opposite the family home, *Wavecrest*. Left to right, Patrick Evans, Andrew Evans, Simon Evans, Elsie Evans (mother of Andrew and Richard), Roderick Evans, unknown and Richard Evans.

COAL, SLATE AND BRICKS - WHEN SCHOONERS SAILED TO GREYSTONES

Though not engaged in importing coal to Greystones, the McGill family's connection to the town was directly linked to the endeavours of John Doyle (1793-1855). The son-in-law of John Doyle, Captain Joseph McGill and his wife, Ellen, were married in Christ Church, Delgany on 2nd December 1848. They lived at *Brighton Lodge*, beside the entrance to *Coolnagreina* YWCA on Trafalgar Road. Captain Joseph McGill was an experienced mariner, having sailed to far flung places including Tristan da Cunha in the 1840s (Book No.5 includes a detailed account of some of his voyages). He was the son of James McGill, who lived in Cockermouth, near Whitehaven in Cumbria. It is believed that he met John Doyle in Whitehaven as a result of the latter importing coal from there. Though living in Greystones, Joseph McGill imported coal from Whitehaven to Dublin so as not to compete with his father-in-law in importing coal into Greystones. The 1876 map of Greystones on the inside of the back cover lists Joseph McGill as the occupier of what is now *Coolnagreina*.

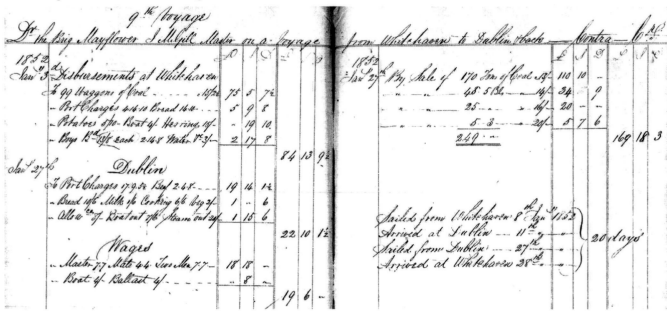

ABOVE: Extract from the 1852 ledger maintained by Joseph McGill, Captain of the brig, *Mayflower,* detailing the receipts and payments relating to the ship's 9th voyage, importing coal from Whitehaven to Dublin. The sale of the cargo of 99 waggons of coal, weighing 249 tons gave rise to an overall profit earned on the voyage of £43, 8 shillings & 4d. The entries also reveal details of the crew's diet, which included beef, herring, potatoes and vegetables.

ABOVE: Photograph taken in the early 1900s showing members of the McGill family in the front garden of *Brighton Lodge* on Trafalgar Road (beside the entrance to *Coolnagreina*). Built in the 1850s, it was the home of Captain Joseph McGill and his wife Ellen (nee Doyle). It remained in the McGill family, with Joseph Edward McGill and his own family regularly visiting Greystones from their home at Rock Ferry in Birkenhead.

ABOVE: Schooner departing Whitehaven harbour in 1850.

RIGHT: The tombstone of Joseph McGill (*"formerly of Whitehaven"*), who died aged 79 in December 1896 and his wife, Ellen, who died aged 56 in May 1878. They lie next to John Doyle (1793-1855), opposite the main door of Christ Church, Delgany.

Joseph Edward McGill, eldest son of Captain Joseph McGill and his wife, Ellen, was born in *Brighton Lodge* on 15th May 1854 and carried on the family's seafaring tradition, going to sea at the age of 15. In May 1869, he set sail aboard the *Recife,* on the first of two voyages he undertook from England to the west coast of South America and back via Cape Horn. He was aged just 15 years 3 months when he rounded Cape Horn for the first time. He completed his apprenticeship in November 1873 in sailing ships owned by Messrs. Ismay Imrie & Co. (parent company of the White Star Line). He subsequently served as second mate and first mate on sailing ships owned by C.T Bowring & Co. and Messrs. Borrowdale & Co., prior to entering service on the steam ships owned by Messrs. T. & J. Harrison in September 1877. In the 1880s, he assumed command of ships for Messrs. Greenshields Cowie & Co., before holding command of the 3,582 ton steamer, *Indra* and the 3,859 ton steamer, *Indrapura,* for T. Royden & Sons until he retired from active service in 1891.

COAL, SLATE AND BRICKS - WHEN SCHOONERS SAILED TO GREYSTONES

The following was written by Dr. Leslie Doyle a number of years ago. "*The McGill man was a very interesting person. I have seen some of his accounts of sea voyages in the 1840s round Cape of Good Hope to India, beautifully detailed. One of his sons, Joseph Edward was born in Greystones in 1854, in the house this side of St. Kilian's Hall, Cloneen is the name of it now. It was Brighton Lodge. He went to sea and I've got a copy of his apprenticeship indentures of 1869. His daughter is still alive. She is in her 80s and lives in Birkenhead. I go to see her occasionally. One time recently she showed me a small journal he kept on his second voyage at sea in the years 1870-71, when he went from London with a mixed cargo including explosives. Starting June 1870, they went to Montevideo I think, round Cape Horn & up to Chile and Peru back again. The voyage took a year and ten days. It's a wonderfully detailed account. As a small boy, I can just remember him as an elderly man with a beard when he used to visit Greystones*".

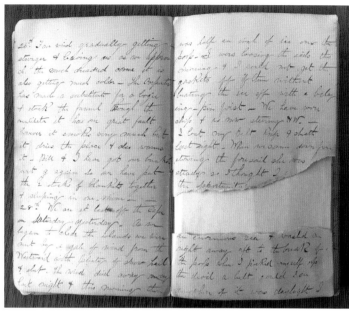

__28th August 1870:__ "*We are at last off the Cape on Saturday yesterday. As we began to clear the islands, we were met by a gale from the westward, with plenty of snow, hail and sleet. The wind died away last night and this morning there was half an inch of ice on the poop. I was loosing the sails this morning and I could not get the gaskets off of them without beating the ice off with a belaying pin first. We have wove ship and we are now steering NW. I lost my belt knife and sheath last night when we came down from stowing the foresail. She was holding steady so I thought.....the opportunity* [3 lines torn out]......*an enormous sea washed me right away aft to the break of the poop. When I picked myself up, the devil a belt, could I see anywhere. If it was daylight, I might have had some chance, but as it was pitch dark, I lost it. The mate sent me up a while ago to grease the fore topgallant and topmast down. I had a nice job, my fingers were that numb, I could scarcely tell I was holding on or not and the ship rolling about in these immense rollers. I had enough to do fair wind, but very little if freezing and snowing.*"

ABOVE: Joseph Edward McGill's journal entry for 28th August 1870 on his 2nd voyage from England to South America aged 16 years 3 months, when he rounded Cape Horn east to west on the 464 ton, three masted sailing barque, *Recife*. Square rigged, the ship called to Valparaiso, before sailing north to Iquique, then part of Peru (now in Chile). Fearing a ship mate was secretly reading his journal and would possibly tear it up when they were approaching Liverpool, Joseph Edward McGill secretly stowed it away.

ABOVE: Early 1900s photograph of Joseph Edward McGill sitting on the verandah of *Coolagreina*, Trafalgar Road, on one of his visits to Greystones from his home in Birkenhead. Sitting in front of him is his son, Philip, with his daughter, Nellie, standing behind, her arm around her brother, Edward's shoulder. Joseph Edward McGill married Elizabeth Musgrave of Cockermouth, Cumbria in the late 1880s and, following her death a decade later, reared his three children himself.

ABOVE RIGHT: Sergeant Edward McGill and his father, Joseph Edward McGill. Sergeant Edward McGill, 1st / 6th Battalion of the King's Liverpool Regiment, was one of 32 men from his battalion killed in action as part of the offensive near Morval at the Battle of the Somme on 25th September 1916. With no known grave, his name is among the 72,337 commemorated on the Thiepval Memorial to the Missing of the Somme. He was 25 years of age.

Captain Joseph Edward McGill never forgot his close ties with his birthplace. He named his home at Egerton Park, Rock Ferry in Birkenhead, *Delgany*. When he died aged 71 in February 1926, his body was brought to Ireland for burial. He lies next to his seafaring father, Captain Joseph McGill and his seafaring grandfather, John Doyle (1793-1855) in Delgany Churchyard.

ABOVE: View from Jones' Hill on Greystones Golf Course around 1900 looking towards Little Sugarloaf. St. Kilian's Church is visible in the centre, with just fields where St. Bridget's Park and Applewood Heights are today. Also visible on the extreme right are houses, including *Ashley House* at the top of Jink's Hill. In the foreground is *Blacklion House* and several other houses, at the intersection between the modern day R761 road through Blacklion and the lower entrance to Applewood Heights. It was around this spot, the first coast guard station in Greystones was established in 1821, close to where Blacklion Pet Hospital is today. It consisted of a cluster of buildings to house the officers and boatmen attached to the station. At that time, the adjacent stream provided a fresh water supply. However it was quite a walk from the station down to the sea. The 1838 Ordnance Survey map on the opposite page shows that there was only one road (what is now Rathdown Road) leading directly to the sea. There was however, a bohereen of sorts, leading from the coast guard station part way down what is now Church Lane as far as where *Knockdolian* is today. It then turned due south and crossed fields on the eastern side of Jones' Hill. From there it was possible to link up with a path that ran along what is now Marine Road on the sea front.

ABOVE: Though the coast guards and its forerunners were established in Greystones a generation before the arrival of the railway, the post office, or any of the town's churches, the site earmarked for the new coast guard building remains undeveloped as of September 2018. This will be the 4th location for the service and its forerunners since its arrival in Greystones almost 200 years ago.

RIGHT: Page from the Establishment Record Book of the Greystones Preventive Station listing the names of the first men to serve under the command of Thomas Lamb Wood. He was transferred from Kent to become the station's first Chief Officer with effect from 1st February 1821. He held the role until 18th September 1822 when Lieutenant T.W. Watkins assumed command, holding the rank of Lieutenant of Station for just over three years.

In 1809, the Preventive Waterguard had been formed in England, with the intention of it becoming a sea-going force, albeit primarily functioning initially as a land based force. By around 1819, it began to operate also in Scotland and Ireland under the command of Sir James Dombrain. The Preventive Waterguard acted as a marine based arm of revenue enforcement on behalf of the government, to crack down on smuggling activities. Watch houses were established around the coast, with crews from the station patrolling the coast each night in cutters. From 1816 it was under the control of the Royal Navy, prior to amalgamating with the Riding Officers (on horseback) and Revenue Cruisers (at sea) to become the Coast Guards under the control of the Board of Customs in 1822. Members of the service were often recruited from the Royal Navy, given that the men were familiar with maritime tasks. Early retirement was quite normal, unless the men targeted promotion to the rank of Chief Officer.

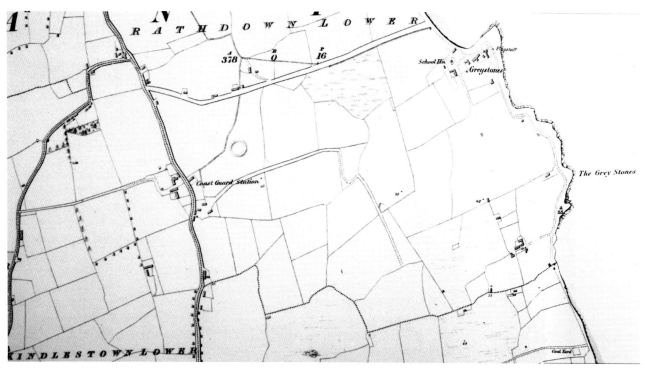

Date of Order for Nomination.	Date of Letter of Nomination or Removal.	From whence Nominated, or Name of the Station removed from.	NAME.	QUALITY.	D. D. D. Removed or Absconded.	Date of Letter directing Discharge or Removal, or Time D. D. or Absconded, &c.	Cause of Discharge or Removal.	Preventive Station Removed to.	REMARKS.
PREVENTIVE STATION. _Grey Stones_	**PORT.** _Dublin_		One — Chief Officer. One — Chief Boatman.	Two — Comd. Boatmen. Eight — Boatmen.					(37) 19
1 Feby 1821		Kent	Thomas Lamb Wood	Chief Officer					
6 Decr 1820		Hartland Quay	Charles Ford	Chief Boatman	Removed	11 March 1822	reduced for Drunkenness	Jack Hole Comn Boatman	
15 March 1822		Pol Skerries	William Smith	Chief Boatman					
6 Decr 1820		Bonsard Bay	John Rogers	Comn Boatman	Promoted	5 April 22		Ballycastle Co Antrim	
30 Jany 1822		Same Station	Thomas Keightley	Comn Boatman	Removed	5 May 22		Downhill	
9 Decr 1820			William Dawsen	Comn Boatman	Removed	30 Jany/22		Five Mile Point	
6 May 1822		Same Station	John Brown	Comn Boatman					
			Michael Ferguson	Comn Boatman					
13 Jany 1820		R.B. Bray	Thomas Keightley	Boatman	Removed	30 Jany 22		Same Station	
26 .. 1821		Ballycotton	William Connelly	Boatman	Promoted	5 May 22		Helvick Head	
9 June ..		R to Arklow	Samuel Ferguson	Boatman	Promoted	5 May 22		Same Station	
10 Apr ..		Co Wexford	Walter Redmond	Boatman	Promoted	5 May 22		Ballycotton	
" "		Do.	Timothy Redmond	Boatman	Removed	24 Jany/1822		Tubane	
19 June 21		Dublin	William Morris	Boatman	Promoted	5 May 22		Dalkey	
26 Oct 1821		Tiger Revd Cruizer	John Brown	Boatman	Promoted	5 May 22		Same Station	
26 Oct 1821		Tiger Revd Cruizer	George Stanbury	Boatman	Promoted	5 May 22		Stanford Loch	
6 Feby 1822		late Harriet Lugger	Philip Calf	Boatman					
16 Jany 1822	12 Feby 1822	Deal	George Arnold	Boatman	Promoted	5 May 22		Newcastle	
17 Apr 1822	13 May 1822	Ipswich	Wm Bird	Boatman					
14 May ..	18 " "	Dublin	John Carolan	Boatman					
" " "	" " "	Dublin	James Dobson	Boatman					
" " "	" " "	HMS Prudova Plymouth	Richard Thornhill	Boatman					
		Do.	William Chapman	Boatman					
16 " "	21 " "	Coffee Grey Stones	John Holmes	Boatman					
26 Apr "	28 May "	Pehes	John Ladner						

As can be seen from the Establishment Record Book entry, the station comprised 12 men under four ranks. There was one Chief Officer, one Chief Boatman, two Commissioned Boatmen and eight Boatmen. It was common for men to be recruited from well outside the local area, as the authorities sought to reduce the risk of the men stationed becoming too familiar with the local population. Likewise, the rate of turnover of men was quite high, with men of all ranks being moved along the coast (the Greystones Station was under the command of six different men during the first seven years of its existence). This helped satisfy the promotion aspirations within the service and also bolstered its independence. It is interesting also to note that the parish records of Christ Church, Delgany, show 18 baptisms recorded between 1830 and 1845, with the fathers' occupation listed as "Waterguard" and living at either Greystones, Blacklion or Windgates.

The role of the preventive guard at this time was thus quite different to the modern day search and rescue operations carried out by the coast guards. The seriousness with which the authorities regarded smuggling along the Irish coast was highlighted by the following account that was published in *Saunders's Newsletter* on 29th January 1821, just days before the establishment of the station at Greystones. Under the header "*Outrage and Reward*" it reported that "*a party of the Preventive Water Guard stationed at Long Island in the district of Baltimore, were lately attacked by smugglers. The Commissioners of his Majesty's Customs do hereby offer a reward of One Hundred Pounds Sterling for the apprehension and prosecuting to conviction of each person who fired at or attacked the Water Guard Men, with any deadly weapon upon this occasion*". One year after its establishment, when smuggling was still prevalent along the Wicklow coast, the Greystones station was already fulfilling its revenue protection role. On 18th February 1822, it was reported that men from the Greystones Preventive Station, together with colleagues from Six Mile Point, apprehended nine smugglers who were subsequently taken under military escort to Wicklow Gaol.

In March 1822, the station's first Chief Boatman, Charles Ford, was reduced in rank to that of Commissioned Boatman, for drunkenness and removed to serve further down the coast at Jack's Hole, just south of Wicklow Head. He had been transferred to Greystones from the Hartland Quay station on the north coast of Devon. He was replaced by William Smith, who joined from the Skerries Station. Close examination of the record reveals that, of the initial eight boatmen who were appointed to serve at the Greystones Preventive Station, six were appointed from within Ireland - Thomas Keightley (Bray), William Connelly (Ballycotton), Samuel Ferguson (Arklow), Walter Redmond (Co. Wexford), Timothy Redmond (Co. Wexford) and William Morris (Dublin). Of particular note, however, are the entries dated 26th October 1821 relating to the appointment of the final two of the initial eight strong compliment of boatmen. Both John Brown and George Hanbury were transferred to Greystones from the *Tiger* revenue cruiser. A key element of enforcement sought by the government was the deployment of revenue cruisers to provide a visible presence along the coast to deter smuggling.

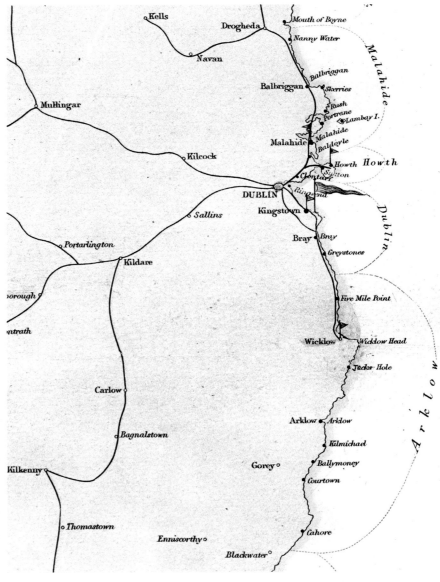

RIGHT: On 14th May 1858, the Admiralty published a map of Ireland showing the 202 coast guard stations, 38 divisions and three districts around the near 2,000 mile length of the country's coastline. The latter were patrolled by district ships (as indicated by a long blue burgee), with the ship stationed at Kingstown (Dún Laoghaire) responsible for the 12 coast guard divisions (indicated by a short blue burgee) and 77 coast guard stations (indicated by a black dot) located along the stretch of coast from Portrush in Antrim to Bar of Lough on the east side of Bannow Bay in County Wexford. The map shows that the Greystones coast guard station was one of five stations, together with Bray, Kingstown, Ringsend and Clontarf under the responsibility of the Dublin division. To the south, nine coast guard stations, from Five Mile Point to Cahore, came under the responsibility of the Arklow division. Note that the railway line did not yet run beyond Wicklow Town.

COAST GUARDS

News of the arrival of men with revenue cruiser experience to serve in the Greystones Preventive Station would undoubtedly have made its way into smuggling circles, particularly those active at the Brandy Hole on Bray Head. It is also interesting to note that John Brown, who was one of those with revenue cruiser experience, was subsequently promoted to become one of the two newly appointed commissioned boatmen at Greystones on 5th May 1822. By that date, all eight of the initial boatmen had either been promoted or transferred to other stations around the coast. The trend to recruit from well outside the local area continued, with some of the replacements arriving from Deal, Ipswich, St Ives and Plymouth.

A decade later, after the formation of the Coast Guards in 1822, the men of the Greystones Coast Guard Station distinguished themselves. The edition of *The Drogheda Journal or Meath & Louth Advertiser* dated 1st September 1832 reported the following. "*On Tuesday evening last, the schooner, Aeolus, John Fellon master, bound to London from Newry with butter and oats, was brought into Kingstown harbour in a very disabled state by the boats of the Greystones and Five Mile Point Coast Guard Stations, the officers of which, by great exertion in towing, succeeded in securing the vessel, just before a gale of wind at E.N.E. came on, which probably would have caused the total loss of vessel and lives.*"

The Newry Telegraph dated 15th February 1855, reported on a storm that lashed the Wicklow coast. "*At Greystones, the coast guard picked up on Saturday morning several pieces of wood, consisting of portions of a cabin and deck planking, with about 10 feet of the lower part of a mast, which led to the inference that a vessel had struck and gone to pieces on the banks. One of the sideboards of the bow with the word Eglington upon it was thrown up by the waves near the Five Mile Point and the corresponding board for the other side was found a little further down the coast. Somewhat later in the day some fragments of a boat floated in to the shore, with the word W. Borland, Ayr carved on what was presumed to be the rail of the steering seat. The figurehead of the same vessel, consisting of a bust of the Earl of Eglington, was also got shortly afterwards, together with a small pillow of very inferior description. The vessel in question is presumed to be the Eglington, of Ayr, 80 tons register, which is known to have been at sea that night with four or five hands on board, all of whom there is too good reason to believe have met a sailor's grave.*"

The Freeman's Journal dated 19th October 1860 reported that "*The Comptroller-General of the Coast Guard, Commodore Yelverton, C.B., accompanied by Captain Boyd, R.N., of her Majesty's ship, Ajax and Captain Young, R.N., the Inspecting Commander of the Coast Guard proceeded at an early hour by train yesterday to Greystones for the purpose of inspecting the Dublin Division of the Coast Guard, the inspection of the North Western Division being completed*". Tragically, less than four months later Captain Boyd was drowned whilst attempting to save the lives of the crew of the schooner, *Industry,* in Dún Laoghaire (refer also to photo on page 82). *The Freeman's Journal* dated 23rd April 1861 reported that "*in less than a week a fine mortar, a twenty four pounder, will be sent to Greystones station of the coast guard. When it has duly arrived and is set in proper order, the men stationed in that locality will be exercised in the use of the mortar for the purpose of rendering prompt assistance in the shape of sending boats on board to vessels driven ashore in foul weather*". It is noteworthy the timing of the arrival of this mortar came just two months after the severe storm that caused significant damage to shipping and loss of life, including that of Captain Boyd, R.N., along the east coast.

The Wicklow Newsletter dated 11th January 1862 reported on the loss of the *Adonis*, a 600 ton screw steamer, owned by the Waterford Steamship Company. Heading from Belfast to Waterford carrying a general cargo, nine steerage passengers and a crew of 24 including her captain, she struck the Muglins Rocks just north of Dalkey Island. As the ship drifted south, the captain ordered two of the three lifeboats to be lowered and 20 of the passengers and crew evacuated the vessel. The captain and the remaining crew stayed on board until five miles east of Bray Head, when he took the decision to abandon ship. The men clambered into the ship's third lifeboat and subsequently landed at Greystones, where the "*crew were treated with every attention at Greystones Coast Guard Station*".

The Dublin Daily Express dated 18th September 1862 reporting on Kingstown shipping noted that the "*Argus, Admiralty screw steam yacht, left harbour this morning at 11 o'clock and cruised southwards as far as Greystones, in pursuance of the coast inspection on which Commodore Yelverton, C.B., is at present engaged*". *The Irish Times* dated 31st May 1864, reporting on naval matters at Kingstown, noted that the "*revenue cutter, Stag, so long lying in the harbour, started this morning on a cruise to Greystones, thence to Dundalk*". *The London Evening Standard* dated 17th January 1882 reported that "*a lifeboat belonging to the Lanarkshire containing thirteen of the missing crew, landed at Greystones at 1.30 on Sunday afternoon. The Lanarkshire was bound from Glasgow to Lisbon and was reported yesterday to have been wrecked on the Codling Bank*".

The Greenock Telegraph and Clyde Shipping Gazette dated 13th May 1886 reported a strong south easterly gale raging in the Irish Sea. It noted that "*at Greystones on the Wicklow coast yesterday morning, two large coasting vessels were driven ashore within a quarter of a mile of each other and the crews were saved by the coast guards with life saving apparatus. The vessels dragged their anchors while trying to ride out the gale in the bay*".

ABOVE: Two coast guards on duty in the watch room of a coast guard station in the 19th century. Tuck sticks can be seen arranged on the wall and the various flags used for signalling can be seen in the wooden pigeon holes. Other signalling and observation equipment such as telescopes, flashing lamps, foghorns and megaphones would also have been kept there.

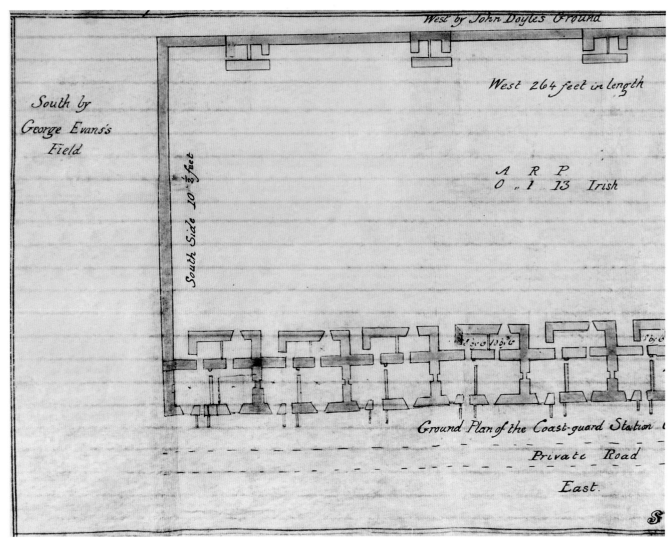

South by
George Evans's
Field

South Side 10½ feet

West by John Doyle's Ground

West 264 feet in length

A R P
0 „ 1 13 Irish

Ground Plan of the Coast-guard Station

Private Road

East

ABOVE: The plans included within the indenture signed on 2ⁿᵈ September 1842 *"between John Doyle of Greystones in the County of Wicklow, coal merchant and Charles Andrew Scovell of the Custom House in the City of London, Secretary to the Commissioners of Her Majesty's Customs"*. H.M. Customs had made a decision to relocate the coast guards from Blacklion closer to the coast. John Doyle (1793-1855) was approached to construct a new coast guard station with accommodation on a plot where Kenmare Terrace on Trafalgar Road is now. At that time it was a private road leading from the sea to the field owned by George Evans. John Doyle built the seven interlinked cottages, the small watch house for the officers on duty, the two storey officer's house next to it and a standalone boathouse. The watch house was also the place where the coast guards were mustered and orders issued. The boathouse stored the station's two boats, a galley and a gig, plus equipment. The galley was a large open boat with oars and most likely a mast and sails. The gig was a smaller, narrower clinker built open boat with oars. The equipment stored in the boathouse also included the station's life saving apparatus, principally its Manby mortar, breeches buoy and rocket cart. The rocket cart formerly used at Greystones is now on permanent loan to the National Maritime Museum in Dún Laoghaire. This is featured in Book No.7.

ABOVE: Photo taken in the 1880s showing the seven white chimneys of the coast guard cottages and the two storey officer's house.

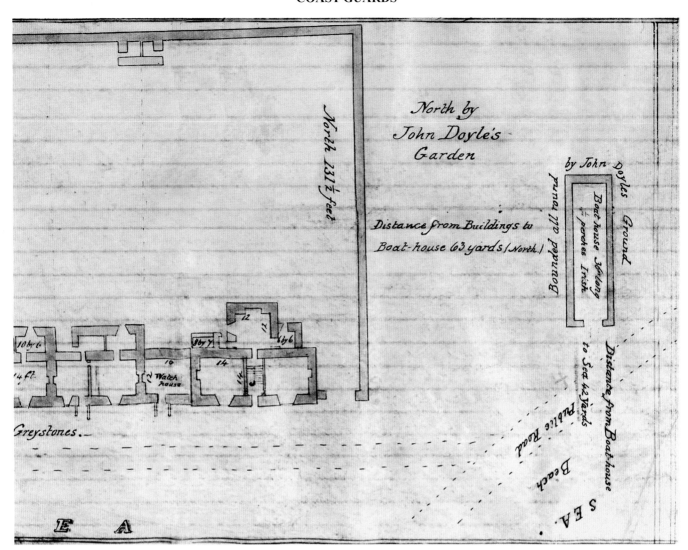

ABOVE: Photograph taken in the early 1900s showing all seven of the original interlinked coast guard cottages, with the small single storey watch house nestling between the last cottage and the two storey officer's house (now Greystones Harbour Family Practice). The Hibernian Bank, with its barred windows is visible in the bottom right of the photograph.

ABOVE & BELOW: Trafalgar Road in 1964 with the coast guard officer's two storey house in the centre. The small single storey building attached to it was the coast guard's watch house, prior to its reconfiguration, when the two storey house with the blue door (shown in the 2017 photograph below) was later built. It was in this small watch house that, according to *The Freeman's Journal* of 17th March 1847, the first plans seeking tenders from interested parties for the construction of a harbour at Greystones were put on public display. In the 2017 photograph below, only the left side of the original 7th coast guard cottage now survives in its original single storey form. The photo shows the coast guard officers' house now as the doctors' practice (with its three window boxes).

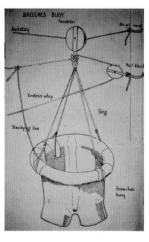

LEFT: The rocket pole on Marine Road, adjacent to the Cove, has been located there for more than a century. Simulating a ship's mast, it was used for practice by the coast guards. They fired the rocket and attached the line carrying the breeches buoy from the tripod (see photo on opposite page) to the top of the pole in order to haul a man across the Cove. The photograph on the far left shows Bob Thompson traversing the Cove in the breeches buoy during a practice in around 1949.

RIGHT: The entry in the Coast Guard Establishment Book for Greystones Coast Guard Station noting the award of the Long Service Medals with the Rocket Life Saving Apparatus to ten recipients on 11th May 1911. The medals were presented by Lord Justice Cherry, former Liberal MP for a Liverpool constituency and later Lord Chief Justice of Ireland. He resided at *Killincarrick House*, which later became the Woodlands Hotel.

LEFT: The medal awarded to Osborne Spurling, No.1 Officer in Charge of the Greystones Coast Life Saving Service. He enrolled in the service at the age of 29 in 1887. He was in charge of the crew of the Greystones Coast Life Saving Service when it was despatched to Bray harbour to effect the rescue of the crew of the *Mary Celine* on 26th January 1926. This was the last time that a rescue using the rocket apparatus and breeches buoy was carried out in Bray.

THE ROCKET-APPARATUS FOR SAVING LIFE FROM SHIPWRECK.

LEFT: The rocket apparatus and breeches buoy was most famously deployed at Greystones harbour during the storm in October 1910 that badly damaged the *Velinheli*, *Federation* and *Reciprocity*. The report in *The Bray and South Dublin Herald* described the dramatic rescue of the crew of the *Reciprocity*.

AND SOUTH DUBLIN
Herald. 15th Oct. 1910.

THE NOR'-EAST GALE.

DAMAGE TO SHIPPING ON WICKLOW COAST.

THREE VESSELS WRECKED AT GREYSTONES.

The crew of the Reciprocity had a most hairbreadth escape from drowning. The vessel was laden with coal, and when she drifted the seas broke over her, and she was driven under the stern of the Velinhelli, where she sank in the harbour. The crew of three took to the rigging, and clambered on board the Velinhelli, which was half submerged, having discharged about half her cargo. The Coastguards at Greystones, under the command of Station Officer M'Carthy, effected a very clever piece of work with the life-saving apparatus. Having got a line to the Velinhelli by means of the rocket, they succeeded in taking off the crew of Reciprocity within four minutes of the line being attached. The rescue was a most thrilling one, and as the men were hauled ashore in a dripping condition, they were heartily cheered. James Hockney, the captain of the Reciprocity, had a very narrow escape. He sustained a wound over one of his eyes, and when landed he was semi-conscious. It was found necessary to have him attended by Dr Ross, Greystones, who dressed the injury.

RIGHT: Derek Ferns leaning against the wall at the top of the boat slip with Bill Spurling, arms folded, in the foreground. Both the Spurling and Ferns families have had a long association with the Greystones Coast Guards. Bill Spurling took over as Officer in Charge following the death of his father, Osborne in 1926, serving in that role until his retirement in 1942. Derek Ferns was Officer in Charge from 1980 until his death in 1992, following which his sons Niall and John filled the role. Also in the photograph is John Redmond.

ABOVE: No.1 Officer in Charge of Greystones Coast Life Saving Service, Osborne Spurling, wearing his trusty bowler hat, preparing to fire the rocket apparatus from the grass above the Cove. Note the observers standing a safe distance away. The photograph was taken on 9th June 1924.

COAST GUARDS

After 30 years at Kenmare Terrace on Trafalgar Road, the coast guards moved to a newly constructed coast guard station on Marine Terrace. The main building included a watch tower which contained a storeroom at ground level. Linked to it was the chief officer's house and six terraced houses for the coast guard men, with the chief boatman's house on the right-hand end.

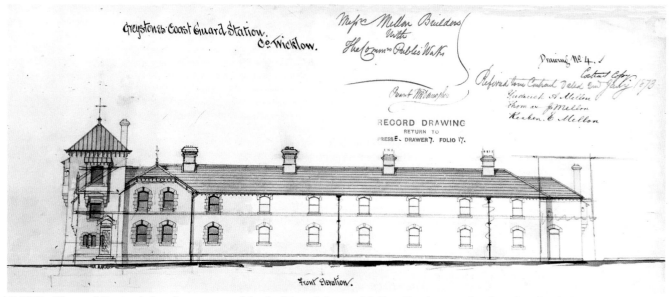

ABOVE: The architectural drawings prepared by builders, Messrs. Mellon Brothers and referred to in their contract with the Commissioners of Public Works dated 2nd January 1873.

ABOVE: Men scything grass in the field opposite the coast guard station in 1886. Behind them, some coast guards can be seen standing in front of the building.

ABOVE: 1880s photograph of the coast guard station with the boathouse and rocket cart house to its left. Note the open access down onto the rocks at the Cove including a set of steps. The timber fence that preceded the present wall had not yet been built.

The obituary for Thomas John Mellon published in *The Irish Builder* in 1913 stated that he was from a family "*long connected with building in Dublin*" and a brother of the contractor, Reuben E. Mellon of Rathgar. The obituary also noted that Thomas Mellon entered the employment of the Board of Works, becoming a District Clerk of Works for Dublin City, before rising to Assistant Surveyor in 1887. In 1893, he was promoted to the rank of Principal Surveyor, responsible for the southern district. On the 1901 census, Thomas Mellon's occupation was listed as "*principal surveyor, Board of Works, Dublin.*" Reuben E. Mellon subsequently had strong links to Greystones. He was the contractor who, in 1898, extended the nave and built the gallery to increase the seating capacity of St. Patrick's Church by 150. A resident of Brighton Square in Rathgar on the census returns for both 1901 and 1911, he also lived in Greystones at *Glencoe* on the North Beach up until the early 1920s.

BELOW: The plan showing the all important access from the Chief Officer's House to the Watch Room.

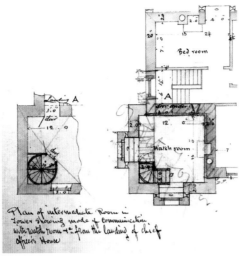

BOARD OF PUBLIC WORKS.
NOTICE TO BUILDERS.

SEALED TENDERS, addressed to the undersigned, will be received up to the hour of 12 o'Clock noon on the 9th December, 1872, for erecting and completing a new
COAST GUARD STATION at GREYSTONES, County Wicklow, according to Plans and Specification to be seen at this Office.
Each Proposal should be for a lump sum, and must be accompanied by a separate Detailed Estimate, giving quantities and prices, and be endorsed "Tender for Greystones Coastguard Station."
Both Tender and Detailed Estimate should bear the name and address of the proposer on the back."
Printed Forms for Tenders can be had at this Office.
N.B.—Persons tendering should send in testimonials as to character and competency, unless previously known to the Board.
The Board will not bind themselves to accept the lowest or any tender.
By Order,
EDWARD HORNSBY, Secretary.
Office of Public Works, Dublin,
13th Nov., 1872.

* If this be not attended to, the Board cannot return detailed quantities to the unsuccessful parties.
14150

ABOVE: The notice seeking tenders for the building of the coast guard station at Marine Terrace, which was placed in *The Freeman's Journal* on Saturday 16th November 1872.

ABOVE: Photo showing the rear of the coast guard station and the flagstaff in the 1880s before the Holy Rosary Church and houses were built on La Touche Road.

RIGHT: The premises presently used by Greystones Coast Guards is the building that used to store the station's boat. The building was also used as an ice cream parlour during the summer, with its Cove Cafe sign above the door and weighing scales outside. Paddy Doyle, who was Officer in Charge for 28 years until 1980, used the building for his cobbler's shop for a number of years.

COAST GUARDS

Whilst the initial purpose of the coast guards and its forerunners was revenue protection to combat smuggling activities, this changed during the 19th century to that of naval reserve. The service also had some life saving responsibilities and by the 1920s this had become its primary role, together with coastal observation. Following the formation of The Irish Free State in 1922, the Coast Life Saving Service was formed. It was placed under the control of the Board of Trade and its role was restricted to lifesaving, salvaging from wrecks and administration of the foreshore. In late 1923, Tom Casement, brother of Sir Roger Casement, became the first Inspector of the new Coast Life Saving Service, visiting Greystones on a number of occasions as part of his duties.

ABOVE: Members of the Greystones Coast Life Saving Service with the Inspector, Captain Tom Casement. Included are O.Spurling, S. Archer, W. Spurling, E. Evans, E. Archer, A. Martin, H.J. Evans, A. Archer, J. Lawless, J. Darcy, C. Evans, M. Keddy, J. Spurling, M. Whiston and J. Evans.

BELOW: During the latter half of the 19th century, rowing races between the local coast guard stations were held as part of the programme of events at regattas. Below are some of the results achieved by the men of the Greystones Coast Guard Station, along with a notable performance by the men of the nearby Five Mile Point Coast Guard Station at the 1880 Wicklow Regatta.

Regatta	Date	Race	Result / Comment	Source
Bray	25th June 1864	Man-of-War & Coast Guard Galleys	1st place, galley from the *Royal George,* prize £5; 2nd place, galley from the revenue cutter, *Fanny,* prize £3. Other placings not reported, 4 boats competed (2 six-oared galleys from the *Royal George* and the *Fanny* revenue cruiser along with 2 four-oared coast guard galleys from Bray and Greystones Coast Guard Stations).	*Bell's Life in London & Sporting Chronicle*
Bray	30th Sept 1878	Coast Guard Race	1st place, Greystones, prize £5; 2nd place, Bray, prize £2; 3rd place, Dalkey.	*The Wicklow Newsletter*
Bray	26th Aug 1879	Coast Guard Race	1st place, Kingstown, prize £4; 2nd place, Greystones, prize £2; 3rd place, Dalkey; 4th place, Bray. Described as a *"well contested race"*.	*The Freeman's Journal*
Wicklow	3rd Aug 1880	Coast Guard Race	Though Greystones were not reported as competing, the race resulted in a rare success for the coast guard men of Five Mile Point over a distance of 2 miles. 1st place, Five Mile Point, prize £5; 2nd place, Arklow, prize £2.	*The Dublin Daily Express*
Dalkey	4th Aug 1881	Coast Guard Race	1st place, Kingstown, prize £4; 2nd place, Dalkey, prize £2. Report noted that the race was *"limited to boats belonging to coast guard stations at Kingstown, Dalkey, Bray, Greystones and Howth"*. The race itself was *"capitally contested"*.	*The Dublin Daily Express*
Greystones	19th Aug 1885	Coast Guard Race	1st place, Wicklow, prize £4; 2nd place, Greystones, prize £2; 3rd place, Bray.	*The Freeman's Journal*
Greystones	23rd Aug 1889	Revenue Race	1st place, the boat of the revenue cutter, *Flora*; 2nd place, Greystones. The report noted that *"the coast guards protested the Flora's boat was not a fair one. The committee gave an extra £1, the crews exchanged boats and Flora's men keel-hauled the gobbies"*.	*The Freeman's Journal*
Bray	7th Aug 1890	Coast Guard Race	1st place, Bray, prize £4; 2nd place, Kingstown, prize £2; 3rd place, Dalkey, prize £1; 4th place, Greystones.	*The Freeman's Journal*
Greystones	16th Aug 1890	Coast Guard Race	1st place, Greystones; 2nd place, Bray.	*The Irish Times*
Bray	15th Aug 1895	Coast Guard Race	1st place, Bray, prize £4; 2nd place, Greystones, prize 2; 3rd place, Kingstown, prize £1.	*The Irish Independent*
Bray	22nd Aug 1903	Coast Guard Race	1st place, Bray; 2nd place, Greystones; 3rd place, Dalkey.	*The Wicklow Newsletter*

ABOVE: A uniformed coast guard watching the shore in the 19th century

ABOVE RIGHT: Coast life saving practice at the rocket pole. Included are Derek Ferns, Paddy Salmon, Bob Martin, Bill Sholedice, Vincent Carroll, Eddie Doyle and the inspector.

ABOVE: Photograph taken in December 1980 marking the retirement of Paddy Doyle as Officer in Charge of Greystones Coast Guards. He had served in the role for 28 years, taking over as Officer in Charge upon the retirement of Herbert Victor Ferns who served from 1942 to 1952. Paddy Doyle is seen handing over the key to Derek Ferns, who served as Officer in Charge until his death in April 1992. Derek's son Niall then assumed the role. Following his appointment to a full time position with the Irish Coast Guards in September 2009, he relinquished the role and his brother John became the new Officer in Charge (the 4th member of the Ferns family to hold the role). Left to right: Bob Martin (without his usual beard), Jimmy Redmond, Paddy Doyle, Eddie Doyle and Derek Ferns.

ABOVE: John Ferns retired from the service in August 2016 after serving with Greystones Coast Guards for 36 years, the last seven as Officer in Charge. In the photo, John, on the left is seen handing over the key to the new Officer in Charge, Dermot McCauley, who has more than 20 years service with the Greystones Coast Guards.

BELOW: The table below has been compiled to show the names and dates (where known) of the men who have held the position of either (i) Chief Officer (ii) Lieutenant of Station (iii) Officer in Charge or (iv) No.1 Officer in the Greystones Coast Guard Station since its inception in 1821. This encompasses also the Coast Life Saving Service formed in 1923. Details are incomplete for the period between 1878 and 1919.

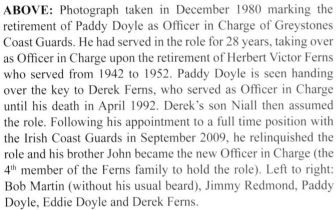

Name	Title	From	To	Comment
Thomas Lamb Wood	Chief Officer	1st February 1821	18th September 1822	Appointed Inspecting Commander of the Coast Guard in Ireland later in his career.
Lieutenant T.W. Watkins	Lieutenant of Station	24th September 1822	14th January 1826	Stationed at Milk Cove in Cork prior to Greystones.
Lieutenant McCormack	Lieutenant of Station	31st January 1826	30th November 1826	Stationed at Mizen Head, prior to Greystones, subsequently to Malahide.
Thomas Share	Chief Officer	30th November 1826	5th January 1877	Stationed at Ballygeary, Co. Wexford, prior to Greystones, subsequently to Rush.
Elijah Lewin	Chief Officer	5th January 1827	20th May 1827	Stationed at Rush prior to Greystones, subsequently to Howth.
William Curties	Lieutenant of Station	31st July 1827	26th March 1840	Stationed at Ballycastle prior to Greystones, subsequently to Kilmichael, Co. Wexford.
Lieutenant Robert Poole	Lieutenant of Station	28th March 1840		Stationed at Balbriggan prior to Greystones.
Lieut. Richard John Turner	Lieutenant of Station	24th September 1847	20th November 1849	Stationed at Oyster Haven, Co. Cork, prior to Greystones.
Lieutenant Arthur Grone	Lieutenant of Station	8th November 1849	28th February 1859	Served aboard *HMS Illustrious* prior to Greystones.
Lieutenant John G. Boilean	Lieutenant of Station	14th February 1859	25th January 1862	Stationed at Fairlight, Sussex, prior to Greystones, subsequently to Howth.
Lieut. William F.A. Harris	Chief Officer	17th May 1862	April 1868	
Richard Doherty	Chief Officer	April 1868	March 1878	Was noted as the Chief Officer in 1873 on the drawings for the new coast guard station.
No Chief Officers are shown in Navy lists for the intervening years through to the end of World War One, but this does not mean that the station could not have been in the charge of a senior rating.				
Charles Bew	Chief Officer	August 1889		Described as such on the front cover of the programme for the 1889 Greystones Regatta, when he was listed as a member of the Sailing Committee involved in organising it.
Robert Jeffers	Chief Officer	October 1892		Noted as such, at the inquiry into the death by drowning of 3 members of the Doyle family, including John Doyle (Coxswain of the Greystones Lifeboat) in October 1892.
Mr McCarthy	Chief Officer	October 1910		Noted as such in various press reports covering the rescue of the crew of the *Reciprocity*.
William Guppy	Officer in Charge	1st September 1919	31st March 1922	
Edward Archer	Officer in Charge			In 1922 the coast guard service was taken over by the Department of Industry & Commerce of the newly formed Irish Free State. From the late 1880s through to the 1920s, Osborne Spurling was a significant figure locally in the coast guard service along with Edward Archer (Coxswain of Greystones Lifeboat), such that both were effectively Officers in Charge within that time period, albeit the exact dates are not known.
Osborne Spurling	Officer in Charge		September 1926	
Bill Spurling	Officer in Charge	September 1926	October 1942	
Herbert Victor Ferns	Officer in Charge	October 1942	1952	
Paddy Doyle	Officer in Charge	1952	December 1980	
Derek Ferns	Officer in Charge	December 1980	April 1992	
Niall Ferns	Officer in Charge	April 1992	September 2009	Relinquished position to take up a full time role with The Irish Coast Guard.
John Ferns	Officer In Charge	September 2009	August 2016	
Dermot McCauley	Officer in Charge	August 2016	Present	

GREYSTONES LIFEBOAT

County Wicklow holds a special place in the history of the lifeboat service in Ireland. Though the Corporation for Preserving & Improving the Port of Dublin had placed their first lifeboat at Clontarf in 1801, it was at Arklow that the country's first lifeboat station was established in 1826 by the forerunner of what is now known as the Royal National Lifeboat Institution. Today there are 45 RNLI Lifeboat Stations on the island of Ireland (15 in Munster, 13 in Ulster, 11 in Leinster and 6 in Connacht). The 45 includes 3 stations on lakes.

While shipwrecks along the stretch of coastline near Greystones were not a common occurrence, there were occasional incidents which resulted in the loss of ships. *Lloyd's List* published the following on 21st March 1871. "*Kingstown, 20th March - The Limerick (S.S.), ashore at Greystones, belongs to Grangemouth and is from Huelva, with ore and oranges, she is full of water and there is little chance of saving her.*" On 3rd December 1867 *The Shields Daily News* under the header, "*Wicklow, Ireland*" reported the following. "*The Rev. Henry Rooks reports that a message was received on Sunday from Newcastle, distant some 5 or 6 miles along the coast, that a dismasted vessel was drifting broadside towards the Greystones and asking for the assistance of the Robert Theophilus Garden Lifeboat of the National Lifeboat Institution. The boat was accordingly got out and dispatched, and found that it was a lighter which had broken away from a vessel. The weather was very thick and rainy and it was blowing fresh at the time.*" The Wicklow Lifeboat, *Robert Theophilus Garden,* was the station's second all weather lifeboat, launched on 82 occasions during her service between 1866 and 1937, saving a total of 137 lives.

In the great storm of February 1861, the 200 ton brig, *Mary*, laden with coal, was wrecked on the shore at Greystones, with the loss of all five crew members, as she broke up into pieces in heavy seas. *The Morning Advertiser* dated 15th December 1849 reported the following. "*Dublin, December 12th, it has been blowing a gale at S.E. and S.S.E., with every appearance of increasing and continuing, several pieces of American timber have washed on shore from Wicklow to Greystones. The Wanderer, on shore at Greystones has broken up*. In another severe storm, *The Lancaster Gazette* dated 9th November 1844 reported that the "*Sovereign, Rogers, from Liverpool to Norfolk, N.S., is on the shore at Greystones with masts cut away and another vessel is on shore at The Breaches, broadside on*".

ABOVE & LEFT: Map and chart published in 1872, the year the Greystones Lifeboat Station was established. At that time there were 31 RNLI lifeboat stations located around the Irish coast. The coverage along the east coast was extensive, however there was only one lifeboat station (at Valentia, Co. Kerry) along the entire western seaboard, between Courtmacsherry in Co. Cork and Greencastle in Co. Donegal.

In September 1871 the Lifeboat Institution's Inspector visited Greystones and interviewed the Chief Officers of both Bray and Greystones Coast Guard Stations. The purpose of the visit was to ascertain the best location for the establishment of a new lifeboat station to be located along the coast between the existing stations at Kingstown and Wicklow. Greystones was duly selected. The Inspector visited William La Touche at his country home, *Bellevue,* who, as the local landowner, immediately threw his support behind the proposal and formed a local committee to create a lifeboat station at Greystones. Fortunately, the late J.J. Tancred, of *Pearville*, Co. Dublin, a man with connections to the area, had stipulated in his will that a large legacy of £1,000 was to be provided to the Lifeboat Institution for the purposes of placing an additional lifeboat on the Irish coast to be named after his late wife, Sarah. By the end of 1871, the committee had accepted an estimate for the construction of the lifeboat house, which was completed during the first half of 1872. Having become the location for the Institution's 233rd lifeboat around the coast of Britain and Ireland, the *Sarah Tancred* was duly launched at Greystones on Saturday 3rd August 1872.

GREYSTONES LIFEBOAT

BELOW: Report from *The Warder* newspaper dated Saturday 10th August 1872 giving a very detailed account of the christening and launch of the first Greystones Lifeboat, *Sarah Tancred.*

"*The little town of Greystones looked its best last Saturday afternoon, on the occasion of the christening and launching of the Sarah Tancred, a lifeboat that has just been built for that station. The boat is the gift of the late Mr Tancred, a gentleman who spent a large portion of his life in the neighbourhood of Bray and Greystones and who saw that in cases of wreck the means of saving life at this particular portion of a wild and dangerous coast were scant indeed. Accordingly, in his will, he bequeathed to the Royal National Lifeboat Institution a sum sufficient to establish a lifeboat station on the coast near Dublin. Greystones was chosen and the humane intentions of Mr Tancred were promptly and energetically supported by the residents. A committee of gentlemen was formed, Mr William R. La Touche acting as chairman and Dr Maunsell as Honorary Secretary. A hardy crew was easily found in Greystones and the praiseworthy efforts of all concerned in the undertaking culminated in the happy proceedings of Saturday. Greystones is usually a quiet place and of course the launch of a lifeboat, even apart from the good results likely to follow, was in itself an event to give a sufficient importance to give a holiday aspect to the town and bring to the place a large number of visitors from Dublin and different parts of Wicklow. Every circumstance favoured the interesting ceremony. The weather was delightful, flags were displayed from one or two of the neat houses in the town, work was generally suspended by the poorer inhabitants while the rank and fashion of the neighbourhood were present in great force to take part in the proceedings. After leaving the railway station, the most prominent object was the lifeboat, a fine specimen of its class, mounted on a large car and manned by thirteen or fourteen sturdy, stalwart men, wearing crimson caps and with their oars upright. The white and blue painting of the vessel, contrasted harmoniously with the red flags displayed by the crew and the rosettes of coloured ribbons and flowers worn by the six horses yolked to the wagon. At two o'clock, a procession was formed under the direction of Captain David Robertson, R.N., one of the inspectors of the Royal National Lifeboat Institution and who superintended the whole proceedings, being ably assisted by Mr Doherty, coast guard officer. The car containing the lifeboat went first, followed by the male and female children of the Greystones schools on foot and the procession was wound up by the carriages and vehicles of resident gentry of the neighbourhood. In this order, the procession passed slowly through the town, the only incident worthy of note being a halt opposite Dr Maunsell's house, followed by three cheers from all present.*

On arriving at that portion of the beach where the launch was to be made, a circle was made by the spectators and Captain Robertson ascended the car for the purpose of presenting the boat to the Bray and Greystones Station, on the part of the Royal National Lifeboat Institution. He said it afforded him great pleasure to hand the boat over to the management of Mr La Touche and the local committee of Greystones and Bray. He alluded to the munificence of the late Mr Tancred in providing a lifeboat for a place in which the Lifeboat Institution thought the necessity for it existed. It was best to be prepared for every emergency and therefore they were thankful that through the munificence of a citizen, they were able to place a lifeboat at Greystones (hear, hear). The National Lifeboat Institution was supported by voluntary contributions and they had thus enabled to place on the coast a large number of boats. He was happy to say that, owing to the harmonious manner in which the different committees worked, there was no difficulty and no want of staff at any station. It was the gentry living along the coast who enabled the Institution to accomplish the work and it was a lesson to them all, that when the work was done hand in hand, it was done well. He believed that all who read the records of the Lifeboat Institution would admit that the crews who manned the boats were brave and zealous, they were always ready by day and by night, to do their work well, regardless of creed or nationality (hear, hear). It was a grand thing to take a broad platform and feel that they were doing a good and humane work. He was proud to present that boat, which would complete the large number of 233 lifeboats which the Institution had under their charge. Captain Robertson then addressed the men in the boat, advising them to be guided by their coxswain, who he said was their appointed leader and concluded by presenting the Sarah Tancred to the Bray and Greystones branch of the National Lifeboat Institution.

Mr William La Touche, in reply, said Captain Robertson, as chairman of the Bray and Greystones Committee, I beg to return you the best thanks of the inhabitants of those localities for the splendid gift of the Royal National Lifeboat Institution and when you consider that the donor was a poor boy born in this neighbourhood, I think I express the feelings of all present in wishing the Sarah Tancred, a prosperous career and that through God's providence, she may be instrumental in saving many lives (applause). I will now call on the Rev. Mr Streane to offer up a prayer for this excellent institution. The Rev. Mr Streane, Rector of Delgany, then gave the 215th hymn, which was sung by local school children under the direction of Mr Harty, after which a prayer was offered up by the reverend gentleman. Lady Meath next advanced towards the lifeboat and christened her in the usual manner by breaking a bottle of wine against her stern, saying, at the same time "God bless the Sarah Tancred." After the singing of the "Lifeboat Song" by the school children, the car was dragged close to the seashore and, the vessel being let loose, she glided swiftly and gracefully into the water, amidst the cheers of the spectators and crew. The lifeboat rode buoyantly over the heavy ground-swells which in all kinds of weather prevail along the Wicklow coast and in a few minutes, in the hands of her able and willing crew, who were seen ploughing gallantly through the surf out towards the sea.

Amongst those present at the launch were: Lady Meath, Lady K. Brabazon, Lady Hodson, W.R. O'Byrne, High Sheriff of Wicklow, Messrs. W. Lindsay, J.P., & the Misses Lindsay, Wm. R. La Touche, D.L. & Miss La Touche, Charles La Touche, Captain La Touche and Octavius La Touche, Dr, Mrs and the Misses Maunsell, Master Pigott, the Rev. Mr Streane, rector, Delgany, the Rev. Maurice Nelligan, the Rev. Mr Seymour, the Rev. St. George French, the Rev. J.A. Galbraith, F.T.D.C, Captain R. Hudson, Wicklow Rifles & the Misses Hudson, Lucius H. Deering, the Rev Henry North, Wm. Corbett, Dr Shaw, TCD, Mrs and Miss Beatty, Mrs and Miss Whitfield, Captain D. Robertson, R.N., James Patterson, John Robertson, Captain Hutchsion, Harbourmaster, Kingstown, Patrick Reid and Mrs Reid, Mr Goddard, the Rev George Scott, the Rev. H. Galbraith, W.B. Orpen, Mr and the Misses Orpen, Charles Ganeen, Richard Graydon, Mrs and Miss Reville, Mr Doherty &c.

The Sarah Tancred is an admirably constructed boat and one well qualified for hand service in case of emergency. Her length is 33 feet, with 8 feet beam and she carries 10 oars. She was built by Mr Wolfe, one of the builders of the Lifeboat Institution and cost between four hundred and five hundred pounds. We should add that the British and Irish Steampacket Company and the Dublin, Wicklow and Wexford Railway carried the boat to its destination free of charge."

RIGHT: Down the years, the Wicklow Lifeboat has been a regular visitor to Greystones harbour. The boat in this photo taken on 17th July 1964 was the *Glencoe*, a Glasgow Lifeboat on relief duty at Wicklow at the time. It was visiting for the annual flag day collection. Upon leaving Greystones harbour, the lifeboat spotted a small rowing boat drifting three miles south east of Greystones, with an occupant waving an oar with a coat tied to it. The other oar had broken and the six relieved occupants of the boat were brought safely back to Greystones by the *Glencoe*.

LEFT: The Wicklow Lifeboat, *JW Archer*, which served as the station's lifeboat from 1956 until 1987, visiting Greystones harbour in the late 1960s. Succeeding the *Lady Kylsant* (1937-1956), the *JW Archer* was the 3rd of Wicklow Lifeboat Station's four permanent all-weather lifeboats to date since its establishment in 1857. Her successor, the *Annie Blaker,* is still in use today. Neither the unpaved car park nor sailing club had yet been built on the North Beach Road. The ruins of the *Yellow House* had been removed by this time, though the remains of *Jubilee Castle / Rosetta Fort,* with a section of its protective wall just above the shoreline can be seen in the background.

ABOVE: On Sunday 18th August 2013, the Wicklow Lifeboat, *Annie Blaker,* visited Greystones harbour. A granite plaque was unveiled on the new pier in memory of John Doyle, Coxswain of the Greystones Lifeboat by his granddaughter, Betty Lowe (standing in front of the plaque). Included in the photograph are great-grandchildren and great-great-grandchildren of John Doyle, as well Frank Doyle (seated in the front row, extreme right), grandson of William Doyle, who along with his nephew, Herbert Doyle, also drowned in the tragedy on 14th October 1892. The RNLI crew present were: Front row (left to right) Dean Mulvilhill, John Vize, Brendan Copeland (Station Mechanic), David O Leary (Deputy Coxswain), Tommy McAulay (Deputy Coxswain), Tommy Murphy (third Mechanic). Back row (left to right) Graham Fitzgerald, John Hayden, John Sillery (Head Launcher), Ciaran Doyle (Second Coxswain) and Wicklow RNLI Operations Manager Des Davitt.

GREYSTONES LIFEBOAT

THE SAD ACCIDENT AT GREYSTONES.

TO THE EDITOR OF THE IRISH TIMES.

SIR,—I appeal to the residents, visitors to this summer resort, and the public generally, on behalf of the poor widows and orphans of John Doyle, coxswain Greystones lifeboat, and William Doyle who, with his eldest son Herbert, lost their lives yesterday off Greystones Pier, whilst assisting to save the schooner Mersey from being wrecked during the fearful easterly gale. They were washed off the pier by a tremendous wave and drowned instantaneously in the sight of many people, none of whom could render the slightest assistance.

Their means of support depended almost entirely on the precarious calling of fishing.

John and William Doyle leave widows and two large families, numbering six and seven respectively, of quite young children, who are entirely unprovided for.

I am sure I will not appeal in vain through your medium in asking aid for these unfortunate families. It is the saddest accident that has occurred here for many years.

The following gentlemen have agreed to act as a committee with me for this good object, and any subscriptions sent to them or to myself will be thankfully received :—David R. Pigot, Esq., Thornbank, Greystones ; R. Cathcart Dobbs, Esq., Knockdolian, Greystones ; J. G. M'Entagart, Esq., The Beach, Greystones.—Yours, &c.,

ARTHUR HUGHES.

St. David's, Greystones, 15th October.

2017 marked 125 years since the tragic event that took place in Greystones harbour on the night of Friday 14th October 1892. Three members of the Doyle family, including John Doyle, Coxswain of the Greystones Lifeboat, were drowned. A very detailed account of the incident and the resultant inquest is included in Book No. 2. In summary, in a raging north easterly, the schooner, *Mersey*, owned by J.G. McEntagart, proprietor of what is now The Beach House, was in danger of being broken up against the pier. A decision was made to attempt to beach her, which first required her stern hawser to be cast off from the granite bollard securing it. *The Dublin Daily Express* reported that *"it was while engaged in this duty that John Doyle, coxswain of the lifeboat, William Doyle and his son Herbert Doyle lost their lives. A green sea came clean over the pier just as they had cast the rope free and carried them away into the surging water in the harbour."*

THE GREYSTONES DISASTER.

TO THE EDITOR OF THE DAILY EXPRESS.

SIR,—I send for publication an extract from a letter I have received from the secretary of the Royal National Lifeboat Institution, and would invite attention to the list of subscribers to the Greystones and Bray Branch of the institution in your advertising columns.— Yours faithfully,

R. CATHCART DOBBS.

18th November, 1892.

" 14 John street, Adelphi, London.

" MY DEAR SIR,—It was with the deepest regret the committee heard of the sad death of their gallant coxswain (J Doyle). They unanimously decided to request that you would convey the expression of their sympathy to Mrs Doyle, and to send for her benefit, and that of her children, in recognition of Doyle's services, the accompanying cheque for £50. You and your (lifeboat) committee will, doubtless, be good enough to see that the money is laid out for the best advantage.—Very faithfully yours,

" CHARLES DIBDIN."

In memory of
JOHN DOYLE
Frankfort, Greystones
Coxswain of the Greystones RNLI Lifeboat
The Sarah Tancred
Drowned at this harbour 15th Oct 1892
while carrying out a rescue on The Mersey
Awarded Scott Medal for saving lives
by the Royal Humane Society

RIGHT: The plaque which was placed on the new pier wall, close to the spot where John Doyle lost his life.

RIGHT: The entry in the RNLI's Greystones Lifeboat records detailing the granting of £50 to be awarded to the widow of John Doyle following the tragedy.

BELOW: Betty Lowe and her son, Richard, (granddaughter and great-grandson) of John Doyle, who travelled from Greystones to attend the unveiling of the RNLI Memorial in September 2009 at the Institution's headquarters in Poole, Dorset. They are photographed standing below the inscription "GREYSTONES - 1892 - J Doyle", which lies close to that of another Irish loss, Finton Sinnott of the Kilmore Quay Lifeboat in Co.Wexford, who lost his life whilst attempting a rescue on 24th December 1977.

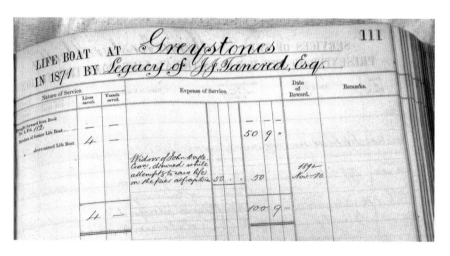

ABOVE: Depicting an RNLI crewman reaching out to save an individual, the RNLI Memorial at the Institution's headquarters at Poole in Dorset, honours the courage of all those lost at sea around the coasts of Britain and Ireland while endeavouring to save the lives of others. The silver bands around its edge carry the names, dates and lifeboat stations of more than 800 crewmen (including John Doyle, Coxswain of Greystones Lifeboat) who have lost their lives over the years.

BELOW & OPPOSITE PAGE: Extract from the Service Ledger of the Greystones Lifeboat Station which recorded details of the four launches undertaken during its years of operation (1872-1895).

Services of the Sarah Tancred

Presented to the Royal National Lifeboat Institution

Date of Wreck	Site of Wreck	Wind & Weather	Name of Vessel
1873 Feb 6th	Off Greystones	N.N.W strong breeze	Dublin Pilot Boat
May 17th	Bray Head	E.N.E fresh gale	Cutter yacht "Nicomi" of Dalkey
1876 Sept 30th	Off Bray	E.N.E. gale heavy sea	Brig, "Leonie" of Charlottetown, Prince Edward's Island
1877 Aug 25th	Off Bray Head	E. fresh gale	Yacht "Cosette" of Kingstown
			Carried forward to Book No.3 Folio 116

Life Boat at Greystones
in 1871 by The late J.J. Tancred Esq. (Legacy)

No. of Lives Saved	Nature of Service	Expense of Service		Date of Reward
	Put off but assistance not required	13 men @ 10s = £6 10s & 0d 22 helpers @ 2s 6d = £2 15s & 0d	£9 5s & 0d	1873 Feb 20th
4	Lives saved	13 men @ 20s = £13 0s & 0d 18 helpers = £2 5s & 0d Expense of bringing lifeboat back from Wicklow = £2 12s & 0d Messenger = £0 7s & 0d	£18 4s & 0d	May 23rd
	Took lifeboat along coast	13 men @ 7s 6d = £4 17s & 6d 18 helpers @ 5s = £4 10s & 0d 4 horses @ 20s = £4 0s & 0d	£13 7s & 6d	1876 Nov 25th
	Services not required	13 men @ 7s = £6 10s & 0d 25 helpers @ 2s 6d = £3 2s & 6d	£9 12s & 6d	1877 Aug 31st
4			£50 9s & 0d	

At first glance, a total of four launches over a quarter of a century for the Greystones Lifeboat does not seem many, but this was not unusual. The RNLI archives at Poole reveal lifeboat stations which operated for a number of years with either a low number or even zero launches. The records for Chapman's Pool Lifeboat Station in Dorset reveal just two launches between 1866 and 1880. The Llanelli Lifeboat Station in South Wales had only one launch between 1852 and 1871. Furthermore, the degree of difficulty, not to say danger in attempting to safely launch a pulling lifeboat off a shingle beach in an easterly gale, cannot be underestimated. For the first 16 years of the Greystones Lifeboat Station, there was also no boat slip. The extended pier and north wall were only in existence for the final eight years of the station's operation. The Wicklow and Kingstown Lifeboats had the benefit of larger, more sheltered harbours than Greystones and this is reflected in their number of launches (for example, between 1866 and 1889, the Wicklow Lifeboat, *Robert Theophilus Garden,* was launched 21 times, rescuing 66 people).

Additional information relating to three of the four launches that were made by the Greystones Lifeboat is contained in newspaper reports of the time, along with other sources. These are summarised below and on the following page as follows:

Sarah Tancred launched 17ᵗʰ May 1873.

THEY BENT THEIR BACKS TO THE OARS.

- *The Irish Times* dated 19ᵗʰ May 1873, under the story header "*Yachting Accident*", reported that "*the Nicomi, a yacht of eight tons, belonging to the R.A.Y.C., went out yesterday for a cruise with 5 gentlemen on board. When abreast of Bray Head, the mast went about two feet under the hounds. The boat becoming unmanageable, all her sails and gear being over her side, the skipper endeavoured to set sail on the stump of her mast, but finding she would not work with it, he let go his anchor. Hoisting his ensign in the rigging, it was seen from the shore and the Greystones Lifeboat was telegraphed for. The occupants were all taken off after being three hours in a most perilous condition. A tug boat brought the vessel into harbour yesterday*".

- *Lloyd's List* dated 20ᵗʰ May 1873 noted "*Dr. Maunsell reports that good service has just been rendered by the Greystones Lifeboat of the National Institution, which boat was placed here about nine months since. The boat was called out on Saturday afternoon. The boat proceeded through a heavy surf and after several hours of hard work, she reached the vessel and rescued four persons on board at the time. The lifeboat then had to run before the gale for Wicklow, which place she made in safety at 11 o'clock on Saturday night*".

- *The Morning Post* dated 6ᵗʰ June 1873, under its column headed "*Royal National Lifeboat Institution*" reported as follows: "*The Greystones (County Wicklow) Lifeboat had been instrumental last month in saving four persons from the yacht, Nicomi of Dalkey, which had been overtaken by a fresh gale from E.N.E., a high sea and was in great danger off Bray Head. The lifeboat was launched through very heavy surf and found that those on board the yacht were about to run her ashore, where she must have gone to pieces among the rocks, with the loss of all hands. After effecting the rescue, the lifeboat had to run for Wicklow, not being able to land at Greystones.*"

RIGHT: Extract from *The Lifeboat*, the journal of The National Lifeboat Institution dated 1ˢᵗ May 1874, which recorded the rescue of the crew of the yacht, *Nicomi.* The four lives saved were part of the overall total of 668 lives saved around the coast of Britain and Ireland, by the Institution's 240 lifeboats during 1873, as also reported in the Institution's 1873 annual report.

> May 17.—The Greystones Life-boat put off, during a fresh gale from the E.N.E., and rescued 4 persons from the cutter yacht *Nicomi*, of Dalkey, which was in distress off Bray Head.—Expense of service, 18*l.* 4*s.*

COMING ASHORE—"ALL SAVED!"

Sarah Tancred launched 30ᵗʰ September 1876.

- The entry in the Service Ledger of the Greystones Lifeboat records the vessel in distress as being the brig, *Leonie*, registered at Charlottetown, Prince Edward Island, Canada. Newspaper reports, as well as the subsequent inquiry into the event, state otherwise. The vessel in distress was the 300 ton brig, *Leona*, heading for Liverpool, with a cargo of timber from St. John, New Brunswick. On the night of Friday 29ᵗʰ September, the ship, built in 1866 at Dorchester, New Brunswick, sailed north past Greystones. The ship's captain, Thomas Richards, took some bearings but miscalculated his ship's position. With the weather deteriorating and believing he was near Dublin Bay, he decided to seek refuge in Dún Laoghaire harbour and sailed landwards.

- *The Weekly Freeman's Journal* dated 7ᵗʰ October 1876 carried a lengthy report on the incident, covering also the inquiry held at Kingstown Coast Guard Station on 3ʳᵈ October (as the Second Coxswain of the Kingstown Lifeboat was drowned taking part in the rescue). "*The first person examined was Thomas Richards, captain of the brig, Leona. He stated that when off the Vanguard lightship, he mistook it for the Kish Light. After making signals for a pilot, the weather was hazy and he was unable to see the land well and ran in for Bray Bay, believing it to be Kingstown. When too late, he ascertained his mistake, then cast anchor. The vessel dragged the two anchors which he put out. A third one was put out and they lay out from the shore from about eleven o'clock. He had a signal of distress flying from the masthead.*" Mr Luxham of Bray Coast Guard Station was first to reply and telegrams were sent to Kingstown and Greystones Lifeboat Stations.

GREYSTONES LIFEBOAT

- Upon receipt of the telegraph at the Postal Telegraph Office located at *Rockport*, the crew of the Greystones Lifeboat quickly mustered. It was decided that it would be better to attempt to launch the lifeboat from the beach at Bray rather than Greystones. The 33 foot *Sarah Tancred* was drawn on her carriage by four horses up Windgates, over the top of Bray Head and down Putland Road to the beach at Bray. The heavy swell rolling in made a beach launch impossible. Shortly after 3pm, the Kingstown Lifeboat, which had battled for two hours through the rough seas, was approaching the *Leona*.

- *The Weekly Freeman's Journal* dated 7th October 1876 further reported. *"After considerable difficulty, the captain and the crew of the Leona were taken on board, the sea running fearfully high at the time & the rain falling in torrents. Notwithstanding the desperate character of the weather, a large crowd was collected on shore, who watched the operations with the most intense interest. After gallantly getting the crew into the lifeboat, the two lug sails were set and the boat immediately set out to return to Kingstown. She made some headway, but began to be driven in towards the shore and as the coxswain seemed about to put her head to the wind, a heavy sea struck the boat when off the Bray Bar, capsizing her, precipitating all the occupants numbering 19 persons into the water. The greatest anxiety prevailed on the shore for the safety of the men. The boat remained bottom up for a considerable time and began to drift landwards, some of the men clinging to the sides, while the larger number were struggling in the water. The men were brought ashore after some difficulty."*

- Among the assembled crowd on the shore who assisted in helping the men were George, Richard and Robert Cuthbert of the Bray schooner owning family. Members of the Greystones Lifeboat remained at the scene and assisted in dragging the men out of the heavy swell as they were washed ashore. *The Dublin Daily Express* dated 3rd December 1886, reporting on the launch of the *Sarah Tancred's* successor, *Richard Browne*, recalled that day just over 10 years earlier in Bray. *"Though it was not necessary to launch the Greystones boat, the crew, led by John Doyle of Greystones afforded great help in saving the lives of the Kingstown crew when their boat capsized"*.

- One of the first to be carried up the beach was coast guard officer, Thomas White. He was also Second Coxswain of the Kingstown Lifeboat. Unconscious, he was taken to a cottage near the strand, *"where every assistance, medical and otherwise"* was rendered, but he was pronounced dead at 7pm. A roll call of the crew of the lifeboat and the *Leona* was conducted on the beach. Sadly three of the *Leona's* crew were missing and were subsequently confirmed as having drowned. The lifeboat was secured and moored at Bray harbour. The next day the *Leona*, which had held fast to her anchor, was towed by a tug into Kingstown harbour. *Lloyd's List* dated 4th October 1876 reported that the ship was in the *"charge of the pilots, who along with the owner of the tug, are procuring a warrant to arrest the vessel for salvage services"*. At the time of her salvage the *Leona's* port of registry, according to *The Mercantile Navy List,* was St. John, New Brunswick, but this was transferred later that year to Dublin. *The Mercantile Navy Lists* for 1880 & 1890 both record her port of registry as Dublin (owner listed as James Carroll).

- At the inquest held at Kingstown Coast Guard Station, the jury returned a verdict that Thomas White, the Second Coxswain of the Kingstown Lifeboat, had drowned as a result of the capsizing of the lifeboat at Bray on 30th September. The RNLI subsequently awarded a £150 legacy payment to be added to the local subscription fund to help provide for his widow and children. In a letter written to the editor of *The Dublin Daily Express* published on 2nd October 1876, William Stapleton, Crofton Road, Kingstown, wrote of the impact that the news of Thomas White's drowning had on the town. *"I never saw such excitement among the population, he being a native of Kingstown. As far as I could judge by their expressions, he was a great favourite with the seamen as well as the landsmen of the town. Every person could tell how he risked his life several times in the lifeboat and otherwise, to rescue his fellow man."*

Sarah Tancred launched 25th August 1877.

- *Lloyd's List* dated 30th August 1877 reported that *"Cosette, of Kingstown, Mr Wilson, owner, was overtaken by the gale when off Bray, with only the owner and two boys on board and was in great danger of being driven ashore. A telegraph was despatched to Greystones, the nearest lifeboat station of the National Lifeboat Institution. In less than 20 minutes of the receipt of the message, the lifeboat was in the water and on her way to assist those on board the endangered vessel. Before however she could reach the spot, the yacht, assisted by the ebb tide, succeeded in getting around the Muglins Rocks and ultimately arrived safely in Kingstown harbour"*.

GREYSTONES LIFEBOAT

The following pages show the entries contained in the Precis Ledger (which details the records of the lifeboat inspectors) for Greystones Lifeboat from the initial entry in 1871 through to the final entry dated 1907. These ledger entries are transcribed in italicised bullet point format below and are supplemented with additional information including press reports, photos and drawings.

1871

- *2ⁿᵈ September: Inspector visited locality to see whether it was practicable to form a lifeboat station thereat, in as much as Mr J.J. Tancred of Pearville, Co. Dublin had bequeathed a legacy of £1,000 to the Institution on condition that it would establish a station in the neighbourhood of Dublin and place a lifeboat thereat to be named the Sarah Tancred. He had interviews with the Chief Officers of the Coast Guard at Bray and Greystones, both of whom stated that, although wrecks were not frequent in the locality, yet they thought that a lifeboat might occasionally be of service and that looking to the long distance between the Kingstown and Wicklow stations, they thought it desirable to place a lifeboat at Greystones as the most convenient point. Having selected the best available position for a lifeboat house, the inspector called on Mr W. La Touche, J.P. of Bellevue, near Greystones, the owner of the land on which the house would be built, when he expressed his readiness to grant a long lease of the site at a nominal rent and to give his support to the undertaking and form a local committee. The inspector therefore recommended that a lifeboat establishment be formed here, the boat to be 33 feet long by 8 feet wide, there being a large number of boatmen in the locality and as she might have long distances to go from the land also she might be provided with a transporting carriage and sails. Captain H.F. Hand R.N. the inspecting Commander of the Coast Guard of the Division, also recommended the formation of a lifeboat station at Greystones.*
- *15ᵗʰ September: Ordered Messrs. Woolfe & Son to proceed with the lifeboat and Messrs. Robinson & Napton with the carriage.*
- *4ᵗʰ October: Received £1,000 being the amount of Mr Tancred's legacy.*
- *12ᵗʰ December: Assistant inspector visited locality to meet the local committee and to see if the new site proposed for the lifeboat was an eligible one. This site was quite as good as that originally selected by the inspector and as Mr La Touche was willing to grant the institution 86 feet by 25 feet, he recommended that the house might be built thereon. From the beach being steep shingle, liable to considerable changes, the lifeboat Assistant Inspector did not think that the station could be made thoroughly efficient until a slipway was made by which the beach might be avoided and the lifeboat launched under the lee of the small pier. This slipway would have to be excavated out of the rock, which was unsatisfied and therefore the expense would be considerable. He told the local committee that the institution had not called on the locality to build the lifeboat house as was usually done in such cases. He thought the locality ought to raise funds enough to do at least a greater part of the work, as the slipway would be a great benefit to the fishermen and that if they raised two thirds of the amount he thought that the inspector would grant the remainder.*
- *28ᵗʰ December: Committee accepted an estimate amounting to £216, 5s & 0d by Mr T. Connolly for erecting the lifeboat house.*

The Lifeboat Institution's income and expenditure account for the year ended 31ˢᵗ December 1871 (contained in the edition of "The Lifeboat" dated 1ˢᵗ May 1872) discloses that the actual cost of the lifeboat house at Greystones was £218 & 5s.

1872

- *1ˢᵗ February: Committee approved the draft lease of the lifeboat house.*
- *7ᵗʰ March: Affixed the corporate seal of the Institution to the lease and counterpart of the lifeboat house.*
- *17ᵗʰ June: Lifeboat had its harbour trial which proved satisfactory.*
- *21ˢᵗ July: Lifeboat and carriage forwarded from London to Dublin free of charge by one of the steamers of the British & Irish Steam Packet Company. The Wexford & Drogheda Railway Company then took the boat and carriage free of charge.*
- *24ᵗʰ July: The lifeboat having arrived at Dublin was removed from the steamer, but from the tides not serving well, it was too late to get her on the trucks at the railway station.*
- *27ᵗʰ July: Assistant inspector had the boat safely removed from her carriage and placed in the house. The railway station not being provided with a crane or suitable siding, the work was heavy. The boathouse was well built, but of a plain character. The local committee expressed a desire to have the lifeboat launched on Saturday 3ʳᵈ August as they could not arrange for an earlier day.*
- *2ⁿᵈ December: The Institution received £350 from the solicitors to the executors of the late Mr Tancred, being the larger portion of the residue of the estate bequeathed to the Institution by the testator.*

1873

- *13ᵗʰ January: Assistant inspector visited station and took lifeboat afloat in a fresh breeze, smooth water & he found all in order.*
- *29ᵗʰ April: Mr La Touche, the Chairman of the branch, asked whether the Institution would be prepared to assist in meeting the expense of making a pier and carrying out other works at this place, one of which was the construction of a slipway, which was considered indispensable for the use of the lifeboat.*
- *30ᵗʰ April: Mr La Touche saw Mr Lewis, the Secretary, who informed him that it would be contrary to the rules of the Institution to assist in carrying out any county work, but that if it could be shown that a slipway was necessary for the lifeboat, he had no doubt the committee would be prepared to grant £30 or £40 in aid of the expense of the same.*
- *27ᵗʰ October: The Revd. Maurice Day accepted the office of Honorary Secretary of the branch on the resignation of Dr. Maunsell.*

1874

- *14ᵗʰ February: Assistant inspector visited station. The after part of the fore carriage had been broken, but it did not interfere with transporting the lifeboat and could easily be repaired by the village carpenter and blacksmith and instructed him to do it at once. Took the lifeboat afloat in fine weather. Everything excepting the above was in good order.*
- *13ᵗʰ April: The Revd. Maurice Day resigned the Honorary Secretaryship of the branch and was succeeded by Mr Patrick Reid.*

- *17ᵗʰ April: Second Assistant Inspector visited station and found everything in good order. Mr Reid who had just succeeded the Revd. M. Day as the honorary secretary took great interest in the work.*

1875

- *5ᵗʰ August: Assistant inspector visited the station and found the coxswain afloat for annual drill and nearly all the men away. He found that the boat had been used before the paint was sufficiently hard and he therefore gave instructions that the inside of the boat be repainted. He also stated that when the boat was first placed at this station, he had reported that a slipway cut out of the rocks for launching the boat would be a great advantage, but he did not recommend it on account of the expense. The Board of Works were now however about to construct a slipway 10 feet wide for the use of the coast guard in exactly the same position as the one contemplated by the assistant inspector and he had applied to them to make the slipway 16 feet wide, so that it could be used by the lifeboat on her carriage and even if the difference of cost should have to be paid by the Institution, the advantage would be very great and the Assistant Inspector therefore recommended it for the favourable consideration of the committee.*
- *2ⁿᵈ September: Committee approved of this recommendation.*

ABOVE: One of the oldest known photographs of the harbour area at Greystones taken during the 1870s. It shows the original basic roof and gable of the lifeboat house built in 1872. This was prior to the subsequent enhancement carried out in 1879, as shown in the photograph on the following page. In the extreme top right corner of the photograph is the large lime kiln. Note the large fishing boats known locally as snuffs pulled high up on the beach. These were open boats of about 24 feet overall, clinker built and double ended, though it appears at least three of them at Greystones were known to have square transoms. They carried around 2 tons of ballast and were sloop rigged. They were mostly built in Greystones, many by Henry Evans (1808-1898) of *Emily House* on Trafalgar Road.

1876

- *4ᵗʰ April: Committee accepted the offer of the Dublin Board of Public Works to widen the slipway at the coast guard station here to make it available for the lifeboat at an expense of £35.*
- *13ᵗʰ June: Second assistant inspector visited station and found all in good order, but he was unable to get a crew to exercise the boat. The work at the joint coast guard and lifeboat slipway had been stopped in consequence of the fishermen having lodged an appeal to the effect that their right of way would be infringed on. It appeared that they would have a very tangible grievance unless the Board of Works built for them a landing quay for fish, as the new works will occupy the only available spot for boats to discharge their cargoes at. The second assistant inspector intended to communicate with the board when in Dublin.*
- *16ᵗʰ July: Second assistant inspector visited station and found that the proposed slipway had been brought to a standstill, the fishermen having removed the work when some weeks in progress. He had interviews with the officials of the Board of Works on the subject. It was quite clear that the fishermen would have a substantial grievance if the works were carried out as originally contemplated. The Board were in communication with the Admiralty and Board of Trade and proposed to build a separate landing place for the fishermen. The second assistant inspector informed them that he would not recommend the Institution to join in any further expense than that originally agreed to for the actual boat slip itself, as the station was not of sufficient importance to call for a large outlay for the purpose contemplated. He thought that ultimately the plan would be abandoned and no slipway would be built.*

1877

- *6th August: Inspector visited station. The coxswain and crew were all absent, but the inspector went over everything with the chief boatman of the coast guard and the coxswain returned shortly before the inspector left. Everything was in excellent order. The boat and house had been repainted and looked very well.*

1878

- *25th June: Lieut. Monteith R.N. inspector visited station and found everything in good order, except that the strings of 7 of the lifebelts were rotten, the end rollers of the carriage rusted into fixtures and the box of one of the small wheels worm eaten. Instructions were given to the Hon. Secretary to have the defects put right at once. Accompanied by the Hon. Secretary, the inspector took the boat afloat.*
- *28th June: Inspector attended meeting of local committee and recommends:*
  1. *That the Board of Works Dublin be communicated with respecting the slipway, as in the event of an easterly gale it would be impossible to launch the lifeboat from such a steep beach.*
  2. *That the name of the branch be changed from Greystones to that of Greystones & Bray.*
  3. *That a tablet be placed over the front door of the boathouse showing the name of the gentleman whose legacy provided the funds for the establishment of the branch.*
  4. *That the space of ground leased to the Institution be enclosed by a stone wall with iron gates at a probable cost of £25.*
- *4th July: Approved by general committee excepting suggestion No.3 which was referred to Chief Inspector.*

1879

- *27th Jan: Captain Sergeant R.N., inspector accompanied by Hon. Secretary visited station and took boat afloat. The boat was left in good order, but considerable dissatisfaction exists amongst the inhabitants as to the selection of the crew.*
- *5th June: Committee accepted Mr T Evans' tender amounting to £73 for various alterations and improvements to the lifeboat house.*

RIGHT: Thomas Evans (1842-1922) was the contractor who added the kneelered gables with granite finials to the roof of the lifeboat house in 1879. According to the records of the Greystones Lifeboat held by the RNLI, there is no entry recording any expenditure incurred for this subsequent enhancement. It is possible that either the local lifeboat committee and or the La Touche family (who were the lessors of the lifeboat house) may have paid privately for the cost of this enhancement to the roof. Today only the northern end of the lifeboat house still retains this architectural addition. The kneelered gable and granite finial on the southern end of the building was removed around the middle of the 20th century. Thomas Evans was also the contractor who built Greystones Presbyterian Church on Trafalgar Road in 1887. He was the son of Henry Evans (1808-1898), of *Emily House* on Trafalgar Road. He resided at *Springmount* on Church Road, beside *Somerset*, where his brother John lived. In 1912, the latter acquired Charlesland Farm to the south of Greystones, which was run as a mixed farm and included Charlesland Dairy until its closure in 1947. The Evans family developed Charlesland Golf Course in the early 1990s and subsequently sold the remainder of the farm for residential development at the turn of the millennium.

ABOVE: 1890s photograph showing the lifeboat house with its two granite finials and kneelered gables added in 1879.

ABOVE: The former lifeboat house in its present use as Sweeney's Take Away & Cafe, photographed in May 2018, with the remaining granite finial on its northern end.

- *7th August: Lieutenant Tipping R.N., District Inspector visited station and found it in good order. The lifeboat had just returned from the Wicklow Regatta where she took the second prize. Chain traces and harness were required.*
- *18th October: Admiral Ward, Chief Inspector visited station accompanied by Lieutenant Tipping R.N., the District Inspector and witnessed the launching of the lifeboat and exercise under oars and sails under the Lieutenant's Superintendents. The Hon. Sec. was also in attendance. The boat was afloat in eleven minutes from leaving the house over a very soft beach which necessitated the parbuckling of the wheels nearly the whole distance. The launch and exercise were very satisfactory. The late improvements in the boathouse had greatly enhanced its appearance and seemed to have been very well executed. The slipway, which had been commenced by the Dublin Board of Works for the use of the coast guards towards which the Institution had offered to give £35 if made wide enough for use by the lifeboat on its carriage, remained in an unfinished state, perfectly useless and had made the landing on the rocks more impracticable than it was before. The coxswain was said to be an excellent man and he had the lifeboat and all pertaining to it in very good order.*

- *20th October:* Chief Inspector went to the office of the Dublin Board of Works and ascertained from the Secretary that the Board had no intention of proceeding with the slipway and that as far as they were concerned the Institution was at liberty to complete it in any manner the committee thought best. He however thought that the Institution had better obtain from the Admiralty an official permission to do so.

- *22nd October:* Chief Inspector and the District Inspector again visited Greystones by appointment to meet Mr La Touche, the landed proprietor, the Hon. Secretary, the contractor to further consider what steps had better be taken with regard to the slipway here. Mr La Touche stated that he was not prepared to make the slipway or to contribute to it himself and both he and Mr Reid, the Hon. Secretary considered that the Admiralty ought to carry out this original intention as the slip was just as necessary as before for launching and hauling up the coast guard boats whilst the unfinished state in which it been left had seriously injured it for the fishermen as a landing place for their nets. The contractor roughly estimated that to make the slipway suitable for taking the lifeboat over it on its carriage in the manner explained by the inspector would cost from £100 to £120. The former amount would in the opinion of the inspector quite cover or more than cover. The inspector considered that the completion of the slipway was necessary but he recommended that further communication from the Admiralty should be awaited.

- *6th November:* Committee approved of the inspector's recommendation.

- *15th December:* The Director of Works of the Navy forwarded to the Institution a copy of a report from the inspecting officer of the Dublin Board of Works on the subject of the proposed coast guard slipway here with accommodation for the lifeboat.

- *23rd December:* Hon. Sec. of the Greystones Branch stated that the local committee had considered this report and that the fishermen had long since withdrawn all opposition to the making of the slipway. An application had however been made by the landed proprietor and the fishermen to the government to make a harbour at Greystones and if this application were acceded to, there would be no necessity to make a lifeboat slipway, as one would be made from which all boats could be launched. It was proposed that the government should contribute £3,000 and the locality £1,000 towards this scheme and the local committee hoped that if the institution were relieved of the expense of making a slipway, it would contribute something towards £1,000 in question on condition that proper accommodation was afforded for launching the lifeboat.

- *30th December:* Committee postponed this matter for further inquiries.

1880

- *15th March:* District Inspector visited station and found it in very good order. He took the lifeboat afloat, the exercise was satisfactory. Nothing more had been done towards making the slipway near the quay. For further details, vide District Inspectors' reports dated 18th January 1881, 27th June 1881 and 20th December 1881.

1881

- *6th October:* Committee accepted Mr Ludlow's services amounting to £13, 5s & 0d and £7, 15s & 0d for cementing the inside walls of the lifeboat house and lining the inside roof of the house.

1883

- *24th October:* Honorary Secretary asked whether the Institution would allow the District Inspector to give evidence before the Harbour Commissioners as to the necessity of constructing a harbour here in order to admit of the safe and speedy launching of the lifeboat.

- *1st November:* Committee decided not to comply with this request.

LAUNCHING THE LIFEBOAT.

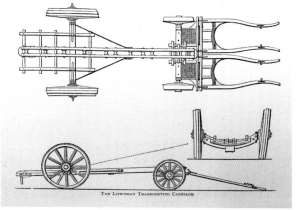

THE LIFE-BOAT TRANSPORTING CARRIAGE.

In his book, "*History of the Lifeboat and its Work*" published in 1874, Richard Lewis described the method for launching one of the RNLI's 33 foot, ten-oared pulling lifeboats of the same specification as the *Sarah Tancred*. "*The lifeboat is drawn to the water's edge, where the carriage is turned round so that its rear end, from which the boat is launched, shall face to seaward. The crew then take their seats in the boat, each rower in his place, with his oar over the side, ready to pull and the coxswain at the helm, or with steering oar in hand. The carriage is then backed by men or horses or both, sufficiently far into the water to ensure the boat being afloat when she is run off the carriage, or if the ground be very soft, or sufficient help unattainable, the carriage is first backed into the water before the crew get into the boat. Self detaching ropes, termed launching ropes, previously hooked to each side of the boat's stern post and rove through sheaves at the rear end of the carriage are then led up the beach and manned either by assistants, or have one or more horses attached to them. When all is ready, the coxswain, watching a favourable moment, gives the word and the boat, the keel of which rests on small iron rollers, is run off rapidly into the water, with her bow facing the surf. The oarsmen then give way, even before her stern has left the carriage and she is at once under command, 'ere the sea has time to throw her back broadside to the shore*".

GREYSTONES LIFEBOAT

1884

- _20th August:_ Chief Inspector accompanied by District Inspector visited this station. He found that the gear had not been replaced since the last time afloat and other signs of neglect for which the coxswain was admonished and the Honorary Secretary's attention called to it.
- _21st August:_ Local Committee to consider the question of whether the Institution should contribute towards the sum of £2,500 to be raised locally in order to secure the government grant of £7,500 for constructing a pier or breakwater. This pier would greatly facilitate the launching of the lifeboat in an onshore gale and in these circumstances he recommended the request to the favourable consideration of the committee.
- _4th September:_ Committee decided to advance £100 in aid of the proposed work.

1885

- _2nd September:_ Committee noted the thanks of the Institution inscribed on vellum to Mr Patrick Reid on his resigning the office of Honorary Secretary of the branch after 11 years service. He was succeeded by Mr R.C. Dobbs.

1886

- _7th January:_ Committee accepted, on the Chief Inspector's recommendation, a tender amounting to £4, 15s &0d enclosing the space between the lifeboat house and the boundary walls of the adjoining property.
- _1st April:_ Committee decided on the recommendation of the Chief Inspector that the lifeboat be replaced by a new water ballast boat, 37 feet by 8 feet. Also to appropriate the new boat to the gift of £500 received by the Institution by Mrs R. F. Browne of Monkstown, Dublin for a lifeboat to be named the Richard Browne.
- _29th June:_ Mrs Browne gave an additional £150 to the Institution, making in all £650.
- _23rd & 26th April:_ Mr James Price, a civil engineer of Dublin, a member of the Greystones Local Committee has asked permission to try the experiment of fitting the lifeboat with electrical accumulators and the necessary machinery with the view to utilising electricity as a supplemental means of propelling the boat.
- _2nd September:_ Lifeboat had its harbour trial which proved satisfactory.
- _11th November:_ Lifeboat and carriage forwarded to their station per British & Irish Steam Packet Company and old boat and carriage returned to London. Boat which is named the Richard Browne is 37ft x 8 ft and was built by Messrs. Forrestt & Son and the carriage by the Bristol Wagon Works Co.

The Greystones Lifeboat Station was one of 16 lifeboat stations located around the coast of Britain and Ireland to receive a new replacement lifeboat during 1886 (Howth was the only other Irish Station to also receive a new lifeboat that year). The £650 gift given to the RNLI by Mrs R.F. Browne of _Annesley Cottage,_ Monkstown stipulated that it should be used to purchase a new lifeboat to be named in memory of her father, Richard Browne, also of Monkstown. In contrast to the warm sunny August day 14 years earlier for the launch of the _Sarah Tancred_, the launch of the _Richard Browne_ at Greystones took place on a bright but frosty morning on Thursday 2nd December 1886. Amongst those in attendance were William La Touche, Robert Cathcart Dobbs, Mrs Joseph Dobbs and the schooner owner, Arthur Evans.

1887

- _14th April:_ District Inspector reported that the lifeboat had been satisfactorily tested at her station.

The Dublin Daily Express dated Saturday 16th April 1887 in its report on the new lifeboat noted that "on Thursday 14th instant her crew were exercised by Captain Tipping, R.N., when the Richard Browne proved herself to be possessed of excellent sailing qualities. In the afternoon, a large number of spectators assembled to witness the measures taken to test the righting powers of the new boat. Several bags filled with stone equal in weight to four or five average men, having been lashed to the thwarts, a rope was pushed under her and by means of a crane on the pier, she was turned nearly right over and allowed to recover herself. Captain Tipping then called for volunteers to remain in her while undergoing a severe test. Mr Frank Dobbs, son of the Hon. Secretary responded when the boat was capsized, made a complete summersault and righted with such energy as to scoop up a large quantity of water. The sole occupant was drenched, but appeared to thoroughly enjoy his shower bath. The boat was next upset with the sails up, the jib and mizzen made fast and in a few seconds, after a little hesitation, she again rode erect. Those present expressed themselves much pleased with the performance of the Richard Browne and, doubtless the experiment has done much to increase and strengthen the confidence of the crew." The then 21 year old Frank Dobbs was none the worse for his dunking in Greystones harbour that day. A civil engineer, like his father, he went on to help build the Ferro-Carril Norte railway line Argentina. He later returned to Greystones, residing in _Knockrath_ on Church Lane from 1913 until 1946.

- _5th May:_ Committee decided that the old lifeboat and carriage be repaired and improved and retained in reserve.

1888

- _1st March:_ Committee instructed the Chief Inspector to communicate with the Local Committee as to the lifeboat being exercised six times in excess of the regular exercises, selecting the suitable days with a view to giving the crew more confidence in the boat.
- _12th April:_ Committee decided on the Chief Inspector's recommendation that two of the six extra exercises of the lifeboat in bad weather ordered by the Committee be dispensed with, the men now having great confidence in the boat after a trial under the District Inspector's Superintendents.

1889

- _11th March:_ District Inspector reported that the small harbour was rapidly filling up and that the slip could only be used at high water.

1890
- _24th December:_ Lifeboat brought to London for alterations and temporary boat sent to station in the meantime.

1891
- _8th May:_ Boat having been altered and improved by Messrs. Forrestt & Son of Limehouse had its harbour trial which proved satisfactory.
- _16th June:_ Boat sent per Great Western Railway to Bristol, thence per Bristol & Wexford Steam Ship Company's steamer to Wexford, thence per Dublin & Wexford Railway to Greystones and temporary boat withdrawn.

1892
- _8th January:_ A new transporting carriage built by the Bristol Wagon Works Company and a set of Tipping's wheel plates were sent to the station. The old carriage was left at the station for disposal.
- _8th February:_ District Inspector reported that he had ordered some slight alterations to the gable of the boathouse to be carried out. As the cost was more than had been anticipated, the Honorary Secretary had obtained an estimate amounting to £8, 10s for the work.
- _11th February:_ Committee sanctioned the repairs being carried out.
- _15th October:_ Honorary Secretary reported the death by drowning of John Doyle who had been coxswain of the lifeboat for 16 years. During that period the boat had been launched once on service. No lives had been saved.
- _11th November:_ Committee voted £50 in aid of the local subscription being raised for the family of the late coxswain.

1894
- _6th February:_ District Inspector reported having authorised the Honorary Inspector to pay 1s, 1d each to the signalman and 4 coast guard men who helped him to put the lifeboat to rights and the hatches in working order.

1895
- _14th March:_ Committee voted a binocular glass with a suitable inscription thereon to Mr R. Cathcart Dobbs in recognition of his long and valuable service as Honorary Secretary of the branch.

Robert Cathcart Dobbs served as Hon. Secretary of the Greystones Lifeboat for 11 years from 1885 until its closure in 1896. He was born in Bangalore in 1836, the son of Major General Richard Stewart Dobbs. Like his father, he spent a number of years working in India where he was with the Madras Civil Service. The Dobbs family eventually settled in Greystones where they played an active role in local affairs. At the inaugural meeting of the newly formed Greystones Improvement Association in held in May 1896, Robert Cathcart Dobbs, fresh from his 11 years service as Hon. Secretary of the Greystones Lifeboat was elected as its Chairman. In the early 1900s, he resided at _Knockdolian_ on Church Lane until his death at the age of 78 in April 1914. At that time his son, Frank Stewart Dobbs, was a neighbour, residing at _Knockrath_.

ABOVE: Photograph taken in the 1890s from Jones' Hill with St. Patrick's Church on the right. To its left in the foreground is _Knockdolian_. The house, designed by James Price who lived at _Knockeevin_ on Church Road, was built in 1879 for Major General Richard Stewart Dobbs upon his retirement. Following his death in 1888 his son, Robert Cathcart Dobbs resided there. The roofs of some of the cottages on the North Beach and the lime kiln are visible in the distance.

- _9th May:_ Committee decided on the recommendation of Sir Richard Williams Baltsley Bart, a member of the Committee of Management of the Institution, who had recently visited this station with the District Inspector that the Local Committee be requested to consider the abolition of the station, the District Inspector to attend their meeting when the subject is considered.
- _13th June:_ The Honorary Secretary reported that the Local Committee had considered the question of abolishing this station. The meeting was attended by the late and present District Inspectors. The Local Committee were of the opinion that under the no circumstances should the station be abolished until telephonic communications along the coast be completed. They were of the opinion that under certain states of the weather, the boat might be very useful. The District Inspector however recommended that the station should be abolished. The Committee decided not to close the station before telephonic communication was completed by the General Post Office.

- *11ᵗʰ July:* The General Post Office, having stated that an arrangement now exists by which messages on life saving service can be exchanged between Greystones and Five Mile Point Coast Guard Station via Dublin & Wicklow Post Offices (there being no coast guard at Six Mile Point), the Committee decided in view of this information to abolish this lifeboat station.

- *3ʳᵈ September:* The Honorary Secretary reported that the owner of the site of the lifeboat house was willing to allow the house to be handed over to the Local Committee to be used as a public recreation room now that the lifeboat station had been discontinued, on condition that the Institution was still responsible for the conditions under which the lease is held (the lease for 200 years from 1872).

- *10ᵗʰ September:* Committee decided that the permission of the lessor be obtained to convey the lease to other parties, together with the house for the above named purposes for a consideration.

- *12ᵗʰ September:* The Chief Inspector reported that the station had been closed and the boat withdrawn. Committee decided that the old lifeboat could be sold.

- *14ᵗʰ November:* The Honorary Secretary, having reported that he had not been able to arrange the disposal of the house on the terms suggested by the Institution the Committee, decided to sell the building to the landlord (Mr La Touche) who had offered to purchase the Institution's interest for £50.

1896

- *9ᵗʰ January:* Committee voted the thanks of the Institution inscribed on vellum to Mr R. Cathcart Dobbs in recognition of his long and valuable service as Honorary Secretary of the branch for 11 years. The Boathouse was sold to the owner of the site for £50.

The Freeman's Journal dated 27ᵗʰ January 1896 reported *"Messrs. McKiernan and Summers of Dublin gave an interesting lantern entertainment in the Greystones schoolhouse for the benefit of the Kingstown Lifeboat Disaster Fund."* Similar fundraising concerts were held in Dalkey and Wicklow. Only eclipsed by the Rye Lifeboat disaster of 1928, the loss of entire 15 strong crew of the Kingstown Lifeboat, *Civil Service Number One,* on Christmas Eve 1895 remains the second greatest loss of life suffered by the lifeboat service around the coasts of Britain and Ireland and is commemorated annually by Dún Laoghaire Lifeboat.

No entries were made in the Precis Ledger over the following 11 years, until the below final entry made.

1907

- *10ᵗʰ January:* Committee considered a letter from Mr R. Cathcart Dobbs, formerly Hon. Sec. of this station forwarding an application from Edward Archer, late coxswain of this lifeboat asking the Institution to consider his case as he understood that pensions were granted by the Institution. He was connected with lifeboats on this station for 23 years. He served as Coxswain Superintendent for three years and 2ⁿᵈ Coxswain for nine years. He was now 62 years of age. Committee voted a gratuity of £10 to Mr Archer (the station was closed nearly three years before the pension scheme was introduced and it was not retrospective).

ABOVE: Edward Archer (1848-1934), Coxswain of the Greystones Lifeboat from 1892 until its closure in 1895.

Under the story *"Old Resident's Death"*, The Wicklow People dated 17ᵗʰ March 1934 included the following:

"The death occurred on Sunday last of Mr Edward Archer, Burlington, Greystones. Mr Archer, who had reached the age of eighty six years, was one of the oldest residents of the district. He was possessed of a very retentive memory and was well versed in the history of Greystones and its environs. He saw the first train run around Bray Head nearly eighty years ago and remembered the accident in which the train was thrown off the line and plunged down the cliff face. He acted as a swimming instructor and at one time held the medal of the Royal Humane Society and also the honour vellum of that body for his gallantry for saving life from drowning. Mr Archer was associated with the Greystones Lifeboat from the time it was established and was appointed coxswain after a previous holder of that post had been drowned together with two other members of the crew in the storm of October 1892. When the lifeboat was transferred from Greystones, the Royal National Lifeboat Institution made Mr Archer a special presentation. He leaves a widow and a daughter, Mrs Pennycook and four sons - Mr George Archer, Mr Edward Archer P.C., Mr William Archer and Mr Albert Archer."

Following in their great-grandfather's role of performing long service in the rescuing of others, both Derek and Robin Archer completed 30 years and 24 years respectively with the Greystones Fire Service.

ABOVE: Cart and loading platform in front of the lifeboat house in the 1890s.

ABOVE: Photo of the Anchor Cafe in the 1960s.

GREYSTONES LIFEBOAT

The Lifeboats

Name of Lifeboat	Period of Service at Greystones	Measurements	Number of Oars	Builder	Lifeboat Cost ***	Carriage Builder	Carriage Cost ***	Number of Launches	Lives Saved
Sarah Tancred	1872-1886	Length: 33 feet Breadth: 8 feet	10 (double-banked)	Messrs. Woolfe & Son, Shadwell, London	£284 & 15s	Messrs. Robinson & Napton	£100 & 0s	4	4
Richard Browne *	1886-1895	Length: 37 feet Breadth: 8 feet	12 (double-banked)	Messrs. Forrestt & Son, Limehouse, London	£373 & 10s	Bristol Wagon Works Co. **	£123 & 10s	-	-

* Between December 1890 and June 1891, the *Richard Browne,* was sent to London for alterations and a temporary, unnamed lifeboat was sent to Greystones.
** In January 1892 a new transporting carriage, built by The Bristol Wagon Works Company and a set of Tipping's wheel plates were despatched to Greystones.
*** As disclosed in the annual report and accounts of The Lifeboat Institution contained in its quarterly publication, "*The Life-Boat Journal*".

The *Sarah Tancred* was one of two lifeboats sent to Ireland by the Royal National Lifeboat Institution in July 1872. The other boat, slightly smaller in length and breadth at 32 feet by 7 feet 6 inches was for a new station located south of the Boyne near Drogheda. Both boats underwent trials at the Regent's Canal Dock at Limehouse in East London where they were satisfactorily tested for stability, self-righting and self-ejecting of water. During the 19th century, around 90% of the RNLI fleet of lifeboats were built by boatyards along the Thames. The complex double diagonal planking used in the construction of their hulls, together with the exacting standards required by the RNLI meant that only a few boatyards were trusted by the RNLI to build their fleet of lifeboats. Messrs Woolfe & Son built 143 lifeboats and Messrs. Forrestt & Son 115 lifeboats. The RNLI had strict specifications for the carriages used to transport their pulling lifeboats.

The Men

Coxswain of the Greystones Lifeboat	Period of Service	Honorary Secretary of the Greystones Lifeboat	Period of Service	Comments
Arthur Evans *	Pre 1876	Dr. Maunsell	1871-1873	
John Doyle	1876-1892	Rev. Maurice Day	1873-1874	
Edward Archer	1892-1895	Patrick Reid	1874-1885	Patrick Reid lived at *Glencarrig*, a large house on the road from Delgany to Temple Carrig.
		Robert Cathcart Dobbs	1885-1896	R.C Dobbs Lived at *Knockdolian* on Church Lane.

* The RNLI records held at Poole do not disclose the identity of the Coxswain of the Greystones Lifeboat prior to John Doyle. In a report on the launching of the second Greystones Lifeboat, *Richard Browne*, contained in *The Dublin Daily Express* dated 3rd December 1886, it noted Arthur Evans, "*former coxswain*" attending the "*substantial and sumptuous dinner in Burlington House*". Arthur Evans, aged 40 when the *Sarah Tancred* was launched, an experienced mariner and more latterly, a coal importer was well qualified for the role. He resided at *Wavecrest* next door to the telegraph office and thus would have been well positioned to muster the lifeboat crew speedily in the event of a telegraph message calling for her assistance being received.

Greystones Lifeboat Regatta Performances

Regatta	Date	Race	Result / Comment	Source
Wicklow	2nd Sept 1878	Lifeboat Race	1st place, Courtown, prize £10 & the Fitzwilliam Prize, 2nd place, Wicklow, prize £5. This was the inaugural Wicklow Regatta, an event which has grown during its 130 years to become one of the foremost regattas held annually in Ireland. The pre regatta notices placed in newspapers stated that there would be a "*lifeboat race, open to Kingstown, Greystones, Wicklow, Arklow, Cahore and Courtown stations*". The report on the race noted that "*only the Wicklow and Courtown boats started this race. After a very close contest, the Courtown boat won by seven seconds*".	*The Wicklow Newsletter*
Wicklow	4th Aug 1879	Lifeboat Race	1st place, Wicklow, 2nd place, Greystones, 3rd place, Kingstown, 4th place, Arklow. The newspaper report noted that the umpire for the race was Captain Robert Halpin, F.R.G.S., the Wicklow born master mariner who captained the Brunel designed *SS Great Eastern*, which laid transatlantic telegraph cables in the 1860s.	*The Dublin Daily Express*
Wicklow	2nd Aug 1880	Lifeboat Race	Distance 4 miles for the Fitzwilliam Prize. Prize fund: 1st place, £10, 2nd place, £7, 3rd place, £3. "*Much interest was centred in this race which was confined to the Greystones and Wicklow boats. The Courtown boat did not appear, though entered. The Wicklow boat came in first, but it had previously fouled Greystones. Greystones subsequently fouled Wicklow and the committee decided on dividing the prizes equally between the 2 boats.*"	*The Dublin Daily Express*
Bray	9th Aug 1882	Lifeboat Race	"*Open to all lifeboats in Ireland, both sailing and rowing, all gear aboard.*" Four lifeboats entered: Ringsend, Kingstown, Greystones and Wicklow. Prize fund: 1st place £10, 2nd place £5 & 3rd place £2 10s. "*This race was very good from the start to the first turn, then Greystones drew ahead and won, Wicklow being second, Kingstown a good third, considering she is the heaviest boat on the coast.*" The report on the regatta also noted that "*it was intended that the lifeboats' crews should display their ability to man them by capsizing them and remaining in them until they righted again. They were offered £5 for the one which would be smartest, but all but Kingstown refused to compete, so that this item fell through*".	*The Freeman's Journal*
Bray	30th Jul 1883	Lifeboat Race	"*After a severe struggle, the Kingstown Lifeboat came in first, Howth second and Greystones third.*"	*The Dublin Daily Express*
Greystones	19th Aug 1885	Lifeboat Race	1st place, Wicklow, prize £8, 2nd place, Greystones, prize £4.	*The Freeman's Journal*
Bray	17th Aug 1885	Lifeboat Race	"*One of the best fought races of the day was the one between the lifeboats of Greystones, Kingstown & Wicklow. The latter, after a capital race, got 1st prize, £10 and Kingstown £4 2nd prize, Greystones got 30s.*"	*The Wicklow Newsletter*
Greystones	19th Aug 1885	Lifeboat Race	"*The signal victory gained by the Wicklow Lifeboat crew at Bray on Monday was repeated on this occasion after a fine race against the Greystones boat for a prize of £8.*"	*The Wicklow Newsletter*
Bray	15th Aug 1888	Lifeboat Race	1st place, Kingstown, prize £8, 2nd place, Wicklow, prize £4, 3rd place, Greystones.	*Belfast Newsletter*
Bray	7th Aug 1890	Lifeboat Race	"*Amongst the boat races, none was more popular than that between the lifeboats from Kingstown, Greystones and Wicklow, each of which carried her full gear as when proceeding to a wreck. The Kingstown men had always had this race their own way and there was not a longshore man who would not have staked his possessions on the crew. It was then no wonder that a loud, excited roar went up from five thousand throats as the Greystones boat rounded the flag boat several lengths ahead of the favourite, which only beat the third or Wicklow boat by a nose.*" Though never launched for an actual rescue during her 10 years of service as the Greystones Lifeboat (1886-1896), the performance that day at Bray was undoubtedly the *Richard Browne's* finest hour and suggested that, had she been called out, she and her crew would have been well up for the task.	*Irish Society*
Greystones	16th Aug 1890	Lifeboat Race	"*Greystones again succeeded in winning the lifeboat race after a hard set-to with Wicklow.*"	*The Irish Times*
Greystones	10th Aug 1891	Lifeboat Race	"*1st prize £5, 2nd £4 & 3rd £3. Wicklow, Greystones and Kingstown started. The pull was a very long one, but in the end, Kingstown pulling an extraordinary good stroke, won a very good race by a length.*"	*The Freeman's Journal*
Bray	12th Aug 1891	Lifeboat Race	"*1st prize £8, 2nd £4, with unsuccessful boats that row the course to get £2 each. 1st place, Kingstown, 2nd place, Wicklow, 3rd place, Greystones. Kingstown held a long lead but there was a good race between the other boats, Wicklow getting ahead just at the finish.*"	*The Wicklow People*

FISHING

In *Topographica Hibernica* published in 1795, the area known as the "Gray Stones" was described as a *"noted fishing place"*. The *"herrings first brought into Dublin"* were, according to William Wenward Seward, *"usually taken by the fishing boats of this place."* In response to a request in 1828 by Peter La Touche Junior for the Commissioners of Irish Fisheries to consider building a harbour at Greystones, a local inspector, James Irvine, was despatched to visit the area and compile a report. Irvine attended Greystones for three days and *"conversed with the most experienced fishermen and obtained every information that could be got."* He noted the following in his report dated 24th January 1828. *"There is excellent fishing ground along this coast extending out as far as the banks about 9 miles. The general take of fish consists of cod and haddock which are caught with the boaters on long lines. Whiting and codlings are taken in great quantities with hand lines. There is also a large take of mackerel in the spring and summer and winter herring fishing and long shore fishing for white trout by seine nets. All of these would afford ample employment to the fishermen if they were able to launch and haul up their boats in the common fishing weather, but whenever it blows a stiff breeze from the northern or eastward they are compelled to be idle although they can see their neighbours employed for they must not launch their boats. There are 41 boats belonging to this place, they are all open row boats manned with 6 men generally, but with 8 during the herring fishery. A capstan has lately been erected which much facilitates the hauling up of the boats."*

RIGHT: *Saunders's Newsletter* dated Thursday 18th November 1830 reported the loss of a Greystones herring boat and her crew of five, which was driven against the North Wall in Dublin.

A herring fishing boat, belonging to Greystones, during the gale on Monday night, unfortunately drove on the wall building by the ballast office, called the New North Wall, and went to pieces. It is melancholy to add that the entire crew, five in number, perished! This is the second boat that has been lost at the same place.

Book No.3 includes transcripts from a fishing register containing details recorded on the counterfoils of 39 Greystones registered fishing boats from 1849 to 1885. During the 1840s, the government introduced the Fisheries Ireland Acts which required formal registration of fishing boats. Information including the name of the boat, its owner, type, mode of fishing, tonnage, length of keel and the number of men and boys usually employed had to be disclosed on the registration application. 30 of the 39 boats registered were yawls (two masted fore and aft rigged vessels, with the fore mast taller than the aft or mizzen mast), between 1 and 3 tons and 18 to 24 feet in length. Five of the boats were larger vessels, known as luggers, up to 42 feet in length and weighing 18 tons. Samuel A. French in his 1964 history of Greystones noted that Greystones boats sailed as far away as Kilkeel in Co. Down and Kinsale in Co. Cork. It is also said that Greystones boats were known in Peel on the Isle of Man. During the timespan covered by the register, a total of 218 men and five boys were employed by the 39 boats, highlighting the status of fishing as the predominant source of employment in Greystones during its initial years of development. Names of registered owners included Doyle, Evans, Darcy, Massey, Carr, Byrne and Farrell. Many of the fishermen were also engaged in farming.

The mode of fishing was principally the use of herring nets, with some of the boats also using seine nets, long lines and hand lines. Upon hearing that mackerel or herring shoals had been sighted, the fishermen would quickly prepare their boats and gear and set sail for the fishing grounds. The men stocked up with food supplies including bread, eggs, butter, milk and vegetables, restocking each time they came ashore to sell their catches. They also supplemented their diet with the fresh fish caught on their trips. Most of the larger boats were either half or quarter decked to provide shelter for the crew. The fishermen's typical 24 hour routine involved shooting their nets at dusk, drifting with them until dawn, then hauling in the catch and proceeding to the nearest harbour to land the catch.

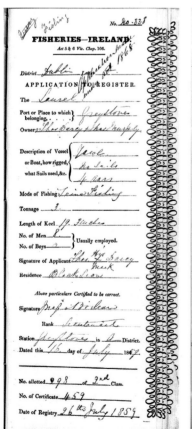
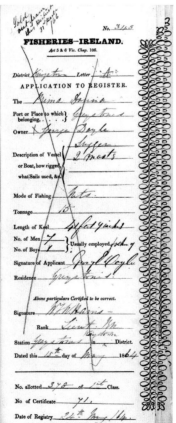

ABOVE & LEFT: The most important document relating to fishing at Greystones during the latter half of the 19th century. The register contains the 39 counterfoils which were completed between 1849 and 1885 to register the fishing boats operating from Greystones between those years. Written in pencil on the inside of the front cover is the following. *"Between 80 and 90 men employed fishing in this division 12th December 1865."* On the left are counterfoils for the yawl, *Laurel*, registered by Thomas Darcy of Blacklion in 1859 along with the lugger, *Prima Donna*, registered by George Enright Doyle in 1864. At 41 feet 9 inches in length, the *Prima Donna* was the largest of the 39 boats. It was built on the Isle of Man where George

Enright Doyle's elder brother, Samuel was a sea captain. It sailed to Greystones in 1864 from where it fished until it was sold in 1866. With the proceeds, George Enright Doyle bought the plot of land on which he built *Bushfield House* on Church Road in 1870.

ABOVE: Fine view of a group of people about to lower a net across the mouth of the dock in the 1940s. The two pipe smoking men wearing hats holding the net are George Archer on the left and Bill Spurling, with his white painter's overalls under his jacket, on the right. It is quite likely the above event coincided with the mackerel chasing fry into the dock.

ABOVE: Landing the catch in the early 1900s at Greystones South Beach (upper photo) and North Beach (lower photo).

ABOVE: Boy sitting on the gunwale of a fishing boat in Greystones harbour in 1911. Note the wicker whelk pots that were used by the fishermen and the oars, ropes and anchors left in the boats.

ABOVE: Early members of The Knights of the Silver Hook Angling Club taken at Greystones harbour. The group includes Captain Dalton and Jim Fields.

ABOVE RIGHT: Jimmy Kearon, Captain of Greystones Ridge Angling Club receiving the John Player Cup on 4th September 1960 from Mr J.M. McNeill, Advertising Manager of John Player & Sons, Dublin. Jimmy's wife Helen is holding a replica of the trophy won by Jimmy, proving that local knowledge went a long way towards seeing off a record field of over 150 anglers. Jimmy and Helen's son, Brod, established the health food shop, Nature's Gold, which has operated on Killincarrig Road for over 40 years, since its opening in 1977. The above angling competition was organised by The Knights of the Silver Hook, an angling club that came regularly to Greystones from the 1940s through to the 1970s. Jim Kinsella looked after their heavy gear and they took out Jim's skiff, *Elsie,* (built by John Spurling) and George Archer's *Daisy Belle,* a heavy 20 foot transom sterned boat on weekends, until the *Daisy Belle* was wrecked in the dock during a storm. In the 1960s, another angling club, Dublin City Sea Angling Club, based their own boats in Greystones. Four or five of them, all transom sterned, beamy boats around 20 foot or more, were a distinctive sight, all painted orange, pulled high up on the beach at the harbour (see pages 56 and 57). By the 1970s, the C.I.E. Anglers' Club moored their boat, a converted ship's lifeboat, *St. Helens,* in the harbour near the north wall.

RIGHT: Close-up of the Greystones Ridge Angling Club metal sign on the exterior wall of its former clubhouse, which was officially opened on the North Beach in October 1977. Also shown is an official postcard for a club meeting during its first year of existence. Greystones Ridge Angling Club takes its name from the line of rocks, known as Reilly's Ridge, that extend out on the seabed close to where the golf driving range is today. The clubhouse was adjacent to the original Greystones Sailing Club pen. With the marina development, Greystones Ridge Angling Club relocated to a new clubhouse, formally opened on 26th June 2016 beside the new sailing club pen.

ABOVE: Fishing competition at Greystones in the mid 1970s with plenty of activity on the shoreline.

ABOVE: Joe Redmond replacing a section of a plank in a fishing boat in front of the fishermen's huts. Among those watching, are Jimmy Nolan and Billy Kinsella. Steam can be seen wafting from the pipe used to steam the oak ribs so they can be bent into shape.

Greystones Ridge Angling Club.

Meeting will take place at Beach House Greystones on Thursday 5·11·59 at 8³⁰ p.m. and your kind attendance will be appreciated.

Agenda:

Chief Officer.

LEFT: Willie Redmond and Jago Hayden cleaning the seaweed from a trammel net on Greystones pier in August 1961. In the background are the steps up onto the parapet storm wall from where shore based anglers cast off.

BELOW: Bill Spurling in 1964, with his grandson, Ian Spurling, standing beside the dock wall at Greystones harbour, giving an oar a fresh coat of paint. The fishing nets with their cork floats draped on the wall drying in the sun were a familiar sight. The ladies' changing room on the approach to the pier was built in 1959.

LEFT & RIGHT: The *Mac Lir,* built by Willie Redmond and owned by Jago Hayden, heading south to lay a trammel net. Jago is steering the boat in the photo on the left, the other photo includes Kevin Dillon.

BELOW: Leslie Spurling and Larry Ryan hauling nets into a boat at the harbour.

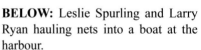

ABOVE: Jimmy Redmond untwisting a net outside the fishermen's huts.

ABOVE: Standing outside the fishermen's huts, Harry Lawless, John Byrne, Brian Sweeney, Paddy Sweeney, Kevin Malone, Noel Belton, Seamus Sweeney and Larry Ryan.

BELOW: What is believed to be the largest ever recorded catch landed at Greystones harbour (weighing over 3 cwt, equivalent to 24 stone or 152 kilograms), was caught by a member of the Archer family, as reported in *The Wicklow Newsletter* dated Saturday 15th November 1913.

ABOVE: Edward Fahy at the fishermen's huts in the 1960s with a spur dogfish caught off Greystones. His father, Ted, was a Dublin barrister and keen angler, who regularly rented a house at Greystones harbour, where the family stayed during the summer months.

CAPTURE OF A SHARK AT GREYSTONES.

Whilst engaged in trawling for herrings during the week at Greystones, the crew of one of the fleet noticed a great commotion in the water around them, which turned out to be a huge fish, evidently enjoying itself immensely among the herrings, which it was devouring by the dozen. As the boat (which was a small one, "The Wave," belonging to Mr Archer), never was originally intended to cope with these monsters, the crew very prudently deemed it advisable to get their nets aboard, so as to save them from possible injury. In the process of getting them into the boat, they were amazed to find that despite all their combined efforts they could not get them, but eventually when they got portion of them in, they found that the cause of the trouble was due to the fact of the shark having got hopelessly entangled in the fine meshes, and as the nets were only new, it was unable to burst it sufficiently to escape. The brute was lashing the sea into a fury with its huge tail, and there was not strong enough tackle to get it aboard, so fortunately one of the crew, who is an expert in the art of working the Semaphore system of sea signalling, succeeded in attracting the attention of the other boats of the fleet by using the electric light as a signalling device. Several of the crews belaboured the brute with their oars, &c, and rendered it harmless; then it was towed ashore. On being landed, it was recognised by a gentleman of great travelling experience, to be the species known as the "Basking shark." It measured ten feet in length, six feet in circumference, and weight over three cwt. On being opened, it contained about a dozen and a-half fishes. A great deal of injury was done to the nets, but the local fleet are glad to be rid of their unwelcome visitor, whose arrival at the harbour created quite a stir by crowds coming to take away pieces as souvenirs of "the visit."

ABOVE: Large skate, weighing over 7 stone, caught by Billy and John Hayden in 1949. The fish was caught on a long-line between the men's bathing place and Swan's Rock on the South Beach. It was too large to haul on board, so was gaffed and towed behind their small rowing boat, *Kathleen,* back to Greystones harbour. In the photo are Eddie Doyle, Jim Hayden, Jack Kinsella, Larry Ryan, Jim Kinsella and Connie Salmon.

ABOVE: Jack Sweeney, father of Joe, Helen, Seamus, Brendan, Paddy, Brigid, John, Bernard and Brian, digging bait at low tide in Greystones harbour. Jack Sweeney was raised by his grandmother, Ellen Darcy, whose fishermen sons, John and James, carried on the family tradition in Greystones.

SAILING

2018 marks 50 years since the foundation of Greystones Sailing Club in 1968 (clubs were established at Wicklow in 1950 and Bray in 1958). Whilst a number of the town's sporting clubs have been in existence for longer, sailing in Greystones, as a pastime and sporting activity has its roots dating back to the time when Greystones was just a tiny fishing hamlet, consisting of a small community of fishermen. In their yawls and luggers, equipped with oars and sails, they were adept sailors, relying mainly on the wind to take them to their fishing grounds and back. In the mid 19th century, regattas began to be held during August and September at a number of venues along the east coast, including Greystones. By 1890, *The Irish Times*, in its report on the Greystones Regatta commented that *"this regatta, which is rapidly becoming one of the pleasantest of all our coast regattas took place on Saturday."*

The Dublin Daily Express dated Tuesday 2nd September 1856 reported on the Greystones Fishermen's Boat Races held the previous day. Unfortunately, it noted that *"the sailing race, for a prize of £6, could not be proceeded with, owing to the want of a sufficient breeze."*

GREYSTONES REGATTA.

A regatta was held yesterday at Greystones. The principal events were two sailing matches and a rowing match. In these matches the only boats allowed to be entered or started were those belonging to the fishermen of Greystones and its vicinity, for whose benefit the regatta was planned and the money to be awarded in prizes was collected. Each race was well contested and won very creditably. The first match was for first-class sailing boats. The little vessels which competed were started at one. The course lay around two flag-boats, placed at the interval of some miles from each other, and though the breeze was very light, the distance was performed in a wonderfully short space of time. The boats arrived in the following order :—

Name.	Owner.	
Robert	C. Evans	1
William	J. Evans	2
John Thomas	B. Barnet	3

The Royal William and Arthur gained the next places.
In the second sailing match the boats were placed as follows :—

Name.	Owner.	
Dove	S. Wither	1
Charles	J. Evans	2
Terror	J. Byrne	3

The first rowing match was for four-oared boats. The winner was the Brownsie, Garret Evans, owner; and the second, the Wave, William Doyle, owner. A third boat started but was not rowed round the course. A second rowing match was won by a boat owned by Garret Evans. There were also a punt race and a duck hunt. The weather was very fine during the day, and although it grew cloudy towards the evening, there was not much rain until after the sports of the day had ended. At nine o'clock there was a brilliant display of fireworks, which were supplied for the occasion by Mr. Robinson, of Grafton-street.

ABOVE: Report on the 1859 Greystones Regatta that appeared in *Saunders's Newsletter & Daily Advertiser* for Wednesday 17th August 1859. Starting at 1pm, it consisted of two sailing races, two rowing races and inshore sports comprising a punt race and a duck hunt. The event was brought to a close by a firework display at 9pm. It is noteworthy that at this early regatta, *"only boats allowed to be entered or started were those belonging to the fishermen of Greystones and its vicinity."*

RIGHT: Extract from the official programme for the 1889 Greystones Regatta held on Thursday 22nd August. The opening *"Sailing Race for Greystones Open Pleasure Boats"* was run over a course of around 8 miles in length. *The Freeman's Journal* dated 23rd August 1889 carried the result, which saw 1st place taken by Osborne Spurling, with Edward Archer (who was Coxswain of the Greystones Lifeboat from 1892 to 1896) taking 2nd place (on time handicap), with John Evans in 3rd place.

The annual boat races and sailing matches, &c., for the benefit of the fishermen, will take place at the picturesque village of Greystones, near Bray, county Wicklow, on Wednesday 10th September, weather permitting. The expenses of this annual "water frolic" are defrayed by the resident gentry of the county, and the visitors to the surrounding districts ; and the poor fishermen are enabled by the prizes distributed to procure nets, put their boats in order, &c., for the better pursuit of their arduous avocation during the winter months.

ABOVE: An Extract from *The Advocate or Irish Industrial Journal* dated Wednesday 10th September 1851 noting the holding of the annual boat races and sailing matches for the benefit of the Greystones fishermen. Already by this time, the event was being described as an *"annual water frolic."*

GREYSTONES REGATTA, TUESDAY, AUGUST 16, 1859.—The Steamship MARS is intended (weather permitting) to sail from the Custom-house-quay, Dublin, on TUESDAY MORNING, the 16th of August, at Ten o'clock precisely, for Kingstown—Fare, 6d. From Kingstown, at Eleven o'clock, by Dalkey Sound, Killiney Bay and Bray Head, for Greystones Offing—Fare, 1s. 6d., including sail round the Course with each Race, and back to Kingstown. Off Greystones she will receive passengers to sail round the Course—Fare, 6d. From Greystones Offing to Kingstown—Fare, 6d. From Kingstown, about Half-past Six o'clock, for Dublin—Fare, 6d. Passengers offering themselves in time by boat can be embarked in Dalkey Sound and off Bray for same Fares as from Kingstown. Tickets can be obtained of CAROLIN and EGAN, 20 Eden-quay, or on board.

ABOVE: Advertisement from *Saunders's Newsletter* dated Saturday 13th August 1859 offering a day excursion aboard the steamship, *Mars*, from Custom House Quay in Dublin for passengers to view the Greystones Regatta. The fare, including return to Kingstown was 1s & 6d. For passengers wishing to embark at Greystones to view the regatta only, the fare was 6d.

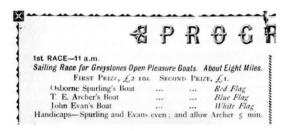

1st RACE—11 a.m.
Sailing Race for Greystones Open Pleasure Boats. About Eight Miles.
FIRST PRIZE, £2 10s.   SECOND PRIZE, £1.

Osborne Spurling's Boat	...	Red Flag
T. E. Archer's Boat	...	Blue Flag
John Evan's Boat	...	White Flag

Handicaps—Spurling and Evans even ; and allow Archer 5 min.

At the 1891 Greystones Regatta, the *Water Wag* race over No.3 course (4½ miles) had three entrants, with *Gladys* of the Dublin Bay Sailing Club taking 1st place and the £3 prize.

It is noteworthy that with the Greystones Regatta taking place on the Monday, immediately followed by the Bray Regatta on the Tuesday and Wednesday, four *Mermaid* boats sailed across the Irish Sea from New Brighton Sailing Club at the mouth of the Mersey. They competed in the sailing race for open boats of the A and B class, twice around No.2 course (8 miles). The English boats proved their superior handling, with *Hazard* and *Deva* taking 1st and 2nd places respectively.

ABOVE: Bill Spurling sailing across Greystones harbour in around 1910.

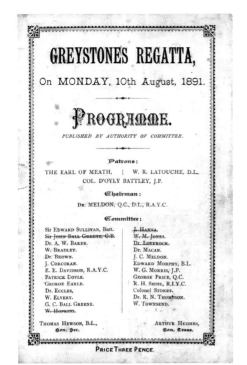

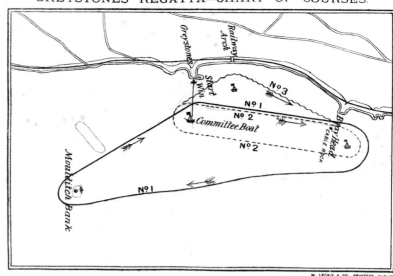

GREYSTONES REGATTA—CHART OF COURSES.

ABOVE & LEFT Programme for the Greystones Regatta held in 1891. Three courses were set, taking in the Moulditch Buoy and up to just beyond the Cable Rock at Bray Head. Note the railway line shown running along the banks over the 2nd Gap Bridge.

The Freeman's Journal dated Tuesday 11th August 1891 carried a report on the regatta. "*This annual water frolic was carried out yesterday and was a considerable improvement on the regattas hitherto held at this favourable watering place. There seems to be an extra amount of energy displayed on the part of the executive to make this event one of the features of the year and if they continue on the lines they are adopting, Greystones will become one of the most popular seaside events.*"

The edition of *Irish Society* dated Saturday 15th August 1891 reported that "*the annual regatta took place at Greystones on Monday in ideal sailing weather. A programme of 18 events was gone through and the vessels went over the course quickly before a steady breeze from the northwest. A very large concourse of spectators witnessed the racing from the shore, where the band of the 28th Glos'ster Regiment played a programme of music. The inshore sports were first class and the evening wound up with a brilliant display of fireworks. By kind permission of the Belleisle, the revenue cutter, Hind (Captain Score) acted as committee boat. The people of Greystones are to be congratulated on the success of the regatta.*" The Greystones Silver Cup, presented by Col. D'Oyly Battley for cruisers over No.1 course, twice around (14 miles), was won by *Fiery Cross* in 4 hrs, 33 mins and 10 seconds.

ABOVE: Photo taken in the 1890s, from an album belonging to the Jeffers family, showing Mr Jeffers senior sailing his boat in Greystones harbour. Mr Jeffers senior was a retired coast guard who came to live in Greystones at *Corraguna*, Eden Road, when his son, Robert, was stationed with Greystones coast guards at Marine Terrace during the 1890s and early 1900s. It was common among coast guards and their families to be interested in sailing and many, like the Jeffers family, brought their own sailing boats with them.

ABOVE: Rochfort Doyle sailing his boat across the mouth of the harbour in the 1890s. A keen sailor, Rochfort Doyle regularly sailed to the Wicklow Regatta every August bank holiday up until 1916. The damage to the section of the north wall closest to the beach can clearly be seen. Signs of subsidence at the end section of the wall are also visible.

ABOVE: Derek Paine sailing in Greystones harbour in his clinker built dinghy, *Joan*, built in 1948-49. It was one of two clinker built boats, built by his father, Ernest Paine and Willie Redmond, one for each of them. It was later lost in a storm that hit Greystones harbour.

ABOVE: Stanley Paine sailing across the entrance of Greystones harbour in a *Cadet* dinghy in 1950 at full tide.

ABOVE: A 1955 photograph of clinker built boats including *Mermaids* owned by Ryan, Fahy, Acheson, Paine and O'Neill. The missing blocks can be seen on the corner of the 1847 jetty, dislodged during the storm of October 1910. These were subsequently replaced when major refurbishment works to the surface of the pier were undertaken in October 1958. Note the wooden fishermen's huts and fishermen's nets neatly draped on the wall opposite *Wavecrest* and Bayswater Terrace.

ABOVE: A number of clinker built yachts moored close to the pier in the mid 1950s. The uneven pier surface and exposed granite bollards prior to their repair can be seen. The corrugated roof of a wooden fishing hut can be seen in the foreground just beyond the fishermen's nets draped on the wall.

ABOVE: *Cadet* dinghy race in Greystones harbour in 1954.

SAILING

In December 1967, at a gathering in the home of Gordon Clarke, a group including Dermod Cafferky, John Roy, Toby Davis and Ian Mitchell toyed with the notion of setting up a sailing club in Greystones. In early 1968, the inaugural meeting took place in John Roy's house and the sailing club was established with the assistance of Derek Paine, Don McClean and Liam Byrne of the Greystones & District Civic Association. The Civic Association was active in regenerating the area adjacent to the North Beach, upon which were the ruins of the houses that were washed away between 1929 and 1931. This necessitated the levelling of the ruins as well as armouring the former North Beach Road with large boulders, to protect the cleared site from being inundated with the shingle from the beach.

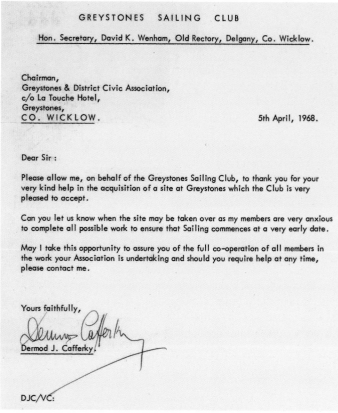

Initially, sailing was confined principally to *Mirror* dinghies, which were transported to and from the harbour by trailer or on car roof racks. Despite not having a clubhouse, Greystones Sailing Club hosted the *Mirror* Dinghy National Championship on 12th and 13th July 1969. Two marquees erected ensured a successful and memorable event. In November 1969, a site plan for the club was measured and drawn up by Derek Paine and Toby Davis. The number of boats sailing continued to increase and during 1970, efforts were focused on securing funding for the proposed construction of a two storey clubhouse to include a bar on the upper floor, as well as a strong wire fence around a pen. In 1971, the clubhouse was constructed at a cost of £6,000. It was formally opened at a ceremony by the Director General of An Bord Fáilte, Eamon Ceannt, alongside Toby Davis (Commodore), John Roy (Vice Commodore) and Dermod Cafferky (Hon. Secretary).

LEFT: This letter is the earliest official correspondence from Greystones Sailing Club. Written three years before the club built its original clubhouse on the North Beach, it was signed by founding member, Dermod Cafferky. It was addressed to Greystones & District Civic Association regarding the acquisition of a site on the North Beach.

RIGHT: Club letter head from 1971 showing the club's original red and black burgee, which incorporated the Kish Lighthouse in recognition of the Kish base at Greystones harbour.

Greystones Sailing Club

Clubhouse, North Beach, Greystones, Co. Wicklow

An opening in the boulders directly opposite the gate to the club facilitated the launching of dinghies on launching trolleys, albeit with difficulty over the steep shingle. A rubber mat was used to better facilitate the launching and in November 1972, *The Wicklow People* reported that for the 1973 season, a pontoon wooden slipway would be used on the beach. This, however, soon proved to be ineffective as it regularly became covered in shingle, defeating its purpose. During 1977, Greystones Sailing Club outlined its development plan, part of which envisaged a permanent slipway on the harbour side of the north wall.

ABOVE: In the initial years following the foundation of Greystones Sailing Club, the *Mirror* Dinghy, with its distinctive red sails, was the dominant class. In 1976, Greystones Sailing Club hosted the *Mirror* Dinghy National Championship for the second time.

In her regular Greystones page in *The Wicklow People,* in April 1978, Gwen McNiff wrote that "*the new sport of windsurfing has come to Ireland. On Sunday, Greystones first wind surfer was spotted off the North Beach.*" At the end of the first decade of the sailing club's existence, she reported on the 1978 club AGM, at which it was noted that there were 45 family memberships and 40 individual memberships. Sailing courses were run at the start of the season under the tuition of IYA instructors. The most popular dinghy class at the club was the *Mirror* dinghy and handicap races were introduced in 1977 so that other sailing classes could participate in races. Nine different classes of dinghy had sailed the previous season - *Mirror*, *Fireball* (these had become the second class of dinghy, after *Mirrors*, to be adopted by the club for racing following a meeting in late 1972), *Laser*, *Wayfarer*, *Enterprise*, *Heron*, *Optimist*, *Skipper* and *Mermaid*. After *Mirrors*, *Optimists* were the second most popular class at the club, reflecting their suitability for young sailors to learn the ropes. The club officers elected at the 1978 AGM were as follows: Louis O'Neill (Commodore), John Caffrey (Vice Commodore), Dermod Cafferky (Hon. Secretary), Eamon Donnelly (Hon. Treasurer). Executive members were John Roy, Ian Mitchell, Harold Avery and Brian Emerson.

In May 1979, two years after it was proposed in the club's development plan, work commenced on the construction of a boat slip on the harbour side of the north wall. Assistance was provided by the Civic Association and An Bord Fáilte to enable the safe launching of boats by Greystones Sailing Club and Greystones Ridge Angling Club. Later that year, a tarmac surface was applied to the road from the old lifeboat house to just beyond the Ridge Angling Club. In June 1996, Minister for the Marine, Sean Barrett TD, opened the club's refurbished clubhouse, with its original front balcony now enclosed and an external semi-circular steel balcony added.

ABOVE: Sailing dinghies pulled up onto the North Beach in front of the old clubhouse in the late 1970s.

ABOVE: Blue is the colour, *Enterprise* is the name, as Greystones Sailing Club hosts the *Enterprise* Dinghy National Championship.

ABOVE: Greystones Sailing Club on the North Beach in 1999.

SAILING

During the 1980s and 1990s, there was a strong active fleet of around 25 *Enterprise* dinghies, with junior members in *Lasers* and *Mirrors*. The club produced a number of Irish Olympian sailors, including Marshall King, helmsman in the *Soling* open keel boat class at the 1996 Olympic Games sailing competition held in Savannah, Georgia, Aisling Bowman (nee Byrne) in the *470* class at the Seoul Olympics in 1988 and the *Europe* class at the 1996 Olympics in Greece and Tim Goodbody in the *Finn* class at the 2008 Olympics in China. Marshall King also won the Dunhill *J24* Match Racing World Championships in Dún Laoghaire in 1988, defeating Jim Brady of the USA. International class sailors produced by Greystones Sailing Club include Roy Van Maanen, Trevor Fisher, Craig Thompson, Sean Craig, Jack Roy and Shane McCarthy.

LEFT: In the 1980s, Greystones Sailing Club's burgee changed design to blue and yellow sails replacing the original red, white and black burgee that featured the Kish Lighthouse. In contrast, Bray Sailing Club, has retained its original white seagull on a blue background burgee since the club's foundation in 1958.

Following the Irish National *Mirror* Dinghy Championships held in 1976, Greystones Sailing Club established a reputation for hosting national and regional Championships and facilitating a number of prestige events. These included the Helmsmen Championships, the *Enterprise* Leinsters and National Championships (1984), the *Mirror* Eastern Championships, the *Wayfarer* Leinsters and National Championships, *Laser* Championships, *GP 14* Purcell Trophy, *420* National Championships, *Mistral* Windsurfing Championships, the inaugural *RS 400* National Championships in 2001 and again in 2002 along with the inaugural *RS 200* National Championships. Both RS classes returned in 2003, 2004, 2005 and again in 2010. For a number of years, Greystones Sailing Club has also offered transition year students of St. David's Secondary School introductory sailing courses.

Commodores of Greystones Sailing Club 1968-2018			
Year	Commodore	Year	Commodore
1968	Dermod Cafferky	1994	Tony Dunphy
1969	Dermod Cafferky	1995	Tony Dunphy
1970	Toby Davis	1996	Dave Diamond
1971	Toby Davis	1997	Dave Diamond
1972	John Roy	1998	Frank O'Rourke
1973	John Roy	1999	David Harris
1974	Ian Mitchell	2000	David Harris
1975	Ian Mitchell	2001	Paul Sunderland
1976	John Byrne	2002	Paul Sunderland
1977	Louis O'Neill	2003	Mark Usher
1978	Louis O'Neill	2004	Mark Usher
1979	John Caffrey	2005	Seamus Gilshinan
1980	John Caffrey	2006	Seamus Gilshinan
1981	Nan Avery	2007	Keith Simpson
1982	Tom Butler	2008	Keith Simpson
1983	Tom Butler	2009	Sarah Byrne
1984	Joe Taylor	2010	Sarah Byrne
1985	Joe Taylor	2011	Simon Herriott
1986	Alan McCracken	2012	Ross Brennan
1987	Alan McCracken	2013	Ross Brennan
1988	Shane Gale	2014	Rodney Beahan
1989	Shane Gale	2015	David Nixon
1990	John Raughter	2016	David Nixon
1991	John Raughter	2017	Daragh Cafferky
1992	Torren Gale	2018	Daragh Cafferky
1993	Torren Gale		

ABOVE: The clubhouse on the North Beach in January 2016, just prior to its demolition.

ABOVE RIGHT: May 2016 photograph showing the remains of the 1971 built clubhouse being removed ahead of the construction of new houses on the site. Greystones Ridge Angling Club in the background is about to suffer the same fate.

RIGHT: Construction of the new clubhouse in August 2015.

154

ABOVE: Despite the ongoing construction works, Greystones Sailing Club dinghies continued to use the harbour for launching, using the newly constructed slipway. In the photograph taken in September 2008, only half the 1889 storm wall is remaining.

ABOVE: The new clubhouse photographed in May 2016, built to lighthouse standards, commands panoramic views of the coast.

ABOVE: Rough sea dowsing the new clubhouse in February 2017.

ABOVE: Local TD and Minister for Health, Simon Harris, flanked by David Nixon, Commodore of Greystones Sailing Club, cutting the ribbon to formally open the club's new premises on Sunday 19th June 2016.

ABOVE: Nan Avery, a stalwart in the running of Greystones Sailing Club for many years and club Commodore in 1981, photographed at the opening club's new premises, with John Caffrey, who served as club Commodore in 1979 and 1980.

ABOVE: Photograph taken at the official opening of the new Greystones Sailing Club premises. The group includes David Nixon, Commodore of the club (bottom left in the blue jacket) and Daragh Cafferky, Vice-Commodore of the club (in the white shirt).

ROWING

Acknowledgements to Jago Hayden, Billy Hayden, Joe Sweeney, Ozzy Spurling, Eric Spurling, Bernard Byrne, John Byrne, Denis Slattery, John Whiston and Bob Gunning for providing information on the history of Greystones Rowing Club.

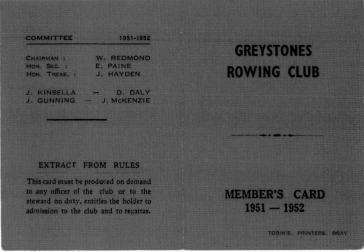

ABOVE: Greystones Rowing Club's distinctive red and black colours. The committee for 1951-1952 comprised Willie Redmond (Chairman), Ernest Paine (Hon. Secretary), Jim Hayden (Hon. Treasurer), Jim Kinsella, D. Daly, J. Gunning and Johnny McKenzie.

ABOVE: No Greystones rowing skiff is remembered with more affection than the first *Colleen Bawn*. Built locally in 1921 by John Spurling, she and her crew were almost unbeatable for nearly ten years from 1922, suffering only two defeats during that time. One of those occasions was a loss to another John Spurling built racing skiff, *Venture*. Her crew in the above photograph were, from left to right: Mick Fields, John "Blacktop" Kinsella, Jim "Lifter" Whiston, John Spurling and Bill Spurling (on the tiller). Though named John Bernard Kinsella on his birth certificate dated 16th November 1873, to everyone who knew him, he was simply "Blacktop". An immensely strong man, he worked for many years with Arthur Evans & Son, Coal Merchants at the harbour - hence the nickname "Blacktop", from the coal dust of his working environment. His duties also included filling the hold of the schooner, *Velinheli*, with 38 tons of ballast using stones from the North Beach. Reputed to have rowed with a 20 foot oar, he was instrumental in the *Colleen Bawn's* dominance at local regattas. In addition to being a very fine racing skiff, the *Colleen Bawn* was also used as a fishing boat by the Spurling family. In the photograph, the damaged end section of the north wall, minus its granite bollard can be seen, as can the three storey *Jubilee Castle / Rosetta Fort,* protruding above the north wall, to right of the bow of the boat.

BELOW: Press clipping showing the *Colleen Bawn* in her pomp, doing what she did best, romping home to victory in the 1926 Bray Regatta.

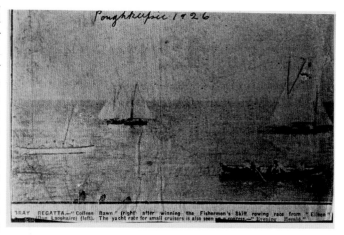

ABOVE: The *Shamrock I's* flag used during her glory days in the mid 1950s when she won four successive Wicklow Regattas (1953-1956).

ABOVE: The old and the modern side by side, with *Shamrocks I, III* and *IV* stored in the club's boathouse in September 2018.

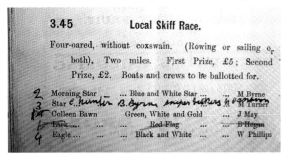

ABOVE: Page from the 1926 Wicklow Regatta programme, showing another 1st place finish for the *Colleen Bawn*.

RIGHT: Joe Sweeney, Chairman of Greystones Rowing Club receiving the Redmond Cup from Jean Redmond in 1971. The presentation of the cup, which was donated by Peter Slattery, took place beside the Greystones skiff, *Shamrock I*, in front of the fishermen's huts, as can be seen in the reflection on the surface of the cup.

RIGHT: Ticket for a 1953 fundraiser.

ABOVE: Jim Hayden, former Hon. Treasurer of Greystones Rowing Club at the top of the boat slip in 1961.

LEFT: The crew of the *Colleen Bawn* including John Spurling, Jim Whiston and John "Blacktop" Kinsella photographed at Kenna's pub in Bray. Other crew members during her golden period of racing included George Archer, Jack Darcy and Jack Kinsella.

ROWING

Together with sailing, rowing can justifiably lay claim to be among the oldest sporting activities in Greystones. Its origins date back to the days when the hamlet of fishermen, who eked out a living from the sea, used to compete against each other in local races. In contrast with today, the competitions were not open to boats from outside of Greystones and this trend continued into the second half of the 19th century. *The Dublin Evening Mail* dated 14th August 1871 included a notice that the Greystones Regatta would take place on Thursday 17th August. The sailing events were scheduled for the morning, with rowing in the afternoon. The notice specifically stated "*the races are only open to fishermen of Greystones and Windgates*". The edition of *Saunders's Newsletter* dated 27th June 1864 reporting on the Bray Regatta, noted that in the race for fishermen's boats, "*it was competed for by four-oared boats from Bullock, Bray and Wicklow*", with no mention of Greystones boats attending.

In 1851, *The Advocate* reported that "*boat races for the benefit of the fishermen will take place at the picturesque village of Greystones, near Bray, County Wicklow, on Wednesday 10th September, weather permitting*". One of its objectives was to ensure that "*the poor fishermen are enabled by the prizes distributed to procure nets, put their boats in order etc*". Five years later, *The Dublin Daily Express* dated Tuesday 2nd September 1856, reported on an event described as the "*Greystones Fishermen's Boat Races*". Its account noted that "*these races came off yesterday afternoon and were favoured by splendid weather. The attendance of spectators was considerable and included, besides many fashionables, a great number of the peasantry of the surrounding district, who seemed in an especial manner, gratified with the spectacle. Few places are more admirably adapted for this description of sport than Greystones, while it must also be said that in no place on our coast can the spectator be afforded a richer treat in the way of scenery. On either side of him, he has the glorious Bay of Dublin and the mountains of Wicklow. The races were gotten up by private subscription amongst the residents, for the benefit of the fishermen, who alone were permitted to contend for the various prizes. Too much praise can scarcely be given for this endeavour to benefit a poor but industrious class of men. The railway company contributed liberally, as they did also in the case of the Bray Regatta, which took place a short time since. The programme comprised several events and the whole proceedings were conducted with a good deal of spirit. The following is a return of the sport:-*"

Race	Boat	Owner	Flags	Result / Comment
First Class Rowing Race for Four-Oared Boats belonging to and pulled by Greystones fishermen - Prize £7, with £4 for 1st, £2 for 2nd & £1 for 3rd	*Kite* *Linnet* *Wave* *Brown Sea*	Thomas Field James Doyle William Doyle R. Garrett Evans	White Red, White, Blue Blue, White, Blue Blue, White, Yellow	"*There were four entries for this race and all started. After a good race, the Kite won cleverly, the 2nd and 3rd boats being Brown Sea and Wave.*" Robert Garrett Evans was the father-in-law of Arthur Evans senior, who established his coal import business at *Wavecrest*, Greystones harbour in 1872.
Second Class Rowing Race, Railway Prize, £5, for Four-Oared Boats belonging to and pulled by Greystones fishermen - £2 10s for 1st, £1 10s for 2nd & £1 for 3rd.	*Martha* *Dove* *Laurel*	James Field Gabriel Farrell Thomas Darcy	Red, White Cross Pink, Black Cross Pink, Yellow	"*This was the best contested race of the day, Dove beating Martha by less than half a boat's length.*"
Third Class Rowing Race for Two-Oared Boats belonging to and pulled by Greystones fishermen - £2 5s for 1st, £1 5s for 2nd.	*Fairy* *Racer* *Rose* *Black Lion*	William Doyle William Keightly Robert Evans William Evans	Yellow, Black, White Yellow Pink, White Red	"*The boat, Racer was declared the winner in this event, the Fairy and the Rose being 2nd and 3rd respectively.*"

The Dublin Evening Mail dated 18th August 1871 reported on the Greystones Regatta, stating that "*a pleasant fete was expected yesterday at the pretty seaside village of Greystones, where some of the local gentry had organised a regatta for the purpose of testing the qualities of the fishing boats of the locality and exciting a healthy emulation among their hardy crews*". Despite inclement weather, with heavy showers during the whole day, "*three or four rowing matches were run off, all of which were stoutly contested, the hardy fishermen, who manned the craft displaying, if not so much science and grace as the members of our metropolitan rowing clubs, an abundance of vigour and determination. In the first race, a match between the Susanna (J. Massey, owner) and another Greystones boat (the property of Mr J. Doyle), the chances seemed to be favour of the former, but, unfortunately, midway in the course, one of her oars broke and her rival came in the winner. Three four-oared boats started for the next race, which was won in excellent style by the Laurel (P. Murphy, owner). Another race for two-oared craft was won by the boat of a man named Woods. The course lay across the mouth of the harbour, between the two flag boats moored about half a mile apart*".

At the Bray Regatta of 1882, whilst some of the rowing races were restricted to Bray fishermen's boats only, others were open to all-comers. In the open pair-oared race for all-comers, J. Evans of Greystones took 2nd place in the boat, *Rose*. Two years later, at the 1884 Greystones Regatta held on Friday 29th August, three fishermen's rowing races were held, including a four-oared skiff race. *The Freeman's Journal* reported that 1st place was taken by W. Dory, followed by Boyd in 2nd place.

The following are the results of the rowing events at the Greystones Regatta held on 22nd August 1889.

Race	Boat	Owner	Flags	Result / Comment
Pair-Oared Race for Fishermen of Greystones in Greystones' Pleasure Boats - Prizes, £2 for 1st & £1 for 2nd.	*Norah* *Linnet* *Snowdrop* *Daisy* *Snowflake*	Edward Archer - William Doyle - Arthur Evans	Red Blue Green White Yellow	1st place, *Norah* (Edward Archer), 2nd place, *Linnet*, 3rd place, *Daisy*.
Four-Oared Race for Fishing Boats - Prizes £2 for 1st & £1 for 2nd.	*Saidi* *Duck* *Happy Return* *Joseph* *May Flower* *Catherine*	William Boyd James Keddy Andrew Bryan William Darcy R. Humphries John Darcy	Red Blue White Green Yellow Dark Blue	1st place, *Duck* (James Keddy), 2nd place, *Linnet* (Andrew Bryan), 3rd place, *Saidi* (William Boyd).
Four-Oared Pleasure Boat Race - Prizes, £2 10s for 1st, £1 10s for 2nd, £1 for 3rd & 10s for 4th.	*Phoenix* *Welter* *Lily* *Posey* *Blossom* *Violet* *Angler* *Gannet*	William Murphy John Doyle Osborne Spurling William Doyle Edward Doyle Charles Evans Thomas Hewson J. Archer	Yellow & White Blue Red Yellow White Dark Blue Green Red & White	1st place, *Welter* (James Doyle), 2nd place, *Violet* (Charles Evans), 3rd place, *Lily* (Osborne Spurling), 4th place, *Posey* (William Doyle).
Four-Oared Seining Boats - Prizes, £3 for 1st, £1 10s for 2nd.	*Laurel*	William Darcy	-	No result

ABOVE: *Shamrock II* being launched at the harbour in March 1971.

Made of deal, *Shamrock II* was much lighter than *Shamrock I* and performed very well in calm seas but, in rougher conditions, *Shamrock I* handled better and she continued to be used as and when the conditions demanded. From the early 1970s, raffles were held every Sunday morning in The Beach House to raise funds for the upkeep of the club and its skiffs. Thanks to the generous sponsorship of local businesses, annual regattas continued to be held. The 1971 rowing season is remembered for the performance of the minor crew who won all nine races and captured the East Coast Rowing Council Plaque. The club's junior crew did well with a number of top three placings. The following year an intermediate grade was also introduced, as the sport had become very popular in all of the east coast rowing clubs. Other individuals including Paddy Sweeney, John Byrne, Bernard Byrne, Billy Kinsella and Denis Slattery (as Honorary Secretary) got involved in the running of the club. In July 1973 Greystones again hosted an All Ireland senior skiff race and through the mid 1970s the club continued to do well in both the intermediate and junior grades. Alas, success at the senior grade proved elusive. By 1977 the club's fortunes had waned and it again folded.

Around 1980 yet another revival of the club was attempted, led by Ronan Sweeney, Jim Woods, Niall Hayden and Pat Keogh. The latter liaised with the Kavanagh brothers (Arklow boatbuilders) to commission the building of a new racing skiff as the *Shamrock I* fallen into disrepair. Although the new skiff was completed, the builder eventually sold it to the Ringsend based club, Stella Maris. Despite this set back, the club limped on until the mid 1980s when it again fell on hard times. No races were won by Greystones during the early 1980s. To the credit of the committee the club continued, however success at regattas proved elusive. In 1999, the Byrne brothers, Willie and Anto, together with Alan Monahan and Conor O'Neill got the club up and running again. By 2003, a new committee was formed comprising of Ciaran Demery (Chairman), Brendan Quinn (Secretary), Bernard Byrne (Treasurer), along with Ciaran Hayden, Willie Byrne, Anto Byrne and Vanessa Kemp. In 2000, after a gap of nearly 30 years, the club bought a new skiff.

In 2007, coxed by Anto Byrne, the Greystones Ladies' Crew (Vanessa Kemp, Sue O'Neill, Shona Murphy and Ciara Hatton) became the club's first ladies' crew to win an East Coast medal for the most junior races won in a season. The crew went on to achieve two regatta wins at senior level in 2009 (both on the same day at Wicklow, which also doubled as the Greystones Regatta due to the harbour being closed for the marina works). In 2007, the club started up a kayak section aimed at introducing youngsters to the sport of kayaking, with a view to bringing them through to the rowing ranks. Two new skiffs (*Shamrock III* & *Shamrock IV*) were acquired in 2007 and 2009, as interest in rowing again began to grow. In 2016 the club lost a valued member of the committee, Stephen Kinsella, brother of John Kinsella (Chairman of the club in the early 1970s). In April 2016, the club took possession of its new clubhouse and with the aid of a grant from builders, Sisk, hired a Wicklow Town builder, TASK to fit it out. It was officially opened in April 2017 by Joe Sweeney and John Byrne (Chairman). Today, Greystones Rowing Club has over 90 members in its kayaking section and over 30 rowers. The present committee comprises: John Byrne (Chairman), Bob Gunning (Secretary), Bernard Byrne (Treasurer), Anto Byrne (Vice-Chairman), Alan Smullen, Shane Mulford, Sharon Hughes and Karl Canavan.

Greystones Rowing Club Skiffs			
Skiff	**Builder**	**Year Built / Launched**	**Achievements / Comments**
Colleen Bawn	John Spurling (Greystones)	1921	Greystones senior crew suffered only two defeats over a ten year period from 1922.
Colleen Bawn II	John Spurling (Greystones)	1951	Raced just the one season (1951), used for training the following season and then converted into a fishing boat.
Shamrock I	Smith (Dublin)	1952	Greystones senior crew won four successive Wicklow Regattas (1953-1956). Her last senior crew victory came at the 1957 Greystones Regatta. *Shamrock I* underwent substantial repairs in 2004 at Howth Boatyard and she currently remains in the club pen.
Shamrock II	Patrick Whelan (Dublin)	1971	Her lightweight (deal) construction was not suited to longevity, she rotted away and was broken up in the 1980s.
Clocha Liatha	FÁS Team (Dublin)	2000	Skiff was built at the old Smith's yard at Eastwall, Dublin where *Shamrock I* was built. *Clocha Liatha* gained a number of regatta victories at junior and intermediate level. She was sold by the club to Courtown Rowing Club for a nominal sum in 2010.
Shamrock III	Maurice Hunkin (Fowey, Cornwall)	2007	Purchased with the aid of a grant from the Department of Arts, Sports & Tourism. Greystones senior crew achieved their first regatta win in 49 years at the 2016 Skerries Regatta. The crew was: Sam Byrne (cox), Patrick Byrne (stroke), Alan Monahan (beam), John Byrne (midship) and Tommy Hammil (bow).
Shamrock IV	Maurice Hunkin (Fowey, Cornwall)	2009	

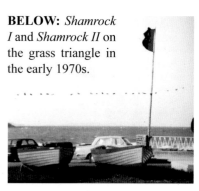

BELOW: *Shamrock I* and *Shamrock II* on the grass triangle in the early 1970s.

ABOVE: In 1970, after an absence of many years, *Shamrock I* (in the foreground) was back racing on the Liffey at the start of the Ringsend Regatta. The Greystones senior crew was Joe Sweeney (cox), Eamonn Brosnan (stroke), Dessie Redmond (beam), John Redmond (midship) and John Sweeney (bow).

RIGHT: Six skiffs positioned at the start line at the Greystones Regatta in the 1990s. At low tide the steep bank of shingle on the North Beach made for an excellent viewing point. The braver spectators clambered over the seaweed-clad remains of the north wall for a head-on view.

ABOVE: Photographs taken at the Greystones Rowing Regatta held on Saturday 30th July 2016. The *Shamrock III* and her crew returning to the harbour after finishing 5th out of ten skiffs entered in the novices' race. Left to right: Robbie Doyle, Shane Mulford, Caolan Doyle, Ciaran Doyle and John Byrne (cox).

LEFT: Skiffs heading past the Cove towards the finish line at the flagstaff during the 2016 Greystones Regatta.

BELOW: Crowds throng the finish line at the flagstaff for the 2016 regatta. More than a century before, the edition of *Irish Society* dated 23rd August 1890 remarked that "*for seeing a regatta, no place along the coast can compare with Greystones and on Saturday, the best positions were taken up at an early hour by a large number of local people*".

The Sea Rangers were founded in Britain in 1920 and were similar to girl guides, but with a focus on all things nautical.

ABOVE: Sea Rangers beside the *Irish Cedar* in August 1963.

ABOVE: Included are Daphne Bowden, Hazel Archer, Sheila Griffin, Joyce Lee, Hazel Griffin and Barbara McLean standing beside their boat.

ABOVE: Crew of the *Irish Cedar* hauling her up the beach at Greystones harbour.

ABOVE: Harbour scene from the 1960s. The boat on the left was the *Irish Cedar*, built by Willie Redmond and used by the Sea Rangers.

LEFT: Though it is now more than 20 years since the last mast was removed, the area adjacent to the rocks overlooking the harbour is still referred to as the flagstaff. The close-up section of the harbour area on the 1838 Ordnance Survey map already marked the existence of a flagstaff at this point. With the arrival of the coast guards and their two boats in 1821, it is likely that a mast or flagstaff would have been placed near the sea as a means of indicating wind direction and strength. In 1870, the Rev. William Urwick, an antiquarian chronicler, published a book about his father, *The Life and Letters of William Urwick, D.D. of Dublin.* In it he mentions his father bringing the family to stay at Greystones in the summer of 1830. Describing the locality, he noted a number of the geographical features, including what he refers to as "*the flagstaff rocks*" on a "*promontory of rock|*".

BELOW: The flagstaff during the era when the coal schooners used to import coal to Greystones harbour.

ABOVE: The flagstaff festooned with flags in the early 1900s.

ABOVE: After an absence of many years, Greystones & District Civic Association erected a mast at the flagstaff in March 1971. This followed a meeting in 1967 at which it had indicated its intention to reintroduce a flagstaff at the spot where one had once stood. In April 1989, the circular base, metal stays and yardarm were damaged in a car crash and the flagstaff was subsequently removed.

ABOVE & BELOW: Photographs taken in the 1970s showing the flagstaff mast about to be re-erected after being taken down for varnishing. The volunteers included Herbie Hill, Don McLean, Jimmy Kearon, Stanley Paine, Derek Paine and Harry Acheson.

ABOVE: Jimmy Kearon on the left and Richard Miller on the right at the base of the flagstaff in the 1980 assisting with the RNLI flag day collection. A ship's anchor today lies adjacent to the spot where the flagstaff stood. The anchor was discovered during dredging of Dún Laoghaire harbour. Its history is unknown, but was believed to be around 150 years old when it was raised from the sea bed and acquired by Greystones & District Civic Association in November 1972. It was originally placed beside the lifeboat house.

ABOVE: View of the flagstaff in the 1970s. The lower mast belonged to a steam tug called the *Southampton*, which had assisted in the evacuation of troops from Dunkirk in May 1940 during World War Two. When acquired, the mast bore scorch marks from the tug's funnel. The vessel was scrapped by the Hammond Lane Metal Company Limited in Dublin. The upper mast was made from the mast of an old sailing boat and the yardarm was fashioned from a mast belonging to a *Mermaid*.

ABOVE: View of the Cove showing a rough path short cut leading down the slope from the end of the wall to the wooden bathing boxes on the beach. A woman can be seen resting on the plank of wood, driven into the beach, from which swimmers could jump in at high tide. At the time the above photo was taken, the building painted white comprised two adjoining houses (*East House* and *West House*, later renamed *Ferney East* and *Ferney West*). The two separate front doors differ to the stepped porch which now fronts the building.

ABOVE: View of the Cove with the wooden bathing boxes on the concrete embankment. Note the two Victorian ladies, one holding a parasol, sitting on the rocks.

ABOVE: Victorian fashions in the Cove, with just a timber fence on Cliff Road.

LEFT: Aerial view in the 1980s prior to the addition of the annexe extension to the La Touche Hotel.

BELOW In recent years shingle has returned to the Cove, enhancing its appeal for swimmers. Stripped back to its bed rock as shown in this late 1970s photo, its seaweed and rock pools were a haven for sea life.

RIGHT: Written on the reverse of the photograph taken in the Cove is "E. Kean, 9 Top Street, Middleton, Lancashire". Note the timber bathing box in the background.

BELOW: Colourtone postcard showing the extent of the grass at the Cove in 1908.

The 1876 map of Greystones on the inside of the back cover shows that residential development along Marine Road was still sparse. It was during the 1880s that most of the houses were built. Two of the substantial detached residences built, both now demolished, were *St. David's* and *Liscarrig*. The former was built around 1888 and its first resident was Arthur Hughes, a corn merchant originally from County Tipperary. He became a prominent figure in Greystones society at that time. When the drowning tragedy befell the Doyles in 1892, it was Arthur Hughes who coordinated the appeal to help the families affected. He was also active in establishing Greystones Golf Club, serving, albeit briefly, as its first Hon. Secretary upon its formation in 1895. The following year the Greystones Improvement Association was formed (the first local voluntary body formed for the advancement and improvement of the local area). Arthur Hughes attended its inaugural meeting in May 1896, becoming its Hon. Secretary.

LEFT: Extract from the minute book of the Greystones Improvement Association showing the minutes written up by Arthur Hughes. The activities of the Greystones Improvement Association and its successors, the Greystones & District Development Society (formed in 1925), the Greystones Utility Society (formed in 1929) and the Greystones & District Civic Association (formed in 1957) are covered in Book No.4.

ABOVE: Postcard of *St. David's* house, with the rear of *Teevinore* and *Burrishoole* on La Touche Road visible on the left. The card was written in December 1903 by Arthur Hughes to a friend in Dublin wishing him a happy Christmas and new year. At the time it was common for householders of fine residences locally to have picture postcards produced of their houses. The postcard featuring *The Gables* on page 277 is a similar example.

* * * *

On Sunday a fire broke out at St. David's, Greystones, belonging to Surgeon Heuston, which caused damage roughly estimated at £500, stated to be covered by insurance. About 1 p.m. smoke was seen issuing from the roof, and immediately the alarm was raised, when in ten minutes upwards of 100 of the local people assembled and worked hard, carrying water from a fish pond. When the pond supply gave out sea water was conveyed by strings of willing workers to be poured on the roof, some 300 or 400 persons assisting in the work. It was afterwards discovered that a very valuable Pekinese dog, which recently cost 300 gns., had been burned to death. The outbreak has aroused local interest in the question of providing the town with fire-extinguishing appliances. Dr. Heuston desires to acknowledge, with thanks, those who so ably assisted in extinguishing the fire, especially the constabulary, coastguards, and hotel employees.

* * * *

ABOVE: Report from *The Wicklow Newsletter* dated Saturday 9th April 1910 on a major fire at St. David's which resulted sadly in the loss of a prize Pekinese dog.

By late 1905 the Hughes family decided to sell *St David's* and placed the following auction notice in *The Irish Times* dated 30th December 1905. "*To be sold, that charming residence known as "St. David's" Greystones, built in Queen Anne style. St. David's is a most substantially built house, on which no expense has been spared in erection and upkeep; it is situated in the best position on the sea front, commanding unrivalled views. Accommodation - 3 sitting rooms, study, 6 bedrooms, attic, bathroom, kitchen, sculleries, pantries, servants' apartments, 2 lavatories etc; hot and cold water throughout. Also coach house, 3 horse stables (one loose box), harness man's rooms, large hayloft, dairy, boathouse, fowl yards, dog kennels, workshop etc, all enclosed. Flower garden tastefully laid out, fish pond, shrubberies etc. Ground rent only £14 per annum. Adjoining is a large field and vegetable garden which have always paid a handsome annual profit.*"

Thom's Directory for 1908 listed *St. David's* being occupied by the Heuston family. Dr. Francis T. Heuston and his family (including his twin sons, Fred and Frank) also lived at No.15 St. Stephen's Green, Dublin. Members of the extended Heuston family also resided at *St David's* and the family is credited with introducing the first Pekinese breed of dog into Ireland. In recognition of a relative's work in establishing smallpox vaccine clinics in China, the Chinese minister, Li Hongzhang, presented the Heuston family with a pair of Pekinese dogs. Miss L.M. Heuston, a family member, established a famous kennels based at *St. David's*. Her prowess was reported in *The Wicklow Newsletter* dated 1st June 1912 when it noted that "*Miss L. Heuston, St. David's, Greystones is one of the leading exhibitors and breeders of Pekingese spaniels in Ireland. The first lady to own a Peke in this country, she has spared neither time nor money to popularise the popular spaniel. In her kennels at Greystones are many big winners at most of the leading shows".* The prefix *"of Greystones"* became renowned for the breed, with many English based owners acquiring Greystones bred puppies from Miss Heuston.

Miss Heuston's Pekinese need no introduction to us. The photograph is of the lovely dog, Ouen Sha of Greystones, at the age of eighteen months. He was bred by Miss Heuston, who is justly proud of him. Ouen Sha is not only a beautiful dog, but has a most attractive character; this is his favourite pose. As we all know, many good dogs have come from the famous "of Greystones" kennels.

OUEN SHA OF GREYSTONES
Bred and owned by Miss Heuston

ABOVE: Photograph taken in the 1890s from the Grand Hotel looking towards Marine Road with *Carrigart* and *Carriglea* on the extreme right. What today is Kimberley Road is no more than a rough lane. On the left of the photograph is the substantial residence, *St. David's,* with a creeper growing on its lower north facing facade. To its right is *Liscarrig*, built in the early 1880s. Like *East House* and *West House* which overlooked the Cove, *Liscarrig's* front door faced north.

SWEET STALL.
(Royal Blue Badge.)
President :—MISS COLLINS.
Assisted by Mrs. HAZLETT, Miss JACKSON, Miss KATHLEEN COLLINS, Mr. H. A. COLLINS, Masters FRED and FRANK HEUSTON.
"Ye Old Time Sweeterie,"
Who will with high-class Sweets be fed,
" Sweets to the sweet " will oft have read ;
Come buy, come buy,
Our wares come try,
Your cravings we will satisfy.

ABOVE: Advertisement from the programme for the Greystones Summer Fete held at the cricket ground on 24th July 1909. Assisting Miss Collins on the sweet stall were Masters Fred and Frank Heuston, twins who had just celebrated their 16th birthdays the previous month. Less than seven years later, both had been killed in action during World War One. 2nd Lieutenant Fred Heuston, 6th Battalion, Royal Irish Fusiliers was killed aged 22 on 15th August 1915 at Gallipoli. Ironically, the following day, the two Duggan brothers also of Marine Road were both killed at Gallipoli (aged just 20 and 29). Lieutenant Frank Heuston, 1st Royal Montreal Regiment was killed by a sniper near Ypres in Western Flanders on 6th April 1916.

Frank Heuston.

Frederic G. Heuston.

ABOVE: Letter written on 16th December 1916 by Frances Heuston to the War Office seeking a public awarding of the Military Cross won by her son, Fred. It read *"In reply to your letter of November 30th I beg to say I would like to have the Military Cross awarded to my son, the late Lieutenant F.G. Heuston presented to me publicly on His Majesty's behalf. I have the honour to be Sir, yours faithfully, Frances Heuston".* It is not known whether the medal was awarded at a public presentation. The file at The National Archives merely contains a note stating that the Military Cross had been forwarded to GHQ Home Forces in January 1917 for a public presentation.

LEFT: *St. David's* was acquired by the Holy Faith Sisters in 1941 and converted into a secondary school for girls. The photograph shows Sister Imelda and Miss Caslin. In 1961, with the town's population increasing, the Sisters bought another house on Marine Road, *Silverstream,* which was reconfigured as part of the junior school.

Liscarrig was built before *St David's*. An advert placed in *The Dublin Daily Express* dated 20th June 1884 listed *Liscarrig* as "*a charming residence to be let, fully and handsomely furnished for the season, conveniently situated close to the sea and rail station*". A similar advert in May 1888 offered the house for let at £35 per month. By 1904 the Dobbs family were living in the house, with the 1906 *Thom's Directory* listing Joseph Dobbs as its occupant, also of *Coolbawn*, Castlecomer in Kilkenny. According to the 1901 and 1911 census returns, Joseph Dobbs' occupation was listed as a colliery owner (he owned the Massford coal mine in Castlecomer). He and his wife had seven children, including four boys. The second eldest of these, George born on 21st July 1884, gained a mathematics scholarship to attend Shrewsbury School. From there he went to the Royal Military Academy at Woolwich, prior to being gazetted as a 2nd Lieutenant in the Royal Engineers in March 1904.

His skills with the oval ball did not go unnoticed. As his military career progressed, he gained a lengthy list of teams that he represented. Stationed in Devon and South Wales, as well as representing the Army, his rugby career included appearances for Plymouth Albion, Devonport Albion, Devon, Llanelli and the Barbarians. Impressing as a versatile flank forward, he was one of seven debutants selected to play for England at home to Wales. The match, played at the Athletic Ground on Kew Road in Richmond on 13th January 1906, saw Wales win 16-3. Dobbs won his 2nd and final England cap, ironically in the 16-6 home defeat against Ireland, at Leicester on 11th February 1906. Despite the result, the match report carried in *The Sporting Life,* noted "*Dobbs dribbling in splendid style*". The following month saw Dobbs achieve success in the County Championship, the RFU's oldest established rugby tournament. Devon met Durham in the final for the 3rd time in seven years. The match at Exeter saw Devon seal victory early in the 2nd half. Dobbs threw the ball to Kelly to go over for the decisive try in the 16-3 victory to win the Championship for the side affectionately known as the *Dumplings*. In his final game that year, he played for Llanelli against the touring South Africa team on the latter's inaugural overseas tour. A record crowd of 16,000 packed into a snowy Stradey Park to see the Springboks run out 16-3 winners. The scoreline did not reflect that the game was neck and neck for long periods. In its match report, *The Sporting Life* noted "*it is almost unfair to single out any of the rival forwards, but the sterling display of Lieutenant Dobbs, the old Devon and England international and Dan Walters, the Llanelli captain on the one side and Paul Roos, Brink and Raaf on the other must be commended*".

ABOVE: Fine view of *Liscarrig* with its verandah on its south facing side with *Carriglea* and *Carrigart* in the foreground.

ABOVE: View looking towards *Liscarrig* on a summer day, with a number of cars parked beside the bathing place.

ABOVE: An etching showing the southern side of *Liscarrig* from an early 1900s card.

At the outbreak of World War One, Lieutenant George Dobbs was immediately sent to the front as part of the British Expeditionary Force. He fought at the first engagement of the war for British troops, the Battle of Mons, in August 1914. His speciality was in signalling and communications. His skill in helping to keep communication lines open during the retreat from Mons was recognised by the French. In November 1914 he was made a *Chevalier de la Légion d'honneur* (Knight of the Legion of Honour). He was promoted to Captain in 1914 and the following year was made Brevet Major. Mentioned in despatches on three occasions, including by Sir Douglas Haig, his rapid rise through the ranks continued and by 1917 he was a Lieutenant Colonel and appointed as an assistant director of signals. On 17th June 1917, near Poperinge in Belgium, when prospecting for a trench to carry a communications line in preparation for what was to become the 3rd Battle of Ypres (better known as the Battle of Passchendaele), he was hit by a shell and died from his wounds shortly afterwards. He was 32 years of age. Lieutenant Colonel George E.B. Dobbs, Royal Engineers is among the near 11,000 war dead buried in Lijssenthoek Military Cemetery in Western Flanders. His Marine Road neighbour, Lieutenant Frank Heuston, 1st Royal Montreal Regiment, is also among the casualties buried there.

ABOVE: Lieutenant Colonel George Eric Burroughs Dobbs in uniform.

ABOVE: The telegram every parent hoped they would never receive during the war. Sent on 17th June 1917 from the Secretary of the War Office to the Dobbs family, *Liscarrig*, Greystones, Co. Wicklow it read *"Deeply regret to inform you Lt. Colonel G.E.B. Dobbs R.E. has died of wounds June seventeenth. The Army Council express their sympathy"*.

1914 - 1918

RUGBY FOOTBALL UNION
IN MEMORIAM

H. ALEXANDER	H.A. HODGES	E.R. MOBBS	L.A.N. SLOCOCK
H. BERRY	R.E. INGLIS	W.M.B. NANSON	F.N. TARR
A.J. DINGLE	P.D. KENDALL	F.E. OAKELEY	A.F. TODD
G.E.B. DOBBS	J.A. KING	R.L. PILLMAN	J.H.D. WATSON
L. HAIGH	R.O. LAGDEN	R.W. POULTON PALMER	A.J. WILSON
R.H.M. HANDS	D. LAMBERT	J.E. RAPHAEL	C.E. WILSON
A.L. HARRISON	A.F. MAYNARD	R.O. SCHWARZ	

LIEUT.-COL G. E. B. DOBBS, R.E. Son of Mr. and Mrs. Joseph Dobbs, The Chalet, Temple Road, and Liscarrig, Greystones.

ABOVE: The Memorial Board at Twickenham which commemorates the 27 England rugby internationals who were killed in World War One. Six of the players played in England's final game before the war when the side defeated France at Stade Colombes in April 1914 to win the Grand Slam. The two Irish born players among the 27 hold separate distinctions. Lt. Colonel George Dobbs was the first of them to see action in the war. Cork born Captain Adjt. Charles Edward Wilson was the first of the 27 men to be killed, when he was hit by a shell on 17th September 1914 in the First Battle of the Aisne. A veteran of the Boer War, at which he saw action and was mentioned in despatches at the Relief of Ladysmith as well as Spion Kop, Wilson won his solitary England cap in a 6-9 defeat at home to Ireland in February 1898.

ABOVE: Taken from of a montage of 18 photographs of officers killed in World War One during the previous month published by *The Illustrated London News* in its 7th July 1917 edition.

BELOW: The former site of *Liscarrig*, now part of St. David's Holy Faith School.

ABOVE LEFT: During World War Two, when food rationing was introduced, many gardens were converted to produce food. The above 1942 photograph shows Mr Fox ploughing the lawn of *Liscarrig*, with the gable of its front porch just visible in the background. *Thom's Directory* for 1933 shows Dr. Robert Blake McVittie living in *Liscarrig*. His widow, Violet, later bequeathed the house to be used as a home for retired clergy and missionaries. The St. Patrick's Church Summer Fete was held annually in its grounds throughout the early 1970s and the house was also used as the CSSM's headquarters during their annual visit to Greystones. It was sold in 1975 to the Holy Faith Sisters, subsequently demolished and its grounds incorporated into St David's School.

EUGENE DAVY

Down the years there has been a long tradition of families holidaying in Greystones. In the latter part of the 19th century and particularly through the first half of the 20th century, this was especially so. With the benefit of the railway link to Dublin, many families would rent houses for part of the summer months, others purchased houses in Greystones to use as holiday homes. The Davy family has a long association with Greystones, ever since Thomas Davy and his family rented *West House* at the Cove in the summer of 1901. Thomas Davy subsequently purchased *Carrigart* on Marine Road in 1906 and since then five generations of the family have enjoyed holidays in Greystones staying there. Upon the death of Thomas Davy in 1923, ownership of *Carrigart* passed to his widow, Alice, who continued to use it as a holiday home until her death in the mid-1950s. It then passed into the ownership of Eugene Davy and following his death in 1996, passed to his son, the present owner, Joseph Davy.

Eugene Davy took a keen interest in Greystones and was a strong supporter of the tennis club, playing an active role in both its relocation from the rugby club to opposite the La Touche Hotel in the mid-1960s and in its subsequent revamp in the mid-1970s. A keen swimmer, he contacted Wicklow County Council each year to ensure that the diving board and raft at the bathing place opposite *Carrigart* were in situ for the summer months, regularly having a morning swim there before travelling to work in Dublin.

ABOVE: Thomas Davy, who purchased *Carrigart* on Marine Road in 1906. Originally from Tipperary, Thomas Davy was a successful publican, at one time owning four Dublin pubs, including Portobello House in Rathmines.

ABOVE: The Ireland rugby team captained by Eugene Davy, holding the ball, photographed before the match against Wales at Ravenhill on 11th March 1933. Eugene Davy scored a drop goal in a 10-5 win for Ireland.

ABOVE: Eugene Davy and his wife, Geraldine, at the South Beach with the linked houses *Carriglea* and *Carrigart* and St. David's Holy Faith Secondary School in the distance.

EUGENE DAVY

Educated at Belvedere College, Dublin, Eugene Davy captained the team that won the Leinster Schools Junior Cup in 1919. He achieved subsequent success on the rugby field with UCD, helping the university win its first Leinster Senior Cup in 1924. He was fly-half in the Lansdowne team that won five successive Leinster Senior Cups between 1927 and 1931 and three Bateman Cups, the then All-Ireland Championship. He was ever present in the Ireland team for nine years, from when he won the first of his 34 caps (4 as captain) at the age of 20, playing at outside-half in a 19-3 win against Wales at Ravenhill, until his final cap in February 1934 against England in a 13-3 defeat at Lansdowne Road. His finest moment in the green of Ireland came at Murrayfield in February 1930, when he scored a hat-trick of tries in a 20 minute period, to earn Ireland a famous win in the then Five Nations Championship.

The year before, he was a member of the Ireland team that achieved a first ever victory over England at Twickenham. In total, he scored nine international tries for Ireland. When Greystones Rugby Club was formed in 1937, Eugene Davy presented the club with its first official ball. A former president of the IRFU, he also served as manager of the Ireland rugby team that toured Australia in 1967. The tour was notable, as Ireland became the first team from the four home rugby nations to win a rugby test in the southern hemisphere, defeating Australia 11-5 at the Sydney Cricket Ground. Eugene Davy, together with his brother James (who was also a former Chairman of the La Touche Hotel) established Davy Stockbrokers in 1926.

ABOVE: Eugene Davy shaking hands with H.R.H. Duke of York, later King George VI, at Twickenham on 9th February 1929. Eugene Davy scored Ireland's opening try in a 6-5 win, the team's first ever against England at Twickenham. In the match between the sides at the same venue two years later, Eugene Davy captained Ireland in a 17-6 defeat.

ABOVE: *Carrigart* has been used to host many Davy family events down the years, including the marriage of Eugene Davy's granddaughter, Kate Carton, to former Leinster and Ireland rugby international, Kevin McLaughlin, in July 2015.

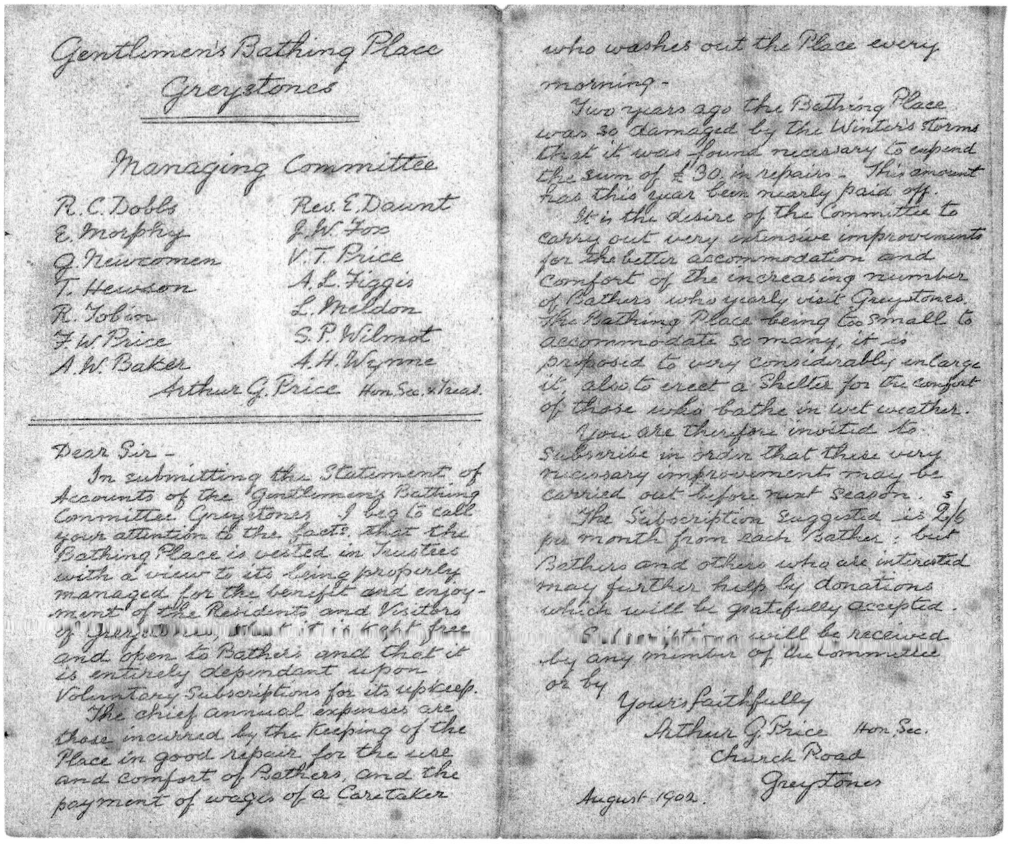

Gentlemen's Bathing Place
Greystones

Managing Committee

R.C. Dobbs — Rev. E. Daunt
E. Morphy — J.W. Fox
J. Newcomen — V.T. Price
T. Hewson — A.L. Figgis
R. Tobin — L. Meldon
F.W. Price — S.P. Wilmot
A.W. Baker — A.H. Wynne

Arthur G. Price Hon. Sec. & Treas.

Dear Sir -
In submitting the Statement of Accounts of the 'Gentlemen's Bathing Committee' Greystones I beg to call your attention to the facts, that the Bathing Place is vested in Trustees with a view to its being properly managed for the benefit and enjoyment of the Residents and Visitors of Greystones, that it is kept free and open to Bathers and that it is entirely dependent upon Voluntary Subscriptions for its upkeep.
The chief annual expenses are those incurred by the keeping of the Place in good repair for the use and comfort of Bathers, and the payment of wages of a Caretaker who washes out the Place every morning -
Two years ago the Bathing Place was so damaged by the Winter's storms that it was found necessary to expend the sum of £30 in repairs. This amount has this year been nearly paid off.
It is the desire of the Committee to carry out very extensive improvements for the better accommodation and comfort of the increasing number of Bathers who yearly visit Greystones. The Bathing Place being too small to accommodate so many, it is proposed to very considerably enlarge it, also to erect a Shelter for the comfort of those who bathe in wet weather.
You are therefore invited to subscribe in order that these very necessary improvements may be carried out before next season.
The Subscription suggested is 2/6 per month from each Bather; but Bathers and others who are interested may further help by donations which will be gratefully accepted.
Subscriptions will be received by any member of the Committee or by
Yours faithfully
Arthur G. Price Hon. Sec.
Church Road
Greystones
August 1902.

Gentlemen's Bathing Place
Greystones

===========================

Managing Committee

R.C. Dobbs	Rev. E. Daunt
E. Morphy	J.W. Fox
J. Newcomen	V.T. Price
T. Hewson	A.L. Figgis
R. Tobin	L. Meldon
F.W. Price	S.P. Wilmot
A.W. Baker	A.H. Wynne

Arthur G. Price Hon. Sec. & Treas.

===

Dear Sir,

In submitting the Statement of Accounts of the Gentlemen's Bathing Committee Greystones, I beg to call your attention to the fact that the Bathing Place is vested in Trustees with the view to its being properly managed for the benefit and enjoyment of the residents and visitors of Greystones, that it is kept free and open to bathers and that it is entirely dependent upon voluntary subscriptions for its upkeep. The chief annual expenses are those incurred by the keeping of the place in good repair for the use and comfort of bathers and the payment of wages of a caretaker, who washes out the place every morning.

Two years ago, the bathing place was so damaged by the winter's storms that it was found necessary to expend the sum of £30 in repairs. This amount has this year been nearly paid off. It is the desire of the committee to carry out very extensive improvements for the better accommodation and comfort of the increasing number of bathers who yearly visit Greystones. The bathing place being too small to accommodate so many, it is proposed to very considerably enlarge it, also to erect a shelter for the comfort of those who bathe in wet weather.

You are therefore invited to subscribe in order that these very necessary improvements may be carried out before next season. The subscription suggested is 2s & 6d per month from each bather, but bathers and others who are interested may further help by donations which will be gratefully accepted.

Subscriptions will be received by any member of the committee or by

Yours faithfully

Arthur G. Price, Hon. Sec.

Church Road

Greystones

August 1902

THE GENTLEMEN'S BATHING PLACE

LEFT: Copy of the report of Arthur Price, the Hon. Sec. of the Gentlemen's Bathing Place, which accompanied the statement of accounts for the year ended 1st June 1902. The income and expenditure account disclosed that subscriptions for the year totalled £9 12s & 6d. Items of expenditure included £3 15s & 6d in wages for a caretaker, the sum of 10s for help in placing and removing the springboard and 5s & 11d on chemicals for the removal of weed. A full transcript of the report is also shown. Arthur Price was a keen swimmer and in the 1885 swimming race over a 200 yard course, held as part of the Greystones Regatta, he took third place and the 10 shilling prize. *The Freeman's Journal* reported that *"about five yards separated first from third."*

In his history of Greystones written in 1964, Samuel A. French wrote of the period 1889 to 1914 that *"for nine months of the year, the City Fathers met each morning at 7am in the Men's bathing place for a morning plunge before breakfast at 8am and catching the 8.45am train to Dublin. Those who missed this train had to join the Wexford train at 10am which usually ran late. It is impossible, it was said, to be late for the ten o'clock train!".*

Gentlemen's Bathing Place, Greystones.

LEFT: Locally published postcard dated 1913 showing a large group of spectators along the wall of the Gentlemen's Bathing Place. Swan's Rock can be seen protruding out from the South Beach, as a result of the absence of shingle on the beach when this photograph was taken.

Published by St. Aubyns, Greystones.

ABOVE: The reverse of the postcard reveals it was taken and published by local photographer, Jesse St. Aubyn.

The Bathing Place, Greystones. Co. Wicklow.

ABOVE: Colourtone postcard sent in 1906.

RIGHT: Gentlemen's Bathing Place from the South Beach on a summer day with wooden diving board in place and the bathing flag flying. Several old cars can be seen parked opposite *Carrigart*.

BELOW: Fine view of the plank traversing the rock gully, with swimmers and sunbathers enjoying a summer day.

BELOW: Taken in 1940, a view of the diving board showing a rope suspended from its end and the wooden plank traversing the rock gully just visible in the top right corner.

175

GREYSTONES SWIMMING CLUB
PROGRAMME OF
EVENTS, ETC., FOR SEASON 1957

Squadron Races will also be held, as announced
on swimming nights.
Open Gala   Saturday, 17th August
Open Half-Mile Race   Tuesday, 9th July
Round-the-Harbour Race
                          Sunday, 21st July, at 4.30
Club Harbour-to-Gents' Race
                          Sunday, 7th July, at 4.30
DIVING and WATER POLO
Sun., 30th June, 12.0   Sun., 4th Aug.,   6.0
SAT., 6th July,   6.0   Sun., 11th Aug., 12.0
Sun., 14th July, 12.0   Sun., 18th Aug.,   6.0
Sun., 21st July, 6.0   Sun., 25th Aug., 12.0
Sun., 28th July, 12.0

ABOVE: A large number of spectators on the rocks to see the end of the 1948 *"Harbour-to-Gents' Race"*. The annual event was always one of the highlights of the Greystones Swimming Club calendar.

ABOVE: Kathleen and Rita Wynne with the Gilbert children photographed at the Gentlemen's Bathing Place in 1924. The fixings to secure the diving board can be seen protruding above the shingle. Taken just three years prior to the photo below, it shows that the build up of shingle on the beach is thus not just a modern occurrence.

ABOVE: 1927 photo of a swimmer diving in. The rope attached to the end of the diving board is clearly visible here.

ABOVE: In 1990, works were undertaken to expand the seating area on the rocks. A wooden chute was constructed and quick drying cement was pumped down it at low tide into a specially designed timber frame. At the far side of the low wall was a popular diving area known locally as the "blue spot". Its name was derived from the blue hue of the rock at this location.

ABOVE: Wide expanse of beach in April 2015. Only the upper part of the wall of the old shelter is visible, protruding above the shingle, in sharp contrast to the photograph below, which was taken in April 2010.

ABOVE: The South Beach car park on the site of the former railway turntable photographed in 2012. Visible to the left are the four chimneys of *Carriglea* and *Carrigart* on Marine Road.

ABOVE: Photograph dated 26th April 1955 showing a train driver operating the lever of the railway turntable to turn *Engine 608*. The turntable remained in use until the 1960s and was later preserved as a sunken stone feature in the 1970s and 1980s prior to it being filled in when the car park was built.

LEFT: Driver operating the lever to turn the engine.

BELOW: Another photo of an engine being turned on the railway turntable.

LEFT: Aerial view in 1987 showing the railway turntable as a sunken concrete feature within the grassy area next to the green copper roofed public toilets. Note the depth of water at the bathing place and almost no beach at high tide.

RIGHT: 1941 photograph of a train driver operating the turntable lever at the front of *Engine 346*.

ABOVE: The siding that led to the railway turntable.

ABOVE: Lucan Dairy depot in 1964 which was located where the car park is today.

ABOVE: 1880s view of the level crossing before the railway footbridge was built. *Malvern House* is visible next to the railway bridge on La Touche place.

ABOVE: View of Greystones railway station in the early 1900s from the footbridge, with the stable yard where the horses and carriages waited on the seaward side.

ABOVE: 1880s view of La Touche Road with a railway worker in conversation with a man before any houses or the Holy Rosary Church had been built. Note the thatched roof on the house beside the railway bridge.

ABOVE: View from the pedestrian bridge at the station in the early 1900s. A horse and cart is waiting on La Touche Road. The cross on the top of the wooden spire of the Holy Rosary Church built in 1903/1904 is visible beyond the roofs of the houses.

ABOVE: Swan's Rock visible on the shoreline.

ABOVE: Summer fashions on the South Beach with a diver on the wooden mobile diving board, which had a wheel at the other end, so that it could be adjusted for the change in the tide. The now demolished *Liscarrig House* is visible on the left.

ABOVE: The end of a day at the South Beach as a family make their way back up the steps.

ABOVE: Donkey rides on the South Beach were always a popular attraction on a summer day.

ABOVE: Aerial photograph taken in 1953 with fields where now there are housing estates.

ABOVE: Photograph taken on Christmas Day 2014 of the Christmas morning swim on the South Beach which has become an increasingly popular event in recent years.

THE R101 AIRSHIP FLYING OVER GREYSTONES IN 1929

ABOVE: This photo was taken by Willie Hughes standing at the entrance to Stanley Stores on Church Road, Greystones between 8.30am and 9.00am on Monday 18th November 1929. The airship *R101* was on its endurance test flight, flying south directly over the Holy Rosary Church. The timber spire which was on the church tower at this time can clearly be seen. To its right is the very high telegraph pole which was located near the sea. *Bushfield House* on La Touche Place can be seen on the right. The flight, which lasted 30 hours and 41 minutes and took in England, Scotland, Ireland and Wales, was to be the longest achieved by the *R101*. The airship crashed on its maiden overseas voyage the following year. This photo is one of two taken of the airship as it passed over Greystones. The other, taken several seconds later, is featured in Book No.1.

When built in 1929, the *R101*, measuring 731 feet in length and 131 feet in diameter (prior to its subsequent extension to 777 feet in June 1930) was the world's largest flying craft. It was constructed under a British government programme to develop civil airships capable of servicing long-distance passenger routes to Canada, India and Australia, as these distances were too great for the heavier-than-air aircraft of the period. It had a cruising speed of 63mph, with a range of around 4,000 miles on a full fuel load. Accommodation for up to 100 passengers was on two decks within the airship envelope and comprised 50 cabins. The dining room, complete with wicker furniture and aluminium cutlery to minimise weight, could seat 60 people. Two promenade decks with windows ran down the sides of the airship and there was an asbestos lined smoking room for 24 people. The bulk of the passenger space was on the upper deck, with the smoking room, kitchen, washrooms, crew accommodation, the chartroom and radio cabin on the lower deck. The control car was directly under the forward section of the lower deck and was accessible via a ladder from the chartroom. In normal service the *R101* carried a crew of 42. This consisted of the captain and two watches of 13 men under the officer of the watch, as well as other crew members including chief engineer, meteorological officer and wireless operator.

The *R101* made its first test flight on 14th October 1929, flying over Westminster from its base at Cardington in Bedfordshire. A further five test flights took place over the subsequent four weeks. A planned flight on 16th November 1929 for 100 Members of Parliament had to be cancelled and rescheduled for the following week due to adverse weather. On 17th November 1929, the weather cleared and the opportunity was taken to quickly arrange an endurance test flight for the *R101* to last at least 30 hours. At 10.33am, the airship lifted off, heading over York and Durham before flying as far north as Edinburgh, where it turned west towards Glasgow. During the night a series of turning trials was made over the Irish Sea, after which the airship was flown south to fly over Dublin, the birthplace of its captain, Herbert Carmichael Irwin. According to the diary of the First Officer, Noel Atherstone, as the *R101* approached Dublin Bay at 08.00am on 18th November 1929, Irwin *"took over for the Forenoon Watch and flew the ship in majestic sweeps over his native land and city."* The *R101* then headed down the coast to Bray and Greystones. Atherstone noted that the airship *"gave the Kingstown-Holyhead mail boat a good start and then whooshed past her headed for the same place."* In Anglesey, it flew over Rhosneigr, where Irwin's mother lived, before passing Chester and eventually landing at Cardington at 5.14pm.

Irwin was born in 1894 in Dundrum, Co. Dublin and was educated at St. Andrews College, Dublin. A talented athlete, he was a member of Clonliffe Harriers, who commemorate him through the Irwin Cup. Long time Greystones resident and former All-Ireland marathon champion and fellow Clonliffe Harrier, the late Noel Henry, was a winner of the Irwin Cup in 1958. Irwin competed in the 1920 Olympics in Antwerp, where he made the 5,000 metres final, finishing out of the medals. He had joined the Royal Naval Air Service in 1915 and commanded a number of airships. He was captain of the *R101* on its ill-fated maiden overseas voyage to India, via a planned refuelling stop in Egypt. The *R101* took off from Cardington in Bedfordshire but crashed in adverse weather conditions near Beauvais in northern France at 2.00am on 5th October 1930, killing 48 of the 54 people on board, including Irwin. The crash effectively ended British airship development and was one of the worst airship accidents of the 1930s. The loss of life was greater than the 36 killed in the more famous Hindenburg disaster of 1937 in New York, though fewer than the 52 killed in the French military Dixmude in 1923 and the 73 killed when the USS Akron broke up over the sea in 1933. According to the report of the subsequent inquiry into the *R101* disaster, the *R101*'s performance on the endurance test flight that overflew Greystones *"gave much satisfaction"* to Irwin.

PROPOSED GREYSTONES TO GLENDALOUGH RAILWAY 1874

In July 1874, plans were drawn up for a proposed railway line from Greystones to Glendalough. From the mid 19th century, railway excursions to the mountains and lakes had become a popular pastime for city dwellers in Britain, arranged through a number of excursion agents that sprang up to meet the growing day tripper demand. In 1850, over the Whitsun weekend, the Lancashire & Yorkshire Railway advertised excursions from Manchester to Windermere in the Lake District, where the line had opened in 1847. That a quarter of century later, proposed plans which would have seen passengers having the opportunity to take a railway excursion from Dublin to Glendalough, via Greystones, was not altogether unsurprising. That the near 18 mile railway line, starting at close to sea level and gradually ascending to reach a maximum elevation of 730 feet above sea level near Roundwood never made it beyond the drawing board is equally unsurprising. The civil engineer, James Andrews, identified a number of challenges to the proposed project. Chief amongst these was a planned 1,400 feet long tunnel to be constructed near Altidore. In addition, two multi-span bridges were envisaged, a 500 feet long bridge comprising 10 spans of 50 feet at Delgany and a bridge of 300 feet, with 10 spans of 30 feet over the Vartry reservoir on the approach to Roundwood.

LEFT: Section of the plan showing the proposed 1,400 feet long tunnel at Altidore.

RIGHT: Section showing the proposed six span bridge over the Vartry reservoir.

BELOW: A diagram to scale showing the route of the proposed railway line which would have seen the construction of seven new stations as marked. The longest section of the line was that between Altidore and Roundwood, a distance between stations of just under six miles.

Glendalough	Laragh	Annamoe	Roundwood	Altidore	Kilpedder	Delgany	Greystones
17 miles 7 furlongs	16 miles 6 furlongs	13 miles 7 furlongs	10 miles 4 furlongs	4 miles 5 furlongs	3 miles 2 furlongs	1 mile 3 furlongs	

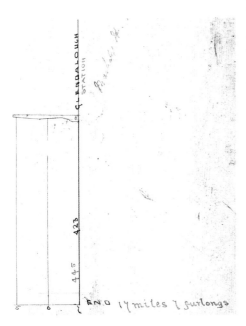

LEFT: The end of the proposed railway line, terminating after 17 miles and 7 furlongs at an elevation of 445 feet above sea level at Glendalough station. The original 1874 plans of the proposed Greystones to Glendalough railway line, unrolled, measure 10 feet by 1 foot and were drawn to a scale of 6 inches to 1 mile. The following two pages show the section commencing from Greystones station, running through Killincarrig, with its first proposed stop after 1 mile and 3 furlongs at (a to be constructed) Delgany station.

RIGHT: A decade after the proposed plans for the railway line to Glendalough were drawn up, day trippers from Dublin's Harcourt Street station could visit the beauty spot, choosing from return fares ranging from 5 shillings for 3rd class to 11 shillings for 1st class. Passengers went by train as far as Rathdrum, from where they were met by Mr Cowley's "*well appointed car*" for onward conveyance to and from Glendalough. The advert appeared in *The Dublin Daily Express* dated 25th July 1884.

DUBLIN, WICKLOW, AND WEXFORD RAILWAY.
NOTICE.
Arrangements have been made with Mr Cowley to despatch, on Week days, from Rathdrum Station, on arrival of 9.5 a m Train from Harcourt street,
A WELL-APPOINTED CAR FOR GLENDALOUGH, SEVEN CHURCHES,
Returning in time to meet the Train due to leave Rathdrum at 7.38 p m for Dublin.
FARES (including Driver's Fees):—

	1st Class.	2nd Class.	3rd Class.
Dublin to Glendalough (Single Journey)	8s	6s 6d	5s
Dublin to Glendalough (Return Journey)	11s	8s	6s

ON SUNDAYS
A limited number of Passengers will be booked Through to Glendalough by the 9 a m Train from Harcourt street, getting Return Tickets at the Fares above quoted for the Single Journey, viz—First Class, 8s; Second Class, 6s 6d; Third Class, 5s.
WILLIAM L PAYNE, Traffic Manager.
Harcourt street Terminus, 11th June, 1884.

Feature	Number	Comment
Bridges	19	Including 1 footbridge and 2 multi-span bridges of 10 x 50 feet spans at Delgany & 6 x 30 feet spans over the Vartry reservoir.
Level Crossings	5	The first of which was planned for Drummin, where the N11 is now.
Tunnels	1	1,400 feet tunnel at Altidore.
New Stations	7	

LEFT: Summary of the number of features which the proposed 1874 Greystones to Glendalough railway line encompassed.

RIGHT: In the end, the closest Glendalough ever got to the railway was having a steam locomotive named after it. The *Glendalough* (No.33), photographed in the railway shed at Bray station on 25th May 1924, was one of two passenger locomotives built by Sharp, Stewart & Co., Glasgow in 1873. The *Glendalough*, like her sister locomotive, *Glenmalure*, was subsequently rebuilt in 1898/1899 for use on the mail train service. Both engines were withdrawn by the Dublin & South Eastern Railway in 1925.

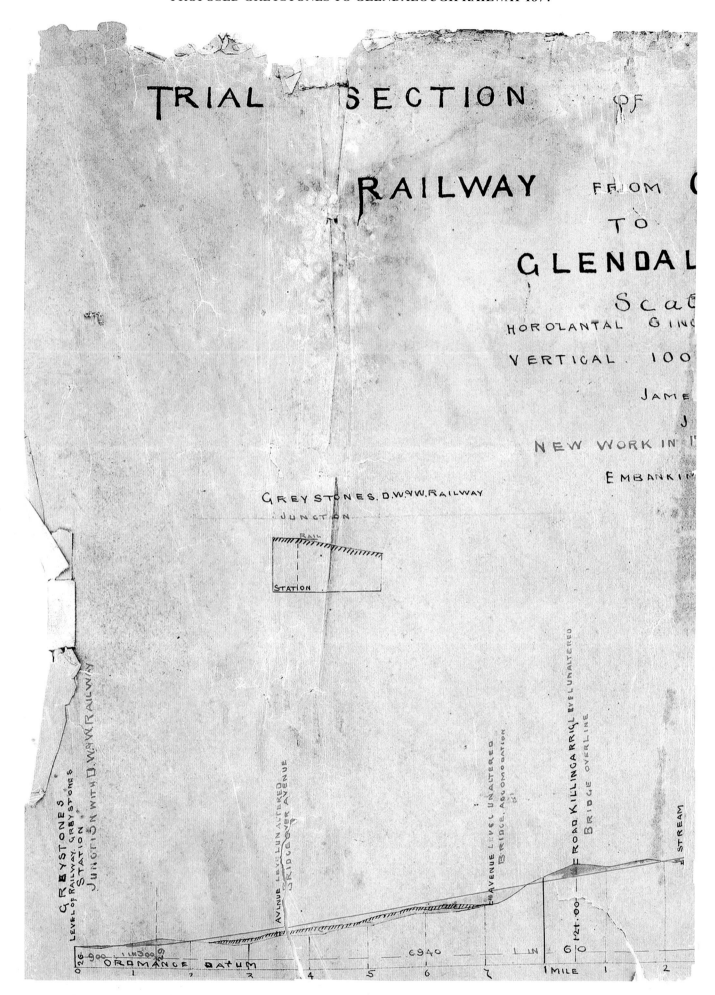

ABOVE: Plan showing the start of the proposed 1874 railway line from Greystones to Glendalough running through Killincarrig at a 1 in 60 incline. It was envisaged that three bridges would be constructed over this section.

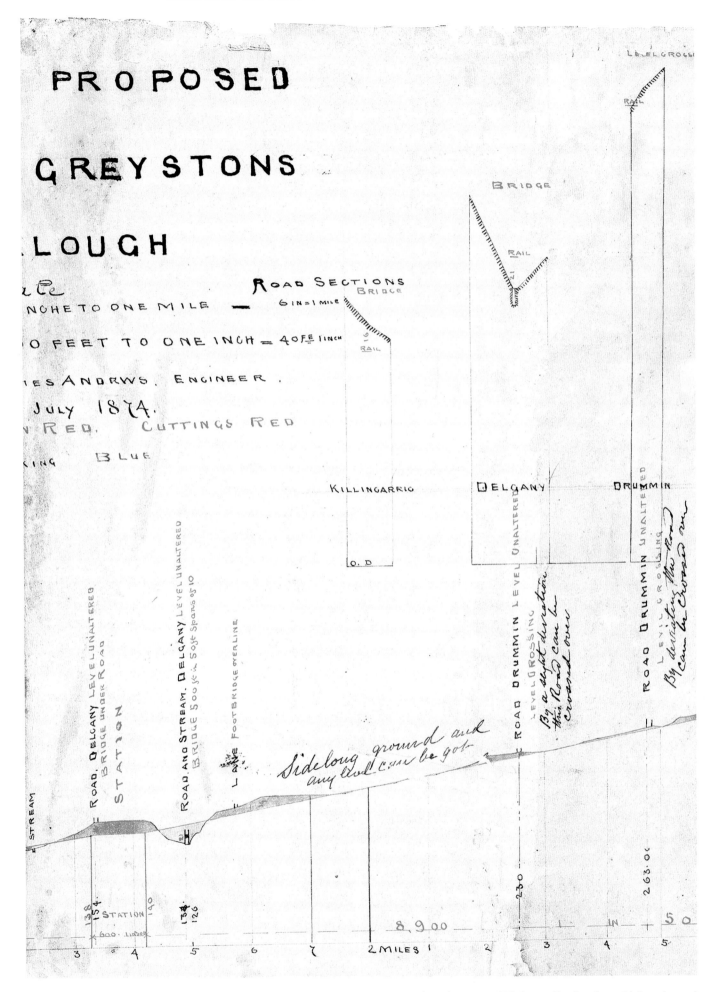

ABOVE: The plan showing the station to be constructed at Delgany, as mentioned on page 185, immediately after which a planned 500 feet bridge comprising 10 spans of 50 feet was proposed to carry the railway line over the Three Trouts Stream. It was envisaged that a level crossing would be built at Drummin, where the N11 is today.

Six companies have operated the railway line to Greystones since its opening in 1855.

Years	Name of Company
1855-1860	Waterford, Wexford, Wicklow & Dublin Railway Company
1860-1906	Dublin, Wicklow & Wexford Railway Company
1906-1924	Dublin & South Eastern Railway
1925-1944	Great Southern Railways
1945-1987	CIÉ / Córas Iompair Éireann
1987- Present	Irish Rail / Iarnród Éireann

ABOVE: Dublin, Wicklow & Wexford Railway 2nd class evening return ticket from Greystones to Bray dated 5th September 1906.

ABOVE: Dublin Wicklow & Wexford Railway ticket for one bicycle accompanied by passenger between Westland Row and any station dated 14th November 1904 costing 6d.

ABOVE: Dublin Wicklow & Wexford Railway ticket for one dog to travel from Westland Row to Bray dated 29th November 1906 costing 3d. Note the company's liability *"not exceeding £2."*

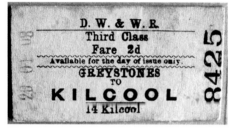

ABOVE: Dublin Wicklow & Wexford Railway 3rd class from Greystones to Kilcool dated 20th January 1908 costing 2d. Despite the change in operating company, it still had D.W.& W.R. lettering when issued.

ABOVE: Dublin & South Eastern Railway 1st class single ticket from Greystones to Bray dated 17th July 1918 costing 10d.

ABOVE: Great Southern Railways 1st class return ticket from Greystones to Tara Street dated 17th April 1944 and a CIÉ 1st class Dublin to Greystones return ticket dated 26th April 1947.

ABOVE: CIÉ 3rd class single ticket from Harcourt Street to Greystones dated 7th August 1947 costing 1s & 2d.

ABOVE: CIÉ 3rd class single ticket from Tara Street to Greystones dated 15th July 1951 costing 1s & 6d.

ABOVE: CIÉ 2nd class return ticket from Greystones to Dun Laoire dated 1st June 1958.

ABOVE: Costing 5d, CIÉ 2nd class single child ticket from Bray to Greystones dated 29th May 1964 .

ABOVE: CIÉ 2nd class ticket from Greystones to Amiens Street dated 10th September 1968 costing 2s & 4d.

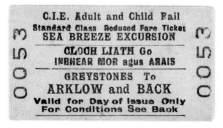

ABOVE: Greystones to Arklow CIÉ Sea Breeze Excursion return ticket.

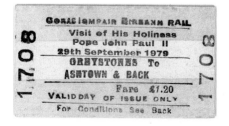

ABOVE: Special CIÉ ticket from Greystones to Ashtown & back dated 29th September 1979 for the visit of His Holiness, Pope John Paul II, costing £1.20.

ABOVE: Letter, newspaper and parcel stamps issued by the Dublin, Wicklow & Wexford Railway.

BELOW: Immediately after the Easter Rising in 1916, travel restrictions were imposed. *The Wicklow Newsletter* dated 29th April 1916 noted that "*in consequence of the Sinn Fein Rising, the train service from Wicklow, either ways, has been greatly disturbed and only two trains are running daily.*" The below rail pass, signed by Major C.P.M., was issued on 8th May 1916 to Leonard Evans granting him permission to travel between Greystones and Dublin via Kingstown (Dún Laoghaire) "*till further orders.*" Leonard Evans, who was 14 years old at the time, lived at *Wavecrest* at the harbour. He was the son of Arthur Patrick Evans who ran the family coal business started by his father, Arthur Evans.

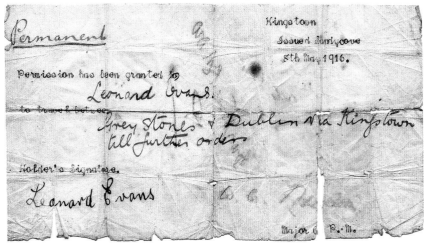

ABOVE: Dublin & South Eastern Railway consignment receipt dated 29th November 1919 for the conveyance of four gallons of milk from Greystones to Harcourt Street station. In 1912 John Evans of *Somerset*, Church Road, Greystones bought the 112 acre dairy farm at Charlesland and regularly supplied milk to the Hazelbrook Dairy in Rathfarnham. Run by the Hughes family, Hazelbrook Dairy grew and in 1926 became Hughes Brothers Dairy, from which the famous *HB Ice Cream* brand was created. John Evans was the son of Henry Evans who built and lived at *Emily House* on Trafalgar Road and is featured in the Charlesland section of Book No.7.

RIGHT: Bill head dated 1914 for Charlesland Dairy, owned by John Evans.

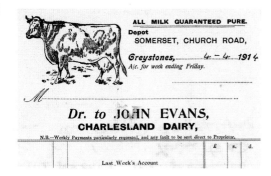

ABOVE: A luggage label for destination Greystones issued by the Great Western Railway in Britain.

ABOVE: CIÉ 2nd class rail monthly season ticket for December 1961 between Greystones and Amiens Street costing 66s.

ABOVE: CIÉ adult 10 Journey Card valid between Greystones and Dublin bought on 31st January 1984 for £4.38.

ABOVE: Irish Rail DART adult return ticket from Greystones to Pearse Station bought on 29th July 2017 for €10.80.

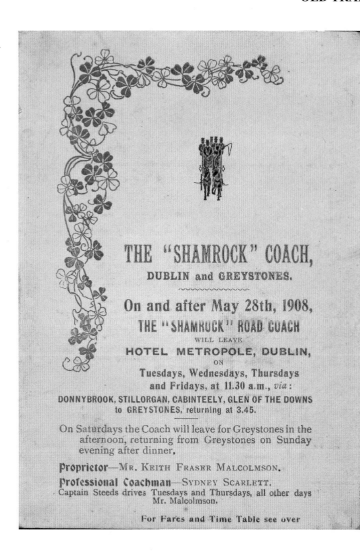

THE "SHAMROCK" COACH,

DUBLIN and GREYSTONES.

On and after May 28th, 1908,

THE "SHAMROCK" ROAD COACH

WILL LEAVE

HOTEL METROPOLE, DUBLIN,

ON

Tuesdays, Wednesdays, Thursdays
and Fridays, at 11.30 a.m., via:

DONNYBROOK, STILLORGAN, CABINTEELY, GLEN OF THE DOWNS
to GREYSTONES, returning at 3.45.

On Saturdays the Coach will leave for Greystones in the
afternoon, returning from Greystones on Sunday
evening after dinner,

Proprietor—MR. KEITH FRASER MALCOLMSON.

Professional Coachman—SYDNEY SCARLETT.
Captain Steeds drives Tuesdays and Thursdays, all other days
Mr. Malcolmson.

For Fares and Time Table see over

BELOW & LEFT: Timetable for the Shamrock Coach which operated from 28th May 1908 between the Hotel Metropole in Dublin and the Grand Hotel in Greystones. It ran on Tuesdays, Wednesdays, Thursdays and Fridays, departing Dublin at 11.30am, with the return journey departing Greystones at 3.45pm. On Saturdays, the coach departed for Greystones at 3.30pm and returned to Dublin on Sunday evenings, arriving at the Hotel Metropole at 8.30pm. The 23 mile journey, via Delgany and the Glen of the Downs, took two and half hours and involved two changes of horses at Cabinteely and Kilmacanogue. On the outbound journey, lunch was ready upon arrival at the Grand Hotel at 2pm. The full single fare, inside or outside the coach cost 6 shillings or 10 shillings return. The minimum fare for any distance requested was 1 shilling. Note the reference to "box seat" on both the seating plan and the fare information. It is from stage coaches that the derivation of the expression "in the box seat" originates, as the driver or coachman at the front usually sat on a box for an elevated view over the two pairs of horses he was driving. Passengers who wished to sit in the box seat had to pay an extra 2s & 6d.

APPROACH TO GLEN-OF-THE-DOWNS. CO. WICKLOW. 21

THE DUBLIN AND GREYSTONES COACH

TEA can be had at Cabinteely on Return Journey.

Fares Inside or Outside	Miles	DOWN (Daily)	Hour	Fares Inside or Out-ide	Miles	UP (Daily)	Hour
		Dublin (Hotel Metropole) ...	11.30			Greystones (Grand Hotel) ...	3.45
		Donnybrook				Delgany	
1/6	5	Stillorgan				Glen of the Downs ...	
2/-	8	Cabinteely (Change Horses) ...	12.30	4/-	7	Kilmacanogue (Change Horses)...	4.30
		Little Bray (Dargle Bridge) ...				Little Bray (Dargle Bridge) ...	
5/-	16	Kilmacanogue (Change Horses)...	1.15		15	Cabinteely (Change Horses) ...	5.15
		Glen of the Downs				Stillorgan	
		Delgany				Donnybrook	
6/-	23	Greystones (Grand Hotel) ...	2.0	6/-	23	Dublin (Hotel Metropole) ...	6.15
		(Lunch ready on arrival).					

Coach leaves Hotel Metropole on Saturdays, at 3.30
Returning from Greystones on Sunday evening,
at 8.30 p.m.

PLAN OF COACH.

Return Tickets, 10s.; Box Seat, 2/6 extra.

The whole of the Coach for the double Journey, taking twelve passengers, £5. To secure places please book in advance. Seats can only be engaged for distances beyond Cabinteely. Intermediate fares at the rate of 4d. per mile, but not less than 1s. taken

Booking Offices:

DUBLIN—HOTEL METROPOLE.
GREYSTONES—GRAND HOTEL.

Headquarters and Stabling—68 Fitzwilliam Lane, DUBLIN.

Telegraphic Address—"COACH, DUBLIN."

Coach runs to all Local Race Meetings.

WHOLE COACH, £4.

ABOVE: Stage coach outside the Grand Hotel, Greystones around 1900.

BELOW: The Blackrock and Cabinteely Express stage coach about to depart from the Grand Hotel.

ABOVE: "Greystones and Delgany" railway station, as stated by the name on the sign further along the platform.

BUS & traein
Dublin District Timetable

CIE

April 1st—June 13th 1965 (inclusive)

FOURPENCE

84 | COLLEGE ST.—DELGANY, KILCOOLE, NEWCASTLE
Via STILLORGAN, BRAY and GREYSTONES

From DUBLIN—WEEKDAYS

Dublin	Bray	Greystones	Delgany	Kilcoole	Newcastle
4.45	5.25	5.45	5.55	—	—
5.15†	5.55†	6.15†	—	6.30†	—
5.35	6.15	6.36	—	6.50	—
5.45	6.25	6.45	6.55	—	—
—	6.35	6.55	—	7.10	—
6.0†	6.40†	7.0†	7.10†	—	—

ABOVE: Weekday timetable from 1965 for the 84 bus from Dublin (College Street) to Greystones. The bus departing College Street at 4.45pm arrived into Greystones at 5.45pm. Today, the equivalent Dublin Bus 84X departing Dublin (Hawkins Street) also at 4.45pm arrives into Greystones at 5.35pm.

Delgany Parish Magazine.

APRIL 1878.

DUBLIN, WICKLOW, AND WEXFORD RAILWAY.

Trains leave Delgany	9·10 a.m.	10·26 a.m.	3·28 p.m.	9.0 p.m.
„ Arrive at Harcourt-street	10·0 „	11·15 a.m.	4·20 p.m.	9·50 p.m.
„ Leave Harcourt-street	9·0 „	2·0 p.m.	5·10 p.m.	....
„ Arrive at Delgany,	9·52 „	2·52 p.m.	5·57 p.m.	....

ABOVE: The 1878 railway timetable from Delgany (Greystones) station to Harcourt Street which was published in the April 1878 edition of *Delgany Parish Magazine*.

RIGHT: Brass button from the Dublin, Wicklow & Wexford Railway.

LEFT: 1970s Kilcoole bound 84 bus.

SHIPPING.

GREYSTONES.

A SPECIAL SEASIDE EXCURSION
(The last Trip of the Season)
TO
GREYSTONES (COUNTY WICKLOW) AND
BACK
On WEDNESDAY, 25th Sept., 1878
(Weather, &c., permitting),

For the accommodation of tourists and others wishing to sail through the beautiful Sound of Dalkey and view the winding shore-line that stretches from the opening of Killiney Bay. dotted with picturesque villas reaching to the water's edge, until it terminates at the base of the heather-clothed bluff of Bray Head, and reaching Greystones about 1 o'clock.

The steamer will leave the Custom House-quay at 11 a.m., Kingstown 12 Noon, arriving back to Kingstown about 6, Dublin about 7 p.m.

N.B.—Passengers will be afforded an opportunity of landing at the Pier if possible, allowing about three hours at Greystones.

Return Tickets—First class, 3s; second, 2s 6d. Children half price.

Parties should bring their own refreshments.
13090   Office—29 EDEN-QUAY.

LEFT: An advert from *The Freeman's Journal* dated Monday 23rd September 1878 for a trip by steamer from Custom House Quay to Greystones and back. It was noted that "*passengers will be afforded an opportunity of landing at the pier if possible, allowing about three hours at Greystones*".

In June 1886, *The Dublin Daily Express* advertised a more upmarket version of the same excursion, this time with refreshments served on board. Under the banner "*Grand Seaside Excursion by sea to Greystones Co. Wicklow and back*", it was operated by J. Renwick & Co., with the advert also stating that an "*Austrian String Band will accompany this excursion*".

During the following decade, *The Wicklow People* in its edition of Saturday 1st September 1894 included a clip entitled "*Excursion to Greystones*" which read as follows: "*The pleasure steamer, Erin's King, carried a large number of excursionists to Greystones on Wednesday. They were allowed a sufficient time on shore to thoroughly enjoy the splendid scenery with which the neighbourhood abounds*".

RIGHT: Photograph taken from the South Beach of *Engine 672* firing up and preparing to proceed to Greystones station.

BELOW: Harris' cycle depot beside the national school in Delgany. In the photograph are Minnie, Cissie and Dickie Harris. The other two gentlemen are unknown.

ABOVE: Old car driving along a dusty La Touche Road, with its ornate electric lamp standards and neatly swept piles of dirt along the edge of the road.

ABOVE: Old photograph of Mrs Sarah Scott with daughters, Maida and Betty in a side car. The Scott family were pharmacists and had a pharmacy located where Mooneys shop is on Trafalgar Road, moving later to the premises on Church Road where McGleenan's pharmacy is today.

ABOVE: Pat Fields and his wife of Ennis' Lane. The Fields family was one of the oldest Greystones families and part of the original fishing community of the Greystones / Windgates area. Throughout the 22 year period from 1839 to 1861 when John Doyle's schooner, *Belle Vue,* imported coal into Greystones, her crew of four included members of the Fields family. By the late 1850s, the *Belle Vue's* master's name was Fields. Book No.7 features Michael Fields, who carried on the family tradition as a commercial fishermen through into the second half of the 20th century. The family was part of the community whose houses on the North Beach were washed away between 1929 and 1931, following which they were relocated to cottages at The Grove on Ennis' Lane. As there was no family member to carry the name forward, the Fields family name disappeared.

LEFT: Kodak van delivering to Scott's chemist on Church Road, with Deacon's shop (where Cafe Gray is today) in the background.

ABOVE: The Archer family in 1921, in their Daimler car outside the family home, *Ard-Na-Ree* on La Touche Road opposite the railway footbridge. The car was sourced in England, with Ted Archer along with Tom Batey (refer to 234) travelling over from Greystones in 1919 to complete its purchase and importation. The car later caught fire and burned itself out on Sea Road in Kilcoole. The children are Reggie, Lily, Connie, Elsie and baby Eric. The Archer family is one of the oldest in Greystones, with Eric taking over the builders business established by his father, Ted. Today Eric's sons, Derek, Robin and Douglas continue the family building and glazing businesses.

ABOVE: Derek Paine wearing the cap in his TC MG car with friends including Isabel, Olive and Derek Gregory at the top of the boat slip in the mid 1950s. In the background, standing beside the bow of a rowing boat is Bill Spurling, son of Osborne and father of Cyril, Noreen, Neville and David.

ABOVE: St. Patrick's Church built in 1857 via private subscription, enhanced by a £1,500 contribution to its cost from the La Touche family. As no endowment existed to support the appointment of a rector, it was not consecrated until 1864. The land upon which the church was built was provided by William Robert La Touche. In 1875 the north transept was added, followed in 1885 by the south transept and in 1898 the nave was extended and the gallery added (increasing the seating capacity by 150). The contractor for the 1898 works was Reuben E. Mellon, who had connections with Greystones. His name appears on the drawings / plans dated 1873 for the construction of Greystones Coast Guard Station. He also resided for many years at *Glencoe* on the North Beach Road, in addition to having a Dublin residence at Brighton Square, Rathgar.

ABOVE: St. Kilian's Church built in 1866. Its site was bequeathed in 1857 by Thomas Phelan, whose desire was that a church be built upon it "*for people in outlying areas working on the farms*". The church was extended in 1886.

ABOVE: Unusual view of the Holy Rosary Church with its wooden spire, taken from Marine Road with the Holy Faith Convent on the right. The site for the Holy Rosary Church was originally obtained in 1895 from Mr Francis La Touche at an annual rent of £25, upon which an iron pre-fabricated chapel complete with bell, was constructed at a cost of £405. In 1903, the well-known local builder, P.J. Kinlen commenced building the present Holy Rosary Church, which opened for worship in 1904.

RIGHT: Greystones Presbyterian Church on Trafalgar Road was built in 1887. The contractor was the local builder, Thomas Evans, who in 1879 had carried out the roof enhancements to the lifeboat house. The architects for the church were the Belfast based firm, Young & MacKenzie, who are best known for their work designing the former Anderson & McAuley department store in Belfast.

ABOVE: In 1909 the tower and timber spire above the Holy Rosary Church were added, though the latter was subsequently removed.

ABOVE: Hillside Evangelical Church on Hillside Road, originally called the Ebenezer Hall.

RIGHT: Nazerene Community Church at Burnaby Lawns.

SUFFRAGETTES

In 1866 a petition for women's suffrage, presented to the House of Commons in Westminster, met with rejection. Its failure led to suffragette societies being started in Edinburgh, London and Manchester. The following year, the Second Reform Bill petition from women was presented to Parliament, but again failed to register support and this prompted the formation of the National Society for Women's Suffrage. In 1881, the Isle of Man granted votes to women. Three years later, an amendment to the Third Reform Bill to grant women the vote was again rejected. In 1897, the National Union of Women's Suffrage Societies (NUWSS) was founded in London, with more than 20 national societies in support. In 1903, Emmeline Pankhurst, a member of the Manchester suffragette set, frustrated at the lack of progress being made by the NUWSS, formed an alternative movement called the Women's Social and Political Union (WSPU) with her daughters, Christabel and Sylvia. In 1905, a militant campaign began and Christabel Pankhurst was arrested and imprisoned. The following year, a daily newspaper coined the term "suffragette" and an increasing number of marches were held over the subsequent two years. Following one such march, protesters chained themselves to the railings of Downing Street, attracting much media attention. In 1910, the Conciliation Bill, which gave women the vote, succeeded in the House of Commons, but the Prime Minister, Herbert Asquith, failed to carry it through.

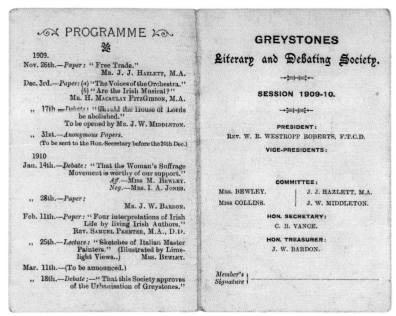

ABOVE: Emmeline Pankhurst

LEFT: The Greystones Literary and Debating Society was founded by Mr C.B. Vance, who served as its Hon. Secretary. It met fortnightly during the winter months in the schoolhouse at La Touche Place (where *La Touche Court* apartments are now located). As can be seen from the programme for the Society's 1909-1910 debating session, the debates and literary papers read covered a wide breadth of subjects, some of which remain very topical today. Of note, was the debate held on 14th January 1910 *"That the Woman's Suffrage Movement is worthy of our support"*.

The Wicklow Newsletter regularly covered the Society's debates and its edition of Saturday 22nd January 1910 included a detailed account of the debate on the suffragette movement held at the schoolhouse. It reported that *"there was a large attendance of members and of the general public, many being unable to obtain seats"*. Arguing for the affirmative was Miss M. Bewley (the Bewley family ran the Seapatrick Private Hotel, now Greystones Nursing Home), who said *"the subject of women's suffrage was one of the greatest subjects at the present day"*. Mrs Ireton A. Jones argued for the negative and *"proposed briefly to grant some arguments against the grant of female suffrage, taking two points of view:- (i) would the State benefit ? and (ii) is a woman naturally and generally fitted for political activity?"*. After some lively debate, interspersed at times by cheering and laughter, *"the Chairman, in summing up the debate, expressed his appreciation of the eloquent speeches of the ladies that they had just heard. He was not in favour of the innovation and one of his objections was that the granting of votes to women would cause an immense increase in the electorate, which he thought was much too high as it was. He might be old-fashioned and out of date, but that was his opinion. He grieved to see illiterate voters or persons without education exercising votes affecting great matters in the State. They always acted in a parochial manner and he was above all an Imperialist. The motion was then put to the meeting by the Chairman, who declared the noes had it"*.

Book No. 4 contains a report from *The Irish Times* dated 26th October 1910 under the headline, *"Chief Secretary and the Suffragettes, Amusing Scene at Greystones"*. Following a storm in which three trading vessels were badly damaged in the harbour, the Chief Secretary for Ireland, Augustine Birrell, visited Greystones together with the Under Secretary and the MP, William Redmond. During the course of inspecting the pier, Birrell was approached by two suffragettes, a Mrs Sheehy-Skeffington and a Miss Webb, who began to protest in favour of their cause. *"You are a disgrace to your sex"*, shouted one of the inspection party, to which one of the women retorted *"You are a disgrace to humanity"*. Eventually, William Redmond intervened and brokered an agreement that the Chief Secretary would *"receive a deputation from the Women's Suffrage Association on the following Friday"*. The police constable on duty was quoted as saying *"How could I tell that them ones would turn up at Greystones?"*. Birrell was a known opponent of women's suffrage and he strongly disapproved of the militancy and violence which its supporters were increasingly resorting to. The following month when walking alone in a street near the House of Commons in Westminster, he was accosted by a group of around 20 suffragettes who recognised him. In the incident, he suffered injuries to his knee, which he told a colleague prevented him from taking strong exercise.

On Whit Weekend in May 1913 another incident relating to the suffragette movement occurred in Greystones. *The Wicklow Newsletter* newspaper dated Saturday 17th May 1913 reported the following. *"The suffragettes have been engaged in terrorising the United Kingdom and demonstrating to Mr Asquith and Mr Redmond that they, single-handed, are not afraid of the coalition. It is a case of The Balkan War, only that the single power is more successful in her attacks upon the allied ones. On Sunday night, Greystones made a feeble effort to retaliate on the betrayers and some of their number, it is supposed, did their best to destroy letters in the pillar boxes, regardless of the consequences. The police were assured a busy and anxious time for the remainder of the Sabbath and also throughout Whit Monday"*. It was recorded that on the Monday, a large number of ladies descended on the town and the local police were alerted to investigate reports that a number of letter boxes had been tampered with as part of a protest.

SUFFRAGETTES

BELOW: Pages taken from the notebook belonging to Constable Alfred Webb, who was stationed at the Royal Irish Constabulary barracks, then based at *Glen Lodge*, Church Road, Greystones. In 1913, he recorded that "*Whit Monday was a very wet day in Greystones and a lot of people came to the seaside for the day but had to stay indoors all the time it rained.*" Specifically, he noted that "*a desperate attack was made to destroy a number of letters at Greystones Sub Post Office on May 11th 1913. It is believed to be the work of suffragettes. A pillar box was tampered with outside the Grand Hotel. It is hoped that the police will be able to locate the culprits. Public information is very strong. Hearing that a lot of ladies are stopping at local hotels, a warrant has been issued to search thoroughly. I remain, yours sincerely, Alfred Luke Webb, May 1913.*"

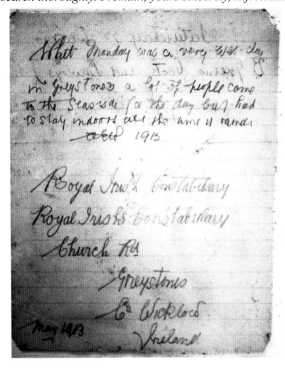

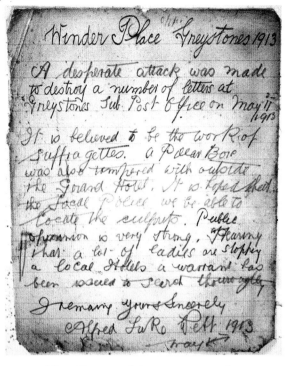

"Be militant each in your own way."
Emmeline Pankhurst, Royal Albert Hall, London, 17th Oct 1912

"I want you to not see these as isolated acts of hysterical women."
Emmeline Pankhurst, Hampstead, 14th February 1913

ABOVE: *Rinneroom* on Church Road, Greystones. The house was previously called *Glen Lodge* and was rented by the Royal Irish Constabulary as their barracks from 1903 until 1922.

ABOVE & BELOW: Similar attacks on pillar boxes took place in Britain.

ABOVE: The pillar box located outside the La Touche Hotel, prior to its removal a several years ago.

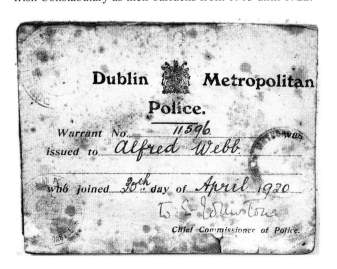

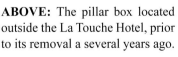

LEFT: The police warrant card issued to Alfred Webb when he joined the Dublin Metropolitan Police in April 1920. Constable Webb together with Constable Dalton arrived on the scene of the Kilcoole gun running incident on 31st July 1914. Both men were briefly held captive by the Irish Volunteers until the arms were landed and moved away, with Constable Webb then taking the train to Bray where he raised the alarm.

A GREYSTONES CONNECTION WITH THE 1916 EASTER RISING

We are grateful to the National Library of Ireland for the kind permission to reproduce the MacDonagh family photographs.

In September 1915, the Dublin literary figure, Thomas MacDonagh, his wife Muriel (nee Gifford) and their two children, Donagh and Barbara holidayed in Greystones, staying at *Annaville* on Church Road. The series of photos on the following pages show the family around the harbour, seafront and on the South Beach and socialising with friends. They bely the events which would impact the family just seven months later and also the following year.

Thomas MacDonagh was born in County Tipperary in 1878. Whilst teaching in Kilkenny in 1901, he joined the Gaelic League and was thus introduced to Irish nationalism. In 1908, he moved to Dublin to assume the role of Assistant Headmaster to Pádraig Pearse, Headmaster at St. Enda's College and moved within literary, theatrical and nationalist circles, where he met James Connolly. In 1911, he founded *The Irish Review* with the poet, Pádraic Colum, author James Stephens and Professor David Houston. This was a monthly literary and current affairs journal that ran from March 1911 until November 1914. The publication featured contributions from many literary figures of the time, including W.B. Yeats and Padraic O'Connaire. It was around that time that Thomas MacDonagh also became friends with Joseph Plunkett, to whom he gave private lessons in Irish.

Muriel MacDonagh was the daughter of a prominent Dublin solicitor, Frederick Gifford. As a child, she had holidayed in Greystones, where she took swimming lessons and became a strong swimmer. It is probable that the MacDonaghs chose to holiday in Greystones because Muriel MacDonagh knew it from her childhood. She met Thomas MacDonagh at St. Enda's College when she visited it in 1908 and they were married in January 1912, by which time he had taken a better paid job at UCD. Their son, Donagh, was born in November 1912 and daughter, Barbara, was born in March 1915, by which time the family had moved from Baggott Street to Oakley Road in Ranelagh.

Thomas MacDonagh joined the Irish Volunteers in 1913 and was sworn into the IRB in 1915. In Easter 1916, he was one of the seven signatories to the Irish Proclamation and commanded the garrison at Jacob's biscuit factory during the Easter Rising, where his garrison was one of the last to surrender. He was found guilty and sentenced to death at his court martial on 2nd May. Although messengers were despatched to his wife, she could not be contacted in time and his last visitor was his sister, Mary MacDonagh, Sister Francesca. One of his final acts was to hand his sister the photographs featured on page 203, taken of his wife and children on the family holiday in Greystones seven months earlier. At 3.30am on 3rd May, in Kilmainham Jail, he was executed by firing squad.

On 9th July 1917, on a trip to Skerries, with a number of the widows of the leaders of the 1916 Easter Rising, including her sister, Grace Plunkett (nee Gifford), Muriel MacDonagh drowned whilst swimming off the South Strand Beach, leaving her two children orphaned.

ABOVE & LEFT: *Annaville* on Church Road Greystones, where the MacDonagh family stayed on holiday in September 1915. In an era when there was more than one postal delivery a day, this envelope, addressed by Thomas MacDonagh to his wife was the equivalent of modern day text message. Written on the reverse of the envelope was a message simply stating that he hoped he "*shall be able to get back at 6.37.*"

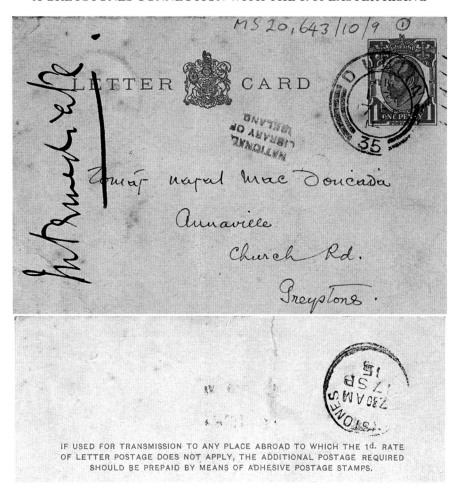

ABOVE & RIGHT: Envelope and letter written by Eamon De Valera to Thomas MacDonagh, updating him on events in headquarters. The letter was posted to him on 17ᵗʰ September 1915 when he was staying at *Annaville* on Church Road. Eamon de Valera also had connections to Greystones. Following his release from prison in July 1917 he lived in a house, known at that time as *Craig Liath,* on Kinlen Road in The Burnaby.

The letter reads:

> *"Midnight Thurs.-Fri.*

I was at H.Q tonight. Walsh had not during week left any note for me, as promised, specifying what materials he needed, so I was quite prepared for a denouement.

It came by his being absent. He told Capt. Breen that he would not be able to attend and I was glad of it. I handed the class over to Breen and things were got going. One man by means of broom handles and some fine rope demonstrated how upright and horizontal poles should be lashed together - the other men trying their hand at it after him. We are beginning to move.

Capt. Breen showed me a note from the Chief of Engineers from which I gathered that he was communicating with you - we are progressing.

Classes will be in full swing working automatically after next week."

The operation orders for Sunday are not yet to hand."

Eamon de Valera

ABOVE LEFT & RIGHT: Donagh MacDonagh on Greystones pier in September 1915, with a schooner in the background discharging its cargo. Note the horse, blinkered and with a thick neck harness. Donagh MacDonagh sitting on the granite bollard, a man (possibly a member of the crew or a coal man, given the dirt on his hands) attempts to get him to look at the camera.

ABOVE: Thomas MacDonagh in a suit and bow tie sitting on the rocks at Greystones beside Mary Maguire Colum holding Barbara, with Donagh partly obscured behind Edith Alderton. Mary Maguire Colum was the wife of the poet Pádraic Colum.

ABOVE: Photograph of Professor David Houston on the rocks at Greystones with Donagh MacDonagh. A fellow co-founder of *The Irish Review*, Professor Houston was a mentor to Thomas MacDonagh.

ABOVE: Thomas MacDonagh holding Donagh on the South Beach, Greystones in September 1915. Part of Swan's Rock is visible on the left protruding from the water.

ABOVE: The above two photos have particular historical significance. The one on the right shows Donagh MacDonagh standing against the wall, with the Cove and Bray Head in the background. The one on the left shows Muriel MacDonagh bathing Barbara in the sea on Greystones South Beach. Written on the reverse of each photo is the following: "*This photo was taken by my brother Tom out of his pocket book and kissed before he gave it to me in Kilmainham Gaol on [the] morning he was shot, May 3rd 1916, Mary [MacDonagh] in religion, Sr. Francesca, Irish S[ister] of Purity.*"

In his last letter home from Kilmainham Gaol, Thomas MacDonagh lamented that his impending death would leave his family in poor circumstances. He wrote that "*the one bitterness that death has for me is the separation it brings from my beloved wife Muriel and my beloved children, Donagh and Barbara. My country will treat them as wards, I hope. I have devoted myself too much to national work and too little to the making of money to leave them a competence. God help them and support them and give them a happy and prosperous life*".

Barbara MacDonagh married the Dublin born actor, Liam Redmond, who began his career at the Abbey Theatre, playing Cúchullain in W.B. Yeats' play, *Death of Cúchullain.* He later appeared in a number of films including *The Cruel Sea* with Jack Hawkins and Virginia McKenna, *Ice Cold in Alex* with John Mills and Anthony Quale and *Tobruk* with Rock Hudson and George Peppard. He also appeared in a number of television series including *The Avengers*, *The Saint* and *Z-Cars*.

ABOVE: Muriel tending to Barbara with Donagh and their dog Flip looking on.

ABOVE: On the rocks at Greystones with Flip.

ABOVE & LEFT: Donagh MacDonagh playing and paddling on Greystones South Beach watched by Muriel. Educated at Belvedere College and UCD, Donagh MacDonagh studied law and was called to the Bar in 1935, serving on the Western Circuit. In 1941 he was appointed as a District Justice in County Mayo and was the youngest person to be appointed as a judge in Ireland. He served as a Justice for the Dublin Metropolitan Courts up until his death at the age of 55 in 1968. In addition to his legal career he followed in his father's literary footsteps, publishing three volumes of poetry as well as writing poetic dramas and ballad operas. He was also a broadcaster on Radio Éireann.

RIGHT: Playing with a St. Bernard dog on the South Beach with wooden bathing boxes adjacent to the railway arch in the background.

RIGHT: Donagh and Flip enjoying a donkey ride on Greystones South Beach.

ABOVE: Donagh standing on a seat on the South Beach path in Greystones.

RIGHT: Thomas MacDonagh, Mary Maguire Colum and Edith Alderton with Barbara and Donagh on the rocks at Greystones.

LEFT: The Greystones 1916 Memorial Garden which was built to mark the centenary of the Easter Rising. Situated at the southeast corner of Burnaby Park, it contains a granite stone with the Proclamation in both Irish and English. A tree was planted in honour of each of the seven signatories to the Proclamation, including Thomas MacDonagh. The tree ironically lies just metres from where he and his family had enjoyed spending time on Greystones South Beach during their holiday in September 1915, just seven months prior to the Easter Rising.

RIGHT: On Sunday 24th April 2016, exactly 100 years after the Easter Rising, a Memorial Garden with seven trees and a granite stone with the Proclamation was unveiled in Kilmacanogue by Tony Lawlor, Secretary of the organising committee, together with Lieutenant Lar O'Carroll of The Irish Army. The photograph shows well-known singer and local resident Mary Coughlan performing a rendition of the song *James Connolly*.

LEFT: Pupils from the Christian Brothers School, Blacklion (located near where the lower entrance to Applewood Heights is today) in around 1943. The photo was taken in the grounds of St. Kilian's Roman Catholic Church in Blacklion.

Seated in the front row, left to right: Nicholas O'Connor, Kevin Kelly, Sean Roche, Billy Hayden, Victor Landers, Eddie O'Gorman and John Connolly (standing).

Second row, left to right includes: Gerry Fallon, Ned Russell, Tommy Dunne, Eric Crinion and Joe Sweeney.

Third row, left to right: Seamus O'Hara, Jimmy Whiston, Jimmy Magee, Rev. Brother S.F. Buckley, Billy Kinsella, Joey Hoey and Dempsey Connolly.

ABOVE: Patricia Moynihan (2nd from the left), Vice Principal of St. Brigid's School on Trafalgar Road, photographed in July 1976 making a presentation to Sister Mary Melania, Principal for the preceding nine years, on her departure to a new teaching post in New Ross, Co. Wexford. She was replaced by Sister Mary Joachim from Finglas.

ABOVE: Blacklion before the road was widened.

ABOVE: Holy Faith Convent on Trafalgar Road which was built by Patrick J. Kinlen at a cost of £6,000 in 1906. The building took exactly 12 months to complete and was formally opened on Monday 10th September 1906.

RIGHT: Temple Carrig School under construction in April 2015, with its backdrop of Coolagad. The school was established in 2012, following a grant from the Department of Education. It took its first intake of 132 pupils in September 2014 in temporary buildings housed on the current school site. In August 2015, the school moved to its new school buildings and welcomed an additional 132 pupils.

BELOW LEFT: Garrett Fennel (Chairman of the Board of Management), An Taoiseach Enda Kenny, Archbishop Michael Jackson and Alan Cox (School Principal) photographed at the official opening of Temple Carrig School on 7th October 2016.

RIGHT: An Taoiseach Enda Kenny addressing a full assembly hall of pupils and teachers.

BELOW: Harvest time at Temple Carrig, with Coolagad in the background. Taken during a break in the work or perhaps before the start or at the end of the day, it shows 22 people having refreshments.

ABOVE: School children in Greystones around 1929. It includes Gilbert Orme (back row, 4th from the left), Maud Orme (front row, 1st on the left), Helene Orme (front row, 3rd from the left) and Eoin Ryan (front row, 6th from the left). Eoin Ryan went on to become a Fianna Fáil TD and Senator. His father, James Ryan was a former Fianna Fáil Minister for Finance and Minister for Agriculture in the governments of Éamon de Valera and Seán Lemass. At the time of the above photo, the Ryans lived in *Kindelstown House* (refer also to page 262).

ABOVE: Delgany School 1954. Included are Brian Cox, Cecil Somers, Robin Evans, Neville Elliott, Stuart Evans, George Evans, Daphne Evans, Charlie Fowler, Dorothy Evans and Leslie Somers.

At the time of writing the town's former principal hotel, the La Touche Hotel, derelict for a decade, is undergoing redevelopment for residential purposes. Despite the growth in Greystones over recent decades, no new large-sized hotels have been built. It is interesting to look back 50 years to a time when Greystones and its surrounding area was served a by number of hotels. The 1967 accommodation list (below) was issued by the Greystones Tourist Promotion Group, which operated under the auspices of the Greystones & District Civic Association. It was aimed at driving tourist numbers to the town. The accommodation list also comprised 16 local participating B&B establishments, with a combined total of 72 bedrooms. These lists were made available to passing tourists and visitors at the centrally-located Copper Kettle restaurant, adjacent to the library.

The list reveals that the total number of guest bedrooms across the five hotels listed was 128. The list did not include either Seapatrick Hotel (now Greystones Nursing Home) or Trenarren Hotel (now *Trenarren Court*) on Church Road. Both hotels were shown on a similar list in 1969, with Seapatrick Hotel having 18 rooms and Trenarren Hotel having 14 rooms. Accordingly, in the late 1960s, Greystones and its surrounds had around 160 hotel bedrooms. In 1969, the charge per head per week to stay at Seapatrick Hotel was 189 shillings in high season and 147 shillings in low season, whilst the respective charges at Trenarren Hotel were 168 shillings and 147 shillings. Of the 16 B&Bs on the 1967 list, only one, *Slievemore House*, on Bayswater Terrace at the harbour still operates as a B&B in 2018. It is run by the Parkinson family, who on the 1967 list ran a B&B at the adjoining property, *Sharavogue*. Other B&Bs on the list included *Burlington House* on Victoria Road and *Ashley House* in Blacklion.

GREYSTONES TOURIST PROMOTION GROUP

Greystones, County Wicklow, Ireland

ACCOMMODATION LIST 1967

Name of Establishment	Grade	Telephone Number	Number of Guest Bedrooms	CHARGES PER PERSON					
				Per Week (Full Board)			Per Day		Bed & B'fast
				*1	2*	1*	2*	1*	2*
Registered with Irish Tourist Board:									
La Touche Hotel	A	874401	52	£22-15-0	£20	(e)75/-	70/-	40/-	37/6
Woodlands Hotel	B	874164	30	(f)392/-	369/6	66/-	60/-	37/6	32/6
Burnaby Hotel	B	874015	15	£16-16-0	£14-14-0	52/6	(e)48/6	30/- - 32/6	27/6 - 30/-
Cliff House Hotel, Windgates	B/C	863157	16	(g)320/-	260/-	55/-	45/-	31/6	28/6
Horse & Hound Hotel, Delgany	B/C	874642	15	14gns.	12gns.	48/-	42/-	27/6	25/6

NOTES : (1) *High Season June to September incl., unless otherwise stated. (2) *Low Season rest of year.
(a) Prices include evening meal. (b) B/B and evening meal rate is 168/- per week. (c) 4 course dinner 13/6; tea 7/6. (d) High Season July /August only. (e) Hotel daily rates apply to minimum stay of 3 days. (f) High Season May/ September incl. (g) High Season June/August incl. (h) Evening meal available 7/6.

You are cordially invited to write to the Secretary, Greystones Tourist Promotion Group, for further information.

In January 1969, the Greystones Tourist Promotion Group travelled to Belfast. Over a ten day period, a special promotion of Greystones as a tourist destination to attract northern visitors was held inside the Anderson & McAuley department store. Brochures and accommodation lists of hotels and B&Bs were handed out. The Greystones Art Group lent a number of oil paintings of local beauty spots to help in the promotion. The group was led by Gordon Clarke, Kathleen Scuffil (Hon. Sec.), Charlie McCormack (Hon. Treasurer) and a committee including, Alan Bell, David Fitzgerald, Liam Byrne, Don McLean and Mrs D. Finnegan.

ABOVE: The advertisements shown above date from, left to right, 1922, 1978 and 1922.

ABOVE: Samuel A. French aged five, with his mother, Margaret and sister, Henrietta in 1904, with the lawn on the seaward side of the Grand Hotel set up for croquet for the guests. The French family lived at *Trippleton Cottage* on Bellevue Road, where Sam and Henrietta's grandfather, Robert French the landscape photographer, was a regular visitor.

Hot and Cold Sea Water Baths

Golf Links in connection with this Hotel

Grand · Hotel · Greystones
Co WICKLOW

21st Aug. 1898.

Dear Sir,

I am instructed by my directors to inform you that they have been offered by a large farmer of the neighbourhood the supply of milk for eight pence

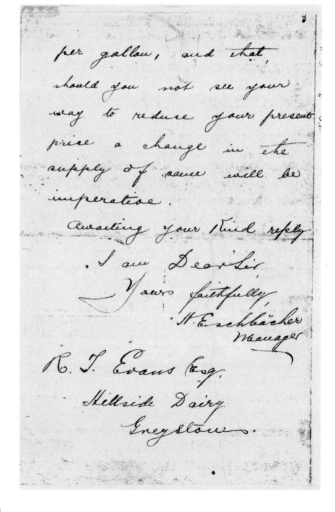

per gallon, and that, should you not see your way to reduce your present price a change in the supply of same will be imperative.

Awaiting your kind reply.

I am Dear Sir,

Yours faithfully,

H. Eschbächer
Manager

R. T. Evans Esq,
Hillside Dairy
Greystones.

210

CROQUET.

GREYSTONES TOURNAMENT.

Greystones, Friday.

Yesterday this tournament was continued on the grounds of the Grand Hotel, and to-day the finals in the handicap matches will be played and the prizes distributed. This is the first croquet tournament held here, and it has proved a great success although organised in a very few days. Almost 100 entries were received, rather more than one half being from ladies, and nearly 70 matches had to be played. In the Gentlemen's Singles Championship of Greystones the winner, Mr R N Roper, Sutton, vanquished all his opponents with ease, and made a break of 8 points in the final. In the Ladies' Singles Championship of Greystones excellent play was exhibited by the winner, Mrs E T Stewart, of Mount Temple Club. The Doubles Championship of Greystones was well won by Capt J and Mrs Preston, Athlone, the brilliant and rapid strokes of Mrs Preston eliciting great applause. She made several breaks, one of these securing for her side no less than 7 points. It is expected that a who took part in the tournament, especially the winners, will attend the distribution of prizes this afternoon, when the grounds will be open to the public.

Report on the opening of the Grand Hotel, Greystones in June 1894

The Freeman's Journal dated 4th June 1894 reported that *"the Grand Hotel, which has just been built at Greystones, has just been opened and on Saturday, a large number of gentlemen, in response to invitations issued by the Directors, attended at a dinner given in the hotel in honour of the occasion. The new hotel is quite near to the sea, so that when the tide is in, the water comes within a few yards of it. The archictect was Mr W.M. Mitchell, while the building etc, was carried out by Mr Kiernan and Mr Baird. The hotel reflects credit on everybody associated with it. There are no fewer than forty rooms in it and these include billiard and smoking rooms, a commodious coffee room and a ladies' dining room. The entire hotel is furnished in the most luxurious style and beyond all doubt this splendid edifice adds a fresh element of beauty to a district which is singularly rich in its possession of those picturesque combinations of hill and dale for which Wicklow is renowned. From the north, Bray Head frowns down upon it, westward the wooded slopes of the Wicklow mountains and on the south and east, the mighty sea. Nobody could pitch upon a lovelier spot for a hotel. Hitherto, Greystones has been rather neglected, now with a hotel like this and the cordial co-operation of the railway company, it may fairly be said to be raised to a position of friendly rivalry with Bray. During the summer months, coaches will be run at frequent intervals between the Grand Hotel and Glendalough."*

ABOVE: Report in *The Freeman's Journal* dated 17th September 1898 on the inaugural Greystones croquet tournament held at the Grand Hotel.

DRAWING ROOM, GRAND HOTEL, GREYSTONES

PHOTO : DR. GERSTENBERG

ABOVE: Old postcard published for sale to guests of the hotel.

ABOVE: Excellent view of the La Touche Hotel in the 1980s, prior to its modern annexe extension.

BELOW: Photo taken on 24th June 2018 showing the demolition of the former La Touche Hotel, with the retention of part of the original shell of the 1894 constructed building.

OPPOSITE PAGE: Letter on Grand Hotel Greystones headed notepaper dated 21st August 1898. In addition to offering guests the attraction of a *"golf links in connection with this hotel"*, the hotel also offered the pleasures of *"hot and cold sea water baths."*

The letter itself, written by the Manager of the hotel, H. Eschbächer, to Robert Thomas Evans of the Hillside Dairy, Greystones complaining about the 1p per pint wholesale price of milk being charged reads as follows: *"I am instructed by my directors to inform you that they have been offered, by a large farmer of the neighbourhood, the supply of milk for eight pence per gallon and that should you not see your way to reduce your present price, a change in the supply of same will be imperative. Awaiting your kind reply, I am, yours faithfully, H. Eschbächer, Manager."*

ABOVE & BELOW: Fine views of the Trafalgar Road side of the Grand Hotel in its heyday, with its name emblazoned within the balustrade of the upper balcony. From its opening in 1894, the hotel straddled the conveyancing of guests by horse and carriage through to the advent of the motor car.

LEFT: A floodlit view of the Grand Hotel in the 1930s.

ABOVE: 1915 postcard view of the Grand Hotel from the field on Trafalgar Road.

ABOVE: A postcard sent in 1965 showing a fine view of the seaward side of the hotel with its lawn tennis court, wrought iron garden furniture and wooden arbours for the guests. The change in the name of the hotel from Grand Hotel to La Touche Hotel occurred in July 1959. This coincided with the improvements carried out that year at the harbour. The hotel, whose manager at that time was David Fitzgerald, spent £3,000 on renovations as part of its revamp. This included a new green and white carpet with a shamrock design by the Dublin born artist, Louis le Brocquy, covering the entrance, reception and lounges. The head waiter at this time was Stephen Pye.

OPPOSITE PAGE BOTTOM RIGHT: Photograph taken in the 1890s of the seaward side of the hotel shortly after its completion. This shows the original ground floor design prior to the extension shown in the colour postcard above.

ABOVE: Envelope addressed to a member of the Whitshed family, Killincarrick, Greystones, posted from Fareham, Hampshire on 2nd November 1862.

ABOVE: Elizabeth Hawkins-Whitshed (1860-1934) inherited *Killincarrick House* (later Woodlands Hotel) upon the death of her father, Captain Hawkins-Whitshed. She married her first husband, Captain Fred Burnaby in 1879 and through this marriage, the large portion of Greystones known as The Burnaby Estate was so named

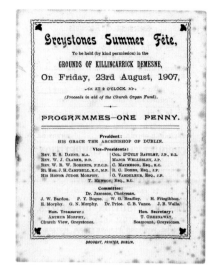

ABOVE: Programme for the 1907 Greystones Summer Fete held in the grounds of Killincarrick Demesne.

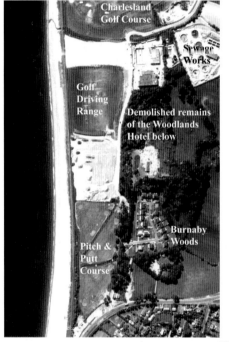

ABOVE: Aerial photograph taken in 1995 showing the demolished remains of Woodlands Hotel.

WOODLANDS HOTEL, GREYSTONES.

ABOVE: 1962 postcard published specially for sale to guests of the hotel. In 1916, the property was the residence of the Rt. Hon. Richard Robert Cherry. He was a former liberal MP for a Liverpool constituency. As Lord Chief Justice of Ireland in 1916, he argued in vain against the execution of the leaders of the Easter Rising.

ABOVE: Woodlands Hotel and its garden in its halcyon days. Prior to this, it was also called the International Hotel in the 1940s and the Clydagh Hotel in the 1930s. It was originally *Killincarrick House*, the home of the Hawkins-Whitshed family.

ABOVE: Photograph taken of the derelict former hotel, shortly after it was gutted by fire on 12th September 1993.

CLYDAGH HOTEL
GREYSTONES
A.A. & R.I.A.C.
ON 25 ACRES FACING SEA.
Three Tennis Courts New Dance Pavilion.
Moderate Terms. Fully Licensed. Garage.
New Smoking Lounge now open in which
a la carte meals are served until 11 p.m.

LEFT: 1933 advert for the hotel when it was called the Clydagh Hotel. During World War Two, the grounds were used by the army. Cabanas nightclub became a popular night spot when it opened in a building adjacent to the hotel in 1983.

ABOVE: A once fine house and hotel reduced to rubble in 1994.

CLIFF HOUSE HOTEL. BRAY HEAD, BRAY, CO. WICKLOW.

ABOVE: Cliff House Hotel in 1960. The hotel was built in 1959 by the Murphy family, who ran it until 1964 when they sold it to the Kopik family. It remained under the proprietorship of the Kopik family until 1983, when it was sold and never operated as a hotel after that. A popular location, it hosted more than 1,000 wedding receptions during the two decades it was owned by the Kopik family.

LEFT: Cliff House Hotel in 1973.

CLIFF HOUSE HOTEL

This Hotel, ideally situated on 250 acres, faces south and overlooks a panoramic sweep of the bay. It is a splendid centre from which to tour Co. Wicklow ("The Garden of Ireland") and is convenient to the seaside resorts of Bray and Greystones, and only 15 miles from Dublin City.
Guests will enjoy a ramble on the scenic "Cliff Walk" and the breathtaking beauty of the surrounding scenery. The sea lying below the Hotel is within a few minutes' walk.

BRAY HEAD, WINDGATES, CO. WICKLOW, IRELAND
Telephone: 863157 / Visitors 867375
FULLY LICENSED - EXCELLENT CUISINE
EVENING ENTERTAINMENT - OPEN ALL YEAR

ABOVE: Cliff House Hotel in 1963. With its proximity to Dublin, quiet setting and sea views, the hotel attracted a number of famous guests down the years. These included Stanley Baker and Tommy Steele in 1966, Doris Day in 1968 and John Alderton, Pauline Collins and Peter Sellars in 1970.

RIGHT: Cliff House Hotel in 1978.

ABOVE: Trenarren Hotel on Church Road, opposite where Centra is today.

ABOVE: *Trenarren Court* on Church Road in July 2017.

RIGHT & BELOW: Hotel information card.

TRENARREN HOTEL
GREYSTONES, CO. WICKLOW

A.A.   R.I.A.C.

TARIFF

October–May ... ... Per week £5 5s. 0d.

June–September ... ... „ „ £6 9s. 0d.

Bed and Breakfast ... 7s. 6d. to 10s. 6d.

SPECIAL TERMS EASTER AND CHRISTMAS.

Children according to age.

The Hotel is under the personal supervision
of the Proprietors,

Messrs. McLellan and Robinson

Telephone : 74 Greystones

The Dublin-Delgany Bus passes door.
Open all the year round.

BATHING, FISHING, GOLF, TENNIS

Mild and sheltered position.

EXCELLENT CUISINE   GARAGE

Greystones Nursing Home, previously known as Castle Clare, has operated as a nursing home since the 1960s. In the 1970s and 1980s it was run by the Peet family. The building was originally the Seapatrick Private Hotel, run by the Bewley family of Dublin coffee company fame. The Greystones census returns for 1901 and 1911 reveal Mrs Emma Bewley, a widow, as the head of the family, with her occupation listed as hotel owner and proprietor with her daughters, Irene, Alice and Olive also listed as residing there. Members of the wider Bewley family were regular summer visitors from Dublin. The Greystones branch of the family played an active role in local society. Mrs Emma Bewley ran sewing classes to help clear the debt associated with the building of Greystones Presbyterian Church on Trafalgar Road. In addition, she was a committee member of the Greystones Literary & Debating Society and delivered a lecture "*Sketches of Italian Master Painters*" as part of the 1909-1910 programme (refer to page 198). They were also involved in the running of the annual Greystones Summer Fete, as seen in the programme below for the 1909 event held at the cricket ground. Afternoon tea at the refreshment pavilion was provided by the Bewleys.

LEFT: It is noted that the 1909 Fete was formally opened by Mrs Aubrey Le Blond. She was the former Miss Elizabeth Hawkins-Whitshed and Mrs Fred Burnaby. At the time she was back in Greystones preparing for the forthcoming auction of the contents of her home, *Killincarrick House* (later the Woodlands Hotel) which took place on 21st September 1909.

SEAPATRICK PRIVATE HOTEL, GREYSTONES, CO. WICKLOW, IRELAND.

ABOVE: Postcard sent on 8th October 1904 featuring a group of ladies playing croquet. The front of the card has a message written to a friend by the hotel proprietor, Mrs Emma Bewley, inviting her to come and see her and her daughter, Irene, when passing through the following week on the morning mail train.

ABOVE: Two old postcards featuring different views of the Seapatrick Hotel from different sides.

ABOVE: Two old postcards featuring different views of the Seapatrick Hotel from different sides.

LEFT: Postcard sent in 1910 showing the hotel's lawn tennis court. The card was published locally by Moore & Co. Stationers of Killincarrig Road (refer also to page 229).

ABOVE: Greystones Nursing Home in 2016.

ABOVE: Hotel information card for Lewis's Hotel (also known as Lewis's Central Hotel) on Trafalgar Road, which included a colourful description of Greystones as the "*Bognor of Ireland*". The hotel was located on the site where St. Brigid's National School is located today. In 1955, the Holy Faith Sisters acquired the former Lewis's Hotel to provide a boarding facility for school girls.

LEFT: View of Lewis's Central Hotel, with its fully licensed status and garage facility promoted by the sign on its end wall. The hotel's petrol pump, with its white spherical sign can be seen beside the pavement at its entrance. Beyond it, protruding from the trees is the Grand Hotel, its flag flying from its roof top.

RIGHT: Henry Joseph Evans of *Prospect House*, ran a restaurant on the site, prior to the establishment of Lewis's Hotel. His father Thomas Evans built Greystones Presbyterian Church and his grandfather Henry Evans built *Emily House*.

BELOW: St. Brigid's National School, built on the site of the former Lewis's Hotel.

ABOVE: View of Lewis's Hotel from Greystones Presbyterian Church on the opposite side of Trafalgar Road.

Coolnagreina was mentioned in the Griffith's Survey dated 1854, listed under its original name, *Brighton House*. Built and owned by John Doyle (1793-1855) it was listed as having lodgers occupying it at the time. On the 1883 Ordnance Survey sheet, the house marked as *Brighton House,* with the house on the left-hand side of its driveway entrance known as *Brighton Lodge*. On the 1876 town plan for the construction of the water supply to Greystones, both *Brighton House* and *Brighton Lodge* were recorded as being occupied by Joseph McGill, son-in-law of John Doyle (1793-1855). In 1890, the house was rented by the Young Women's Christian Association (YWCA) to be operated as a holiday centre *"for those in need of a change or at the seaside"*. This arrangement continued through the turn of the century and by the early 1900s the establishment was managed by Miss M. Going and Miss Matilda Kennedy. Eventually in 1928, the YWCA acquired the property outright and today it still remains part of the YWCA and the complex has been expanded to offer accommodation for around 70 guests.

ABOVE: An early 1900s photograph of *Coolnagreina* on a summer's day bathed in sunshine with all its windows open and featuring a number of young ladies enjoying their outdoor activities, while some sit and have afternoon tea on the verandah.

RIGHT: *Coolnagreina* (originally called *Brighton House* on the 1883 Ordnance Survey sheet).

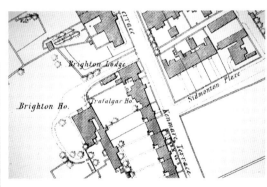

ABOVE & BELOW: Complimentary comment from a guest.

Already marked on the 1876 town plan for the construction of the Greystones water supply, Carrig Eden comprised two separate semi-detached houses. At that time both properties were occupied by Robert H. Pennick, with William R. La Touche noted as the lessor. The Pennick family had a long association with the La Touche family. Book No.7 highlights the role played by Michael Pennick, gardener on the Bellevue Estate in the late 18th century. Following the demise of *Bellevue*, the Pennick family carried on the family business, running a garden nursery business in Delgany through much of the 20th century. The houses which today comprise Carrig Eden were originally known as *East House* and *West House* and later as *Ferney East* and *Ferney West*. In their book, *The Wicklow War Dead*, Tom and Seamus Burnell note that during World War One, George Duggan senior was living in *Ferney East*, with Colonel Ribton Gore living in *Ferney West*. Both families were to suffer the horror of war through the loss of sons. Private Gerard Ribton Gore was killed aged 20 on the Western Front in France on 20th December 1914 and Captain George Grant Duggan and his younger brother Lieutenant Jack Duggan were both killed, aged 29 and 20 respectively, at Gallipoli on 16th August 1915.

Ferney East and Ferney West were subsequently enlarged and combined to become Carrig Eden, which opened in Easter 1936 and was a popular place to stay during the summer months for visitors from the north of Ireland. During the 1970s it was managed by the Cardoo family before being sold to The Irish Assemblies of God in 1991, following which it was used as a Theological College and retreat centre. In 2009, it ceased to be a Theological College and in 2010 it formed a partnership with the Tiglin Challenge outreach organisation. In July 2017 it was announced that the owners of Carrig Eden,The Irish Assemblies of God, had accepted an offer from the Department of Housing and Wicklow County Council for the purchase of Carrig Eden, thereby reducing the uncertainty over the future of the building.

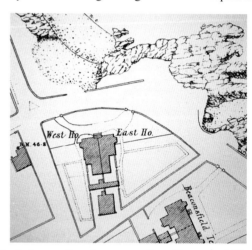

BELOW: Section from the 1883 Ordnance Survey sheet for the town of Greystones showing Carrig Eden as two separate houses.

ABOVE: Photograph taken in the late 1890s with the imposing houses of what were then known as *East House* and *West House* rising above the dock to the left of the flagstaff.

TENNIS COURT "CARRIG EDEN" WITH BRAY HEAD IN BACKGROUND

ABOVE: Old view of Carrig Eden. Its porch entrance contrasts with the original two door entrances when the building comprised two adjoining houses (refer also to page 166).

ABOVE & BELOW: Postcards published specially for sale to guests. The upper card was posted in 1938.

DINING ROOM—CARRIG EDEN

ABOVE: View towards the Cove in the mid 1960s with a croquet match on the lawn of Carrig Eden.

RIGHT: *Brooklands House* on Trafalgar Road, with Mrs Doyle and a maid, Miss Watson, standing in the doorway. At one time, Michael Collins (who stayed at the Grand Hotel just down the road the night before he departed to London to sign the Treaty in 1921) was interested in acquiring the house.

COMFORTABLE
Furnished Apartments.

Good Cooking and Attendance.

Mrs. JESSE ST. AUBYN, Proprietress.

BROOKLANDS, Trafalgar Rd., Greystones.

ABOVE: Advertisement from 1914.

RIGHT: Advertisement from 1922 for the Braemar Private Hotel which was located on the corner of Trafalgar Road and Sidmonton Place. It was completely destroyed in a fire with just the four walls remaining and was subsequently demolished. At the time of its loss, it was owned by a Scotsman, Alexander Knight, who had only acquired it six months before. Prior to this it was owned and run by the Gorman family.

◊ Braemar Private Hotel ◊

Overlooking the Sea; Very Comfortable and Homely; Close to Rail, Golf Links and Churches

CABS, CARS, AND VICTORIAS FOR HIRE.

The Golf Hotel
GREYSTONES.

OPEN ALL THE YEAR ROUND'

Special Terms for Residential Visitors.

⇨ CLOSE TO SEA, RAIL, AND LINKS. ⇨

TENNIS; GARAGE
'Phone—52 Greystones.

ABOVE & BELOW: Advertisement for The Golf Hotel and list of Portland Road residents dated 1922.

Mrs. GORMAN,
PROPRIETRESS.

PORTLAND ROAD

G T Parsons, Dromore	Mrs A Leigh, Knockbawn
F H Gethin, Moorfield	H Wilson, K C, Holmhurst
H N Walker, Glenart	G P Moore, Blairfinde
Colonel McCloghry, Carbery	C P Whelan, Rochfort
Justin MacCarthy, Golf Private Hotel	S F Jones, Portland House

The Golf Hotel
GREYSTONES.

Ideal for a Golfing Holiday.
Near Links, Sea and Rail.
:: Quiet and Comfortable. ::
Excellent Cooking.
Tennis Court. :: Moderate.
Continuous Hot Water.
'PHONE 52.

Delgany.

ABOVE: Old postcard of a horse and carriage outside the Horse & Hound Hotel in Delgany.

LEFT: Old advertisement for The Greystones Golf Hotel, with its attraction of "*continuous hot water.*"

SUMMER OR WINTER
STAY AT
DELGANY HOTEL
DELGANY

Fully Licensed —◦— Bus Terminus

Enjoy GOOD CATERING, COMFORT & SERVICE.
Adjacent to GOLF COURSE & RIDING SCHOOL.

(M. M. SWEENEY, Proprietress)

Telephone: Greystones 42.

HORSE & HOUND HOTEL	Delgany,
(Licensed)	Co. Wicklow
GOLF (18 Holes)	*In the Garden*
TENNIS	*of Ireland*
SEA BATHING	WRITE FOR TERMS
RIDING ACADEMY	
(All Adjacent)	Proprietor: W. NOLAN

THE LIGHTING OF GREYSTONES

Thom's Directory for 1869 in its description of Bray noted that "*gas works have been erected near the shore and the town and beach are now lighted with gas*". However, it was not until the early 1900s that proposals for the provision of both public street lighting and private lighting for households in Greystones were made. In late 1901, Victor Price, a committee member of The Greystones Improvement Association, of *Knockeevin* on Church Road at the entrance to the turnpike, instructed The Sunlight Gas Company Limited to provide the Association with two estimates, one for public lighting only, the other for both public and private lighting.

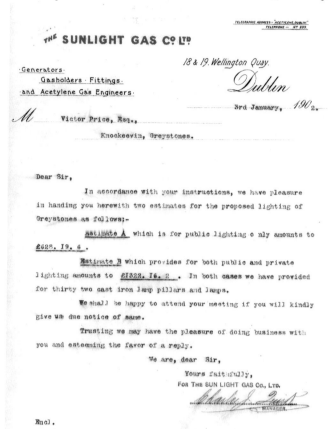

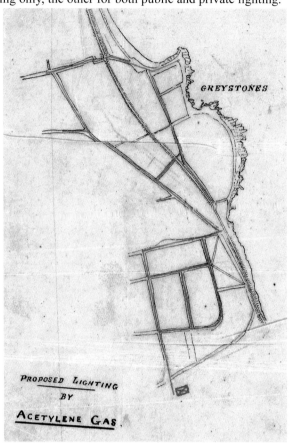

ABOVE: The letter dated 3rd January 1902 from The Sunlight Gas Company Limited and accompanying hand drawn map on tracing paper. The latter indicated the proposed roads coloured red which were earmarked to be lit by street lighting powered by an acetylene gas plant opposite the end of St. Vincent's Road where the red box is drawn on the map. At this time, it was noted that the Grand Hotel already had its own complete installation of acetylene gas for its indoor requirements as well the ornate lamps outside.

As outlined in the letter, "Estimate A" was £628, 19 shillings & 6d for public lighting only, whilst "Estimate B" was £1,322 16 shillings & 2d in respect of both public and private lighting. Both envisaged a total of 32 cast iron lamp pillars with lamps being placed at various points on the roads indicated. The lighting was to be powered by an acetylene gas plant comprising a steel gas holder of 150 cubic feet capacity for public lighting only or 1,000 cubic feet for both public and private lighting.

After much consideration, The Greystones Improvement Association opted in the end to provide public street lighting through the cheaper method of oil lamps which were required to be lit manually each evening. The Association's cash book reveals that the overwhelming number of subscriptions received from residents during the winter months of 1902 and 1903 were noted as "*Lighting Fund.*" There was a clear desire for Greystones not to remain in darkness during the winter evenings. The entry in the cash book for 27th December 1902 notes expenditure of 8 shillings & 9d in respect of "*4 lamp pillars from Dublin.*" It was thus apparent that there was a need to employ a lamp lighter. On 7th January 1903, 1 shilling was spent on placing an advertisement in *The Wicklow People* newspaper "*for a man to light street lamps.*" During the remainder of January 1903, further expenses were incurred in respect of carriage for an additional eight street lamps from Dublin, including the return of a sample street lamp back to the supplier, Wright & Butler. In the first week of February, 12 more street lamps were delivered from Dublin. Sam Evans applied for the job as lamp lighter and was duly appointed to the role at a wage of 8 shillings per week. He commenced work on 1st February 1903. The cash book notes that on 6th March Henry Evans was paid £5 for painting lamp pillars in addition to also making a special ladder for the lamp lighter. During March, a further four lamp pillars arrived from Dublin. On 16th April, Sam Evans received a further six weeks pay of 8 shillings a week for his work as lamp lighter. On the same day, Edwards & Co., which traded as The Greystones Supply Stores (from the premises where O'Brien's Wines is today), were paid £1, 3 shillings & 11d for 41 gallons of oil used between 31st January 1903 and 31st March 1903, as well as wicks, chimneys, oil cans and matches required for lighting and maintaining the lamps. During May, a further four lamp pillars were delivered from Dublin.

By the autumn of 1903, Sam Evans was unhappy with the wages he was paid as lamp lighter and was growing tired of going out each night in all weathers with his ladder, oil can, replacement wicks and matches in hand. He was replaced as lamp lighter by J. Carroll, who took on the job at an increased weekly salary of 10 shillings. Lamps were lit each night from 23rd September throughout the autumn and winter. In January 1904, six more lamp pillars arrived from Wright & Butler in Dublin. By April, the weekly wage paid to J. Carroll as lamp lighter had risen to 12 shillings a week, reflecting the increased number of lamps required to be lit on a nightly basis. During May 1904, six more lamps were supplied by Wright and Butler. Lighting of the lamps each evening recommenced during the last week of September 1904, with J. Carroll continuing in the role of lamp lighter. A number of friends of

Sam Evans, who had become tired of hearing his constant complaints about his job as lamp lighter, penned a poem entitled "*The Greystones Lamps*."

"On Greystones when the sun was low,
Brave Sam Evans prepared to go,
With ladder, can and donkey cart,
To make the darkness all depart.

He started out quite brave and strong,
and thought it would not take him long,
to trim and fill and light each lamp,
although the night was wild and damp.

But 'ere his task was well begun,
He saw it would not be quite fun,
The work that seemed so light before,
now was to him an awful bore.

The Greystones folks stayed up that night,
To gaze upon the wondrous sight,
And as they gazed their minds did fill,
With thoughts of who would pay the bill?

The committee they did flit about,
to see their plans were carried out,
Their many breasts with pride did dwell
To hear their praises sung so well,

The little stars their light did shed,
When the Greystones lamps were put to bed,
And Sam went home with his empty can,
A sadder and a wiser man."

On 8th November 1904, Edwards & Co. was paid £7, 13 shillings & 1d for oil, wicks, chimneys and matches for the period running from 16th April 1903 through 14th May 1904 and a further £7, 3 shillings & 7d was paid to them on 2nd February 1905 for similar items from 15th September 1904 through 31st January 1905. In March 1909, Greystones still had a lamp lighter, Michael O'Leary.

Book No.7 describes a proposal made in 1907 to bring town gas to Greystones. Formal notice was given on 14th November 1907 of the intended application to the 1908 session of Parliament at Westminster, which would have seen the construction of gasometers on a site between Victoria Road and the railway line. This aroused a great deal of discussion among the residents of Greystones and a meeting of rate payers was held in the Grand Hotel on Saturday 1st February 1908. The proceedings were extensively covered in *The Wicklow People* newspaper dated 8th February 1908. Prior to the February meeting, a public meeting had been held in October 1907, with one of the key agenda items being *"the advisability of introducing a system of public and private lighting for Greystones."* A local committee of rate payers was formed and, at the February 1908 meeting, it was noted that nine various schemes to provide lighting had been submitted by firms and individuals in reply to an advertisement placed in the newspaper by the Rural District Council. The nine schemes were narrowed down to three for discussion by the committee at the meeting:

Scheme No.1, submitted by Messrs. Wm. Coates & Son Limited of Dublin, provided for public and private lighting by electricity. It proposed the construction of a gas suction electricity generating plant with engines and dynamos, which would not result in noise, smell or vibration. The current would be distributed via underground cables. It was envisaged that it would include 70 lamp standards for public lighting, with two lamps on each standard, with light being supplied all year round between the hours of dusk and 1am. The proposed plant would have capacity to provide sufficient electricity to power 4,000 lamps across houses, shops, etc. in Greystones. The overall cost of the scheme was estimated at £3,000, with Messrs. Wm. Coates & Son agreeing to subscribe £1,000 towards the capital of a company to be formed to supply electricity to Greystones, in return for an agreement with the local authority to supply electricity for at least 15 years.

Scheme No.2 provided for public and private lighting by coal gas and was submitted by Anderson Bros. of Westminster and was *"subject to the Greystones Gas Act, 1908, receiving the consent of Parliament."* In respect of public lighting, the scheme provided for maintaining 68 standard lamps for 168 nights per annum, from sunset until 12.30am. In addition, the scheme proposed supplying gas to private households through a limited company to be set up for this purpose.

Scheme No.3 was for public lighting only. It recommended improving the present system of lighting by oil lamps, using the 22 paraffin oil lamps currently in operation for a period of seven months during the year. It was to be funded via a levy of one penny in the £ and it was envisaged that an increase in the rate to three pennies in the £ would be sufficient to install and maintain an additional 20 oil lamps during the first year, 16 in the second year and eight in the third year. This proposal would increase the total number of lamps to 66 by the end of the third year, incurring an estimated annual total running cost of £77.

THE LIGHT FOR GREYSTONES

RATEPAYERS UNANIMOUS FOR ELECTRICITY.

STRENUOUS OBJECTION TO GAS.

PARLIAMENTARY BILL TO BE OPPOSED.

On Saturday evening a meeting of ratepayers was held in the Grand Hotel, Greystones, for the purpose of considering the report of the ratepayers' committee regarding the proposed public and private lighting of Greystones.

LEFT: Some residents were concerned that the lower ceilings of their houses in Greystones versus their larger Dublin houses would adversely affect the atmosphere of their sitting rooms if gas were used.

THE LIGHTING OF GREYSTONES

The committee was of the opinion that of the three schemes, Scheme No.1 was the most suitable, provided that the balance of the capital necessary for the formation of a company to supply electricity to Greystones could be raised. In the event that it was not possible to raise the necessary capital and the committee recommended implementing Scheme No.3 to improve and expand the existing system of lighting by paraffin oil lamps.

Committee member, Ivon Price, voiced the widespread objections amongst Greystones residents to the introduction of gas to Greystones. He stated that "*in this matter he represented the views of about 30 owners and occupiers of between 90 and 100 of the best houses in Greystones*". Furthermore, he stated that "*these people had absolutely declined to take gas into their houses or residences. Many of these owners were gentlemen who had been accustomed to the use of gas in their residences in Dublin and many of them state they would not take gas into their houses in Greystones, even if they got it for nothing. They didn't want the gas because they considered it unsuitable to the classes of houses in Greystones. The rooms in these houses were very low in comparison to Dublin houses. Gas would render their sitting rooms unendurable and it would be unhealthy. One gas burner consumed as much as five persons in a room, whereas electric light consumed none whatever. Gas would discolour their ceilings and paintwork and spoil furniture*". The meeting also noted that a further objection to the implementation of Scheme No.2 was "*the unsightly gas works proposed to be erected in Greystones*". There was thus already strong opposition to the introduction of town gas to Greystones. That around £600 had already been contributed towards the formation of a limited company to supply electricity was also a significant factor. The resolution that was put to the meeting for Scheme No.1 to provide Greystones with public and private lighting by electricity was unanimously approved.

BELOW: Letter dated August 1909 sent to households in Greystones confirming that the Greystones Electric Light & Power Co. Limited had "*great hopes of being in a position to supply electricity before the end of this year*".

BELOW: This circular was sent to all households seeking their support for the provision of electric lighting for Greystones. The final paragraph made clear the result if the requisite support from households was not forthcoming.

ABOVE RIGHT: Callender Cables Limited truck outside W.H.Dann at the harbour, with the handles of the winding reels for the cable protruding above it. The company was engaged in the provision of electric cables around Greystones.

LEFT: Callender Cables Limited truck in Greystones.

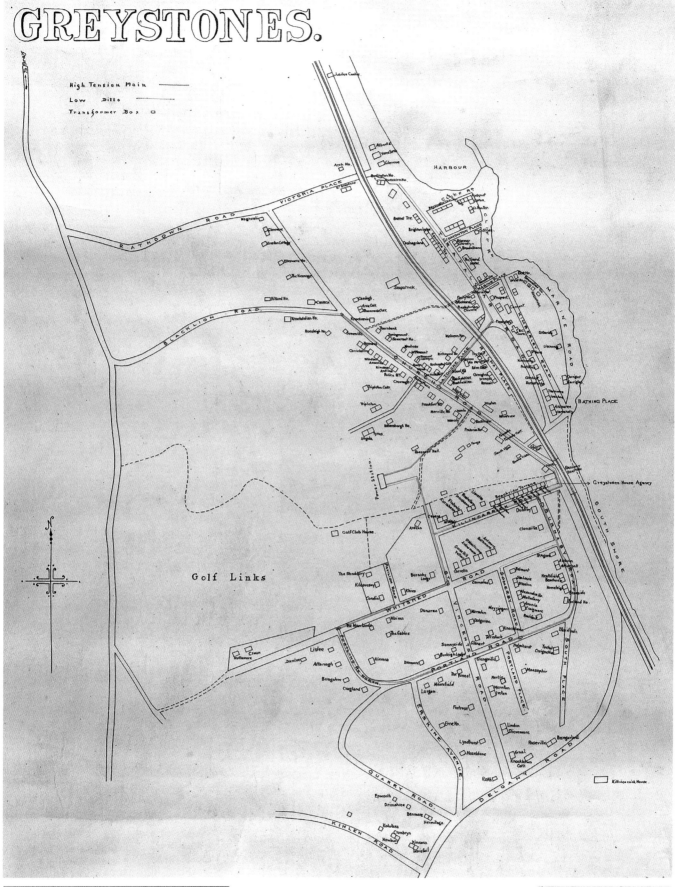

GREYSTONES.

High Tension Main ——————
Low   Ditto   ——————
Transformer Box   ▢

Golf Links

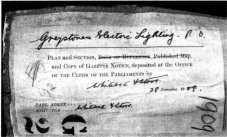

ABOVE, LEFT & RIGHT: Plan of Greystones dated 1908 submitted by Whitelock & Storr, solicitors, Chancery Lane, London as part of the application by the Greystones Electric Light & Power Company Limited to seek parliamentary approval at Westminster to bring electricity to Greystones. The power station is marked on Hillside Road, close to where the pedestrian entrance into Heathervue is today.

THE LIGHTING OF GREYSTONES

The Greystones Electric Light & Power Company Limited was incorporated in 1909, with an issued share capital of £1,201, 5s & 0d, raised from a number of Greystones residents keen to see the town progress. The company's seven directors were: Charles L. Matheson, K.C., of 20 Fitzwilliam Square, Dublin and *Nirvana*, Greystones, H. Macaulay Fitzgibbon, Barrister-at-Law, of *The Bungalow*, Greystones, Arthur Lennox Figgis, of *Gorse Hill*, Greystones, Frederick Batchelor, of *The Gables*, Greystones, Arthur Archer, J.P., of *Bellevue*, Delgany, Eustace Stanley Dashwood, electrical engineer, of Carrickfergus and Robert N. Tweedy, electrical engineer of 5 Leinster Street, Dublin. Due to onerous terms imposed by the County Council, in May 1909 the company announced that it was "*obliged for the present to abandon the public lighting of these roads and streets.*"

The Irish Times of 23rd November 1909 reported that "*the electric lighting of Greystones will, it is expected, be an accomplished fact by Christmas Day. It is proposed to have general illumination of the town that day. The works are now far advanced and the new system will be in complete working order by 1st January 1910. Within a fortnight, the electric power house, which is being erected by Mr P.J. Kinlen, contractor, will be handed over to Messrs. William Coates and Sons, who have the contract for the installation of the electric system. The power house consists of a main building, 43 feet by 22 feet and an annex, in which will be located the generating plant. This comprises two suction gas engines of 90 horse power each. One of these engines is capable of generating electric power sufficient to meet the needs of the entire system. The second engine, will, serve as an alternative, should occasion arise. A home industry will be benefited by the use of suction gas, as Kilkenny anthracite coal is the material employed in working these machines. Within three weeks, cables will be laid over the La Touche Estate, which includes the older portion of Greystones, while on The Burnaby Estate, the cable system is already complete. The public lighting part of the scheme will be immediately begun under the permit of the Wicklow County Council. The system has the advantage of being wholly an underground installation system. It will, therefore, in no way detract from the appearance of the pretty town by day and at night, will be a very welcome improvement. The Greystones Electric Light & Power Company Limited are the promoters and owners of the installation, the Resident Engineer being Mr R.F. Fry, of Lynnwood, Greystones.*"

ABOVE & LEFT: In 1909 P.J. Kinlen built Greystones Power Station, the small building in the foreground (with the white gable end). The year before, he built the Holy Rosary Church, which can be seen with its wooden spire above the tower. The Ebenezer Hall (Hillside Evangelical Church) on what is now Hillside Road can be seen beyond the power station.

On 19th February 1910, *The Wicklow Newsletter & County Advertiser* reported that "*a deputation of the Rathdown No.2 Rural District Council, consisting of Mr John Murphy, J.P., Chairman, Dr Archer, Mr Thomas Hewson, Mr J. Healy, with Mr R. Butler, engineer and Mr B. Cunniam, secretary, in attendance, waited on the Greystones Electric Light Company, who were represented by Mr Charles Matheson, K.C., Mr J.K. Figgis, Mr McCormack Fitzgibbon and Mr Fry, secretary, with reference to the public lighting of Greystones. The deputation, in the first instance, mentioned that the rate payers of the district would not sanction a higher rate than 3d in the £1 for public lighting. The financing of new lamp posts and fittings and the transforming of existing fixtures into electrical standards etc. was then discussed. A rough calculation showed that this would cost several hundred pounds which would amount to a rate of nearly 1s in the £1. It was suggested that the capital cost of the standards and fittings could be raised on a loan for a period of ten years and thus the cost would not amount to more than ½d in the £1. The meeting appointed Mr Butler and Mr Fry, Secretary to The Electric Light Company, to investigate the number and position of the intended lamps and to estimate the cost of their installation, etc. Further consideration was postponed to the next meeting of the council, when it was hoped that a satisfactory arrangement, securing the public lighting of Greystones at a cost not to exceed 3d in the £1*".

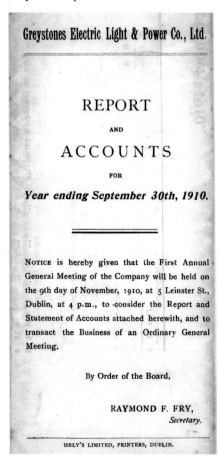

RIGHT: The first AGM of the Greystones Electric Light & Power Company Limited took place at 5 Leinster Street, Dublin. The company's financial statements for its initial six month period ended 30th September 1910 were presented.

The company's financial statements for its initial six month trading period ended 30th September 1910, showed total sales of £88, 11s & 9d, with the company's largest expenses comprising coals and water (£52, 19s& 0d) and wages at its power house (£45, 12s & 11d). It incurred a loss of £66, 4s & 6d. The directors' report noted that the first few houses in Greystones received electric power during April 1910 and that by August and September 1910 *"there were 45 private houses and shops lighted by the company and also two churches."* The report further noted, that by November 1910, there were *"55 buildings wired to receive electric light, a number which the directors have ascertained is almost a record number in the history of small electric light companies."* By the year ended 30th September 1919, the company's annual revenues exceeded £1,000 and by the year ended 30th September, 1924, revenues exceeded £2,400.

Book No. 2 includes details of an interview between Derek Paine and Mabel Evans who worked as a bookkeeper and typist at The Greystones Electric Power Company Limited for ten years. She described that during her time the number of customers had grown to around 500. Apart from Raymond Fry and herself, the other staff employed there at that time were Thomas Barry, Ben Hayden, Edward Barry, Kevin Gunning and Mr Goodehill, who was an engineer. She recalled an occasion when Edward Barry was electrocuted while painting the light poles. He thought he had checked the power was off, but as soon as the metal bucket touched the wires he was electrocuted and fell to the ground. He was rushed to hospital and was attended to by the house doctor who happened to be Dr. Kenneth Evans, also from Greystones, the grandson of Arthur Evans senior of *Wavecrest* at the harbour, who helped him recover. Mabel Evans recalled another occasion when she found Tom Barry unconscious on the floor of the engine room, overcome by fumes. With the help of an apprentice, she managed to get him into the fresh air, where he soon recovered.

Report of the Directors to the Shareholders.

In presenting their First Annual Report to the Shareholders, the Directors feel that a short statement should be made by them as to the position and prospects of the Company.

Notwithstanding the many unforeseen difficulties that arose in establishing the Company as a working Company, the Directors at length succeeded, in the month of April last, in supplying as a tentative matter a few houses with Electric Light, and the light supplied was so good, and the boon of having it was so highly appreciated, that in the months of August and September there were 45 private houses and shops lighted by the Company, and also two Churches. At the present time, although the Company has been barely six months working, there are 55 buildings wired to receive the Electric Light, a number which the Directors have ascertained is almost a record number in the history of small Electric Light Companies.

Of course, for several months the Company were obliged to work at a loss, while the number of houses receiving the light was small; and the Profit and Loss Account which is attached to this Report consequently shows a loss on the working of the Company for the six months ending September 30th, 1910. The period of working at a loss which every new Company has to pass through is, the Directors believe, now over. For some months the Company has been able to meet all its expenses out of its income, and though several houses which used the Electric Light will be closed for a great part of the winter, the Directors calculate that the necessarily longer hours of consumption of light during the winter months will entirely make up for the loss of summer consumers.

ABOVE: A note written by Raymond Fry, Resident Engineer and Secretary of the Greystones Electric Light & Power Company Limited to Mr Scott of Scott's Pharmacy, requesting the supply of H2SO4, otherwise known as sulphuric acid.

ABOVE: Greystones Electric Light & Power Co. Limited bill.

RIGHT: Jack Sweeney, switching on the first public Christmas tree lights in Greystones, at the harbour in front of The Beach House in December 1978. A group of local business people, including Jack's son, Joe, Bernard Darcy, Johnny Burke, P. Hickey and The Beach House clubbed together to fund the display of the tree, which was sourced from Kilmurray forest, near Newtown. Also in the photograph are Jimmy Reilly, bar manager of The Beach House and Johnny Burke.

SPORTING INTELLIGENCE

BRAY RACES—YESTERDAY.

Yesterday the above races, under the management of the members of the Bray Harrier Hunt Club, took place at Greystones, and passed off with a fair amount of success. The day was fine, but rather chilly, and the attendance good. The course, which is situated near the Greystones Station, is the same as used upon the last occasion, but many improvements have been effected under the supervision of Mr. Waters. The course takes a lot of "doing," and contains seven fences in the round. The stands were well filled, and the stewards exerted themselves to the utmost to show sport. Six events made up the card, but the fields were small, and the racing altogether of a very moderate description. Punctuality, we are sorry to say, was not observed. Three did battle for the opening event, which fell to Sweetheart. Of the eleven coloured for the Hunters' Plate only four came to the scratch, and the well-bred R. D. won easily. The Handicap brought five out, and Sultana was made favourite, but, after New Purchase having been heavily backed, and landing far into the run home, the smart Salamis, most artistically handled by D. Canavan, upset the calculations of the *cognoscenti* of the Eyrefield Lodge stable and secured a pretty easy win from Sultana, who fought out the finish instead of New Purchase. Sobersides went well for two miles, but the pace was only middling. The remaining events call for few remarks. Tomboy and Pretty Girl falling, Ruby had no trouble in cantering in for the light weights of the Members Plate. The Stand Plate, as we anticipated, was a race between The Colonel and Mrs. Gladstone, the former winning by a head. An objection was lodged against the winner for not carrying proper weight, which remains in abeyance. The moderate day's sport wound up with the welter portion of the Members' Plate, and Tomboy, this time not falling, won easily.

Race	Distance	Result / Prize (where disclosed) / Comments
Selling Plate	2 miles	1st *Sweetheart* (30 sovereigns), 2nd *Tomboy* (£3). Winner sold £68.
Hunters' Plate	3 miles	1st *RD*, 2nd *Honest Ralph*, 3rd *Gertrude*. Total prize 30 sovereigns.
Bray Handicap	2½ miles	1st *Salamis* (98 sovereigns), 2nd *Sultana*,(10 sovereigns), 3rd *New Purchase*.
Members' Plate	3 miles	1st *Ruby*, 2nd *Pretty Girl*. Total prize 30 sovereigns. Race for light weights.
Grand Plate	2 miles	1st *The Colonel* (19 sovereigns), 2nd *Mrs Gladstone* (6 sovereigns).
Members' Plate	3 miles	1st *Tomboy* (£15), 2nd *Percy* (5 sovereigns). Race for welter weights.

LEFT: Report from *The Freeman's Journal* dated 13th September 1876 of horse races held at Greystones under the management of the Bray Harrier Hunt Club. The race course used was "*situated near the Greystones railway station.*" Given that the detailed report of the races noted that part of the race course included a descent, its location was likely to have been where The Burnaby Estate and lower slopes of Jones' Hill on Greystones Golf Club is today. During the 1870s horse races held at Greystones were popular events, with special trains run from Harcourt Street station. For the 1876 race meeting, two special trains were laid on. The first train, comprising 1st, 2nd and 3rd class carriages, departed Dublin at 10.45am for Greystones and stopped en route at Bray station only. The second train had 1st class carriages only, departed at 12 noon and ran direct to Greystones.

ABOVE: Results of the horse races held at Greystones on 12th September 1876.

RIGHT: Photographs taken in December 1944 showing Bray Harriers Hunt Club meeting up at the Grand Hotel before heading up Trafalgar Road.

ABOVE: Three generations of the Evans family of Hillside Road, Greystones (Edward senior, his son, Norman and Edward junior). The photograph was taken in the early 1980s on the set for the filming of the TV series, *The Irish RM*.

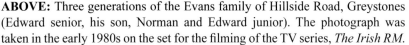

ABOVE: Vincent Carroll, Brendan Sweeney, E. Brosnan, Willie Evans and Norman Evans in front of the Anchor Cafe in September 1958.

LEFT: Pony rides on the beach. The paddock field, located where *Harbour View* apartments are today, was a popular attraction at the harbour up until the end of the 1970s.

In April 1963, outline planning permission was sought by Mrs H.A.G. Burnaby of *Killincarrig Manor* to build a shopping centre in Burnaby Park. She was the widow of Harry Arthur Gustavus Burnaby, son of Colonel Fred Burnaby and Elizabeth Hawkins-Whitshed. As a quid pro quo, Mrs Burnaby offered a four acre field (which would serve as a new park space), across from where the Woodlands Hotel was located, adjoining the Delgany Road. *The Sunday Independent* reported that Mrs Burnaby's proposal for the development of Burnaby Park was for "*something colourful and bright, like one would see in California, a white facade to the shops and a portico to protect shoppers from the weather.*" Not surprisingly, the proposed development sparked much local debate, with Greystones & District Civic Association co-ordinating the opposition to the plan. They pointed out that when The Burnaby Estate was developed as a planned residential area, the open space was specifically left to be a park amenity. Furthermore, it was on a such a basis that the houses had originally been sold and those immediately adjoining Burnaby Park had covenants covering the existence of this open space.

MOORE & CO.,
House Agents, Stationery, Newsagency, and Fancy Warehouse,
2 KILLINCARRIG ROAD,
BURNABY ESTATE,
GREYSTONES.
Telephone—Greystones 42.

LEFT: Nos.1, 2 & 3 Beachview Terrace on Killincarrig Road were built in the late 1890s by P.J. Kinlen. This photograph was taken around 1900 and shows the awnings over the front of J.J. Moore & Co. Stationers & House Agents at No.2.

ABOVE: No.2 was acquired by the Ireton family in 1959, with the shop run for many years by Leo Ireton. Prior to this, the shop was M.J. Murphy's tobacconists and stationers. The adjoining shop was originally Howard's Bakery & Cafe and has been Nature's Gold health food shop for the last 40 years.

ABOVE: Mr and Mrs Murphy with their son, Jimmy standing outside their shop. The photograph was taken in August 1938. The newspaper headline posters described events of the day, including "*Forty dead in air accidents*", "*Plane crash at Greystones*", "*England's team for final test*" and "*Queen Mary smashes all records.*" The latter referred to the *Queen Mary* recapturing the *Blue Riband,* for the fastest crossing of the Atlantic by a passenger liner. The plane crash concerned a *Moth* airplane which crash-landed approaching the landing field at the International Hotel (Woodlands Hotel). The pilot, J. Weldon survived.

HOWARD'S
Burnaby
. . Restaurant
(Opposite Railway Station).

LUNCHEONS.
DINNERS.
TEAS.

We Solicit the patronage of Visitors and Residents.

LEFT: 1907 advertisemnet.

BELOW RIGHT: Longtime Greystones resident, Ronnie Drew of *The Dubliners,* holding his daughter Cliodhna, at the RDS in 1968. Also in the photo is his friend and near neighbour, Norman Evans of Hillside Road. The Drew family lived at *Benevenagh* on Killincarrig Road for many years.

BELOW: View looking towards the line of houses and shops on Killincarrig Road in the late 1890s. In the foreground is *Burnaby Gate Lodge*. Note the two large haystacks in Burnaby Park. Prior to the arrival of the motor car, it was common to see stacks of hay around Greystones for horse feed, particularly in the field that was at the rear of what is now The Beach House.

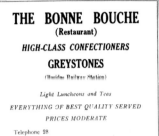

THE BONNE BOUCHE
(Restaurant)
HIGH-CLASS CONFECTIONERS
GREYSTONES
(Beside Railway Station)

Light Luncheons and Teas
EVERYTHING OF BEST QUALITY SERVED
PRICES MODERATE

Telephone 28

ABOVE LEFT: Nancy O'Neill who ran The Bonne Bouche Cafe. She also served for many years on the Greystones and District Civic Association.

ABOVE: 1960s postcard promoting The Bonne Bouche when the building was still single storey. The Bonne Bouche Tea & Luncheons was first listed at the site in the 1928 *Thom's Directory*. Since then, the premises has housed a number of restaurants including The Copper Kettle, Schooners, Vino Pasta and today, Buoy's Kitchen.

LEFT: Old advertisement for The Bonne Bouche, complete with 2 digit Greystones telephone number.

RIGHT The building known as The Copper Kettle restaurant in December 1975, as a large crowd of school children greet the arrival of a helicopter in Burnaby Park for the opening of Liptons Supermarket on the main street. The latter subsequently became The Shopping Basket and was located where Boots pharmacy is today.

THE COPPER KETTLE
CHURCH STREET - GREYSTONES
FOR MORNING COFFEE - LUNCHES - TEAS
We Specialize in Home-made Teas - Parties Catered for
Phone: Greystones 874028
TRY OUR HOME-MADE CAKES.

ABOVE: An advertisement from 1970.

In 1973, The Copper Kettle, which had been owned for a number of years by Evelyn Cox and Dorothy Finnegan was sold to Jim and Angela Molloy, who also owned Molloy's bakery and cafe in Bray. In November that year, the restaurant was revamped under the new management, with various different nationalities of themed evenings introduced, enabling the clientele to enjoy an evening of wine, dine and dance.

ABOVE LEFT & RIGHT: In its guise as Schooners Restaurant under the ownership of Peter and Jackie Dowling (in the photo on the left). As Vino Pasta photographed in April 2010 (now Buoys Kitchen), with Greystones Florist next door in the retail unit once occupied by Punch & Judy, a children's clothing shop.

RIGHT: View from Burnaby Park in 1958 of Watson & Johnson's garage with its lock-up garages at the southern end. The gable roof of the library is visible on the extreme left.

ABOVE: Photograph taken in the 1880s looking up a tree lined Church Road from the railway station.

ABOVE: "CAR FOR HIRE" sign on the shop in the background, behind Jack Doyle of Lower Windgates standing beside his charabanc in the foreground.

ABOVE: Gramophone Supplies shop in the 1920s.

ABOVE: Kevin Scuffil and his wife, Kathleen, who ran their electrical appliances shop beside the railway station for many years.

RIGHT: Scuffil's electrical shop in the 1960s.

BELOW: The shop now as Greystones Antiques.

BELOW: The shop as Pet's Corner photographed in 2013 following the retirement of its owner, Jim Moulton.

ABOVE: 1914 photograph of Burnaby Pharmacy and Burnaby Stores which were built by P.J. Kinlen for Andrew McFarland in the late 1890s.

ABOVE & LEFT: Burnaby Pharmacy receipt and stamp from 1914.

ABOVE: Advertisement from 1922 for The Railway Hotel, owned at that time by the Byrne family. Subsequently it was acquired by the Larkin family and today, known as The Burnaby, it is again owned by another Byrne family.

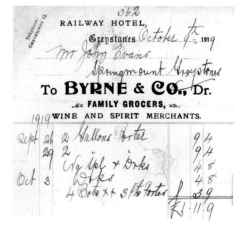

ABOVE: 1890s photograph of three men standing in front of where McFarland's shop was later built. *Buona Vista* (behind where Madison & Co. is today) can be seen just beyond The Railway Hotel, and beyond it is the double gable end of *South View* (where the Hungry Monk is today), the Buckley family's first house on Church Road.

ABOVE: Andrew McFarland opened Burnaby Stores opposite the railway station in May 1898.

A. McFARLAND,
Burnaby Stores,
GREYSTONES.

Finest Irish Butter
and Eggs,
FRESH SUPPLIES DAILY.
Irish hams and Bacon.
TEA a Speciality,
Prices—1/4, 1/8, 1/10 & 2/4.
Are Unsurpassed for Quality
and Value.

ABOVE & BELOW: 1907 Advertisement for Burnaby Stores and a receipt for eight bags of potatoes in 1919.

ABOVE LEFT: AIB Bank photographed in August 2017, with the entrance at the front, similar to where it was when McFarland's shop traded from the premises. The shop on the left, where Sherry Fitzgerald is located today, was originally Burnaby Pharmacy and for many years was Eugene's Newsagents.

LEFT: AIB photographed in 1990 with its entrance at the end of the building.

ABOVE: View up Church Road with four petrol pumps outside Batey's garage which was situated near where the Credit Union is now. Willie Johnson worked at Batey's garage prior to opening his own garage, Watson & Johnson opposite Burnaby Park.

ABOVE: The garage lock-up of the Greystones Motor Company at the rear of the Batey's garage where Meridian Point is today. Jim Hempenstall and Tom Batey are preparing to set off to deliver mail to Newtownmountkennedy, Annamoe, Glendalough and Roundwood for which the company had the mail delivery contract.

MARCONI WIRELESS. :: 'PHONE—57 GREYSTONES. :: AUSTIN CARS.

Thos. W. Batey, M.I.M.T.

MOTOR, ELECTRICAL & WIRELESS ENGINEER.
CHURCH ROAD, GARAGE,
GREYSTONES.

LOCK-UP GARAGE ACCOMMODATION. :: REPAIRS & ACCESSORIES.

11 . 8 . 33

LEFT: Letterhead dated 1933 for Batey's garage.

ABOVE: Photograph taken on 16th August 1928 of stilt walkers belonging to Duffy's Circus walking up Church Road. It was traditional for a circus performing in a town to parade through it. The local shopkeepers can be seen standing outside their shops to watch the horse and cart belonging to the circus lead the way. Just beyond its driver, one of the petrol pumps on the pavement outside Batey's garage can be seen, with its round white top. Dr. Leslie Doyle remembered watching the convoy pass by as an eight year old. He recalled that when the stilt walkers reached Walkers garage, they "sat down" for a rest on an adjacent low roof for a number of minutes, before proceeding on their way.

ABOVE: Two men in conversation outside the hairdressers adjacent to Deacon's shop, with Greystones station in the distance. The hairdressers had pigeon hole shelves where regular customers left their own cut-throat razors. Prior to Deacon's shop operating from the premises, the shop was G.L. Pepper's stationery and confectionery shop.

ABOVE: James Ernest Scott standing in the doorway of his pharmacy on Church Road, where McGleenans pharmacy is today.

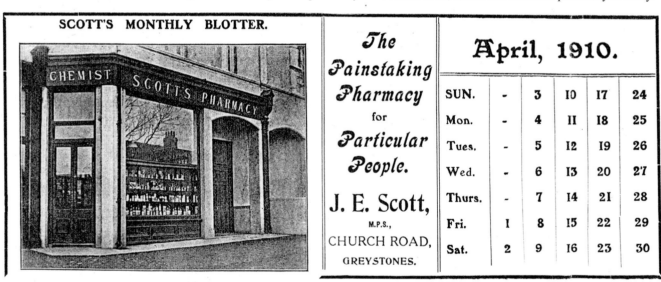

ABOVE: Calendar advertisement for Scott's Pharmacy in 1910.

RIGHT: Staff dispensing in Scott's Pharmacy on Church Road.

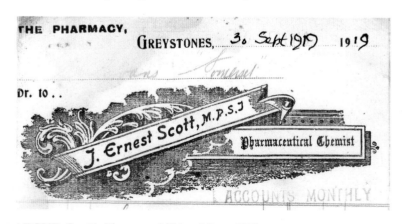

ABOVE: Scott's Pharmacy bill head from 1919.

Edwards & Co.
THE STORES,
GREYSTONES,
Ranelagh & Ballybrack.

There is no doubt Our Teas
are the Best. They are bought
by competition and comparison
selected with the greatest care,
and specially blended to suit
the water of the District.
1/6, 1/8, 2/- Blends also 2/6, 3/-
Per lb.

Telegrams:
EDWARDS, GREYSTONES

Phone:
GREYSTONES No. 5

EDWARDS & COMPANY

FIRST-CLASS FAMILY GROCERS
AND PROVISION MERCHANTS

Best Brands of Wines and Spirits

THE SUPPLY STORES
GREYSTONES

ABOVE: O'Brien's in August 2017.

ABOVE: Old advertisements for Edwards & Company, which traded as The Greystones Supply Stores where O'Brien's off-licence is today. The advertisement on the left is from 1907. Note the single digit Greystones phone number on the right.

BELOW: The shop as O'Brien's Fine Wines, before the extension, when Harper's dry cleaners and Greystones laundrette were located to the rear. The adjoining white house where the Kilkenny shop is today was *Weston House,* previously Doctor Orr's GP practice and, prior to that, the home of the Magee family.

BELOW: Edwards & Company grocery shop with all the staff standing outside. The smaller man in the doorway is George Edwards (who died in 1911), brother of the proprietor, James Edwards. James Edwards was the grandfather of Sean Magee, Mrs Kay Crowe and Mrs Maureen O'Meara. The horse and cart was used to deliver groceries around Greystones. On the wall behind it is a wheel with a pulley to lift and lower heavy goods from the storehouse onto the cart. The well stocked window is crammed with boxes of Jacob's biscuits and cuts of bacon. Two oil lamps can be seen hanging in the windows and a bird cage over the doorway.

LEFT: Frank Clarke, Betty Lowe (nee Fox) and John Fox standing in the doorway of Fox Bros. butchers shop which closed in 1974. The premises then became a delicatessen run by Tino and Claire Cassoni until their retirement in 2008. Frank Clarke's barbers was next door on the right.

ABOVE: Looking towards Frank Clarke's barbers and Fox Bros. butchers shop in March 1971, with a large sign advertising Fenelon's butchers located in the adjoining premises. Note the house on the right, which was originally called *Buona Vista* (painted blue in the photo below), built at a diagonal, to follow the originally intended direction of the road, from near the railway bridge at Trafalgar Road to intersect Church Road in front of the two storey house, *Mount View*, as shown on the next page.

ABOVE: Frank Clarke standing in the doorway of his barbers in 2003 which he opened in March 1942 and ran until his retirement in 2005.

BELOW: View in August 2017 of Rudi & Madison, Amoc Jewellery and the Credit Union.

RIGHT: Section of the Greystones town plan drawn in 1876 for the construction of the town's water supply. It shows the middle section of Church Road, with La Touche Place and the start of Trafalgar Road. The red lines overlaid on the plan show the original road from the harbour. Samuel A. French, in his history of Greystones, written for the centenary of St. Patrick's Church in 1964, noted the original route which the road took from the harbour along Trafalgar Road. He wrote that

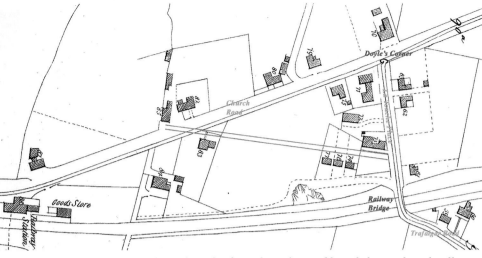

"after passing Emily House and Sweet Briar Cottage you came to the railway bridge, where the road bore left past the schoolhouse, now the teacher's residence to meet Church Road at Mount View". The route of the original road shown on the above map in red pre-dates the building of St. Patrick's Church in 1864. Once it was built, "Church Road", as we know it today started to develop and the original direct road ceased to be used. Samuel A. French summarised that *"the diagonal road from the railway bridge to the station on the west side was abandoned and La Touche Place was made, joining Church Road at Doyle's Corner"*. Accordingly, *Seaview House* (No.73) on the above plan and best known as Moran's fish shop, now Dooley Auctioneers, the original school, which then became the school teacher's house (No.72), *Ivy Cottage* (No.74), *Eden Cottage* (No.77) and *Mount View* (No.83) were all built to run parallel to the original road. Doyle's Corner has been in use for more than a century and half, ever since George Enright Doyle built *Bushfield House* around 1870 (No.77), followed by *Stanley House* (No.70). His cousin, James Doyle, built *Carrick Cottage* (No.63). On the opposite corner, John Doyle, later Coxswain of The Greystones Lifeboat and brother of James, then built *Frankfort House* (not shown on the above map, but shown on the 1883 map at the bottom of the page) where he resided and thus the junction became known locally as "Doyle's Corner".

LEFT: Photograph taken in the 1880s with no houses between the railway station and the two storey *Mount View,* built at an angle to Church Road, as described above. The roofs of other houses built along the same diagonal can be seen towards the centre of the photograph.

BELOW: *Mount View*, the Egan family home for almost half a century photographed just prior to its sale in July 2016.

BELOW: Section from the Ordnance Survey sheet for Greystones drawn in 1883, overlaid with the route of the original road shown by the red line. The schoolhouse, built in 1880, is shown connected to the school teacher's house, the latter following the line of the original road (refer also to page 250).

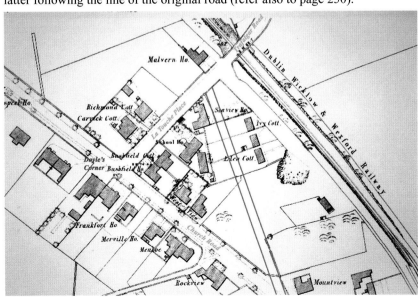

ABOVE: Redevelopment of *Mount View* in progress in May 2018 showing the shell of the house aligned with the original road.

ABOVE: View from the corner of Hillside Road and Church Road in August 2017 towards the shops which now occupy the former site of *Verdella*. *Thom's Directory* for 1906 listed the occupier of *Verdella* as Mrs Ferrar.

RIGHT: View from the corner of Hillside Road and Church Road in the early 1970s of the ivy-clad *Verdella,* originally built by the builder, Patrick Flynn. The family home of Ozzy and Betty Spurling in the early 1960s, the house was demolished in 1975, when it was redeveloped for commercial purposes, with Lipton's supermarket opening on the site. Since then it has been home to a number of other shops including Love's Supermarket, The Shopping Basket and Xtra-vision. On the right, where Las Tapas is today, is Bel's shop, with its awning down.

LEFT: Photo with *Verdella* on the left, next to where Las Tapas is today. The ornate shop front where Edwards & Co. traded as The Greystones Supply Stores can be seen at the end of the row. *Mount View,* built at a diagonal can be seen further along.

BELOW: Sale on at Bel's shop (now Las Tapas restaurant) with the Xtra-vision video rental store next door.

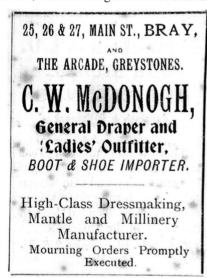

25, 26 & 27, MAIN ST., BRAY,

AND

THE ARCADE, GREYSTONES.

C. W. McDONOGH,

General Draper and 'Ladies' Outfitter,

BOOT & SHOE IMPORTER.

High-Class Dressmaking, Mantle and Millinery Manufacturer.
Mourning Orders Promptly Executed.

ABOVE: 1907 advertisement for McDonogh's general drapery & ladies' outfitters which traded from where Las Tapas is today. Charles Whitelaw McDonogh's main shop was in Bray, where the family resided. The premises was Bel's shop for a number of decades, prior to which it was owned by Miss Coates.

RIGHT: Bel's shoe repair price list from the 1960s.

BELS	GENTS' REPAIRS IN LEATHER		
		s.	d.
	Soles and Heels Stitched On	13	6
	Soles Only	9	0
SHOE REPAIR SERVICE	Heels with Quarter Rubbers or Steels ...	5	0
	Toe Pieces	3	6
	Full-Length Soles and Heels	25	0

ABOVE: 1920s photograph with two modes of horse power! A Walker's Garage Shell petrol pump on the path outside *Rockview* can be seen (where Cafe Delle Stelle is today). Beyond it is the large detached house, *Pretoria*. Just visible is the cobblestone pedestrian crossing. It was put there so the ladies of the town could cross without their garments trailing in the mud.

BELOW: Walker's Garage sign on the gable end wall and two women standing on the cobblestone crossing. The roof of the garage workshop is visible on the right.

ABOVE: April 2010 photograph, with a fine view of the original cobblestone crossing at the junction of Hillside Road and Church Road. On the extreme right is the curved wall and hedge of *Waverly* (undergoing redevelopment in 2018).

RIGHT: Garage proprietor Thomas Walker was the golf professional at Greystones Golf Club from 1907 until 1917. He was a renowned maker of golf clubs prior to leaving to set up his garage on Hillside Road.

ABOVE: Hill's garage in the 1970s with its red brick art deco facade and house next door where Cafe Delle Stelle is today. The garage was demolished in December 2007.

RIGHT: Staff at Walker's garage.

LEFT: *West View House* on Church Road as it was with its walled front garden. It was formerly the home of Isabella and Fred Robb, as well as Alice and Annie Evans, Isabella's sisters. It was originally built by Isabella's brother.

ABOVE: 1883 Ordnance Survey sheet showing *West View*.

ABOVE: *West View House* being converted into commercial use, following which it was the premises of Charlie's Fruit & Vegetables for a number of years. As it is today, the home of The Happy Pear.

ABOVE: The Buckley family of *Pretoria House* on Church Road had a number of shops in the locality, including the butcher's shop beside the Cherry Orchard in Killincarrig.

LEFT: *Pretoria House* on Church Road next to Hill's Garage was the Buckley family home for many years. It was demolished in 1994 ahead of its subsequent commercial redevelopment, with Supervalu now located on its former site.

LEFT: Very old photograph of Buckley's grocery store on Church Road with the shop's delivery cart loaded up and ready to deliver provisions around Greystones. The Buckley family had other shops, one on the opposite side of the road where Supervalu is today, as well as the butcher's shop in Killincarrig shown on the bottom of opposite page.

BELOW: A later photograph of the shop with fully stocked window and baskets of fruit and vegetables outside the front.

BELOW: Horse and cart bearing the livery of Alexander Buckley, Victualler, Greystones opposite the railway station. In the background is the Wine Merchants and Byrne & Co. Family Grocers, which formed part of the The Railway Hotel.

BELOW: Vincent Kelly worked in the butcher's section at the rear of Flynn's Superstore on Victoria Road in the 1970s and later established his own butcher's shop where Buckley's grocery store once stood. This photograph was taken in November 2005 following its closure and subsequent revamp into Bochellis restaurant.

ABOVE: Winter scene from the early 1900s. A horse and cart loaded up with timber is parked outside the shop built and run by George Enright Doyle. Son of John Doyle, he was born in 1840 at No.1 Bethel Terrace. *Bushfield House*, built around 1870, was one of several houses he built in Greystones and was from where he ran his general provisions shop. Its entrance was via the doorway in the high wall as seen on the right of the photo. After he had built *Stanley House*, he transferred his shop across the road to there. His son, Rochfort, followed in his father's footsteps and built the cottages at The Grove in Redford before changing profession to become an auctioneer in 1919, with auction rooms located on Hillside Road. Note also the sign for John Storey's grocery shop just visible high up on the side wall beyond Doyle's Corner.

BELOW: Photo showing the rectangular cement board with Rochfort Doyle's auction notices pasted on it almost a century ago.

ABOVE: Rochfort Doyle, house builder, auctioneer and father of Dr. Leslie Doyle.

TELEPHONE 32.
ROCHFORT DOYLE, 1524
Auctioneer and Estate Agent, GREYSTONES.
18-10-1939

JOHN STOREY,
Church Rd., Greystones,
FOR
**Choice Groceries
and Provisions.**
Agent for FALKINER'S
and MAZAWATTEE TEAS
Fresh Buttered Eggs a Speciality

ABOVE: 1907 advertisement.

ABOVE: July 2017, looking towards Doyle's Corner with Rochfort Doyle's auction noticeboard still preserved as a feature on the wall where Mooch is now.

ABOVE: *Bushfield House* on Doyle's Corner photographed in 1886. George Enright Doyle funded the purchase of the plot through the disposal of his fishing lugger, *Prima Donna*, in 1866 (see page 142). At the time this photograph was taken, the trees on the left in front of his shop were mere saplings and there were no lamp standards on Church Road. Fenton Fires occupies the premises today.

LEFT: Photograph taken c.1885 of George Enright Doyle, his wife Jane (nee Buckley) and their six children. From left to right the children are: Rochfort, George, Florrie (next to her mother), Eleanor Anne (standing at the back), Rupert and Edwin. Following the death of his father in 1903, Edwin Doyle ran the family shop, Stanley Stores on Church Road.

BELOW: 1886 view of *Frankfort House* on the left, built by and resided in by John Doyle.

ABOVE: George Enright Doyle (1840-1903).

ABOVE: George Enright Doyle's shop. On the pavement is one of the oil lamps erected by the Greystones Improvement Association on Church Road in 1903, which a lamplighter ascended a ladder to light manually each evening. Note that the front of the shop had not yet been extended out, in contrast to the photograph below.

ABOVE: Mr Kane with his Dublin Bakery Company horse and cart delivering Gold Medal Vienna bread during a late snowfall in the month of May. By now Edwin's name was over the shop door. He was the father of Enright, who was the last Doyle family proprietor. The shop by then was known as Stanley Stores.

LEFT: Advertisement for "High-Class" accommodation at Stanley House, next door to Stanley Stores. Given the oil lamp standard in front of the house, the advertisement dates from between 1903 and 1910.

STANLEY.

HIGH-CLASS FURNISHED APARTMENTS

GOOD SITUATION.

BATH, HOT AND COLD.

MRS. DOYLE, STANLEY, GREYSTONES.

Household and Builders' Ironmongery, Toilet, Tea and Dinner Sets, Paints, Oils, Colours, Hall's Sanitary Distemper, Varnishes, Chamois, Sponges, Brushes, Wall-paper, Garden Requisites, Royal Daylight Oil, Methylated Spirit, Lamp Chimneys and Wicks. China and Glass for Hire.

Agent for Rudge-Whitworth and Rover Bicycles.

E. DOYLE, Church Road, Greystones.

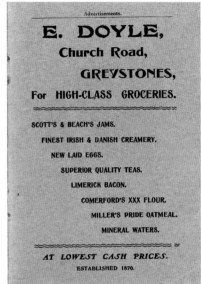

Advertisements.

E. DOYLE,
Church Road,
GREYSTONES,
For HIGH-CLASS GROCERIES.

SCOTT'S & BEACH'S JAMS.

FINEST IRISH & DANISH CREAMERY.

NEW LAID EGGS.

SUPERIOR QUALITY TEAS.

LIMERICK BACON.

COMERFORD'S XXX FLOUR.

MILLER'S PRIDE OATMEAL.

MINERAL WATERS.

AT LOWEST CASH PRICES.

ESTABLISHED 1870.

ABOVE: Stanley Stores, when it was under the proprietorship of Edwin Doyle. The 1914 *Thom's Directory* listed Edwin as a grocer, hardware merchant and house agent. The white horse and cart with Doyle livery on its side is about to set off delivering groceries and other goods around Greystones. Note the change in lamp standard to electricity which was introduced in 1910.

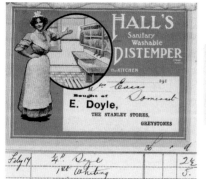

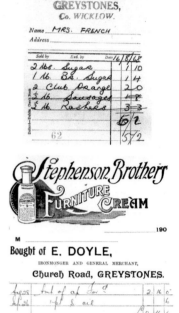

ABOVE: Edwin Doyle.

ABOVE: Photograph taken in 1913 in the back garden of *Stanley House* showing a family gathering. It features Jane, widow of George Enright Doyle and four of their six children, Eleanor Anne, Edwin, Rochfort and Florrie. It shows the inter-linked family connections between four Greystones families, the Doyles, Evans, Buckleys and Watsons. Eleanor Anne Doyle, known as "Nellie" was married to Arthur Evans senior's son, Arthur Patrick Evans. Standing left to right are: Miss Parker, Sidney Evans (1898-1980), unknown, Edwin Doyle (1874-1935), Florrie Doyle (1885-1972) who married Alexander Buckley in 1916, Rochfort Doyle (1876-1945), Nellie Evans (nee Doyle, mother of Sidney, Leonard and Kenneth), Leonard Evans (1902-1987) and George Watson. Seated left to right: Kenneth Evans (1909-1969), Jane Doyle (nee Buckley, 1841-1916)*,* Enright Doyle (1911-1985), Olive Doyle (nee Watson, 1887-1976 and wife of Edwin Doyle).

ABOVE: Stanley House photographed in August 2017.

BELOW: *Iveragh House* on Church Road in 2017. Built no earlier than 1876, the house was originally three storeys, but was damaged by a fire around 1913, following which it was remodelled as a two storey residence. By 1917, it was the family home of William Eagar and his wife, Ida. Their son, also called William was killed at Gallipoli on 21st August 1915 (refer to page 278).

LEFT: Photograph dated around 1907 showing it as the original three storey shop prior to the fire damage.

BELOW: Close-up view of the shop front reveals that some of the well-known food brands around today, such as St. Ivel cheese and Bovril, were also around over 100 years ago. A female shopkeeper, attired in bonnet and apron, can be seen behind the counter looking out the window.

249

ABOVE: View of La Touche Place looking towards Doyle's Corner at the intersection with Church Road. On the left is *Seaview House*, with Charles Evans' shop fronting onto La Touche Place. The shop was later run as a sweet shop and hairdressers by his daughter, Margaret Donnolly (sister of William, John, Isaac and "Allie") and her husband. *Thom's Directory* for 1908 lists "*Telephone Exchange, Seaview House - Mrs La Combre, Caretaker*", a role she held for more than 20 years. *Thom's Directory* for 1933 still lists the telephone exchange at *Seaview House*, but with Mrs E.J. Skehan as caretaker. By 1936 it was no longer listed as located there. During the latter part of the 20th century it operated as Moran's Fish Shop for a number of decades. In recent years, it was for a time a florist and is currently Dooley Auctioneers. This photo gives a clear view of the adjacent living quarters parallel to the original road as detailed on page 239 as well as on the map below.

LEFT: Charles Evans (1858-1941) of *Seaview House*, La Touche Place. A keen boat owner, on the 1901 census, his occupation was listed as "*pleasure boat owner.*" He took 2nd place in the four-oared pleasure boat race at the 1889 Greystones Regatta (see page 158).

RIGHT: Section from the Ordnance Survey sheet for Greystones drawn in 1883, overlaid with the route of the original road indicated by the red lines. Shown on it is *Seaview House*. Also shown is the new schoolhouse built in 1880, aligned parallel to La Touche Place as it was now the main thoroughfare.

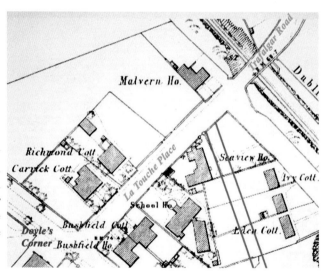

BELOW: Greystones National School. The foundation stone for this school was laid by William R. La Touche on 8th September 1879 and built by R. Ludlow. The building was demolished in 1967. Note on the map above it faces directly onto La Touche Place

ABOVE: Redevelopment of the former St. Patrick's National School site in April 2009, during which the original house shown in the photograph on the left was demolished.

ABOVE: May 2005 photograph of the Thrift Shop in the former St. Patrick's National School. This school building, which was perpendicular to La Touche Place, was opened in April 1968 and replaced the original 1879/1880 built national school. The building ceased to be a school in December 1975 and the current St. Patrick's National School on Church Road opened in January 1976. In addition to the above two class rooms, there was a third class room which was relocated in 1976 to the grounds of St. Patrick's Church. It was used as the parish room, prior to the construction of Swann Hall. Also visible is the house used as the schoolhouse prior to 1880 which was aligned to the original road (refer to property No. 72 on the 1876 plan shown on the inside of the back cover and also map on page 250). When the 1880 school was built, this became the school teacher's house. Belonging to St. Patrick's Parish, this was also used as the sexton's house for a number of decades.

ABOVE: Old photograph of a group of girl guides in the school playground. Directly behind them, on La Touche Place is *Richmond Cottage*. It was when living there that a young Jimmy Magee applied to the Director of Broadcasting at Telefís Éireann in a letter dated 27th March 1956 to become a sports commentator. The rest, as Jimmy would have said, is history!

ABOVE: Demolition in 2000 of Evans Hardware shop, which had been in business for 83 years. It was established by Allen "Allie" Evans, when he returned home to Greystones after being injured at the Battle of the Somme in World War One (see also page 283).

ABOVE: Evans Hardware shop which was established in 1917 by Allen 'Allie' Evans. Subsequently the shop was run by his nephew, Charlie Evans, whose son, Clifford ran the business until its closure in 2000 when the premises was redeveloped. Moran's fish shop is just visible on the extreme right.

ABOVE: La Touche Wines and Ju Ju in May 2018.

During the latter part of the 19th century and early part of the 20th century, the schoolhouse on La Touche Close hosted many meetings and events. On 1st February 1887, a public meeting of residents was held there to discuss the proposed extension of the pier at Greystones harbour. On 22nd May 1896, the inaugural meeting of the Greystones Improvement Association was held in the schoolhouse. On the left is a ticket from 1907 for an ambulance demonstration event. On 28th August 1915, Percy French, the famous songwriter and entertainer gave a memorable performance to a packed schoolhouse.

ABOVE: Gethings sweet shop on La Touche Place.

ABOVE: Dorothy Haughton, photographed in the late 1970s in the doorway of her Olde Curiosity Shoppe. The premises operated as the Thrift Shop from 1974 until early 1976, when it relocated across the road to the former St. Patrick's National school.

ABOVE: La Touche Upholstery photographed in August 2017.

ABOVE: A century ago, upholstery and cabinet making was carried out by Thomas Gethings from the shop adjoining the family home, *Osborne Cottage*, next door. The Gethings family came to Greystones from County Wexford in 1908.

LEFT: Malvern House on La Touche Place in September 2017 with shops, Paraphernalia, La Touche Barbers and Something Nice ice cream. The original premises, which had three upper floor windows, was subsequently extended towards the railway line. The original gable end chimneys were also removed. Paraphernalia was established by Suzy Kenny in 1991 and traded from a premises behind where The Happy Pear is today, prior to moving to its current location on La Touche Place in 2001.

ABOVE: Mrs Evans and two friends standing in the doorway of the family's shop, prior to it becoming Hendy's pharmacy.

ABOVE: A.W. Hendy's pharmacy, which replaced E. Evans' shop. Now home to Paraphernalia.

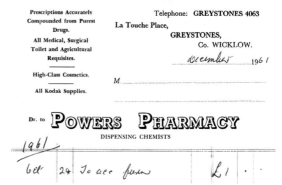

ABOVE: Old advert for Hendy's Pharmacy on La Touche Place.

LEFT: Hendy's Pharmacy in the 1920s. The sign to the right of the door is for Gilbey's Wine.

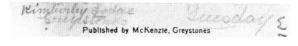

ABOVE: The shop remained as a chemist, under the proprietorship of Eamonn Power.

ABOVE & RIGHT: Postcard sent on 18th September 1923, published by John McKenzie, newsagent and confectioner, Trafalgar Road.

ABOVE: View from the tower of the Holy Rosary Church showing the field (owned by Jack "The Post" Evans) upon which La Touche Close was later built. Note the blackened stonework above the railway arch from the soot emitted from passing steam engines, also the chemist sign painted on the gable end of the *Malvern House* premises from which Hendy's pharmacy operated.

LEFT: View looking up Eden Road towards the shops on La Touche Place in May 2018 (note the cottages built in line with the original road).

ABOVE: 1880s view towards the railway bridge. On the extreme left is *Ivy Cottage*, built at an angle. To its right is the two storey *Malvern House*, in its original form, with three upper floor windows and chimneys on both gable ends. The first cottage on Trafalgar Road, adjacent to the railway bridge has a thatched roof. Neither the Holy Rosary Church nor the shops at No.1 and No.2 Trafalgar Road had yet been built. Greystones Presbyterian Church had not been built, making the two storey *Brooklands House* on the left-hand side of Trafalgar Road quite imposing.

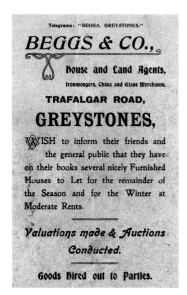

Telegrams: "BEGGS, GREYSTONES."

BEGGS & CO.,

House and Land Agents,

Ironmongers, China and Glass Merchants,

TRAFALGAR ROAD,

GREYSTONES,

WISH to inform their friends and the general public that they have on their books several nicely Furnished Houses to Let for the remainder of the Season and for the Winter at Moderate Rents.

Valuations made & Auctions Conducted.

Goods Hired out to Parties.

BELOW: 1907 advert for Beggs & Company, showing their wide range of businesses.

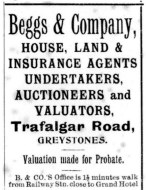

Beggs & Company,
HOUSE, LAND &
INSURANCE AGENTS
UNDERTAKERS,
AUCTIONEERS and
VALUATORS,
Trafalgar Road,
GREYSTONES.

Valuation made for Probate.

B. & CO.'S Office is 1¼ minutes walk from Railway Stn. close to Grand Hotel

ABOVE: Photograph of *Winton House* which comprised No.1 and No.2 Trafalgar Road. The name *Winton House* is believed to be derived from the Beggs family home in Dalkey of the same name in the 1880s. When Edward Beggs came to Greystones and established his business on Trafalgar Road, his shop was known as the Winton Hardware Stores. He operated several businesses, as the advertisements on the left show. The above photograph, taken in the 1930s, looking down Trafalgar Road shows the J. McKenzie sign above the shop front awning. Beside it is Sam Ferns' drapery shop with the S. Ferns sign above the doorway. Note the ornate lamp standard.

FROM S. FERNS
TAILORING, GENTLEMEN'S OUTFITTING
UP-TO-DATE FOOTWEAR, HOSIERY ETC.
TERMS – CASH

RIGHT: Sam Ferns outside his shop. Visible behind is some of the lettering of the McKenzie & Kinsella coal merchants sign on the wall of the adjoining shop, when operated by John McKenzie.

ABOVE: A customer entering Sam Ferns' drapery shop in the 1940s to get suited and booted. The 1914 *Thom's Directory* listed "*Samuel Ferns, draper, Winton House*" as being the occupier, paying annual rates of £26. He originally came to Greystones from Newtown Barry in County Wexford. The drapery business was subsequently carried on by his son Derek and his wife Norah, from March 1965 until the family sold the premises in 1991. It then became a cafe called Poppies, then latterly Summervilles and is now The Baker's Table.

Having made arrangements with Ireland's newest and most up-to-date Tailoring firm for the production of our made-to-measure Suits, we are now in a position to give the last word in Style, Quality and Fit. Our Patterns represent the newest in Tweeds and Serges, whether for Sports or Ordinary Wear. See our Irish Tweeds.
Prices from **50/-** *to* **£6.**

Our Flannel Trousers are made on the same up-to-date lines, in all shades
from **7/6** *up to* **21/-.**

S. FERNS,
TRAFALGAR ROAD, GREYSTONES

ABOVE Norah behind the counter.

ABOVE: Derek and Norah Ferns in 1990 inside the family's drapery shop with boxes of shoes on the shelves beside the step ladder.

RIGHT: 1991 photo of Mooney's shop at No.2 and the neighbouring premises at No.1 Trafalgar Road, showing the S. Ferns sign above the empty shop.

ABOVE: Summerville's in April 2000, where Ferns' shop operated for most of the 20th century.

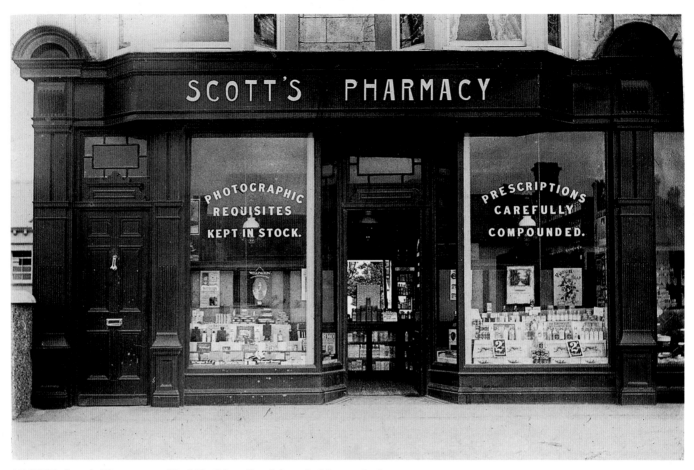

ABOVE: Scott's Pharmacy at No.2 Trafalgar Road, latterly Mooney's shop.

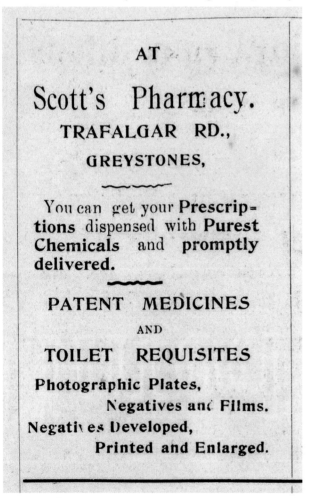

AT

Scott's Pharmacy.

TRAFALGAR RD.,

GREYSTONES,

You can get your **Prescriptions** dispensed with **Purest Chemicals** and **promptly delivered.**

PATENT MEDICINES

AND

TOILET REQUISITES

Photographic Plates, Negatives and Films.
Negatives Developed, Printed and Enlarged.

ABOVE: Advertisement from the 1909 Greystones Summer Fete Programme.

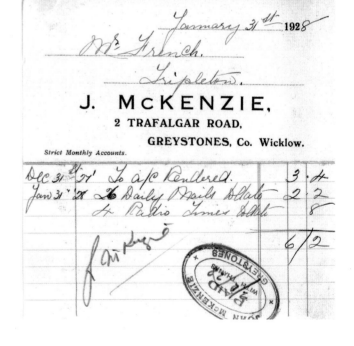

January 31st 1928

Mr French.

Tripleton

J. McKENZIE,
2 TRAFALGAR ROAD,
GREYSTONES, Co. Wicklow.

Strict Monthly Accounts.

November 30th 1933

Mr French.

Dr. to "Tripleton,"

J. McKENZIE,

Newsagent, etc.,

2, TRAFALGAR ROAD,
GREYSTONES, Co. WICKLOW.

LEFT: Close-up photo of the sign above the door of No.2 Trafalgar Road when the shop was owned by John McKenzie. In conversation with Gary Paine in May 2017, Eric Archer, then aged 97 recalled one of his earliest childhood memories in the early 1920s was seeing John McKenzie each morning, regular as clockwork, wheeling a push bike past the Archer family home, *Ard-na-ree* on La Touche Road to the station to meet the 7.20am train from Dublin. With the morning papers loaded onto the bike he would wheel them back to the shop.

Prior to Mooneys acquiring the shop in 1955 it was owned by John McKenzie, who ran his newsagents and confectionery shop there, from the early 1920s until his death in 1953. Born in Liverpool, John McKenzie was brought to Dublin at a young age by his mother, following the death of his father, Edwin, a marine engineer, in an accident in 1915. During his early career he worked as an erector of iron buildings, including one of the first munition works at Trafford Park in Manchester.

He married a Greystones woman, Catherine Kinsella, and after their marriage they settled in Greystones at No.2 Bethel Terrace on the lower part of Trafalgar Road. Sadly Catherine died in 1923 leaving him to raise their two young children. Together with his brother-in-law, he started a coal distribution business, *"McKenzie & Kinsella."* Later he took a lease on the newsagent's shop at No.2 Trafalgar Road and decided to concentrate on running this business, while also rearing his two children, Annie and Johnny. In August 1953 John McKenzie died and the shop was subsequently sold. In memory of his life during difficult times, The John McKenzie Perpetual Challenge Cup was presented by his family to Greystones Rowing Club. His son, Johnny served on the committee of Greystones Rowing Club at the time, along with Willie Redmond (Chairman), Ernest Paine (Hon. Sec.), Jim Hayden (Hon. Treasurer), J. Kinsella, D. Daly and J. Gunning.

ABOVE: John McKenzie standing in front of his newsagents and confectionery shop at No.2 Trafalgar Road in the late 1920s / early 1930s with his daughter, Annie and her friend Peggy Grant, holding her dog. Annie McKenzie married Jim Hayden in 1932 and was the mother of Billy, Jago, John, Kathleen, Eileen and Declan.

LEFT: Photograph of Bridie Mooney raising a glass of champagne after closing her shop for the final time on Christmas Eve 2015. The photograph was taken by her grandson, Eoghan Megannety. Bridie and her late husband, Robert, acquired the shop in 1955. At the age of 86 and after 60 years behind the counter selling newspapers and general provisions she decided to take a well earned retirement. For over a century the shop, along with its neighbouring premises, No.1 Trafalgar Road, has been an integral part of Greystones, with its convenient location between the station and the harbour.

ABOVE: Photo taken around the mid 1890s with the fine red-brick entrance to the Grand Hotel. In the background is the Hibernian Bank building, with the sign in the door indicating that it opened on Wednesdays. The three storey building at the corner of Trafalgar Road and Sidmonton Place later became the Braemar Hotel. Above its bay end window is a Beggs & Co letting sign. Note also the very ornate lamp fittings that befitted a hotel of the Grand Hotel's status. A substantial length of the sea wall, built to protect the railway approach from Bray Head along Morris' Bank can be seen at the far end of the North Beach in the distance. Just visible, protruding from the summit of Bray Head, is the Victoria obelisk erected in 1887 by W. G. Morris of *Windgate House*.

ABOVE: Thatched roof on one of the cottages on Trafalgar Road in the 1890s.

ABOVE: The Hibernian Bank in the 1890s.

Though the first Post Office in Greystones, located in *Rockport* at the harbour, included a "Savings Bank" (refer to page 55), The Hibernian Bank building, with its barred windows on Trafalgar Road was the town's first purpose-built bank. It was first listed in the 1891 *Thom's Directory* (below) as opening on Wednesdays, as a sub-branch of The Hibernian Bank branch in Bray. Bray was served by a country branch of The Hibernian Bank from at least 1874. It is likely that the red-bricked bank building was among the first parts of the Grand Hotel to be built. By 1914, The Hibernian Bank had relocated to *Cremona* on Church Road and the *Thom's Directory* for 1915 showed it now opened on Tuesdays and Fridays. It also included The Northern Bank's advertisement stating that the bank had a sub-branch in Greystones attended to from Bray, also opening on Tuesdays and Fridays. By 1922, *Thom's Directory* was listing The Royal Bank as having a branch in Greystones, located beside MacFarland's shop, where Sherry Fitzgerald is today.

ABOVE: The former bank premises in May 2018 with its original red bricks visible under the cement rendering to the right of the door.

RIGHT: St. Killian's Hall opened in November 1928. The photograph was taken in July 1999 after it had been sold for redevelopment. The lower photo is of its interior at a flower show in the 1980s.

ABOVE: Early 1900s photograph showing Emily Greer's stationery and newsagent's shop in the former coast guard cottage at No.5 Kenmare Terrace.

ABOVE: 1880s photograph looking down Trafalgar Road with just a field opposite the thatched cottage and the former coast guard cottages on Kenmare Terrace. The building which later became the Braemar Hotel on the corner of Sidmonton Place and Trafalgar Road had not yet been built.

RIGHT: August 1959 advertisement for Sharavogue Stores which was located where the Harbour Barber is today.

Ownership of The Beach House	
Year	**Family Ownership**
1850-1884	Doyle
1884-1907	McEntagart
1907-1952	Dann
1952-1963	O'Reilly
1963-present	Byrne

The origins of what is now The Beach House date back to c.1850. In addition to his coal import business, John Doyle (1793-1855) also owned a shop at the harbour. Following his death, his son, John Doyle II (1836-1883) took over the running of his late father's coal import business and, seeing the need for a hotel in the area, opened the Greystones Hotel in what is now The Beach House. It also included a licensed premises and grocery shop.

> **GREYSTONES HOTEL** The numerous tourists and visitors to this delightful outlet having called my attention to the great want of a First-class Hotel in it, I purpose opening a first-class one, and trust by attention to the comfort of my patrons to merit their support.
> JOHN DOYLE, Greystones.
> The Hotel will be Opened on Saturday, the 29th May.

ABOVE: The notice that appeared in *Saunders's Newsletter* on Thursday 27th May 1858 announcing the opening of the Greystones Hotel on Saturday 29th May 1858.

AUCTIONS.

HIGHLY IMPORTANT LICENSED PREMISES,

KNOWN AS

"THE BEACH,"

GREYSTONES, COUNTY WICKLOW,

TOGETHER WITH ADJOINING PROPERTY AND EXTENSIVE COAL TRADE CONNECTED

ANDREW J. KEOGH has received instructions from the Owner, Mr. M'Entaggart (who has his entire attention occupied by his extensive City Catering Establishment, The Empire Restaurant, to SELL BY PUBLIC AUCTION, in his SALEROOMS, 10 LOWER ORMOND QUAY, on FRIDAY, the 8th day of NOVEMBER, 1901, at One o'clock if not previously sold by private treaty, the magnificent 7-day Licensed Premises, known as "THE BEACH," GREYSTONES, facing the Harbour, which is held from the La Touche family for two existing lives, at the nominal rent of £10, and the benefit to the purchaser of a promise from Major La Touche to renew lease at same rent.

This Lot forms one of the most important Licensed Properties in the County of Wicklow, and consists of a large, sightly, two-storey structure, containing spacious Shop, splendidly arranged and appointed for the Family Grocery, Wine, Spirit, and General Provision Business, in which an extensive turn-over is effected throughout the entire year. Adjoining same is a good-sized Spirit Bar, with suitable appointments for the retail trade, with entrance separated from the main shop.

Behind Grocery department is a well-arranged bottled drink store. There is fine cellar and bottle-washing store, with concrete floors, and railed-in yard at the side of building, used for keeping empties.

The dwelling portion, which is most suitably furnished, is entered by hall door, and consists of 11 bedrooms, 4 sittingrooms, bathroom, h. and c. supply, lavatory, 2 w.c.'s, kitchen, with tiled floor, having double oven range, copper cylinder, hot water circulating pipes, larder, etc. There is a garden and small field; also an extensive, walled-in coal yard at the rere of the premises, with large gate entrance, the walls being supported by heavy buttresses. The coal trade, which forms a profitable adjunct to the business, is very extensive. The schooner "Mersey" (of 95 tons burden), the property of the Vendor, conveys coal to the Harbour immediately opposite the premises, and will be included in this Sale. She is well found and in good repair, and at present at sea.

This Lot forms one of the most unique properties to be found in Ireland. The extensive business has realised for both Vendor and his predecessor a substantial fortune. Books have been regularly kept, and the auditor's certificate shows a substantial profit for many years.

The Premises are in a splendid state of preservation, and in addition to forming a most desirable and roomy residence, the rooms yield a large sum of money as a private hotel during the summer and autumn seasons.

Greystones is now the favourite watering-place between Wicklow and Dublin, and the numerous new villas and buildings being erected therein bear testimony to its extraordinary progress and the extensive patronage paid to this beautiful resort.

Further particulars as to trading, etc., can be had from the Auctioneer.

The purchaser can have the Stock-in-trade, Book Debts, and Modern Household Appointments at a valuation if he so desires, so that the business will be carried on without interruption.

For Particulars and Conditions of Sale, and Cards to View, apply to

H. F. STEPHENS, Esq., Solicitor, 33 Dawson street, Dublin; or to

ANDREW J. KEOGH,

AUCTIONEER, 10 LOWER ORMOND QUAY, DUBLIN.

5966

On 23rd January 1883, John Doyle II died at the age of 46. In 1884 his widow, Susanna, sold the business comprising the grocery shop and public house to a Dublin restaurateur, John George McEntagart. The coal schooner, *Mersey*, which was owned by John Nolan of Wicklow, regularly imported coal to Greystones harbour, supplying J.G. McEntagart's coalyard. McEntagart was in direct competition with Arthur Evans & Son, who owned a large coal store to the rear of The Beach. In 1889, with the works nearing completion to extend the pier at Greystones harbour, J.G. McEntagart acquired the schooner, *Mersey* from John Nolan, diversifying his business interests to include shipping. By 1901, J.G. McEntagart needed to devote more time to his Empire Restaurant business in Dublin and put his Greystones business up for auction. However ownership of the premises did not pass from the McEntagart family to the new owners until January 1907

LEFT: *The Irish Independent* dated 21st October 1901 carried the auction notice for the "*highly important licensed premises, known as The Beach, Greystones, Co. Wicklow, together with adjoining property and extensive coal trade connected*". The notice described the lot as "*one of the most unique properties to be found in Ireland.......and that Greystones is now the favourite watering place between Wicklow and Dublin*".

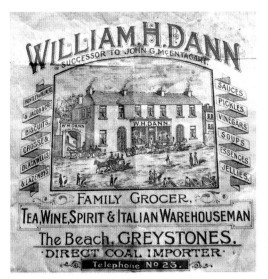

OPPOSITE PAGE LEFT: 1880s photo of the building on Victoria Road, then known as The Beach, Greystones. The entrance archway, with the sign, "*John G. McEntagart, Coal Store*" can be seen to the left of the grocery shop and licensed premises with the name "*J.G. McEntagart*" above the entrance. The large clinker built fishing boats were known locally as snuffs and were used for long line and herring net fishing.

BELOW: William H. Dann, who was manager of *The Beach* when it was owned by J.G. McEntagart, acquired the business from his former boss in 1907.

LEFT: August 1959 advertisement when the premises was owned and run by the O'Reilly family.

ABOVE: Jack Dann, nephew of William H. Dann and son of John T. Dann.

William H. Dann's father, Alexander Dann was from Co. Limerick and moved to Co. Wicklow where he worked as a butler. On the 1901 census, he was listed as a widower, living in Newtownmountkennedy with his son, Alexander, whose occupation was recorded as a grocer's porter. Another son, Nathan was listed on the 1901 census as living in Delgany with an occupation of grocer (Book No.3 includes a photo of Dann's shop in Delgany which was immediately to the right of where The Wicklow Arms was later located). Their elder brother William worked as the manager of The Beach in Greystones for the proprietor, J.G. McEntagart. When the latter eventually disposed of the business, it was William H. Dann who acquired it in January 1907. On the 1911 census, the return for The Beach, Greystones listed William H. Dann, aged 49, with an occupation of grocer and his brother, John T. Dann, aged 44, with an occupation of grocer's assistant.

In August 1932, Arthur Patrick Evans disposed of his coal business at the harbour. This included the large coalyard to the rear of Dann's, which William H. Dann bought for £300. The Danns also acquired the stock, goodwill, implements and one horse which belonged to A. Evans & Son. In March 1936, John T. Dann died and two years later his elder brother, William H. Dann died aged 74. Following this, his nephew, Jack Dann, carried on the business for another 14 years until 1952 when he sold it to James O'Reilly. The O'Reillys ran it for just over a decade, selling the business to Liam Byrne in 1963 and it remains in the Byrne family to the present day. Despite moving to Newbridge in Co. Kildare, Jack Dann maintained his links to Greystones, reminiscing about old times when he attended the exhibition of old photographs held in the annexe of The Burnaby in November 1983.

ABOVE: The Beach House in November 1991, showing the extension being built to its side. On the left, where The Creperie is today, was a betting office run by Bernard Darcy for a number of years from the late 1970s. In the early 1970s this premises was a shop which opened during the summer months selling items for holiday makers such as buckets, spades and beach balls. The building was at one time used by the coast guards to store equipment.

ABOVE: View looking across Victoria Road in the early 1940s with two Austin 10 saloon cars parked opposite Dann's. The original (1855 built) Gap Bridge is visible up the North Beach, as is the long stretch of sea wall and buttresses to protect the original railway line further up the beach towards the Red Rocks.

ABOVE: View of the harbour in the early 1960s at full tide before the arrival of the Kish base. Major repairs and improvements were undertaken in the vicinity of the harbour in 1958-59 under the auspices of Greystones & District Civic Association, with the assistance of both Bord Fáilte and Wicklow County Council. The works undertaken included major repairs to the surface of the pier along with the construction of a bus shelter directly opposite The Beach House and a row of fishermen's huts. The flat roof of the huts doubled as a viewing area. The official opening of the improvements took place on Sunday 9th August 1959 by the Minister for Finance, James Ryan. James Ryan had links to Greystones for many years, having resided at *Kindelstown House* in the 1930s.

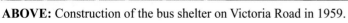

ABOVE: Construction of the bus shelter on Victoria Road in 1959.

ABOVE RIGHT: Lena Pennycook was the daughter of Edward Archer (Coxswain of the Greystones Lifeboat between 1892 and 1896). She and her husband, Charlie Pennycook, ran the Cafe Marina which was a popular venue for a number of years, particularly on Sundays when it did a roaring trade.

Cafe Marina
GREYSTONES

TEAS AND ICES

OUR SPECIALITY
MORNING COFFEE, BISCUITS
AND CIGARETTE

(C. M. Pennycook, Proprietor)

ABOVE: An old advertisement for the Cafe Marina which was ahead of its time, in name at least. Its speciality of *"morning coffee, biscuits and cigarette"* was of the time.

ABOVE: Fine view in the early 1960s looking up Victoria Road from the upstairs of *Wavecrest* towards the original 1855 built railway arch. Just visible between *Burlington House* and the railway embankment is the single storey building that housed the Cafe Marina.

LEFT: Photograph taken in 1948 with a Dublin bound steam train heading over the railway arch. The white "Teas" sign on the gable end of the Cafe Marina is visible to the right of *Burlington House*.

ABOVE: Various photographs taken in October 1971 showing the removal of the original 1855 railway arch on Victoria Road. Its replacement by the steel bridge was to enable the new double-decker buses to pass under the bridge on the number 84 bus route via the harbour.

ABOVE RIGHT: Doreen Thompson, Stan Paine and Flo Thompson in 1939, with the Cafe Marina and railway embankment in the background

ABOVE: Photograph taken in 1886 from the railway bridge with a fishing net drying on the garden wall of *Burlington House*. It was on this plot that the Cafe Marina run by Lena Pennycook was later located.

ABOVE: Brady's Hardware and Flynn's shop on Victoria Road photographed in May 1997, prior to their redevelopment.

In December 1944 John Brady senior acquired a plot of land, establishing a forge and operating as a farrier and general smith. In 1961 he sold a portion of the site to John Darcy who, the following year, sold it to Anthony and May Monks. They established a grocery shop which was known as May's shop.

Today, the Flynn brothers, twins David and Stephen are prominent Greystones retailers. Just under half a century ago, three Flynn brothers (no relation) were about to put their own stamp on the town's retailing history. In September 1969, John Flynn bought May's shop from the Monks, initially keeping on the name May's, before subsequently renaming it Flynns. He was joined by his two brothers, Pat and Kevin, with all three brothers working in the shop at the same time.

In April 1973, the brothers opened a second grocery shop in Kilcoole, which operated for a short period. In 1975, Pat Flynn acquired the grocery shop at the entrance to Grattan Park from Clare man, Mr McMahon, who had run the store for a decade. He had acquired it from the Dunne family, who had owned it for many years.

ABOVE: 1948 John Brady invoice.

BELOW: Pat, John and Kevin Flynn, originally from County Longford, photographed outside their shop on Victoria Road in around 1970. Spot the Spot Dogfood advert for just 7p!

ABOVE: 1960s advert for Monk's.

LEFT: Three photos showing the shops occupying the site opposite Tesco, where Donnybrook Fair is today. The upper photo shows Dunne's grocery shop. Note the enamel *"Foyles' 2d Library"* sign above the entrance. The shop operated a small library in conjunction with Foyle's, the famous London bookshop, whereby customers could borrow books for 2d. Pat Flynn acquired the shop in 1975 and remodelled it as Pat's Foodmarket. After running it for 29 years, he closed the shop in December 2004. Subsequently, the premises has been redeveloped into a two storey commercial unit where Donnybrook Fair is today.

RIGHT: Photo of Flynn's Superstore on Victoria Road beside the former Ormonde cinema during a St. Patrick's Day parade in the 1980s. The shop was run by John Flynn from 1969 until 1998, following which it was redeveloped into the Rosa Apartments, named after John's wife, Rosa.

ABOVE: Staff photographed in Flynn's newly opened shop in Kilcoole in April 1973. Left to right, Eleanor Semple, John Flynn, proprietor, Kevin Flynn and Michael Doyle.

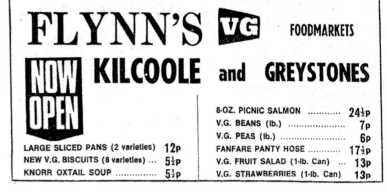

ABOVE: August 1959 advertisement.

ABOVE: April 1973 advertisement, with prices to match!

BELOW: Three generations of the Brady family, Kevin, Sean and John. The shop celebrated 50 years in the hardware business in July 2018.

ABOVE: Actors Ardal O'Hanlon and Dermot Morgan photographed outside the Ormonde cinema filming an episode of *Father Ted*.....down with this sort of thing!

BELOW RIGHT: In 1965, expensive seats were 3 shillings, with the cheap seats at 1 shilling & 6d to watch films including *Wild and Wonderful* (starring Tony Curtis), *The Chalk Garden* (starring Deborah Kerr & John Mills) and *633 Squadron* (starring Cliff Robertson).

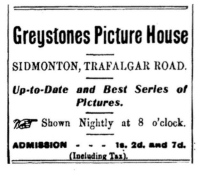

LEFT: Advertisement from *The Wicklow Newsletter* dated 22nd September 1917.

ABOVE: Photograph taken in 1947 during the construction of the Ormonde Cinema. The Morris car belonged to Mr Jones who was the electrician.

Prior to the construction of the Ormonde cinema, movies were shown at the Greystones Picture House. This was also known as Hipple's cinema and was located on Sidmonton Road, where *Harbour Court* apartments are today. Small and compact, it could accommodate around 80 movie goers, with a choice of 3 seating categories. The two rows of benches at the front comprised the cheap seats, at 2d, with the seats behind those costing 4d and the upstairs seats 1 Shilling.

ABOVE: Greystones R.F.C. and Ireland scrum half John Robbie making his test debut for the British & Irish Lions against South Africa in the 4th test on 12th July 1980. The match, played in front of 68,000 at the Loftus Versfeld Stadium in Pretoria, saw the Lions defeat the Springboks 17-13, with John Robbie becoming the first Greystones R.F.C. player to be capped by the Lions in a full test. Capped 9 times by Ireland, he made his debut as a 20 year old against Australia at Lansdowne Road in January 1976 and gained the last of his caps against Scotland at Murrayfield in March 1981. The Robbie family lived for many years in *Fernside* on Church Road, Greystones, prior to its demolition and redevelopment into commercial use close to where the Sam McCauley / Supervalu development is today.

ABOVE: Greystones R.F.C. senior team in October 1986. Back row, left to right: B. O'Connor (Chairman), J. Doyle (President), S. Dunne (Manager), N. Popplewell, J. Murphy, P. Madigan, N. Avery, R. Boyd, B. McCauley, H. Kealy, J. Boyle, S. Ryan, T. Diaper (Coach), Front row, left to right: J. O'Brien, D. O'Kelly, T. Ward, T. Doyle, H. Gallagher, S. Doyle, J. Murphy.

In 1993, Nick Popplewell followed in John Robbie's footsteps, becoming only the second Greystones R.F.C. player to date to win a full test cap with the British & Irish Lions, when he played in all three test matches on the tour to New Zealand. Also in the above photograph is Tony Ward, who earlier in 1986 as a Greystones R.F.C. player, was recalled to the Ireland team at home to Scotland. Tony Ward also played on the British & Irish Lions tour to South Africa in 1980, though he was attached to Garryowen R.F.C. at the time. His tally of 18 points in a narrow opening 26-22 test defeat to the Springboks in Cape Town set a new individual points scoring record at the time in a test match for the British & Irish Lions.

ABOVE: Greystones R.F.C. 1978 Leinster Senior Cup squad. Back row, left to right: Willow Murray (coach), Anton O'Carroll, Eddie O'Beirne, Fergus Dunphy, Pierce Power, Tim Kelly, Tom Ryan, Pat Kenny, Joe Boyle, Brian O'Neill, Robin Daly, Ken Ging (team manager), Dick Beamish (referee). Middle row, left to right: Jerome O'Brien, Jack O'Driscoll, Paul McNaughton (captain), Eric Archer (president), Simon Doyle, John Murphy. Front row, left to right: Tony Doyle, Des O'Leary, Cormac Megannety.
Eric Archer was president of the club in 1977 and 1978. At the time of his passing aged 97 in June 2017, he was the last surviving founding member of Greystones R.F.C. which was established in 1937. He was captain of the club's 2nd XV in 1939, playing on the wing and at centre.

ABOVE: Former New Zealand world cup winning coach, Graham Henry, being interviewed on the pitch at Dr. Hickey Park. In August 2016, the Leinster team held an open training session at the home of Greystones R.F.C. Henry, who coached the All Blacks to world cup victory in 2011, was working as a coaching consultant to Leinster at the time.

267

ABOVE: Donal O'Sullivan, President of Greystones Rugby Club and one of its founding members, making a speech at the opening of the club's new pavilion in 1969. Also included in the photo are Derby Kelly and players, Jackie O'Driscoll and Jack Murphy.

ABOVE: The Greystones rugby team photographed at the opening of the new pavilion in 1969. Back row, left to right includes: Pat Kerr, Jimmy O'Driscoll, Ken Spellman, Eddie O'Byrne, Jackie O'Driscoll, Eddie Russell and Colm Corcoran. Middle row, left to right includes: John Russell, Jack Murphy, Paul O'Brien, Dan Parkinson, Joe Nolan, Tony Bellew, Des Guilfoyle and Neil Keeney. Front row, seated on the ground, on the right, Tino Cassoni.

ABOVE: Greystones XV on a tour to Liverpool. Back row, left to right: Mick Dunne, Jack Murphy, Eamonn Clohessy, Ken Spellman, John Russell, Seamus Ryan, Ken Ging, John O'Gorman. Front row, left to right: Tom Lloyd, Gene Parkinson, Mick Maher, John Doyle (Captain), Stan Parkinson, Dave Noble, Bob Coffey.

ABOVE: Greystones 3rd XV 1965-66 cup semi finalists and league finalists. Back row, left to right: B. Tyrell, E. Flynn, F. Savage, J. Sweeney, D. Scullion, P. Doyle, J. Russell, B. O'Beirne, D. McAlister. Front row, left to right: M. Dunne, F. Davey, S. McCaul, R. Lynch, P. Elliott, P. Fitzgerald, B. Driver, G. Hennessy.

ABOVE: Greystones 1st XV rugby team 1946. Back row, left to right: J. Molloy, S. Hudson, J. Madden, A. Channing, M. Dempsey, P. Dooley, A. Coleman, N. Moore. Front row, left to right: D. Paul, S. O'Neill, E. Black, L. O'Brien, P. Kerr, R. Walsh, F. Keogh.

ABOVE: Greystones XV team in the early 1970s. Back row, left to right includes: Dan McAlester, Rory Murphy, Willie Dunne, Jack McGowan, Peter Doyle, Des Guilfoyle and Jack McVitty. Middle row, left to right: Jack Murphy, Kevin Byrne, Ken Ging (Captain), Tony Bellew, Aubrey Shaw and Fergus Dunphy. Front row, left to right: Paul O'Brien and Mickey Maher.

ABOVE: 1953 team photograph of St. Killian's GAA team of Blacklion. Back row, left to right: Willie Mitchell, Bro. Bolger, Jim Gregory Andy Byrne, Tom Carrigy, Jimmy O'Toole, John Byrne, Kevin O'Kelly. Front row, left to right: Matt Murphy, Jimmy O'Keefe, Jimmy Whiston, Noel Foley, David Fox, Declan Clarke, Jimmy Kelly and Willie Earls.

ABOVE: A junior St. Killian's GAA team taken in the late 1940s. Included in the group is Vincent Carroll.

CRICKET

Cricket's origins in County Wicklow date back to the 1830s, when John Henry Parnell played cricket matches on the lawns of *Avondale House*, near Rathdrum. Educated at Eton, John Henry Parnell studied at Cambridge University, for whom he played First Class cricket in 1831. Through the 1840s and 1850s, he regularly turned out for Avondale, as well for the Wicklow County Club against clubs from Carlow and Enniscorthy. His second son, the land reform agitator and leader of the Home Rule League, Charles Stewart Parnell, born in June 1846, showed a similar liking for cricket. He played regularly as a boy for Avondale and also at Cambridge during his university studies. On occasions, he captained a Wicklow XI and also represented the Dublin club, Phoenix.

In the north of the county, Bray Cricket Club was established in the early 1860s, with one of their earliest recorded matches being against a South of Wicklow XI, captained by Charles Stewart Parnell at Avondale. *The Wicklow Newsletter* dated 15th August 1863, in its report on the match noted that "*there was a large attendance of the neighbouring ladies and gentry.*" The South of Wicklow XI won by 123 runs, with the reporter highlighting Charles Stewart Parnell for "*making a splendid hit to leg for 6.*"

By the 1880s, a cricket club in Greystones had been established, with regular fixtures versus Wicklow and Delgany played where Burnaby Park is now. In the late 1890s, mixed cricket matches involving Ladies XI v Gentlemens XI, were held at *Bellevue*, the home of the La Touche family. From those early years, the game in Greystones has witnessed periods of varying popularity. Securing a ground upon which to play, proved difficult at times. In the 1940s and 1950s, cricket was played on the rugby club pitch during the summer months. From the mid 1950s, there was a resurgence of cricket in Bray, but by 1976, Bray Cricket Club had lost its ground and went out of existence. Its reincarnation as the North Wicklow Cricket Club based in Greystones in 1986, had a number of new local members, including Robin Flemming, Frank Kenny and Bobby Cross. This club played at Greystones Rugby Club and then at the nearby reserve pitch at Farrankelly, until it was sold in 1994. In 2010, North Wicklow Cricket Club merged with Avondale to form Wicklow County Cricket Club, which today plays at Presentation College, Bray. In 2011, a new Greystones Cricket Club was also formed locally, playing at Druid's Glen.

> **GREYSTONES C C V. DELGANY VISITERS.**
> This match was played on Monday, August 15th, and was won by 34 runs and 8 wickets to spare. The double figures for Greystones were Messrs E Waller 24 and 23, not out, A D Price 0 and 20, not out, H Stephens 13, and J H Pigot 12, while Messrs, Taylor and Collis for Delgany, played well for their respective scores of 17 and 20, and 21.
>
> Score :—
>
> | | 1st Inns | | 2nd Inns |
> |---|---|---|---|
> | G C C | ... 76 | ... | 58 for 2 wkt |
> | D V C C | ... 38 | ... | 64 |

ABOVE: A report from *The Dublin Daily Express* dated Wednesday 17th August 1881 on a match between Greystones and Delgany.

BELOW: 1904 photograph of Samuel H. French standing with his son, Samuel A. French at the gates of the family home, *Trippleton Cottage* on Bellevue Road, Greystones. Samuel H. French was the son of the celebrated landscape photographer, Robert French who uniquely captured images of rural Ireland in the late 19th century.

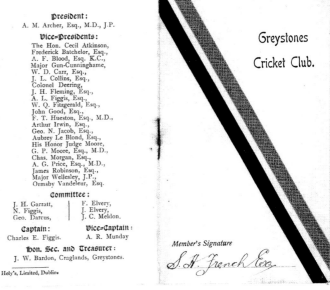

President:
A. M. Archer, Esq., M.D., J.P.

Vice-Presidents:
The Hon. Cecil Atkinson,
Frederick Batchelor, Esq.,
A. F. Blood, Esq. K.C.,
Major Gun-Cunninghame,
W. D. Carr, Esq.,
J. L. Collins, Esq.,
Colonel Deering,
J. H. Fleming, Esq.,
A. L. Figgis, Esq.,
W. Q. Fitzgerald, Esq.,
John Good, Esq.,
F. T. Hueston, Esq., M.D.,
Arthur Irwin, Esq.,
Geo. N. Jacob, Esq.,
Aubrey Le Blond, Esq.,
His Honor Judge Moore,
G. P. Moore, Esq., M.D.,
Chas. Morgan, Esq.,
A. G. Price, Esq., M.D.,
James Robinson, Esq.,
Major Wellesley, J.P.,
Ormsby Vandeleur, Esq.

Committee:

J. H. Garratt,	F. Elvery,
N. Figgis,	J. Elvery,
Geo. Darcus,	J. C. Meldon.

Captain:
Charles E. Figgis

Vice-Captain:
A. R. Munday

Hon. Sec. and Treasurer:
J. W. Bardon, Craglands, Greystones.

Hely's, Limited, Dublin.

Greystones Cricket Club.

Member's Signature
S. H. French Esq.

ABOVE RIGHT: Greystones Cricket Club member's card belonging to Samuel H. French, dated 1910. This contained the rules of the club, Rule II of which stipulated that the club colours shall be black, green and white. Rule XI noted that the subscription rates were as follows: Life Members, £5 5s & 6d, Ordinary Members, £1 & 1s, Boys U-16, 10s & 6d, Visitors for two months, 10s & 6d. The committee included 19 year old Neville Figgis, son of club captain, Charles E. Figgis. Just five years later Neville Figgis, of the 6th Battalion of the Leinster Regiment was killed in World War One on 10th August 1915 at Gallipoli, where he is buried.

ABOVE: Greystones cricket team in 1900.

ABOVE RIGHT: Greystones cricket team in 1950. Included in a team which played a Passionate Fathers selection at the rugby club were: Stan Paine, Derek Paine, Kieran Condell, Tommy Dunne, John Spurling, Billy Thompson, Alan Foster, John Mitchell, Michael Reynolds, Eddie Nichols and Jimmy Magee.

TENNIS

Acknowledgements to Paddy Dunne who wrote the following history of Greystones Tennis Club in 1993 when the club relocated from Trafalgar Road to its current location on Mill Road.

"*The origin of Greystones Lawn Tennis Club is believed to date from the end of the 19th century. Situated only a stone's throw from its new Mill Road home, the club had four grass courts located to the right of the existing rugby club pavilion, with a membership roll of 211 in 1911. During these formative years, competition would seem to have been as keen as it is today, with the club being the host of the East of Ireland Championship, later to move to the Co. Wicklow Lawn Tennis Club in Bray. Notable players included the late Shelia Buttonshaw, Ladies Champion for many years in the forties.*

For reasons unknown, the club ceased for several years, until in 1955, the existing club as we know it was founded at a meeting in St. Killian's Hall, convened by the local Garda Sergeant, Michael Spelman, with 20 members paying an annual subscription of 4 shillings. The club rented the old rugby club pavilion for changing facilities and discos at a rent of 15 shillings from May to September each year.

During the late fifties and early sixties the club grew both in membership and talent. In the summer of 1963, the late Mrs Keefe donated a field which she owned at Trafalgar Road to the local parish priest, Very Rev. J. Fennelly P.P. "for the good of the parish." With the assistance of Bord Fáilte, the La Touche Hotel and Wicklow County Council, a clubhouse, two grass and three hard courts were constructed in 1964 and opened on 8th August 1965".

ABOVE: Ground levelling work being undertaken in 1964 to prepare the laying of the two grass and three hard tennis courts. Photograph of the reception held in the La Touche Hotel in April 1976 for the opening of the floodlit courts. Left to right: James Davy (Director of the La Touche Hotel), Geraldine Davy, who cut the tape, Kevin Menton, No.1 ranked player in Ireland at the time, Jo Donnelly, Secretary of the club and Paddy Dunne, Chairman of the club. Colour photo shows an aerial view of the courts in 1987.

"*Various developments took place over the following years which included the re-surfacing of and installation of the floodlit all-weather court and practice wall in 1976, extension to the clubhouse in 1979 and re-surfacing and floodlighting five all weather courts in 1982. The club held its first Open Tournament, the Hardcourt Championships of South Leinster over a week in May 1966 and subsequently changed the format in 1979 to the current very popular Whit weekend event that it is today. Such was its popularity and success that it is now included in the Irish list of Grand Prix Tournaments.*

On the tennis front, Greystones Lawn Tennis Club can be very proud of its achievements which included wins in the Provincial Towns Cup Competition in 1967 and 1974. In the Summer Leagues, there were wins for the men in Class IV in 1969 (38 teams) and Class II in 1986 (24 teams). Nine members have achieved international honours at various age levels, David Nolan, Nicky Malone, Paul Donnelly, Colm Og Molloy, Bernadette Davy, Conor Woods, Garbhain O'Nuallain, Tom Hamilton and Laura McCracken. However, the growth in membership and town population brought its own problems. With a total of five courts, a small pavilion and a land-locked site, accommodation difficulties arose. Over the past five years, development committees explored many options and possible sites to eliminate the problem. The club members finally agreed to the sale of a portion of the Trafalgar road premises and a mutually beneficial exchange of the balance with Wicklow County Council for a 4 acre site on the Mill Road.

With nine floodlit courts and views of four other sporting clubs from the lounge of the magnificent new clubhouse, the 240 family, 140 senior and 180 junior members today can enjoy their tennis and social functions. Thanks to the hard working development committee comprising Mary Cahill, Tim Cahill, Cathal Cooney, David Doyle, Art Grimes, Ken McAvoy, Susan McNamara and Chris O'Reilly. On 3rd April 1993, the next step in the history of Greystones Tennis Club will be taken with the official opening of the new facilities by the club President, Mr Declan Power. From an annual rent of 75p to a total development cost of approximately £650,000, the club has come a long way to this historic day".

LEFT: Peter Bateman hitting a backhand volley in the late 1960s, with Enright Doyle in the background about to serve. Enright Doyle was the owner of Stanley Stores on Church Road, where Fenton Fires is today. *Emily House* at the corner of the turnpike and Trafalgar Road is also visible in the background.

RIGHT: Group including Patricia Bateman, Eileen Herlihy, Anne Marie Hanna and Mary O'Sullivan sitting outside the clubhouse on Trafalgar road.

LEFT: The field opposite the La Touche Hotel donated by Mrs Keefe, upon which Greystones Tennis Club relocated in 1965. The nets of the two grass courts belonging to the hotel are visible in the top right of the photo.

RIGHT: View from the upper floor of the La Touche Hotel in January 1990 showing the courts, clubhouse and the practice wall at the far end of the lawn.

ABOVE Greystones Lawn Tennis Club Committee in 1905: Harold Price, Captain Jeffreys, Colonel D'Oyley Battley, G. Bradley and H.R. Maunsell. Colonel Battley lived at *Belvedere Hall,* Windgates (now the SEK International Spanish School). He also served as President of Greystones Golf Club from 1900 until his death in 1924.

ABOVE: Liam Byrne, Sheila O'Neill, Carmel Gaffney and Desmond Fogarty at Greystones Lawn Tennis Club in 1936, when it was located beside the rugby club. Liam Byrne served with the Greystones Civic Association for a number of years and was a prominent local businessman. He owned The Burnaby and The Beach House pubs.

GREYSTONES LAWN TENNIS CLUB

Official Opening
of the

CLUBHOUSE AND GROUNDS

at Mill Road, Killincarrig, Greystones
on
Saturday 3rd April 1993

at 2.00 pm
by
Club President *Mr Declan Power*

ABOVE & RIGHT: Construction of the new clubhouse in August 1992 and the programme cover for its opening the following April.

ABOVE LEFT & OPPOSITE PAGE: Playing the 18th hole at Greystones Golf Club. Note the absence of mature trees in The Burnaby, contrasting with the large wooded area around *Killincarrick House* (later appropriately known as the Woodlands Hotel). The large detached house in the foreground above is *The Shrubbery*. To the right of it is *Kilcoursey* and to its right, in the photograph on the top of the facing page is *Corofin*. Note the sheep grazing on the course, a practice that continued up until July 1962.

On 26th January 1895, a meeting was held at the Grand Hotel in Greystones at which it was decided to form a golf club to be known as Greystones Golf Club. During the previous 12 months, the Grand Hotel Company had acquired, through an agreement with the trustees of The Burnaby Estate, certain rights by which guests of the hotel could play golf on the ground surrounding Jones' Hill. By the middle of March 1895 *The Irish Times* reported that the club had been formed with around 100 original members. Its first President was the Right Hon. Viscount Powerscourt, with Arthur Hughes of *St. David's*, Marine Road, Greystones its first Hon. Secretary.

On Saturday 8th June 1895, the then 9 hole golf course, was formally opened. On that day, two handicap competitions were held, one for members of any recognised golf club, the other for the members of the Greystones club only. Over the following two decades, the course gained in popularity amongst both members and visitors, the latter due in part to its association with the Grand Hotel. Consideration was given to a proposal to acquire additional land to expand the course to 18 holes.

ABOVE: View from Jones' Hill on Greystones Golf Course in February 1947. When blanketed in deep snow, the golf course has doubled as a popular place for locals to toboggan down, most notably in 1982 and in March 2018.

The additional 9 holes were laid out by Tom Walker, the club professional and renowned maker of golf clubs, who went on to found Walker's Garage on Church Road. The new 18 hole course was opened on Tuesday 2nd June 1914. The outbreak of World War One however, heralded tough times for the club, with all competitions postponed until further notice. Against the backdrop of a substantial fall in revenue the new 9 holes, opened just two years earlier, were closed in 1916, with the course reverting to its original 9 hole layout until 1920. Since those early days the club has experienced ups and downs but has always pulled through.

ABOVE: A slightly later photograph showing the roof tops of the houses in The Burnaby protruding above the trees.

ABOVE: *Killincarrig Farm House* in around 1924.

ABOVE: *Killincarrig Farm House* prior to its redevelopment.

LEFT: Postcard sent in July 1913. The reverse of the card reveals that it was published by the Grand Hotel, Greystones, with whom the golf club maintained very close links right from its inception. The photo shows the original clubhouse built by Roger Harpur in 1896, which overlooked the 18th green. The photograph also shows the extensions carried out in 1904 (ground floor extension on the west side) and 1909 (smoking room, secretary's office and balcony on the south side with open stairs). On 13th September 1988, a fire gutted the first floor and roof of the old clubhouse, with the remainder badly water damaged.

Undeterred, members arranged for portakabins to be used for temporary bar, kitchen and office accommodation. Three weeks after the fire, plans were displayed for a new clubhouse to be relocated on the site of *Killincarrig Farm House*, also known as *Killincarrig Manor*. In 1984 Greystones Golf Club acquired the property, which had been the home of the Hawkins-Whitshed family prior to them building their new family home, later to become the Woodlands Hotel. Permission to demolish *Killincarrig Farm House* had been refused by An Bord Pleanála in December 1986 and again in August 1988. During 1989 a number of EGMs were held by Greystones Golf Club, culminating in the passing of a motion to construct the new clubhouse incorporating the facade of *Killincarrig Farm House*. An Bord Pleanála granted planning permission in November 1990 and construction work commenced the following month. In October 1991, the new clubhouse was handed over to Greystones Golf Club.

ABOVE: Retention of the Georgian facade of *Killincarrig Farm House* in January 1991.

ABOVE: The new ivy-clad clubhouse photographed in 2002.

ABOVE: Harry Bradshaw.

In 2015, Greystones Golf Club was thrust into the spotlight of the world's sporting media when club member, Paul Dunne, shared the lead after three rounds of the 144th Open Championship. He was the first amateur since 1927 to achieve such a feat. A final round of 78 saw him saw him eventually tie for 30th place. This was the second occasion that a local golfer has come close to capturing the Open Championship. Delgany's Harry Bradshaw, after suffering the misfortune of his ball landing in a broken beer bottle during his 2nd round, famously lost to Bobby Locke in a play off at the 1949 Open.

ABOVE: Paul Dunne talking to the press at the 2015 Open Championship at St. Andrews in Scotland. He gained his first professional tour win at the British Masters in October 2017.

ABOVE: British Prime Minister, David Lloyd George (left) and James H. Campbell, who, as 1st Baron Glenavy, served as President of Greystones Golf Club between 1925 and 1931. His eldest son, Gordon Campbell (who succeeded his father as 2nd Baron Glenavy), served as President of Greystones Golf Club between 1931 and 1950.

ABOVE: A postcard written by a previous resident of the *The Gables*, on Whitshed Road in The Burnaby in 1903. In 1915, James H. Campbell, a former Solicitor General and Attorney General for Ireland, rented the house. In May of that year he wrote the letter on the left to future British Prime Minister, David Lloyd George, in which he invited him to come and stay and play golf at Greystones Golf Club.

The letter was written just two days after Lloyd George was appointed Minister of Munitions, following seven years as Chancellor of the Exchequer in Asquith's government. James H. Campbell wrote *"My Dear Lloyd George, I imagine your new mission may bring you over soon to this distressful country, where in the absence of a Chief Secretary and Lord Lieutenant, I am running the civil side of the show. If so, I would be very glad to put you up as I have taken a very nice house at Greystones, Co. Wicklow, about 16 miles from Dublin, with frequent trains in and out and in emergency, I can always requisition a motor. I have a golf links in front of my door and another excellent links about a mile off, so if you bring your clubs, you may get a chance to use them. I have plenty of spare rooms."*

It is not known whether David Lloyd George took up the above offer. In December 1916 Lloyd George became Prime Minister, serving until October 1922, when he was succeeded by Andrew Bonar Law. The photograph on the left was taken at Greystones Golf Club in 1914 and shows Andrew Bonar Law watched by James Campbell. At the time Bonar Law was Leader of the Opposition in Westminster, though he became Colonial Secretary in May the following year, when a coalition government was formed.

James H. Campbell and Andrew Bonar Law were close acquaintances and corresponded regularly during 1915, as evidenced by the letter reproduced on the following page. Born in 1851, Campbell was admitted as a Member of the Irish Bar in 1873 and rose to become Solicitor General and subsequently Attorney General for Ireland. In December 1916 he was appointed Lord Chief Justice of Ireland and two years later he became Lord Chancellor of Ireland, a role he held until October 1921, when King George V conferred on him the title Baron Glenavy of Milltown. The following month, as Lord Glenavy, he took his seat in the House of Lords. He served as the Chairman of the first Irish Senate from 1922 until 1928. His second son, Cecil, served as a major in the Royal Army Service Corp during World War One. He was a talented tennis player, reaching the Wimbledon Men's Singles quarter finals in 1921, 1922 and 1923. His grandson, Patrick Campbell was a captain, opposite Frank Muir, on the popular BBC programme, *Call My Bluff* during the 1970s.

ABOVE: Future British Prime Minister, Andrew Bonar Law playing at Greystones in 1914, watched by James. H. Campbell.

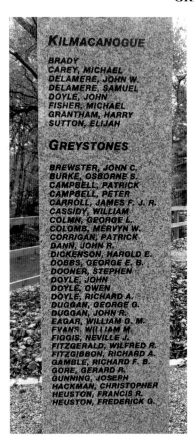

KILMACANOGUE

BRADY
CAREY, MICHAEL
DELAMERE, JOHN W.
DELAMERE, SAMUEL
DOYLE, JOHN
FISHER, MICHAEL
GRANTHAM, HARRY
SUTTON, ELIJAH

GREYSTONES

BREWSTER, JOHN C.
BURKE, OSBORNE S.
CAMPBELL, PATRICK
CAMPBELL, PETER
CARROLL, JAMES F. J. R.
CASSIDY, WILLIAM
COLMN, GEORGE L.
COLOMB, MERVYN W.
CORRIGAN, PATRICK
DANN, JOHN R.
DICKENSON, HAROLD E.
DOBBS, GEORGE E. B.
DOONER, STEPHEN
DOYLE, JOHN
DOYLE, OWEN
DOYLE, RICHARD A.
DUGGAN, GEORGE G.
DUGGAN, JOHN R.
EAGAR, WILLIAM G. M.
EVANS, WILLIAM W.
FIGGIS, NEVILLE J.
FITZGERALD, WILFRED R.
FITZGIBBON, RICHARD A.
GAMBLE, RICHARD F. B.
GORE, GERARD R.
GUNNING, JOSEPH
HACKMAN, CHRISTOPHER
HEUSTON, FRANCIS R.
HEUSTON, FREDERICK G.

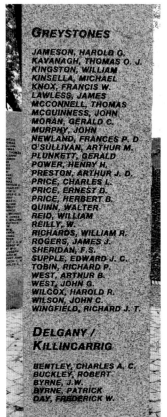

GREYSTONES

JAMESON, HAROLD G.
KAVANAGH, THOMAS O. J.
KINGSTON, WILLIAM
KINSELLA, MICHAEL
KNOX, FRANCIS W.
LAWLESS, JAMES
MCCONNELL, THOMAS
MCGUINNESS, JOHN
MORAN, GERALD C.
MURPHY, JOHN
NEWLAND, FRANCES P. D
O'SULLIVAN, ARTHUR M.
PLUNKETT, GERALD
POWER, HENRY H.
PRESTON, ARTHUR J. D.
PRICE, CHARLES L.
PRICE, ERNEST D.
PRICE, HERBERT B.
QUINN, WALTER
REID, WILLIAM
REILLY, W.
RICHARDS, WILLIAM R.
ROGERS, JAMES J.
SHERIDAN, F.S.
SUPPLE, EDWARD J. C.
TOBIN, RICHARD P.
WEST, ARTHUR B.
WEST, JOHN G.
WILCOX, HAROLD R.
WILSON, JOHN C.
WINGFIELD, RICHARD J. T.

DELGANY /
KILLINCARRIG

BENTLEY, CHARLES A. C.
BUCKLEY, ROBERT
BYRNE, J.W.
BYRNE, PATRICK
DAY, FREDERICK W.

ABOVE: In September 2014, a memorial garden at Woodenbridge was opened honouring the 1,192 men from Co. Wicklow killed in World War One. Inscribed on the two granite columns shown are the names of the 60 men with Greystones connections.

ABOVE: The above photo shows two pages from a ten page letter dated 1st September 1915, written by James H. Campbell to the then Minister for Munitions (and future British Prime Minister) Andrew Bonar Law. Whilst the bulk of the letter relates to political affairs in Ireland, the left-hand page is quite sobering. Campbell writes *"this place Greystones is like a cemetery, as within the last fortnight six young residents who had commissions in the 10th Division were killed in the Dardanelles"*. Also on the left-hand page, Campbell mentions his own son, writing that *"poor Phil has been fighting continuously in the trenches at the Dardanelles since he returned there after his wound in May last."* He also asks Bonar Law about his own sons *"has either Jim or Charlie been [sent to the front yet?]."* By 21st September 1917, all three had been killed in the war. On 13th November 1916 Philip Campbell, by then a Lieutenant Commander in the Drake Battalion of the Royal Naval Division, was killed in action, only a fortnight after being mentioned in despatches for *"very distinguished services."* The following year, on 19th April 1917, Charles Bonar Law, a Lieutenant in the 3rd King's own Scottish Borderers, was killed aged 20 years and 2 months at the Battle of Gaza in Egypt. On 21st September 1917 his brother, Jim Bonar Law, who had joined the Flying Corps and was a member of a fighter squadron, was shot down and killed.

Details of 7 Greystones men killed at Gallipoli in August 1915			
Name	Regiment	Date of Death / Age / Burial / Memorial	Additional Information
Lieut. Neville J. Figgis	6th Battalion, Leinster Regiment.	10th August 1915 / 23 years old / Embarkation Pier Cemetery, Gallipoli Peninsula.	Son of Charles & Augusta Figgis of *Ingle Field*, Whitshed Road, Greystones.
Capt. & Adjutant William R. Richards	6th Battalion, Royal Dublin Fusiliers.	15th August 1915 / 24 years old / Green Hill Cemetery, Suvla Bay, Gallipoli Peninsula.	Son of John W. Richards, J.P., of *Rath* on St. Vincent's Road, Greystones.
Capt. Arthur J.D. Preston	6th Battalion, Royal Dublin Fusiliers.	15th August 1915 / 29 years old / Azmak Cemetery, Suvla Bay, Gallipoli Peninsula.	Husband of Sylvia W. Preston of *Cronbryn*, Kinlen Road, Greystones.
2nd Lieut. Frederick G. Heuston	6th Battalion, Royal Irish Fusiliers.	15th August 1915 / 22 years old / Helles Memorial, Sedd El Bahr, Gallipoli Peninsula.	Son of Dr. Francis T. Heuston and Frances L. Heuston of *St David's*, Marine Road, Greystones.
Capt. George G. Duggan	5th Battalion, Royal Irish Fusiliers.	16th August 1915 / 29 years old / Helles Memorial, Sedd El Bahr, Gallipoli Peninsula.	Son of George & Emilie Duggan of *Ferney East* (later, merged along with *Ferney West* to create Carrig Eden), Marine Road, Greystones.
Lieut. John R. Duggan	5th Battalion, Royal Irish Regiment.	16th August 1915 / 20 years old / Azmak Cemetery, Suvla Bay, Gallipoli Peninsula.	Son of George & Emilie Duggan of *Ferney East* (later merged along with *Ferney West* to create Carrig Eden),Marine Road, Greystones.
Capt. William G.M. Eagar	3rd Battalion, attached to 1st Battalion, Royal Munster Fusiliers.	21st August 1915 / 23 years old / Helles Memorial, Sedd El Bahr, Gallipoli Peninsula.	Son of William Eagar & Ida Eagar, later of *Iveragh*, Church Road, Greystones.

Sources: Website of the Commonwealth War Graves Commission, Thom's Directory and the British Newspaper Archive.

Another name of interest on the memorial at Woodenbridge is that of Private John R. Dann, 113th Company of the Machine Gun Corps (Infantry). The nephew of William H. Dann, who in 1907 bought what is now The Beach House, Private John R. Dann was killed on 31st July 1917 aged 23. He is remembered on the Menin Gate Memorial at Ypres.

The son of John and Catherine Kinsella, Michael Kinsella was born on 29th May 1880 in the gate lodge to Fox's farm (now replaced by a bungalow) opposite Redford Cemetery. His name is commemorated on the memorial to the Wicklow war dead at Woodenbridge and also on the memorial plaque in Bray, next to the Carlisle football ground.

He was a brother of John "Blacktop" Kinsella, a stalwart of Greystones rowing in the 1920s. His sister, Catherine married John McKenzie, who went on to run the newsagent and confectionery shop at No.2 Trafalgar Road. His grand-nephew, Billy Hayden, who lived for a time with his grandfather, John McKenzie, in the 1940s recalls that the photograph on the right was always in a frame on the mantelpiece in the living quarters to the rear of the shop.

ABOVE: Memorial to the dead of World War One in Bray, which includes the name of Private Michael Kinsella.

ABOVE Private Michael Kinsella, along with 1,125 other soldiers is buried in Harlebeke cemetery in West Flanders.

ABOVE: Private Michael Kinsella, 2nd Battalion, Irish Guards, was killed at the Battle of Passchendaele (also known as the 3rd Battle of Ypres) on 13th September 1917. He was 37 years of age.

BELOW: John McKenzie, together with his brother-in-law, started a coal distribution business, McKenzie & Kinsella, which had a coalyard in Greystones and also at Blacklion. Later on the business traded as Kinsella Coal Merchants.

ABOVE: Anne Hayden (nee McKenzie), niece of Private Michael Kinsella, photographed with her husband, Jim Hayden in 1932 in front of her father's shop at No.2, Trafalgar Road, Greystones. Jim and Anne Hayden were the parents of Billy, Jago, John, Kathleen, Eileen and Declan.

ABOVE: Photograph of Bernard Martin in the Vandeleur family car on the driveway of *Windgate House* on the slopes of Bray Head. He had been employed as the family's driver for three years at the time of the outbreak of World War One. He served with the Royal Irish Fusiliers at Gallipoli in August 1915 and later served in Bulgaria, where he was awarded the Military Medal *"for his leadership in a successful attack on Bulgarian trenches at Agamar on the river Struma and later defending an advanced post"*. By coincidence, he won this award on St. Patrick's Day 1917. He subsequently saw action in Southern Palestine, where he was severely wounded, losing his eyesight in 1917 near Gaza when his position was pounded by Turkish howitzers.

Originally from Trim in Co. Meath, Bernard Martin was employed as the chauffeur to Cecil Vandeleur who lived at *Windgate House* in 1914. He died in June 1978, but a few years earlier he was persuaded to write his experiences of the war. During his recuperation and treatment at St Dunstans, the hostel established in Regent's Park, London, to help service men blinded during the war, he learned to read braille and type in both braille and standard typeface. His memoir covered 22 foolscap pages and he commenced his story as follows:

```
                          1.
I, Bernard Martin. still remember the outbreak of the 1st War. Aug. 4th
1914. It was not altogether unexpected, because very many of us knew
that Germany was preparing for War from the time of Bismarck.. In
1910, they had an army of five million men. The first fortress to fall
was Liege, with the loss of over 1,000. men At this time I was a motor
driver with a Mr. Vandeleur, who lived at Windgate House. just across
Windgate's hill, and about half way between Bray, and Greystones. I
was then known as a Chaffeur. I rember going to Dublin with my boss
about the 27th. of August, and stopped somewhere in Grafton St. He went
away for some time, and when he returned. I knew from his changed appear-
ance that there was something badly wrong. He told me that the fortress
of Namur had fallen that the Germans would be here in a fortnight. to
put the car up at the automobile Club in Dawson St, and that he would mee
meet me there at 5.p.m.   I went to the recruiting Office in Brunswick
St. nearly opposite the old Queen's Theatre, and joined up. They wanted
me to join the motor transport. as I was in uniform, but I only wanted
a gun to stop them landing here, and joined my father's old Regiment.,
the Royal Irish Fusiliers It meant giving up a six shillings per day
job for one shilling a day. It was a sacrafice, but we all knew
that England's defeat would be ours as well I bade my boss good bye
next morning, and proceeded to Brunswick St, received there one day's pey
1/9-, and was told to be at Amien's St. tation at 2.40. p.m. There
were quite a number of men waiting there, and an army Sgt. came
along, gave us our tickets, and saw us on to the train for Armagh.
We arrived there about 5.30.p.m. answered our names in the guard room
and shown our sleeping quarters that night. The following aafternoon
we were issued out with a khaki uniform, equipment, and rifle. Later
we dressed in our new uniform, and were shown how to put our equipment
together. Although the War at that time was only a few weeks old. I
noticed women at their doors, and on the streets of Armagh crying, and
people around trying to comfort them After a rew days. we went back
```

Initially stationed at Portobello Barracks near Rathmines, Bernard Martin underwent army training which included a firing course on Dollymount Strand, trench digging near the Grand Canal and regular route marches. Ironically, one of these involved a stopover at Belmont, on the back road at Windgates. On 25th April 1915, his battalion departed Dublin, spending the next two months training in Basingstoke, before sailing from Devonport on 13th July 1915, bound for Suvla Bay, on the Aegean coast of the Gallipoli peninsula. In his memoir, Bernard Martin recalled *"we moved along the west coast of Gallipoli that night and clearly heard the artillery and the sound of bursting shells as we went along. We arrived at Suvla Bay about dawn and immediately rafts or lighters were thrown out to row us to the land..... we would dash forward for about 25 yards, drop down for about 10 seconds and then forward again another 25 yards and down again. The rifle and shell fire were heavy and we were losing men, but we persevered and at about 6pm that evening, had reached and captured the ridge of Chocolate Hill.....every Turkish sniper was allotted a certain piece of*

LEFT: Sgt. Bernard Martin standing to the right of nine men of his battalion in Bulgaria.

ground to watch, so that you got out of the trench at the peril of your life. I remember asking a couple of men to take half a dozen water bottles and bring back some water. Nobody would go. I was in a bad way with thirst and there was nothing for it but go it alone. I had a good idea where there was a well. I made a dive out of the trench. The sniper was on me alright, but he didn't get me.....I continued like this until I got to the well and crawled around until I found some form of cover from the sniper's bullets. It was a horrible sight, there were dead and dying men lying everywhere.....they were in such a state that they risked death to quench it. Anyway, I got 2 bottles of water & zig-zagged my way back, followed all the time by the sniper. I got back to the trench." He recalled that *"in the day time in Gallipoli, it was a burning sun that shone down from a cloudless sky. If you got a bright piece of metal and brought the rays of the sun to bear on it, the heat was so great that you could light a cigarette by touching it with the metal".*

Subsequent to this, Bernard Martin sustained a shrapnel wound to his back and was evacuated to a hospital ship in the harbour to have the piece extracted. From there he rejoined his regiment to the right of Chocolate Hill at Sari Bair, Gallipoli, *"we never advanced a yard from these positions, we had only 2 officers left in the battalion and 1 full rank N.C.O. in our company, the rest were either killed or wounded......our task was to hang on to our positions, to bluff the Turks that we had a lot of troops there."* In October 1915, Bulgaria declared war on the allies and Bernard Martin and his regiment were moved from Gallipoli, landing at Salonika in Greece. After completing an instruction course in the handling and use of hand grenades, he was given the rank of Acting Sergeant and put in charge of the bomb throwers. Ironically the officer in charge was Lieutenant Douglas Figgis, from Greystones, later promoted to Captain. Both men later met up at regimental reunions in Dublin after the war. During the summer of 1916, Bernard Martin and his regiment advanced north to the river Struma in Bulgaria where Bulgarian forces were stationed on its northern bank. In September 1916, he was part of a reconnaissance force that crossed the river to gauge the strength of the Bulgarian positions. There followed a number of counter offences between the Bulgarian forces and the allied forces and in one of these, Sergeant Martin and his regiment *"charged into their trenches and captured about 200 men without a shot being fired."* The Bulgarian army retreated back beyond Kalendra church.

Throughout the winter of 1916, the allies probed the Bulgarian positions. At the end of February 1917, Bernard Martin *"was moved to the outpost position at Kalendra Wood and I was included with Lieutenant Harris, Lieutenant Fitzgerald and Sergeant Atkins and 40 men to take over Kalendra Church. It was the extreme outpost position and our orders were to stay there to the last and no surrender under any circumstances or conditions."* From the church tower, Bernard Martin could observe the Bulgarian forces who regularly approached as far as the barbed wire, on occasions engaging them in gun fire. *"I remember the 17th March 1917, the morning started very peaceful until about 11am until we heard heavy shell fire from the direction of Kavala."* This continued until about 4pm. Bernard Martin assumed command when the N.C.O. in charge, Sergeant Atkins, became ill with shell shock. A number of men were killed at the southern end of the church which suffered heavy shelling. The following day, a message was received *"from H.Q., promising immediate relief if we so desired. Our wish was to stay where we were and that wish was granted. We remained at the church post until the end of March, sending out patrols every night into no-man's land and keeping a sharp look out by day from the church tower......out of a force of 50 men at Kalendra Church, we lost 21, all killed."* Two months later in May 1917 at Wessex Bridge on the river Struma, General George Milne, Commander-in-Chief of the British Salonika Army pinned the ribbon of the Miltary Medal onto the left breast of Sergeant Bernard Martin. *"It was in connection with the action at Church Post, Kalendra. They were all good men that day, a day I shall always remember. The shell fire was fierce and demoralising, but they stood up to it all magnificently."*

In September 1917, Bernard Martin's regiment moved from Salonika to Alexandria in Egypt and within a few weeks had moved into position between Gaza and Beersheeba. In his typed memoir, he recalled *"About one in the afternoon, our artillery came*

ABOVE: Though he had previously received his medal ribbon only from General Milne, on a parade in a field in Bulgaria in May 1917, Sergeant Bernard Martin, 5th Battalion, Royal Irish Fusiliers, formally received his Military Medal at a ceremony in the grounds of St. Dunstan's in Regent's Park, London in June 1919. Gertrude Vandeleur travelled from Windgates to London to attend the award ceremony and mentioned that she was Bernard Martin's "aunt", so she was allowed to stand immediately behind his chair. The photograph above was published at the time in *The Daily Mail* and had a caption which read *"Major-General Fielding presenting the Military Medal to Bernard Martin".*

along at the gallop, loosened the horses and dragged the guns into position in the river bed. This work was carried out at lightening speed and then the guns went into action. Away in the distance, probably about 3 miles away we could see the shells burst and columns of sand pitched high into the air. It looked at times as if the whole desert was going up into the sky, so fierce was the bombardment................when we had advanced about half a mile, the Turkish artillery opened up. They must have been long range howitzers, as the shells seemed to come straight down from the sky and burst with a deafening noise. We had only advanced about a mile when I got hit. I remember going down and I made several attempts to get off the ground, but was unable to do so. I did not know what had happened to me. Then I heard someone shout an act of contrition into my ear. Still I didn't know what had happened, nor where I was. Later I knew that I was being brought somewhere on a camel. Each camel carried 2 men, 1 balancing the other. As the camel moved forward, the stretcher swayed a lot and I was in pain". After several weeks in hospital in Alexandria, Sergeant Bernard Martin went by ship to Marseilles. He spent Christmas Day at sea, before being accompanied on a train to La Harve and onward conveyance to the Royal Victoria Hospital near Southampton, where he remained until 1st March 1918. *"I wrote home to my mother and to my girlfriend. I told her about my condition and that I didn't think it would be wise for us to get married under these circumstances. I had a reply to this letter to say that my condition would make no difference and as long as we loved each other, that was all that mattered.*" He was then moved to St. Dunstan's, the hostel for blind soldiers and sailors in Regent's Park, London. Importantly it was here that, in addition to learning braille, he also learned the skills of basket weaving (for laundry baskets, etc.) and how to make string bags. This would be his post war occupation, supplementing his war pension. His mother visited him in April 1918 and accompanied him on a visit back to Ireland, arriving into Dublin on 25th April 1918, three years to the day since he had departed with his regiment. He stayed as a guest of the Vandeleur family at *Windgate House*, sleeping in his old room until he married Christina Cooling, who lived at the top of Windgates, "*the girl he left behind*", in Greystones on 13th May 1918. Following their wedding, they returned to London, where Bernard Martin continued his programme of convalescence at St. Dunstan's before they settled in Bray in September 1919. Their son, Dick Martin, recalled that his father became good friends with Father Francis Gleeson, the well-known chaplain to the Munster Fusiliers during World War One. He would always arrive early at Mass so he could chat and reminisce with Father Gleeson about their experiences during the war. Bernard Martin's 22 page memoir concluded with a note about Lieutenant Douglas Figgis from Greystones, his old officer in charge, when in Greece. "*I met him 4 times at regimental reunions in Dublin. He told me that in his experience the fiercest and bloodiest combat was the one at Jefferson's Ridge on 16th August 1915. He died in December 1970, but I did not know about this until three months later, nor did I know where he was buried. One summer afternoon in 1972, I went with my wife and son to a churchyard in Enniskerry........my wife was a native of Bray and the names on many of the tombstones brought back to her memories of the past........we came to the grave of Captain Figgis. The following was written on his tombstone. Douglas Figgis, born August 1894, died December 1970, nothing more. My eldest son laid a poppy wreath on his grave last armistice, 1975, with a note attached: From One Who Remembers.*"

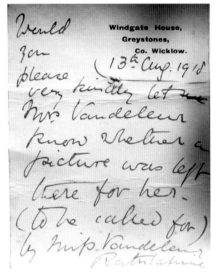

ABOVE: *Windgate House* in better times.

ABOVE: *Windgate House* in its derelict state in March 2017. Originally built by the Morris family of Windgates in the mid 19th century, this large house, on the slopes of Bray Head, with its commanding views over Greystones and south to Wicklow Head, also included a stables and two coach houses. The house was occupied by Cecil Vandeleur, a Land Agent and his wife, Gertrude and three staff per the 1911 census.

ABOVE: A letter on *Windgate House* headed note paper written in 1918. Ormsby Vandeleur and his wife Georgina lived at *Rathlahine* on Church Lane, Greystones and were related to Cecil Vandeleur and his wife Gertrude who resided at *Windgate House*.

The minute book for the Greystones Improvement Association notes that Ormsby Vandeleur took an active interest in Greystones, chairing a meeting at the Grand Hotel in February 1907 to discuss the deteriorating state of the harbour. A General Sir John Ormsby Vandeleur (1763-1849), who was the son of Richard and Elinor Vandeleur of Co. Laois commanded the British cavalry at the Battle of Waterloo in 1815. Members of the Vandeleur family are buried in Redford cemetery at The Grove. *The Freeman's Journal* dated 5th September 1917 contained an advertisement placed by Cecil Vandeleur seeking applications for the position of Matron for the Auxiliary Hospital in Bray for Irish soldiers who had lost their limbs in the war. The post carried an annual salary of £150 and applications were to be sent to Cecil Vandeleur, Hon. Sec., *Windgate House*, Greystones. Aware of the devastating impact of the war on his former driver, Bernard Martin, Cecil Vandeleur was active in raising funds locally for St. Dunstan's, which had greatly helped Bernard Martin in his recovery.

ABOVE: Ticket for a fundraising event in Delgany organised by Cecil Vandeleur.

RIGHT: Private John Cooling, originally from the top of Windgates, brother of Christina Cooling who married Sgt. Bernard Martin. John Cooling emigrated to Australia in 1910 aged 19 and joined the Australian army as a member of the Expeditionary Force, enlisting in Randwick New South Wales. Photographed in the uniform of the 2nd Battalion, Australian Infantry, he was severely wounded at the historic landing at the Dardanelles on 26th April 1915 and later killed in the Gallipoli landing. The record of his death in the Australian Military Archives reads: "*Cooling, Pte. John 379 2nd Battalion, Australian Infantry, killed in action, 6th / 9th August 1915. Age 24. Native of Windgate, Bray, Co. Wicklow, Ireland. Son of John and Sarah Cooling.*" Private John Cooling, 2nd Battalion, B Company, Australian Infantry is buried in Lone Pine Cemetery, Gallipoli.

Aug. 12.	1 Pkt. Steel wool.	1	6.
	2 Prs. T. Hinges.	5	6.
	28 Screws.		11.
	1 lb 3" nails	1	1.

ABOVE RIGHT & LEFT: Allen "Allie" Evans in uniform and in civvies, standing on the railway bridge beside the shop known as The Bridge Stores and more latterly during its history as Evans Hardware. He established the business in 1917 following his return home to Greystones after being severely wounded at the Battle of the Somme in July 1916. He ran the business until the late 1960s, when his nephew, Charlie Evans took it over.

BELOW: Clifford Evans standing in front of the shop established by his great-uncle, Allie Evans, prior to its closure.

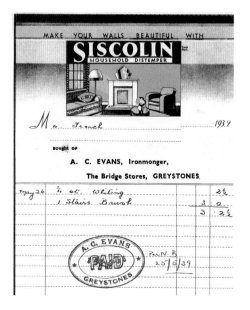

ABOVE: Helene Orme with her sister Yvonne on her lap and the family dog with friends in Greystones harbour in 1933.

ABOVE: Yvonne Orme with the family dog in Greystones harbour in 1933. Note the effort involved in floating the clinker built boat in the silted up harbour at low tide.

ABOVE: Cyril Orme, in the uniform of the Royal Army Medical Corp (RAMC) indicated by the medical cross on his sleeve.

Cyril Orme enlisted in September 1914. He was sent to France with the RAMC soon after and quickly became proficient in French, working as an interpretor for his superior officer. He was initially posted to the Pas de Calais area of northern France and was billeted in a house in the village of Marles sur Canche. There he met one of the daughters of the house, Brigitte Emilie Renne Andrieux, and after a whirlwind romance they married. Their first child, Gilbert, was born in 1916 in Marles sur Canche. One of Brigitte's names was Renne, which is the French for Queen and Cyril always referred to her as "*Queenie.*" During his time in France he saw action on or close to the front line and sustained shrapnel injuries. Although his family knew of his time in the army and had seen photos and his medals, he was always reluctant to speak of the four years he had spent during World War One. One can only surmise what he must have witnessed as a member of the RAMC during that time.

He remained in the army in France until 1919 when he was demobilised, residing at Marles sur Canche, where his second child, Helene, was born. The family then moved to Wasquehal, just outside Lille, where their next two children, Maud and Cyril, were born. They remained there for nine years, coming to Ireland in 1928 and settling in Greystones. They lived in *Hawthorn Cottage* on Trafalgar Road, opposite the Grand Hotel until about 1938. Their fifth and last child, Yvonne, was born there in 1928. The Orme children, three of whom are in the school photo on page 208, described an idyllic childhood in Greystones - summers spent swimming with "the harbour crowd." They were particularly friendly with members of the Evans, Fanning, Ryan and Ferns families. Initially they were seen as quite a novelty, as the children and their mother spoke no English when they first arrived. They soon settled into the community and Cyril became great friends with the local Parish Priest with whom he went fishing on many occasions. Cyril Orme later ran a paint suppliers in Dublin until his retirement in the 1960s. He died in 1970.

LEFT: On first glance an ordinary envelope addressed to the family living at 4 Sidmonton Place, Greystones, Co. Wicklow. Sidmonton Place is one of the oldest rows of houses in Greystones and runs between Trafalgar Road and Cliff Road at the harbour. Upon closer inspection, the envelope reveals a lot of detail. Headed up "*On Active Service*", it has five French stamps, is postmarked "*Army Base Post Office*" and is also stamped "*Passed by No.1985 Censor.*" The date is significant, 31st December 1914, just six days after the unofficial Christmas truce in the trenches on the Western Front. The contents of the envelope have been long lost sadly, but likely contained a letter home from the front. It is possible that it may have even referred to the all too temporary truce in hostilities, enjoyed by the troops during the first Christmas Day of World War One.

RIGHT: Alec Thompson in the uniform of the South Irish Horse Regiment, as indicated on his left shoulder. He served during World War One in northern France, where he suffered from the effects of gas, which affected his lungs in later life. He lived in *Glencoe* on the North Beach for a number of years, which he inherited from his parents, Robert and Mary Thompson.

BELOW RIGHT: Lance Corporal William Moore Evans, 9th Batallion, Royal Inniskilling Fusiliers, killed in action on 16th August 1917. Born in Greystones, he was the second eldest son of John and Elizabeth Evans who lived at *Malvern* on La Touche Place. William Evans has no known grave, but is listed on Panel 70 to 72 on the Tyne Cot Memorial near Passchendaele, West Flanders in Belgium. The other photograph is of Thomas Francis Evans, younger brother of William Evans by four years, wearing mourning suit, indicated by the wearing of a black armband on his left sleeve.

BELOW: The first barber in Greystones was York Fox. If anyone wanted their hair or beard trimmed they would queue up on a Sunday morning on the grass opposite Dann's. In the photograph, he can be seen trimming a man's beard with scissors in hand. York Fox worked on steam ships during World War One. On one particular trip, his ship was torpedoed when heading from China to France. He was coming up the companionway just at the moment the torpedo struck and a box fell on him, severely injuring his back. He was hospitalised when the ship arrived in port. At that time, the British government had a scheme whereby sailors could elect to cash in all or part of their pension in return for a lump sum. York Fox elected to cash in his pension and bought a boat, nets and gear with some of the proceeds. Book No.2 includes a photograph of him standing beside a very large seal landed in Greystones. Eventually he sold the boat, nets and gear and had nothing. He turned his hand to hairdressing, building up a steady business as the barber at the harbour on Sunday mornings. Also visible in the photo below are the cottages along the North Beach and *Jubilee Castle / Rosetta Fort* in the distance.

LEFT: Pottery vase dating from the 1890s, which shows the schooners in Greystones harbour which used to import coal and slate. The vase was originally displayed in J.G. McEntagart's and subsequently in W.H. Dann's (now The Beach House).

ABOVE: A miniature china vase showing the lifeboat house and the cottages along the North Beach before they were washed away. The mark on the base of the vase indicates that it was manufactured in Germany between 1918 and 1939.

RIGHT & BELOW RIGHT: A China dish featuring the Bathing Place. The mark on its base indicates that it was made in Bavaria.

ABOVE & BELOW: A pottery chamber pot from the Grand Hotel (La Touche Hotel) Greystones with the company logo on the front.

BELOW & LEFT: A fine bone china teacup and saucer dating from the early 1900s and specially made for Beggs & Co. with *Manufactured for Beggs & Co. House Agents Greystones* stamped on the base. At that time, Edward Beggs ran a general house furnishing and builders' ironmongers, trading as The Winton Hardware Stores at No.2 Trafalgar Road.

The image on the design shows the lifeboat house, *Glencoe*, *Alberta*, *Yarra Yarra* and the cottages that were washed away during the storms of 1929-1931. Interestingly, it shows *Alberta* without the balcony that was later added to the front of the house.

ABOVE & LEFT: The South Beach was featured as card number 11 of a series of 25 "*Irish Holiday Resorts*" issued in 1924 by W.D. & H.O. Wills. The company was part of The Imperial Tobacco Co. of Great Britain & Ireland Ltd.

ABOVE: View of Greystones from Jones' Hill on the golf course, which was featured as card number 462 of 600 in the "*Irish View Scenery*" series issued by Gallaher Ltd between 1908 and 1910. Many of the photographs, including the one above, were taken by Robert French, others were taken by Strabane born, Robert John Welch, who went on to become the official photographer for Harland & Wolff in Belfast. Other local views in the series included the Glen of the Downs, Kilruddery and Powerscourt. No descriptions were included on the reverse.

Picture postcards became available on the continent in the mid to late 1870s. In Britain and Ireland, the post office produced its own plain postcard with a printed stamp in 1870, but these did not include a picture. Over time, pictures appeared on advertising and commemorative cards, but still with a pre-printed stamp. Eventually, after much lobbying, commercially produced picture postcards, to which a halfpenny stamp could be affixed, were allowed by the post office with effect from 1st September 1894.

The postcards most avidly sought by collectors today, are principally from the "Golden Age" of postcard production, between 1902 and the outbreak of World War One in 1914. What caused the explosion in popularity was the decision, taken in 1902, to divide the back of the card. This meant that for the first time the message and the address could go on the reverse side, leaving the front of the card free for a picture. At a time when there were up to seven postal deliveries a day and before the telephone was in general use, the picture postcard was eagerly taken up as the cheapest and most reliable form of communication.

LEFT: Postcard published by the Dundee based firm, J. Valentine & Son, who were prolific producers of postcards featuring scenes around Britain and Ireland. Although posted in July 1904, the photograph dates from earlier, as, immediately to the right of the lifeboat house, *Alberta* was the only two storey house that had been built. Its porch with balustrade balcony had not yet been added to its front. The reverse of the card includes an amusing, yet complimentary comment about Greystones, "*This place has somewhat drawn away the people from Bray.*"

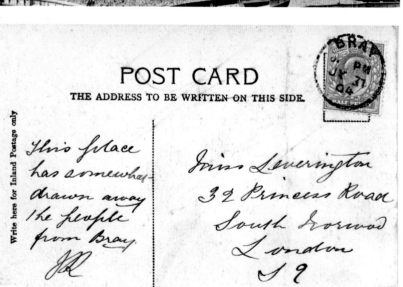

RIGHT: 1912 locally published postcard by G.L. Pepper, whose newsagents was located on Church Road, where Cafe Gray is today. It is an example of one of the rarer postcard images of Greystones produced by independent shops in the town. It provides an excellent view looking across the harbour towards *Rockport*, Watson's shop next door, Arthur Evans coal merchants at *Wavecrest*, Bayswater Terrace and Bethel Terrace at the end of Trafalgar Road. Other newsagents, stationery shops and local publishers that produced their own postcard images of Greystones included, Moore Stationers & Newsagents of Killincarrig Road, E. Greer of Trafalgar Road, J. McKenzie, of Trafalgar Road and photographer, Jesse St. Aubyn of *Brooklands*, Trafalgar Road. These often feature different images to those used by the larger postcard publishers such as J. Valentine & Son.

VIEW FROM GREYSTONES HARBOUR, GREYSTONES.

Published by G. L Pepper, Greystones.

LEFT: Publisher's mark on the reverse of the above rare locally published postcard.

A variation on the traditional picture postcard, was a black and white series produced during the 1950s. These combined greetings and messages, with various views of Greystones contained within objects on the front of the card.

CLASS I.
Pictorial Studies taken in Counties Wicklow or Dublin.

(Confined to Residents, temporary or permanent, within three miles of Greystones Post Office).

1st Prize, 5 Alpine Views (signed), presented by Mrs. Aubrey Le Blond.

2nd Prize, Photographic Apparatus to the value of £1.

3rd Prize,   „   „   „   15/-

CLASS II.
Local Snapshots.

(Confined to Residents, temporary or permanent, within three miles of Greystones Post Office).

1st Prize, 1906 Focussing Hand Camera (presented by Mr. C. B. Vance).

2nd Prize, Kodak Developing Machine (presented by Miss Bewley).

3rd Prize, Album (presented by Mr. Herbert Green).

CLASS III.
Open.

(a) Architectural Studies.
(b) Still Life.
(c) Miscellaneous.

A Silver Medal will be given for the best photo in this class and a Certificate for the best in each division.

CLASS IV.
Snapshots taken by Children under 15 years.

1st Prize, 5/-; 2nd Prize, 4/-; 3rd Prize, 3/-

LOAN COLLECTION.
Pictorial Postcards. (No Entrance Fee).

Prize for best set of 6 Cards:—Two Mounted Photographs, presented by Mrs. Aubrey Le Blond.—"*Larch Woods in Winter*" and "*The Gorge of the Inn*" (St. Moritz, Engadine),

I have just arrived at GREYSTONES

PEBBLES FROM THE BEACH AT GREYSTONES.

Talk about Pebbles,
I found TWO, to-day, such Rippers.
THE Best at Greystones.

THE LOVERS' WALK AT GREYSTONES

ABOVE: Page from the programme of the 1906 Greystones Summer Fete held in the grounds of Killincarrick Demesne on Tuesday 21st August 1906 at which attendees were invited to submit a set of six pictorial postcards. A prize of two mounted photographs was to be awarded by Mrs Aubrey Le Blond (the former Miss Elizabeth Hawkins-Whitshed) for the best entry. Eligibility for the Class I and Class II photographic competitions was restricted to residents "*within 3 miles of Greystones Post Office*".

The postcards on this and the following page were post marked between 1908 and 1937. Whilst some of the wording may not be viewed as appropriate in the modern day, they nevertheless represent the era when cartoon-style saucy seaside postcards were in vogue. Huge numbers of these postcards were mass produced for sale at seaside resorts around Britain and Ireland in the early to mid 20th century, with annual sales peaking at over 16 million. Greystones was not immune from the phenomenon.

RIGHT & OPPOSITE PAGE:

The pull-out card format proved a very popular format. Though more expensive than the standard single image postcard, their attraction lay in the dozen small pull-out images contained under the flap. These featured local scenes, which in the case of the six postcards of this type shown here included the Grand Hotel, the South Beach, the Cove, schooners in the harbour, the railway station, the golf course and a view of the North Beach with Bray Head and Sugarloaf.

Full of Messages from GREYSTONES

Here's a packet full of news,
Stored as well with lots of views;
All the prettiest scenes around
Within this pillar box are found.

A MOUTHFUL OF GREYSTONES

A Little Irish Colleen from Greystones

I send this Irish colleen,
    With her bewitching smile;
And in the basket on her arm
    Are views of Erin's Isle.

Regd. No. 582,456
779

GREYSTONES is doing me good.

I am just able to sit up and take nourishment

This place makes one feel like a Spring Chicken.

At GREYSTONES.

PRINTED IN ENGLAND

ABOVE: View from Jones' Hill in the 1880s looking towards Little Sugarloaf. Sheets and washing can be seen drying on the hedge of the field where Tesco is located today. The roof of *Blacklion House* can be seen amongst the copse of trees at the top of where Church Lane now runs. St. Kilian's church in Blacklion can be seen directly in line, beyond *Blacklion House* and beyond it, *Belvedere Hall*, surrounded by trees. Just right of centre, *Ashley House,* at the top of Jink's Hill is visible.

RIGHT: Jink's Hill with thatched cottages in the 1880s prior to the construction of the Grand Hotel. In the top left of the photograph are *Duncairn* and *Burlington* at the harbour.

ABOVE: 1880s close-up section of a view of the harbour with a yacht entering it. Only the two storey house, *Alberta* had at this time been built on this section of the North Beach. The lifeboat house roof is slightly obscured by a tree in the paddock field adjacent to it. Note the kink in Victoria Road at the approach to the railway arch. Haystacks can be seen in the field beside *Arch House*, which at this time was owned by the Carr family who ran a farm from there.

ABOVE: Another view from Jones' Hill on Greystones golf course around 1918 looking towards Bray Head. The railway cutting at the approach to the mile long tunnel is just visible. Evans' farm at Hillside is in the foreground on the right with only a few houses on Church Lane. Just off centre are the first two houses built on New Road, on the left, *The Chalet* (now *Woodbrook*) and on the right, with the double gable roof, originally named *Barbaville* (then *The Firs* and now *Sentosa*). Both built in 1911/1912 by Ted Archer, *Barbaville*, completed first, was sold for £1,200 and *The Chalet* for £1,100. In the 1960s, the British actor, Richard Greene, who played the lead role in the long running television series, *The Adventures of Robin Hood,* resided at *The Chalet* for a number of years. His prior film acting career in Holywood saw him play Henry Baskerville in the 1939 movie, *The Hound of the Baskervilles* and in the same year, he also appeared alongside Spencer Tracy in *Stanley and Livingstone,* before starring alongside Douglas Fairbanks Junior in *The Fighting O'Flynn* a decade later. Another former resident of *The Chalet* was Manliffe Barrington, who won the Isle of Man TT motorcycle race in the lightweight (250cc) classification in 1947 and 1949, the latter forming the opening round of the 1949 World Championship in which he eventually finished 6th. To the right of *The Chalet* and *Barbaville* is the railway linesmen's cottage built by the Dublin, Wicklow & Wexford Railway (refer also to page 29). Towards the left of the photo is the single storey *Killeen Cottage*, that stood on Rathdown Road, where the Martin family lived.

ABOVE: An earlier view than the photo at the top of the page, taken in the 1880s from Jones' Hill on Greystones golf course looking towards Bray Head. The railway line still ran along the cliff edge and no houses had yet been built on New Road. In the centre of the photograph is *Killard* on Church Lane and to its right, *Knockdolian* and St. Patrick's Church. The roofs of some of the cottages in The Bawn as well as those on the North Beach are just visible, as is the lime kiln further north upon which *Jubilee Castle / Rosetta Fort* was later built.

ABOVE: View from Coolagad in the late 1890s with St. Kilian's Church, Blacklion in the foreground and mainly fields either side of Rathdown Road. The roofs of some of the houses in Strand Cottages (The Bawn) can just be seen protruding on the seaward side of the railway embankment and two of the houses on the North Beach Road are visible on the extreme left. Only *Alberta* has been built between them and the lifeboat house. On the corner of Church Road and Rathdown Road is *Magheralin*. St. Patrick's Church is visible in the top right of the photo, with the modern day Greystones Nursing Home (formerly the Seapatrick Private Hotel) and its curving driveway to its left. Beyond it, with its flag flying is the Grand Hotel. *Brooklands House* and Greystones Presbyterian Church can be seen in the top right of the photo.

ABOVE & OPPOSITE PAGE: 1880s photo from the top of Jones' Hill on the golf course. The lime kiln upon which *Jubilee Castle / Rosetta Fort* was later built can be seen in the top left of the photo along with the roofs of the single storey houses on the North Beach. *Arch House* is visible on Victoria Road, but no houses have yet been built opposite it. The tops of the cottages in The Bawn can just be seen above the railway arch, with only *Alberta* built at the lifeboat house end of the North Beach. *Eyrefield House* with its four chimneys can be seen at the bottom of Church Lane. Haystacks can be seen in the field directly opposite St. Patrick's Church.

ABOVE: View from Coolagad in the late 1890s looking southeast. *Blacklion House*, which was once a coaching inn on the main coast road from Bray to Wicklow can be seen left of centre. Greystones railway station is visible on the horizon just right of centre. The early houses built in The Burnaby are visible in the top right corner. Bordering the fields to the right of this photo was the land belonging to *Kindelstown House*. *Saunders's Newsletter* dated 17th November 1821 carried an advertisement for the letting of *Kindelstown House* and its 30 to 40 acres. It noted that the land was "*excellent sporting country*" and that a "*pack of hounds are constantly kept in the neighbourhood*".

ABOVE: McEntagart's, later Dann's and now The Beach House, is visible in the top left of the photo. Further to the right on the horizon are the roofs of Bayswater Terrace, *Wavecrest* and *Rockport*. Parallel to them is Sidmonton Terrace, the roofs of *Carrig House* and *Cliff House* can be seen. Inland of Sidmonton Terrace is the whitewashed two storey *Trafalgar House* on Trafalgar Road, originally the coast guard chief officer's house (now Greystones Harbour Family Practice). The Grand Hotel had not yet been built. The rears of the houses on Church Road can be seen in the foreground.

ABOVE: Fine close-up view from the golf course in the 1890s over the roof tops to the Grand Hotel with its flag billowing in the sea breeze. The pyramid shaped roof of the coast guard station watch tower on Marine Terrace is just visible against the sea towards the right of the photograph.

ABOVE: Photo taken in the 1880s from the top of Jink's Hill on Rathdown Road, with just fields extending to St Patrick's Church on the left and *Killard House* to its right.

Section of the plan drawn in 1876 which formed part of the "Book of Reference" that was presented to The House of Con

No.	Description	Owner	Occupier	No.	Description	Owner	Occupier	No.	Description
5	Pasture Field	William La Touche	Robert H. Pennick	24	House, Offices & Garden	William La Touche	Andrew Byrne	42	House, Offices & Garde
6	Pasture Field	William La Touche	William Evans	25	House, Offices & Garden	William La Touche	John Fields	43	House, Offices & Garde
11	House & Garden	William La Touche	James Fields	26	House, Offices & Garden	William La Touche	Michael Fields	44	House, Offices & Garde
12	House & Garden	William La Touche	Michael Whiston	27	House, Offices & Garden	William La Touche	William Hackman	45	House, Offices & Garde
13	House & Garden	William La Touche	William Boyd	28	House, Offices & Garden	William La Touche	George Ennis	46	House, Offices & Garde
14	House, Offices & Garden	William La Touche	William D'Arcy	29	House, Offices & Field	William La Touche	Stephen Carr	47	House, Offices & Garde
15	House, Offices & Garden	William La Touche	Lawrence Ryan	30	House, Offices & Garden	William La Touche	John Doyle	48	House, Offices & Garde
16	House, Offices & Garden	William La Touche	Thomas D'Arcy	31	House, Offices & Garden	William La Touche	Edward Chapman	50	House, Offices & Garde
17	House, Offices & Garden	William La Touche	Michael Kinsella	32	House, Offices & Garden	William La Touche	Mrs Doyle	51	House, Offices & Garde
18	House, Offices & Garden	William La Touche	Michael Fields	36	House & Field	William La Touche	Susan Furlong	53	House, Offices & Garde
19	House, Offices & Garden	William La Touche	Patrick Doyle & John Doyle	37	House, Offices & Garden	William La Touche	Rev. E. Daunt	54	House, Offices & Garde
20	House, Offices & Garden	William La Touche	Philip Smyth	38	Church	William La Touche	Rev. E. Daunt	55	House, Offices & Garde
21	House, Offices & Garden	William La Touche	Patrick Doyle	39	House, Offices & Garden	William La Touche	John Doyle	56	House, Offices & Garde
22	House, Offices & Garden	William La Touche	William Doyle	40	House, Offices & Garden	William La Touche	William Doyle	57	House, Offices & Garde
23	House, Offices & Garden	William La Touche	Hugh Lawless	41	House, Offices & Garden	William La Touche	Joseph McGill	58	House, Offices & Garde

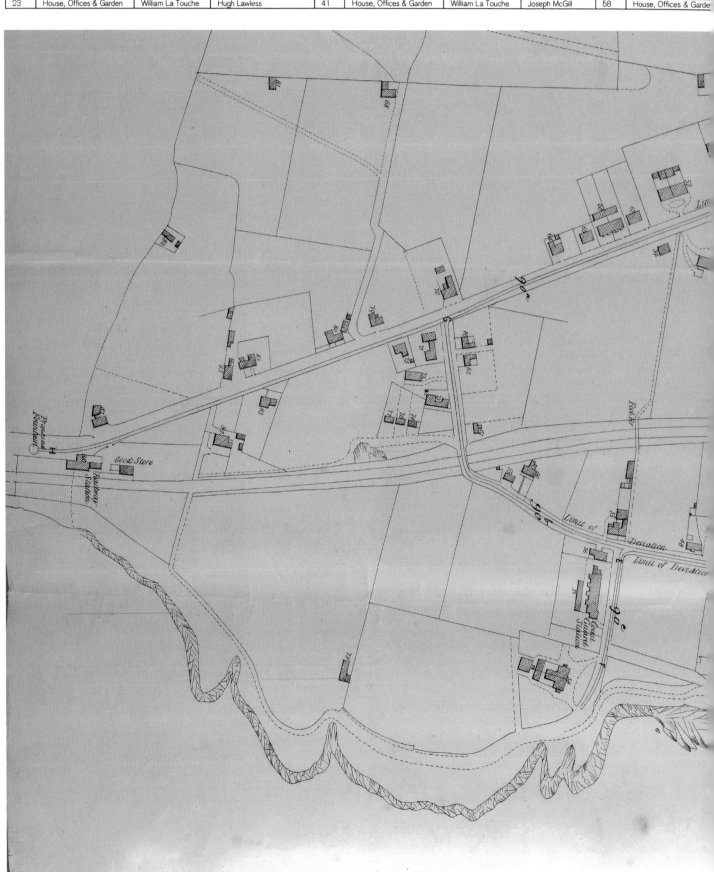